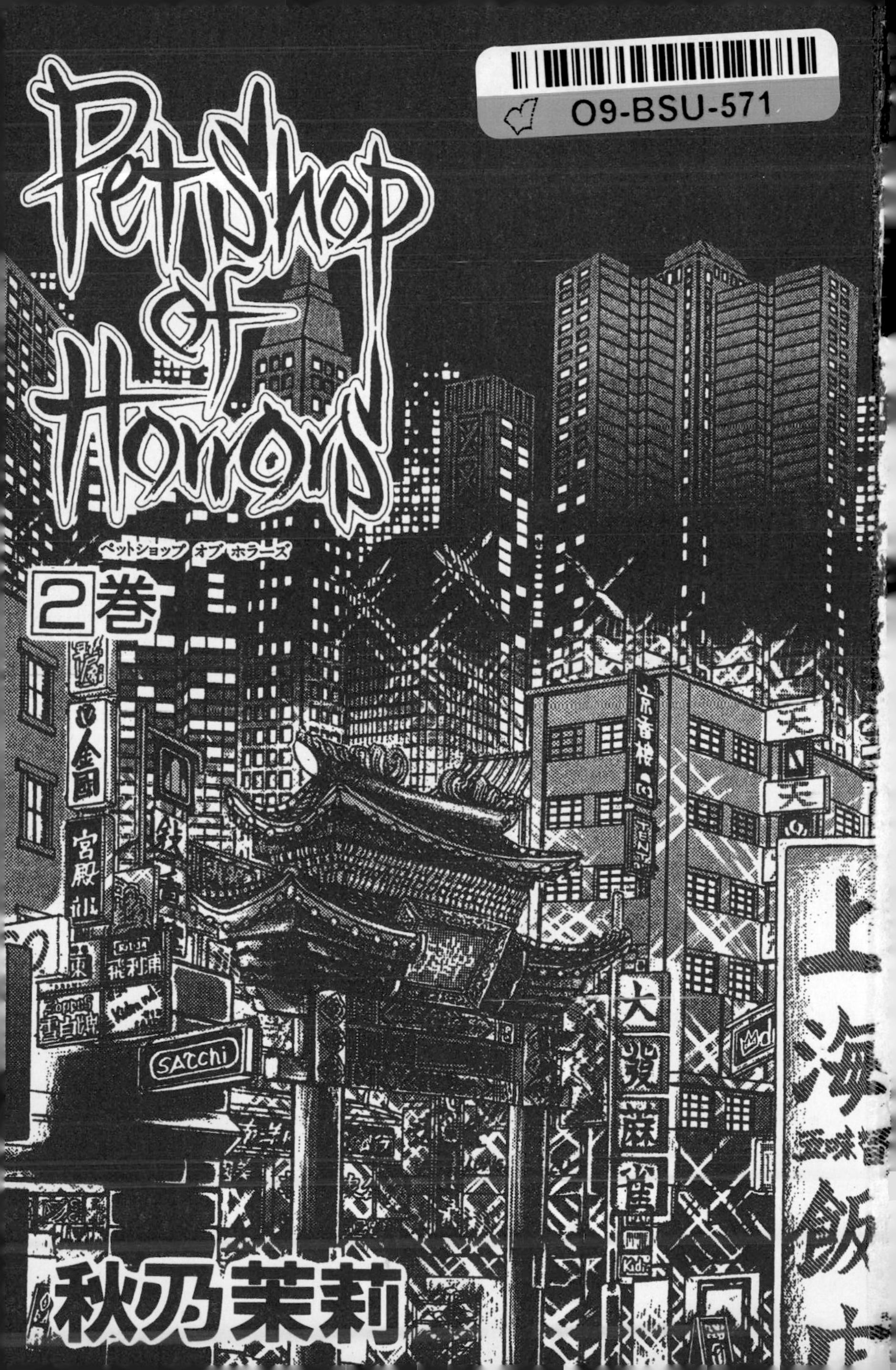

Pet Shop of Horrors
ペットショップ オブ ホラーズ
2巻
秋乃茉莉

ALSO AVAILABLE FROM

MANGA

.HACK//LEGEND OF THE TWILIGHT*
@LARGE (December 2003)
ANGELIC LAYER*
BABY BIRTH*
BATTLE ROYALE*
BRAIN POWERED*
BRIGADOON*
CARDCAPTOR SAKURA
CARDCAPTOR SAKURA: MASTER OF THE CLOW*
CHOBITS*
CHRONICLES OF THE CURSED SWORD
CLAMP SCHOOL DETECTIVES*
CLOVER
CONFIDENTIAL CONFESSIONS*
CORRECTOR YUI
COWBOY BEBOP*
COWBOY BEBOP: SHOOTING STAR*
CYBORG 009*
DEMON DIARY
DIGIMON*
DRAGON HUNTER
DRAGON KNIGHTS*
DUKLYON: CLAMP SCHOOL DEFENDERS*
ERICA SAKURAZAWA*
FAKE*
FLCL*
FORBIDDEN DANCE*
GATE KEEPERS*
G GUNDAM*
GRAVITATION*
GTO*
GUNDAM WING
GUNDAM WING: BATTLEFIELD OF PACIFISTS
GUNDAM WING: ENDLESS WALTZ*
GUNDAM WING: THE LAST OUTPOST*
HAPPY MANIA*
HARLEM BEAT
I.N.V.U.
INITIAL D*
ISLAND
JING: KING OF BANDITS*
JULINE
KARE KANO*
KINDAICHI CASE FILES, THE*
KING OF HELL
KODOCHA: SANA'S STAGE*
LOVE HINA*
LUPIN III*
MAGIC KNIGHT RAYEARTH*

MAGIC KNIGHT RAYEARTH II* (COMING SOON)
MAN OF MANY FACES*
MARMALADE BOY*
MARS*
MIRACLE GIRLS
MIYUKI-CHAN IN WONDERLAND*
MONSTERS, INC.
PARADISE KISS*
PARASYTE
PEACH GIRL
PEACH GIRL: CHANGE OF HEART*
PET SHOP OF HORRORS*
PLANET LADDER*
PLANETES*
PRIEST
RAGNAROK
RAVE MASTER*
REALITY CHECK
REBIRTH
REBOUND*
RISING STARS OF MANGA
SABER MARIONETTE J*
SAILOR MOON
SAINT TAIL
SAMURAI DEEPER KYO*
SAMURAI GIRL: REAL BOUT HIGH SCHOOL*
SCRYED*
SHAOLIN SISTERS*
SHIRAHIME-SYO: SNOW GODDESS TALES* (Dec. 2003)
SHUTTERBOX
SORCERER HUNTERS
THE SKULL MAN*
THE VISION OF ESCAFLOWNE*
TOKYO MEW MEW*
UNDER THE GLASS MOON
VAMPIRE GAME*
WILD ACT*
WISH*
WORLD OF HARTZ
X-DAY*
ZODIAC P.I. *

For more information visit www.TOKYOPOP.com

*INDICATES 100% AUTHENTIC MANGA (RIGHT-TO-LEFT FORMAT)

CINE-MANGA™

CARDCAPTORS
JACKIE CHAN ADVENTURES
JIMMY NEUTRON
KIM POSSIBLE
LIZZIE MCGUIRE
POWER RANGERS: NINJA STORM
SPONGEBOB SQUAREPANTS
SPY KIDS 2

NOVELS

KARMA CLUB (April 2004)
SAILOR MOON

TOKYOPOP KIDS

STRAY SHEEP

ART BOOKS

CARDCAPTOR SAKURA*
MAGIC KNIGHT RAYEARTH*

ANIME GUIDES

COWBOY BEBOP ANIME GUIDES
GUNDAM TECHNICAL MANUALS
SAILOR MOON SCOUT GUIDES

090503

Pet Shop of Horrors

Volume 2

by Matsuri Akino

TOKYOPOP®

LOS ANGELES • TOKYO • LONDON

Translator - Tomoharu Iwo and Bryan Masumoto
English Adaptation - James Lucas Jones
Contributing Editor - Tim Beedle
Retouch and Lettering - Jennifer Nunn
Cover Layout - Raymond Makowski

Editor - Luis Reyes
Managing Editor - Jill Freshney
Production Coordinator - Antonio DePietro
Production Manager - Jennifer Miller
Art Director - Matt Alford
Editorial Director - Jeremy Ross
VP of Production - Ron Klamert
President & C.O.O. - John Parker
Publisher & C.E.O. - Stuart Levy

Email: editor@TOKYOPOP.com
Come visit us online at www.TOKYOPOP.com

A  Manga

TOKYOPOP Inc.
5900 Wilshire Blvd. Suite 2000
Los Angeles, CA 90036

PETSHOP OF HORRORS VOLUME 2

ISBN: 1-59182-364-1

First TOKYOPOP® printing: August 2003

10 9 8 7 6 5 4 3 2

Printed in the USA

The Story so far

Plumes of mist billow up from the back alleys of Chinatown, home to a variety of merchants of the occult and mystical. A sharp breeze drives the mist out into the crowded streets, revealing here, in the crevices of the concrete jungle, a solitary pet shop. Its proprietor, an enigmatic figure known only as Count D, beckons through his doors the injured and the scarred, introducing them to creatures friendly and bizarre.

Our guide through this mysterious landscape is one Detective Leon Orcot who has traced a series of seemingly unrelated crimes to Count D and his Pet Shop of Horrors. A steadfast skeptic, Leon dismisses as trickery the inexplicable events he witnesses. However, this hard-boiled dick is driven to prove Count D's guilt, or to catch a glimpse of the magic he wields.

Prepare yourselves for four tales of wonder and woe in which lessons are learned and fates foretold.

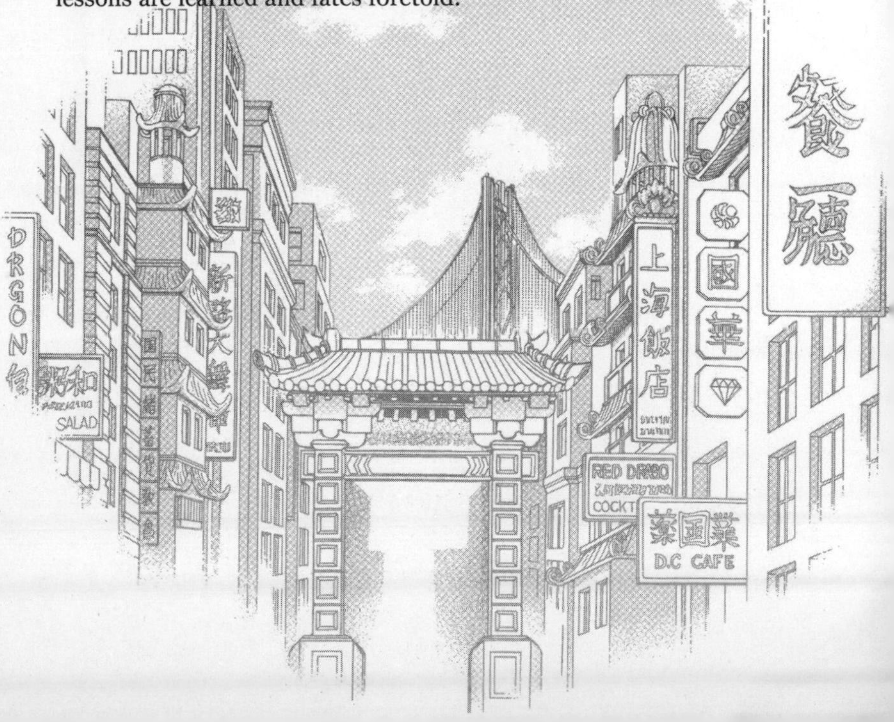
DRGON
SALAD
上海飯店
RED DRAGO
COCKT
D.C CAFE

CONTENTS

第1話／Dragon

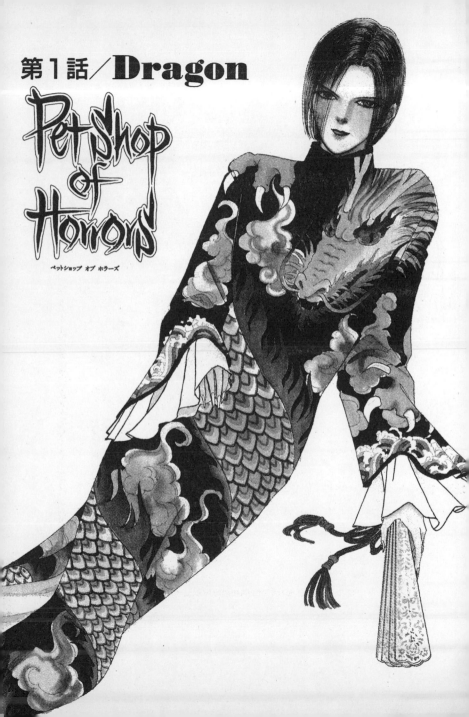

Pet Shop
of
Horrors

ペットショップ オブ ホラーズ

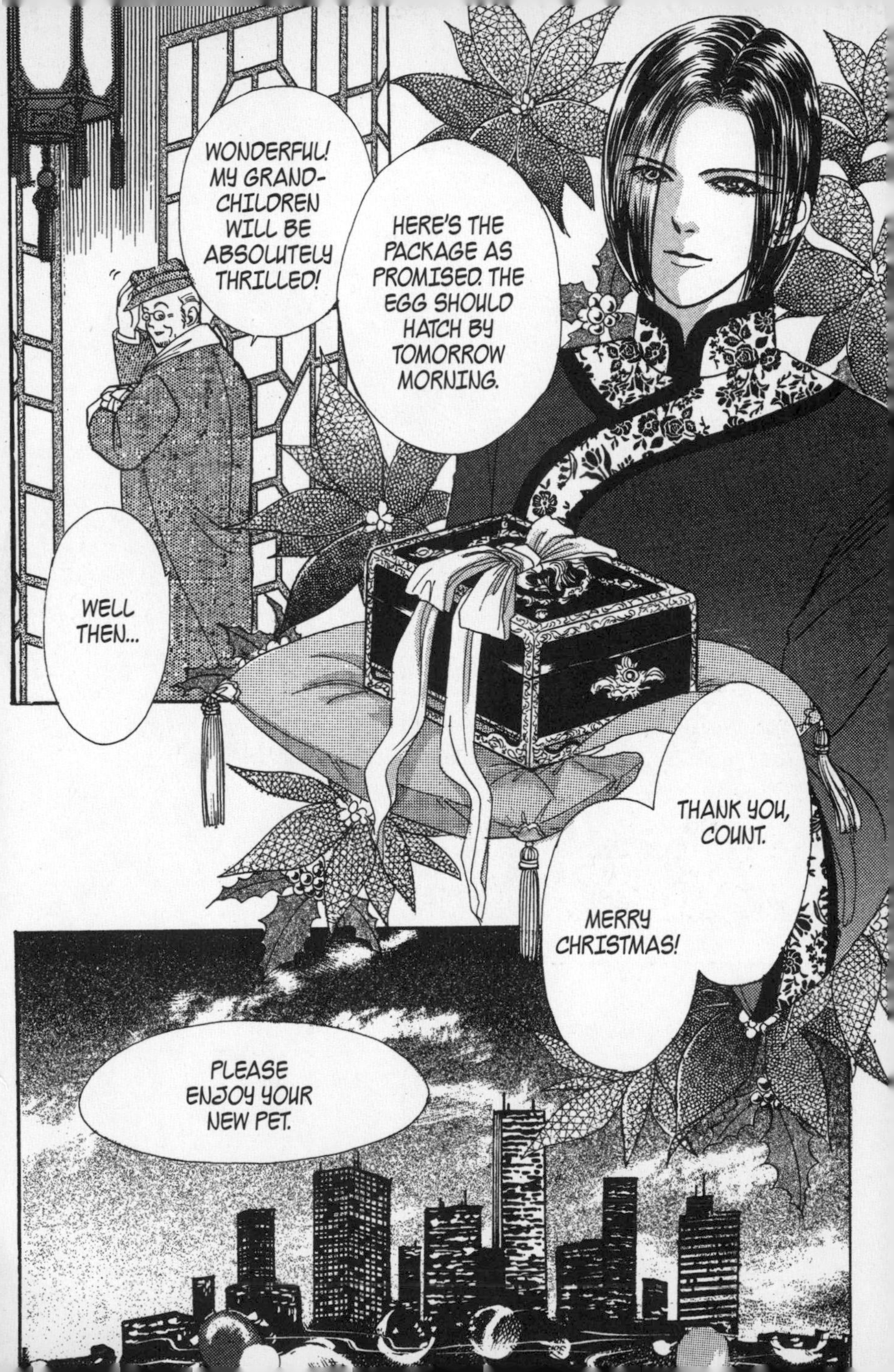
HERE'S THE PACKAGE AS PROMISED. THE EGG SHOULD HATCH BY TOMORROW MORNING.
WONDERFUL! MY GRAND-CHILDREN WILL BE ABSOLUTELY THRILLED!
WELL THEN...
THANK YOU, COUNT.
MERRY CHRISTMAS!
PLEASE ENJOY YOUR NEW PET.

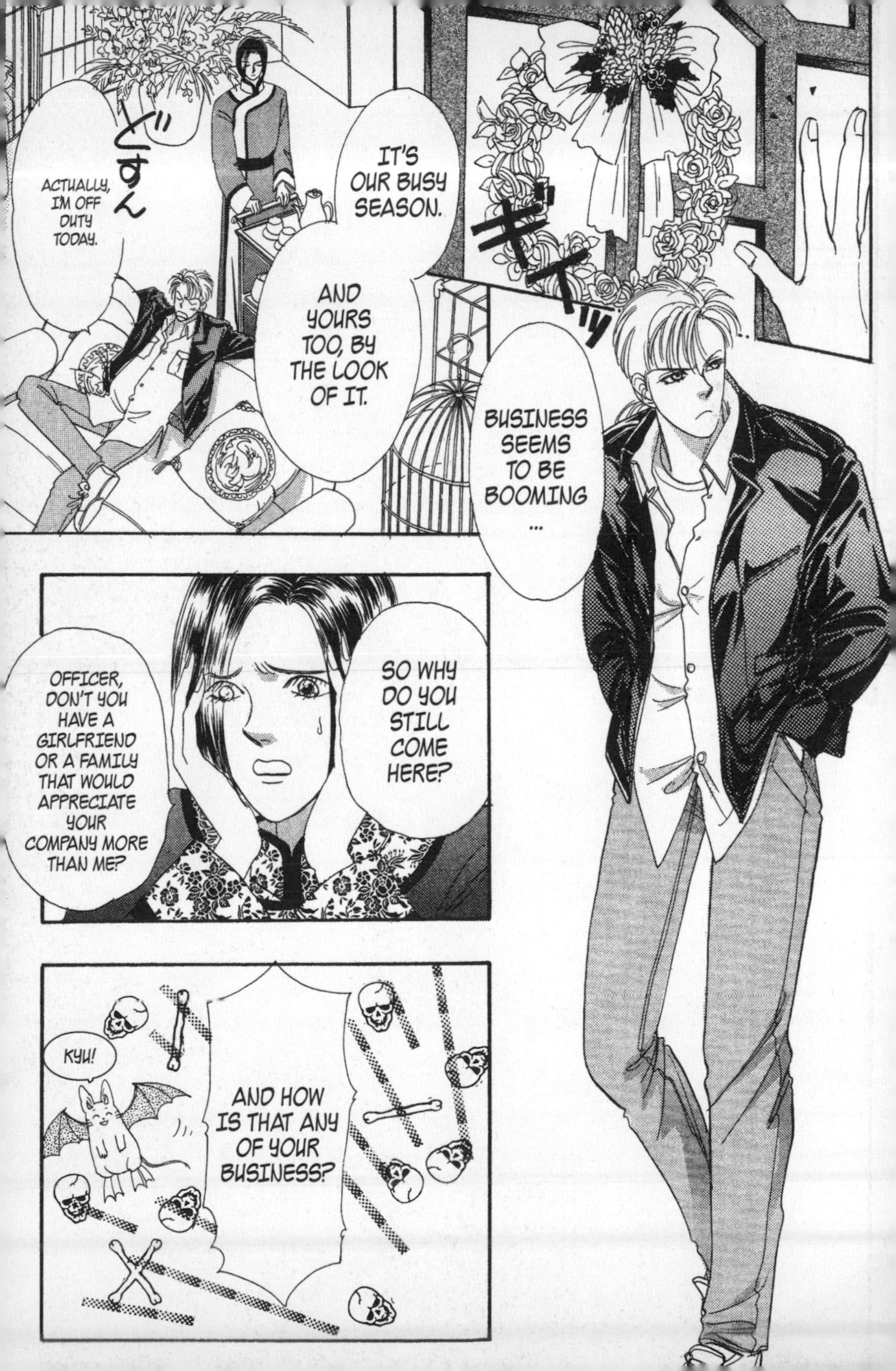
ギイッ
BUSINESS SEEMS TO BE BOOMING ...
IT'S OUR BUSY SEASON.
AND YOURS TOO, BY THE LOOK OF IT.
どすん
ACTUALLY, I'M OFF DUTY TODAY.
SO WHY DO YOU STILL COME HERE?
OFFICER, DON'T YOU HAVE A GIRLFRIEND OR A FAMILY THAT WOULD APPRECIATE YOUR COMPANY MORE THAN ME?
AND HOW IS THAT ANY OF YOUR BUSINESS?
KYU!

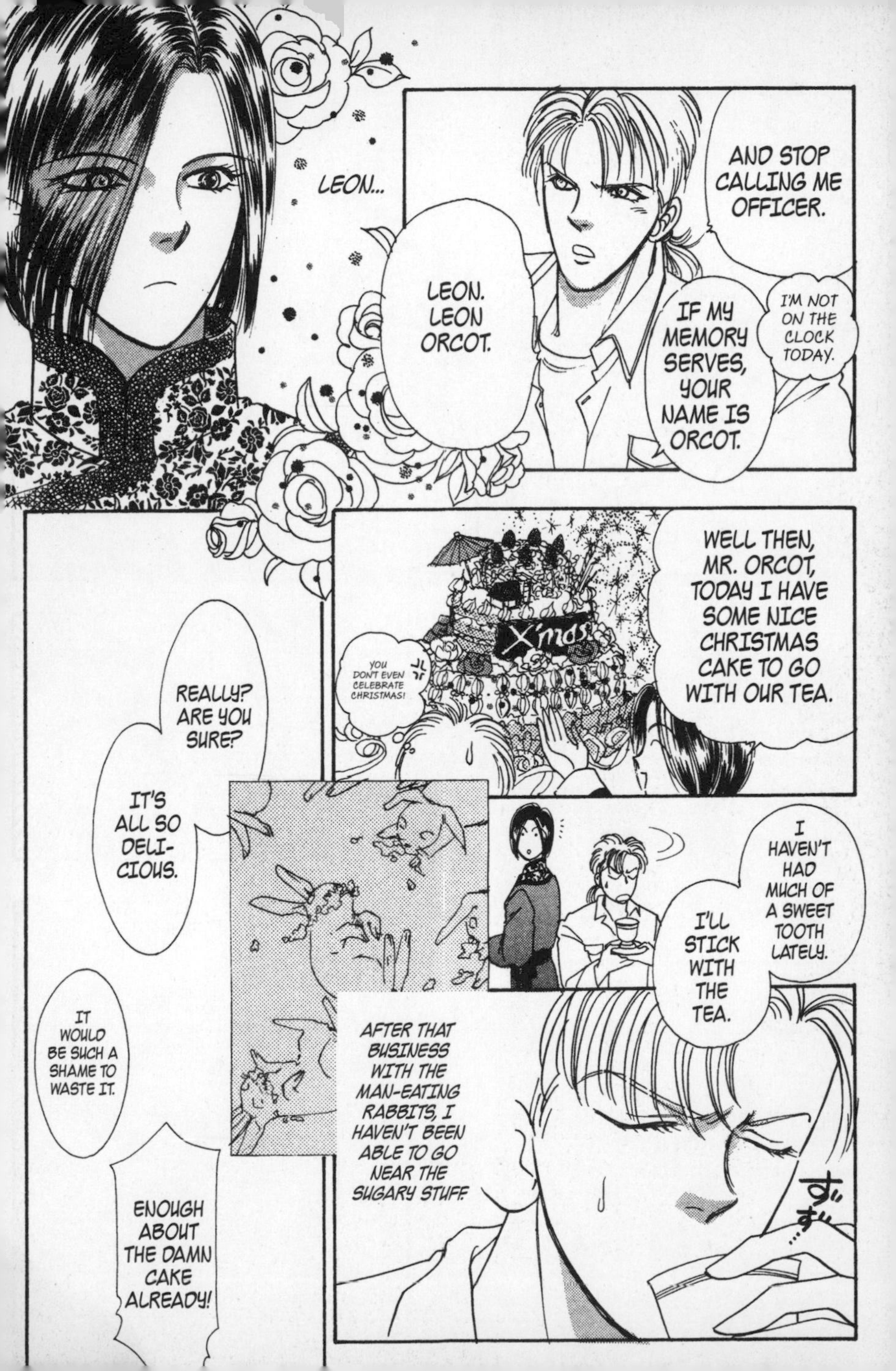
AND STOP CALLING ME OFFICER.
I'M NOT ON THE CLOCK TODAY.
IF MY MEMORY SERVES, YOUR NAME IS ORCOT.
LEON. LEON ORCOT.
LEON...
WELL THEN, MR. ORCOT, TODAY I HAVE SOME NICE CHRISTMAS CAKE TO GO WITH OUR TEA.
X'mas
YOU DON'T EVEN CELEBRATE CHRISTMAS!
I HAVEN'T HAD MUCH OF A SWEET TOOTH LATELY.
I'LL STICK WITH THE TEA.
REALLY? ARE YOU SURE?
IT'S ALL SO DELI-CIOUS.
AFTER THAT BUSINESS WITH THE MAN-EATING RABBITS, I HAVEN'T BEEN ABLE TO GO NEAR THE SUGARY STUFF.
ずず ずず...
IT WOULD BE SUCH A SHAME TO WASTE IT.
ENOUGH ABOUT THE DAMN CAKE ALREADY!

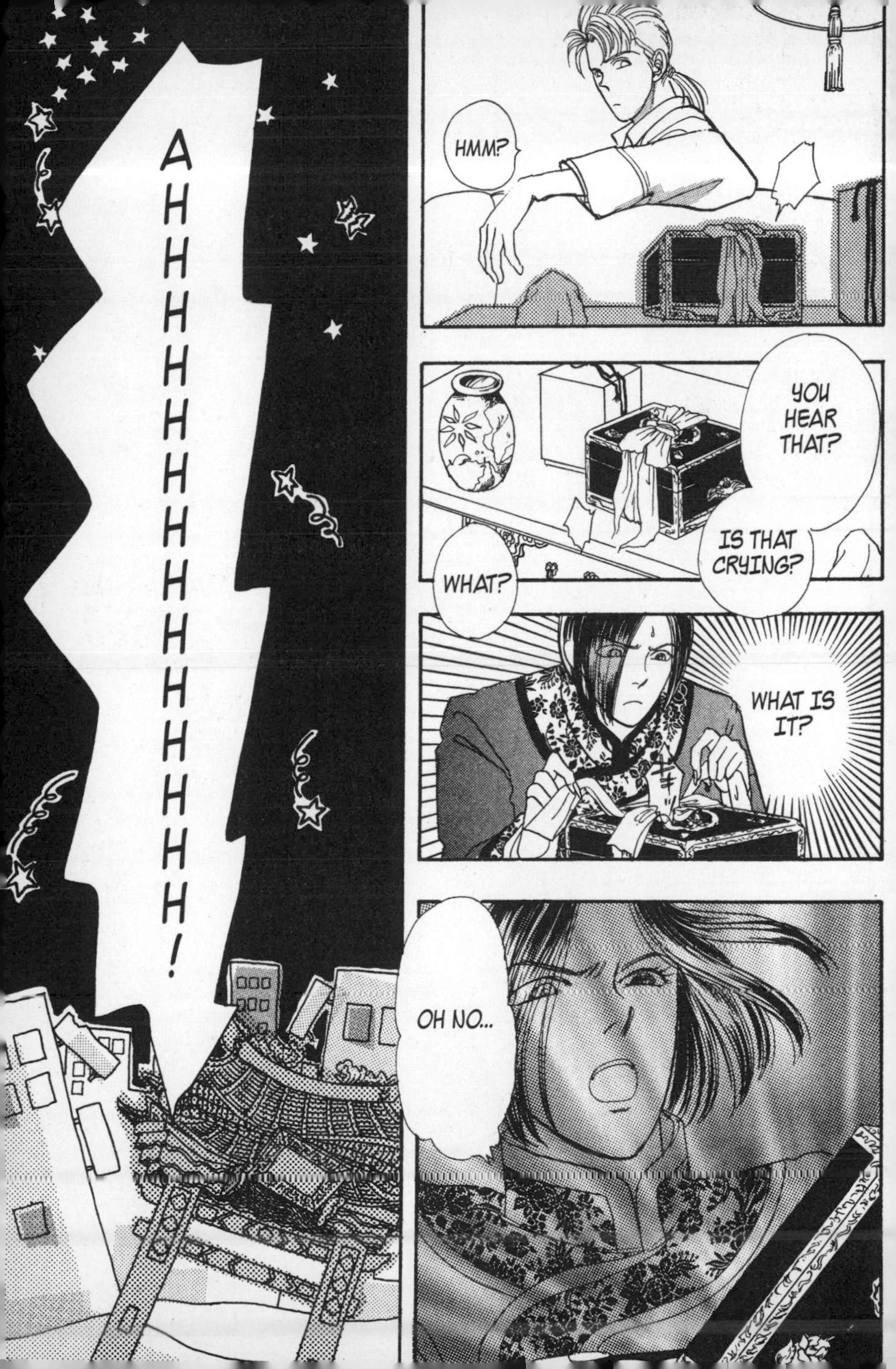
HMM?
YOU HEAR THAT?
IS THAT CRYING?
WHAT?
WHAT IS IT?
OH NO...
AHHHHHHHHHHHHHH!

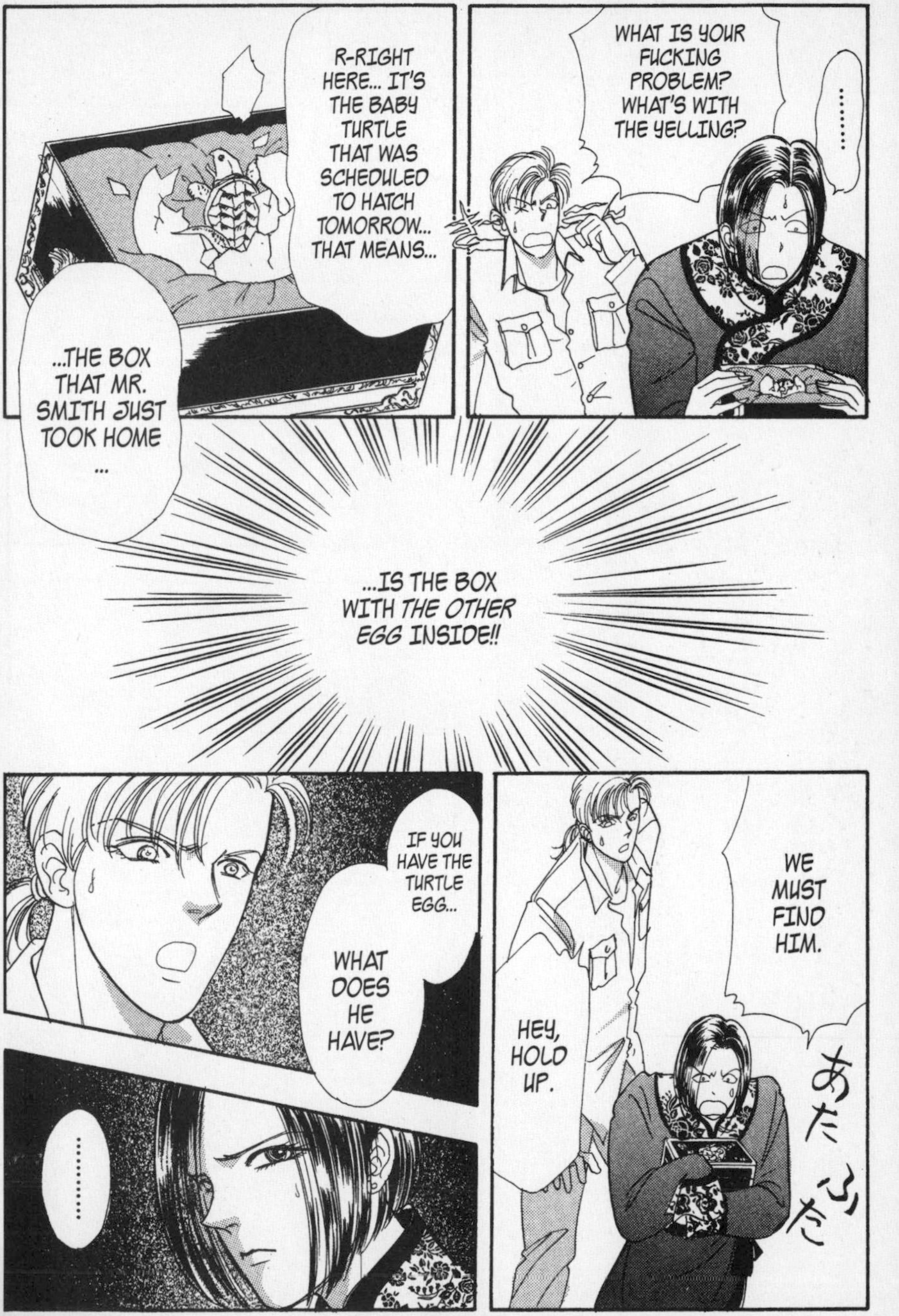

......
WHAT IS YOUR FUCKING PROBLEM? WHAT'S WITH THE YELLING?
R-RIGHT HERE... IT'S THE BABY TURTLE THAT WAS SCHEDULED TO HATCH TOMORROW... THAT MEANS...
...THE BOX THAT MR. SMITH JUST TOOK HOME ...
...IS THE BOX WITH *THE OTHER EGG* INSIDE!!
WE MUST FIND HIM.
あたふた
HEY, HOLD UP.
IF YOU HAVE THE TURTLE EGG...
WHAT DOES HE HAVE?
......

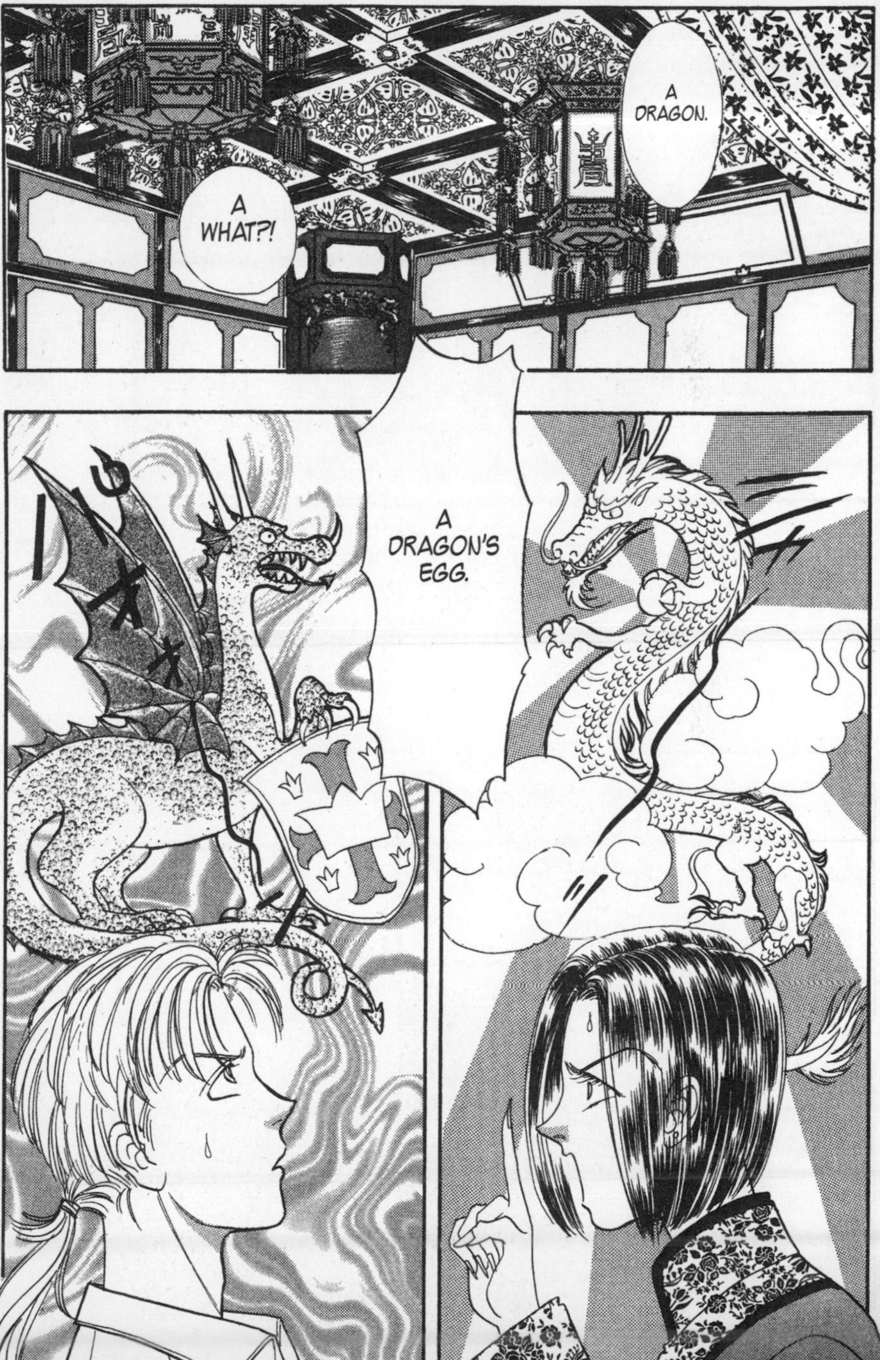
A DRAGON.
A WHAT?!
A DRAGON'S EGG.

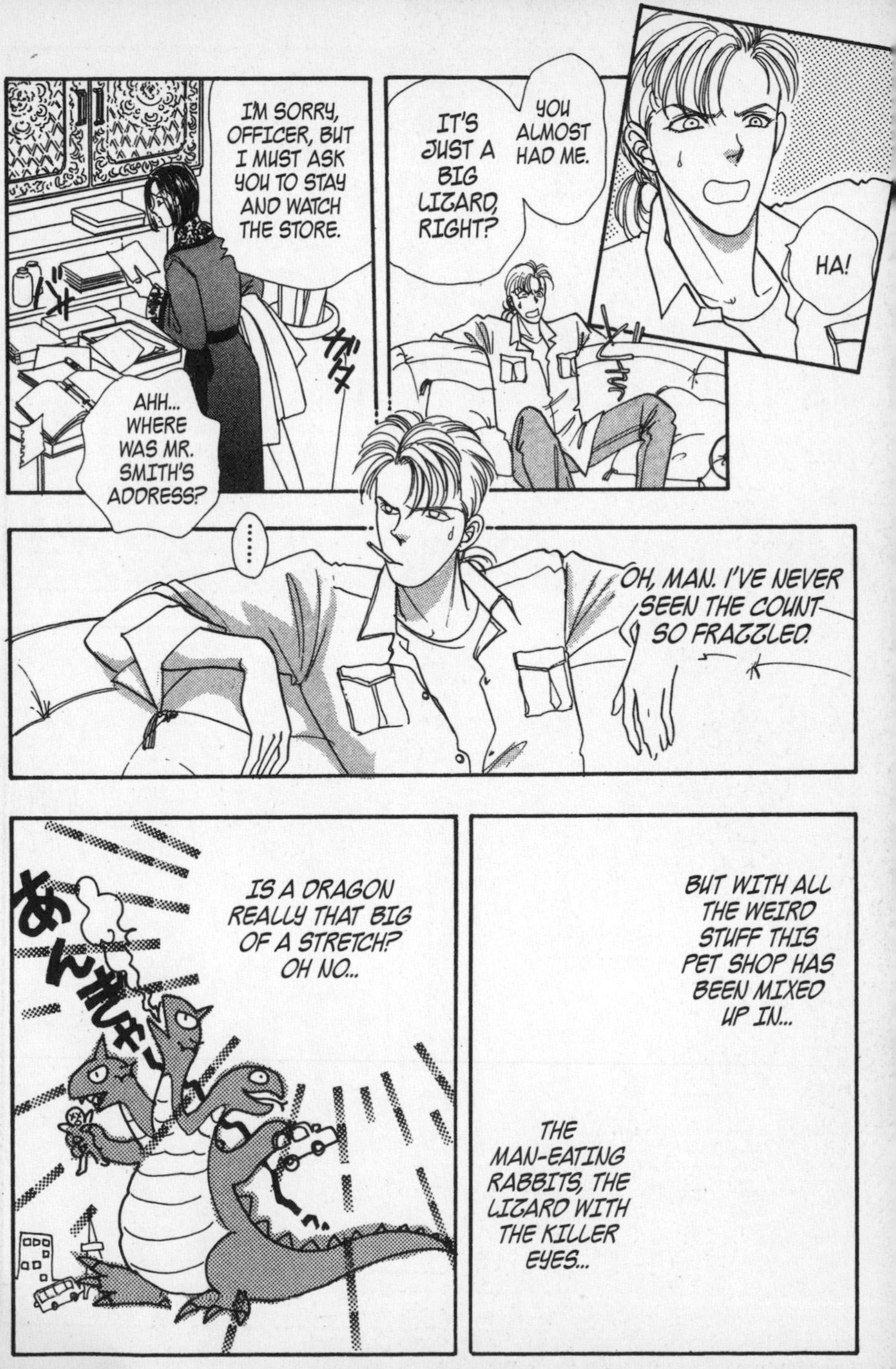
HA!
YOU ALMOST HAD ME.
IT'S JUST A BIG LIZARD, RIGHT?
I'M SORRY, OFFICER, BUT I MUST ASK YOU TO STAY AND WATCH THE STORE.
AHH... WHERE WAS MR. SMITH'S ADDRESS?
......
OH, MAN. I'VE NEVER SEEN THE COUNT SO FRAZZLED.
BUT WITH ALL THE WEIRD STUFF THIS PET SHOP HAS BEEN MIXED UP IN...
THE MAN-EATING RABBITS, THE LIZARD WITH THE KILLER EYES...
IS A DRAGON REALLY THAT BIG OF A STRETCH? OH NO...

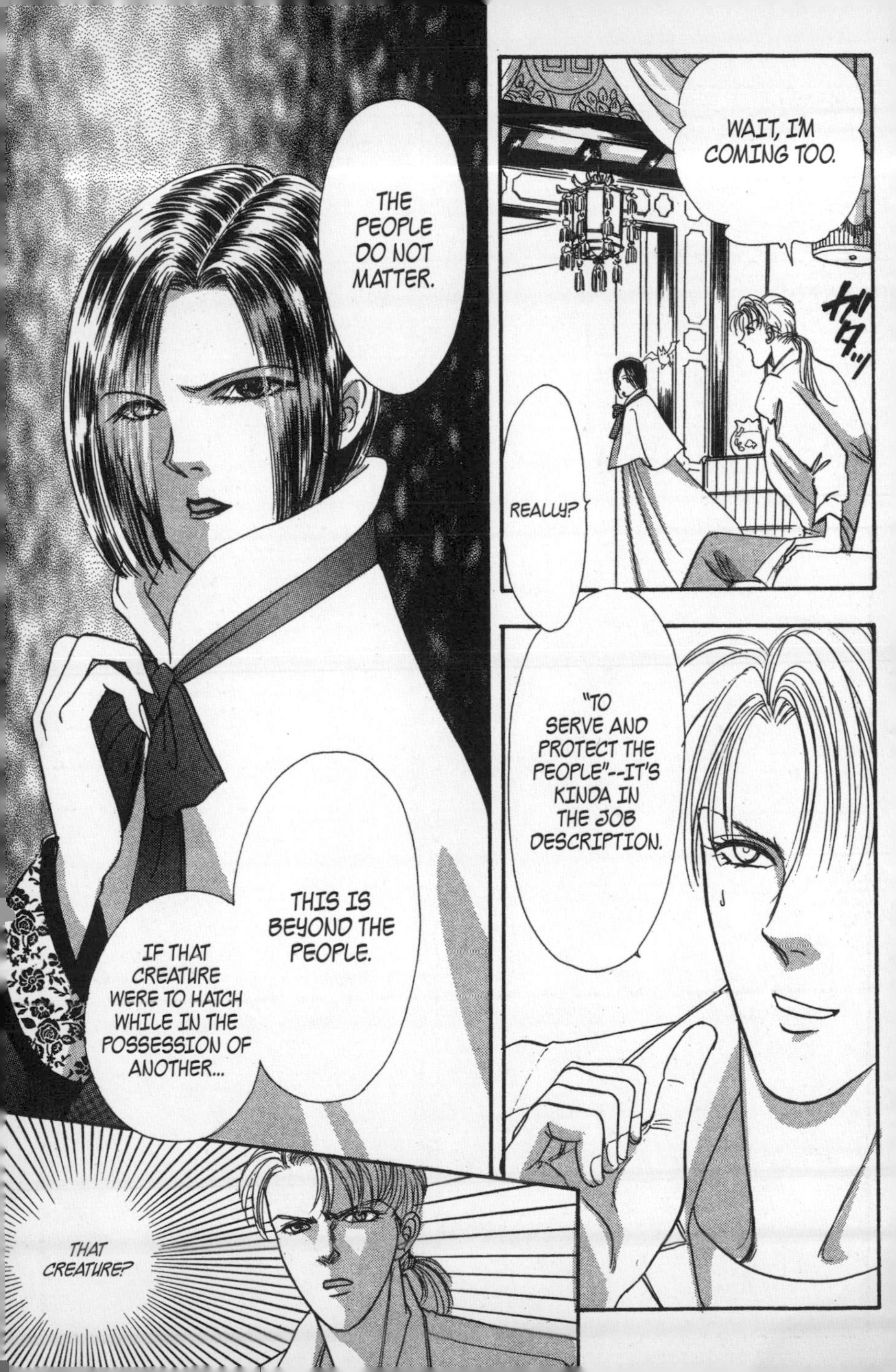

WAIT, I'M COMING TOO.
ガタッ
REALLY?
"TO SERVE AND PROTECT THE PEOPLE"--IT'S KINDA IN THE JOB DESCRIPTION.
THE PEOPLE DO NOT MATTER.
THIS IS BEYOND THE PEOPLE.
IF THAT CREATURE WERE TO HATCH WHILE IN THE POSSESSION OF ANOTHER...
THAT CREATURE?

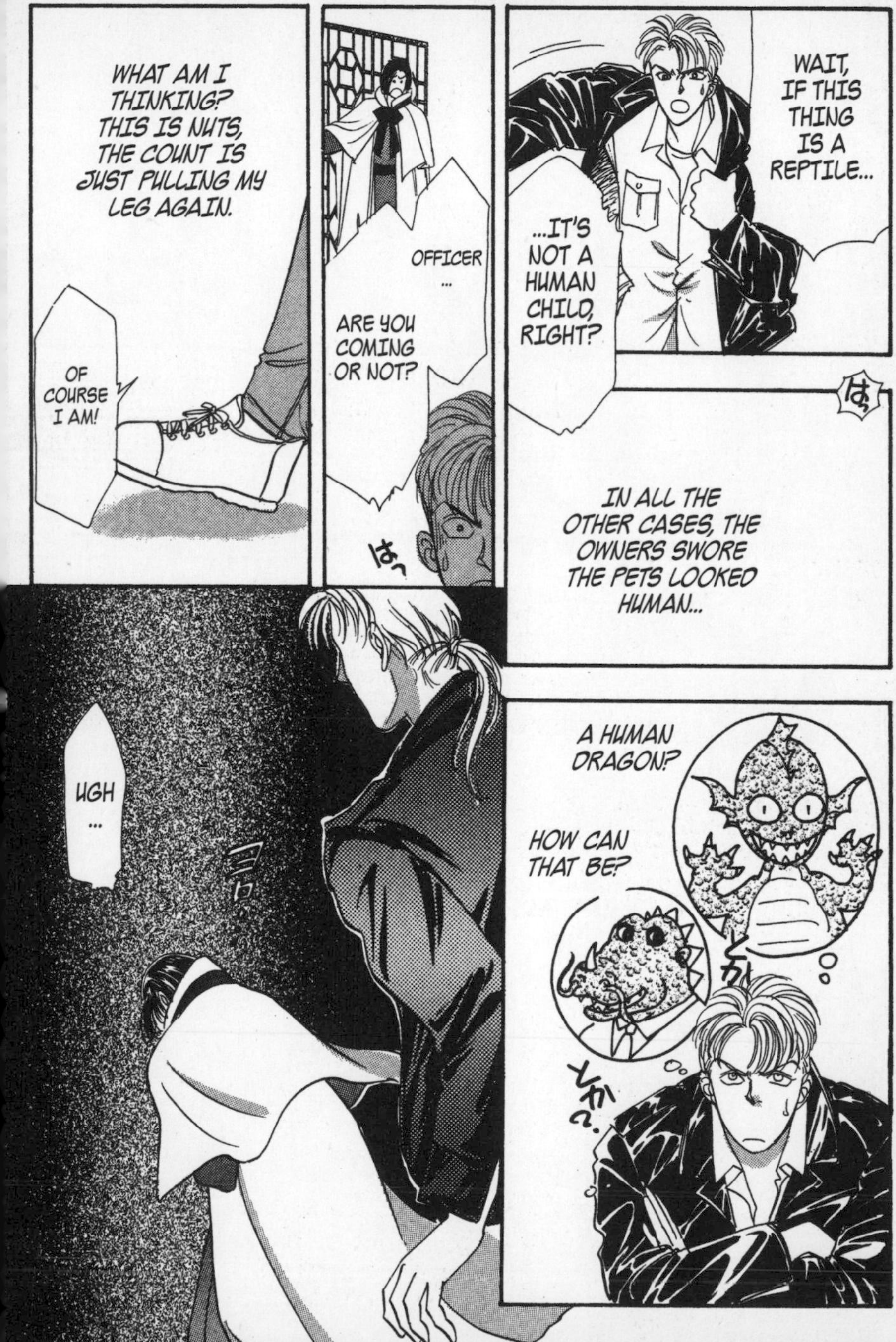

WAIT, IF THIS THING IS A REPTILE...
...IT'S NOT A HUMAN CHILD, RIGHT?
は
IN ALL THE OTHER CASES, THE OWNERS SWORE THE PETS LOOKED HUMAN...
A HUMAN DRAGON?
HOW CAN THAT BE?
OFFICER ...
ARE YOU COMING OR NOT?
はっ
WHAT AM I THINKING? THIS IS NUTS, THE COUNT IS JUST PULLING MY LEG AGAIN.
OF COURSE I AM!
UGH ...

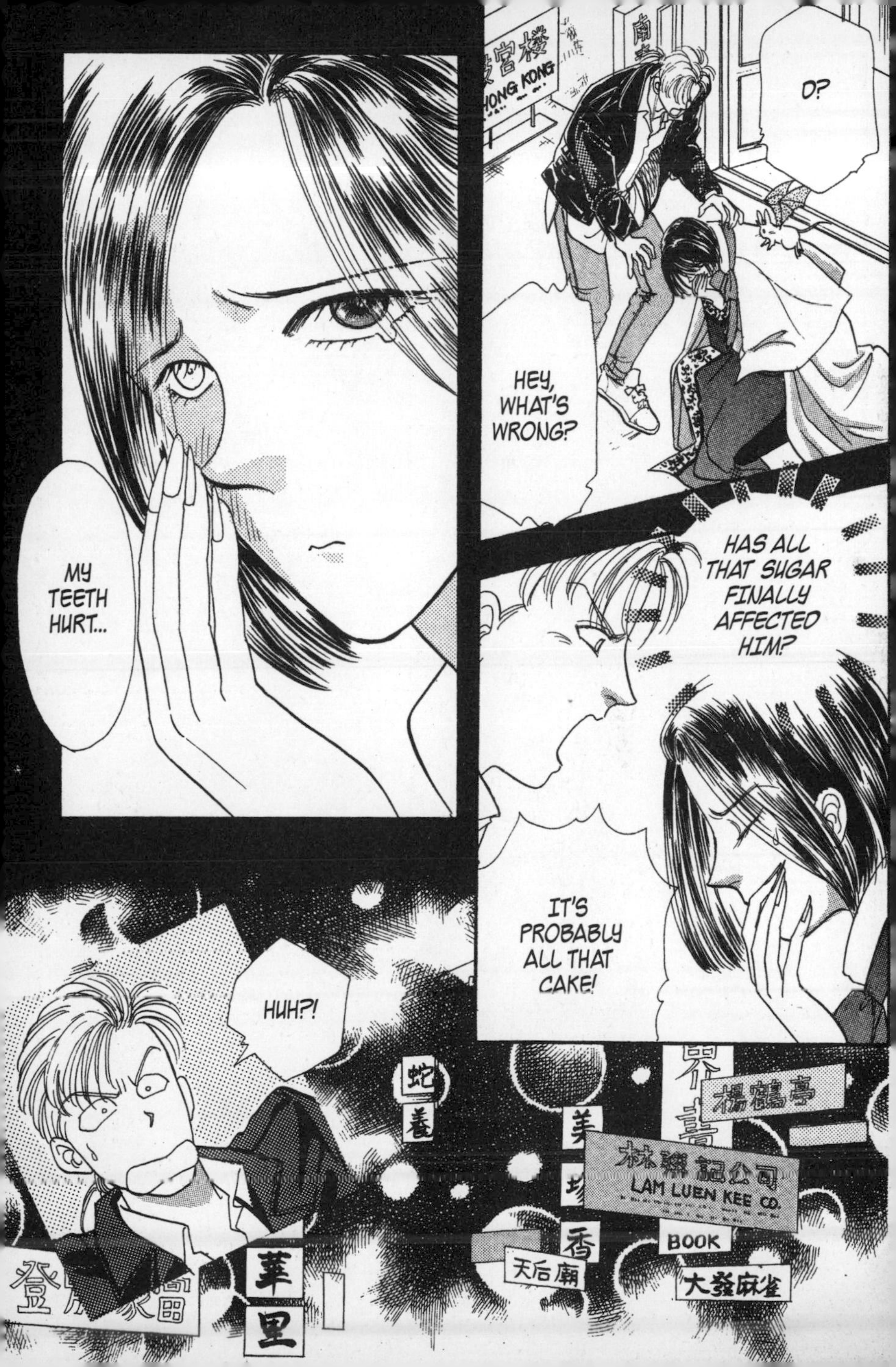
HONG KONG
O?
HEY, WHAT'S WRONG?
HAS ALL THAT SUGAR FINALLY AFFECTED HIM?
IT'S PROBABLY ALL THAT CAKE!
MY TEETH HURT...
HUH?!
LAM LUEN KEE CO.
BOOK
天后廟
大發麻雀

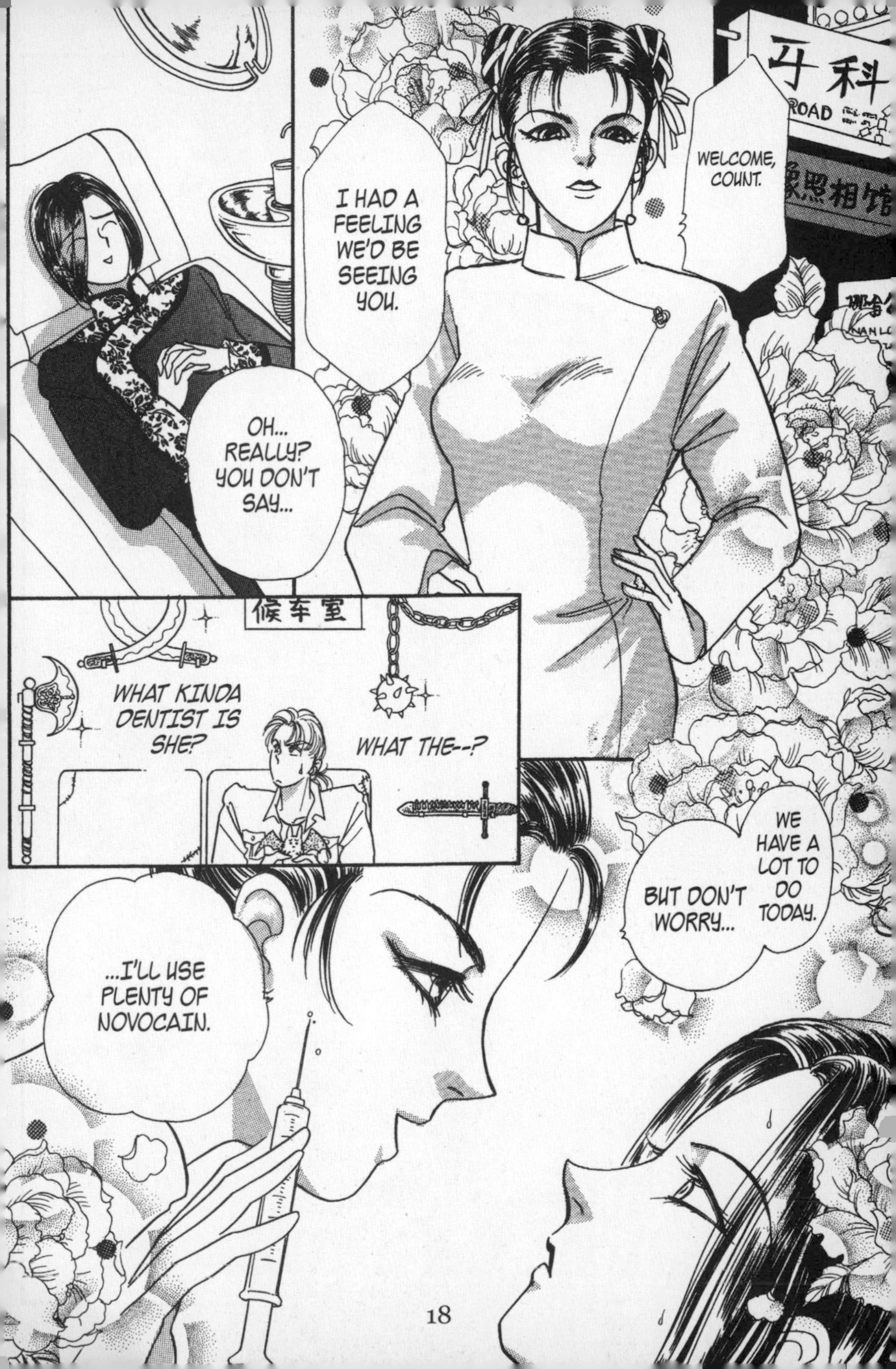

牙科
ROAD
WELCOME, COUNT.
I HAD A FEELING WE'D BE SEEING YOU.
OH... REALLY? YOU DON'T SAY...
候车室
WHAT THE--?
WHAT KINDA DENTIST IS SHE?
WE HAVE A LOT TO DO TODAY.
BUT DON'T WORRY...
...I'LL USE PLENTY OF NOVOCAIN.

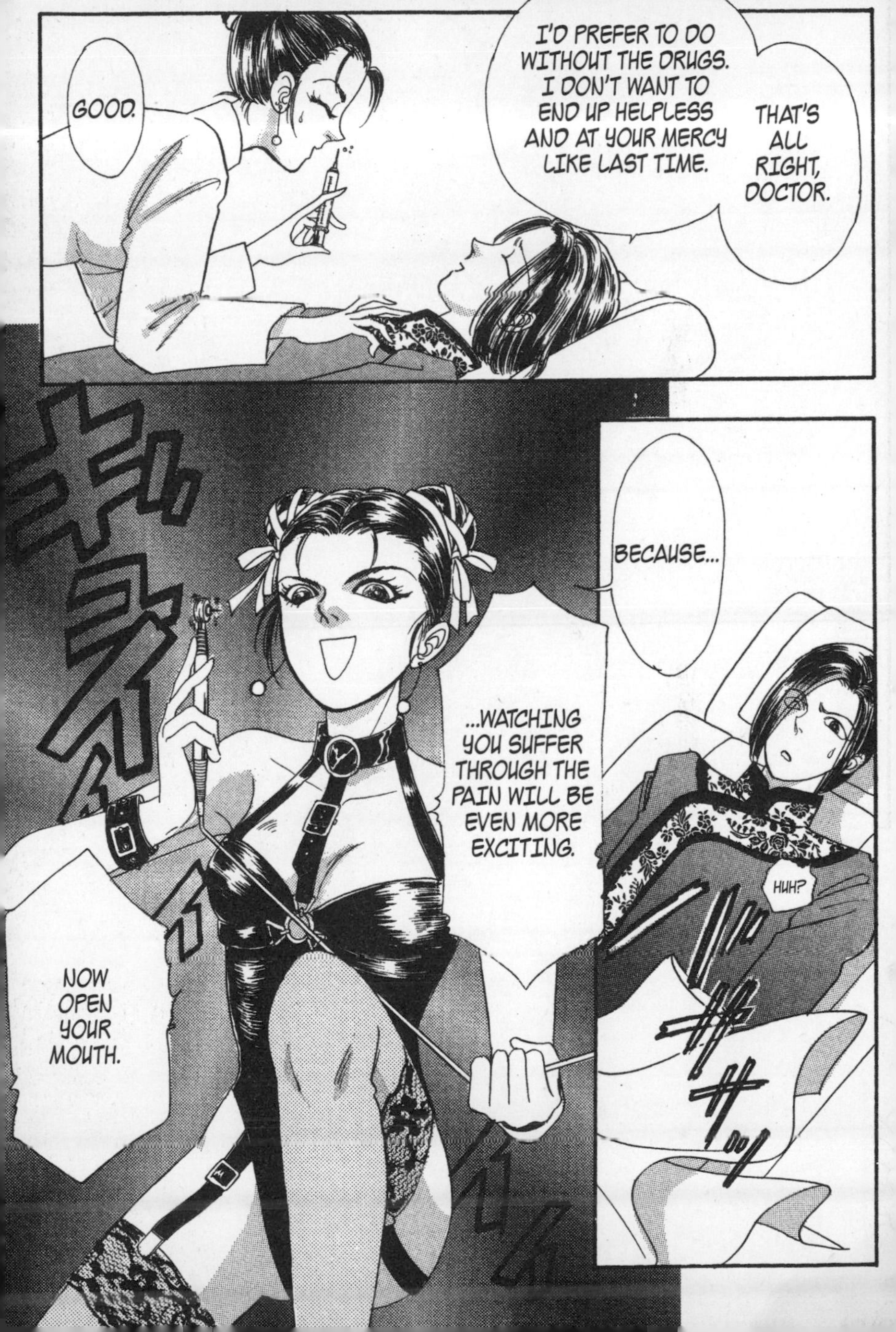
THAT'S ALL RIGHT, DOCTOR.
I'D PREFER TO DO WITHOUT THE DRUGS. I DON'T WANT TO END UP HELPLESS AND AT YOUR MERCY LIKE LAST TIME.
GOOD.
BECAUSE...
HUH?
...WATCHING YOU SUFFER THROUGH THE PAIN WILL BE EVEN MORE EXCITING.
NOW OPEN YOUR MOUTH.

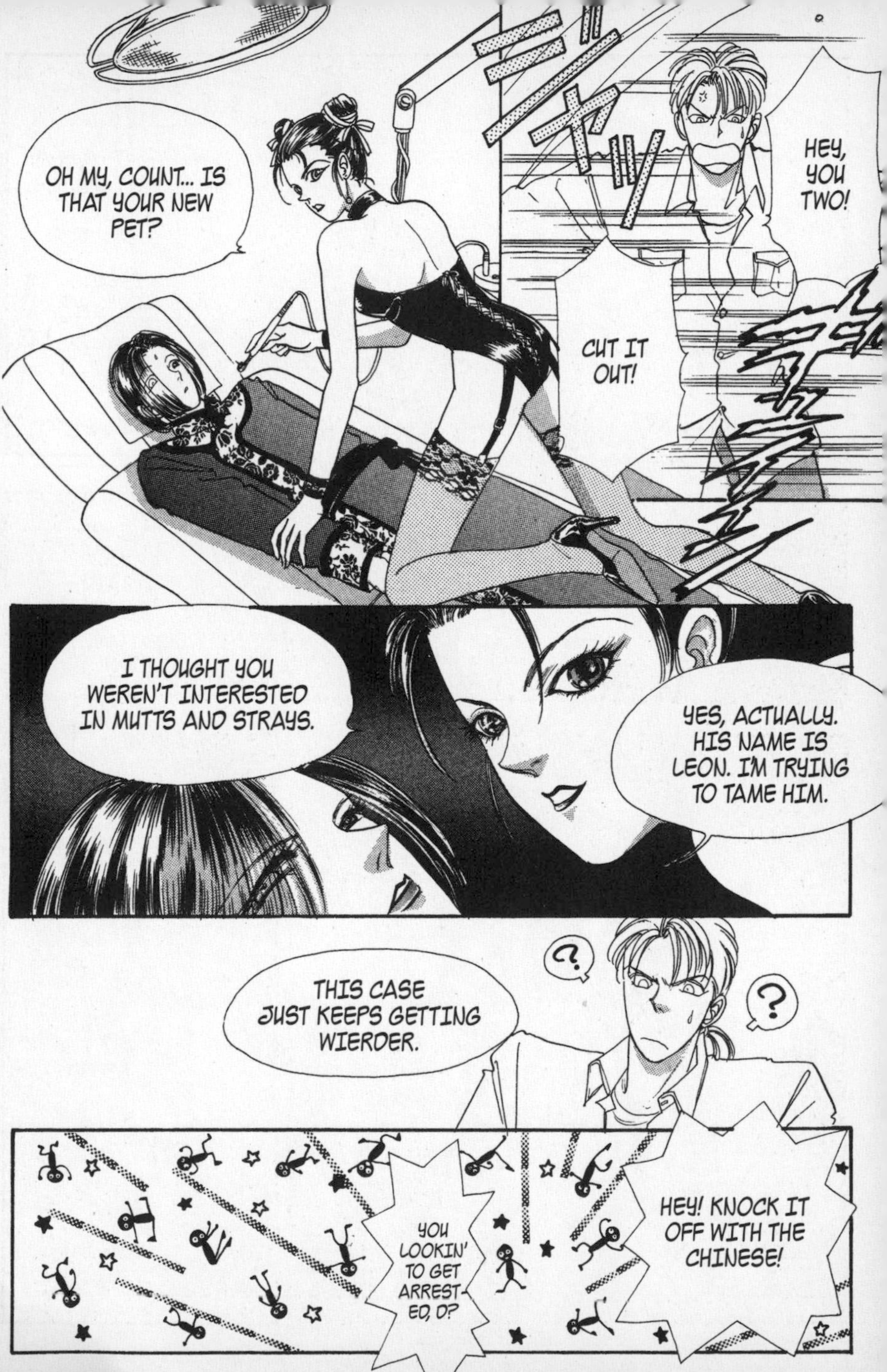
HEY, YOU TWO!
CUT IT OUT!
OH MY, COUNT... IS THAT YOUR NEW PET?
YES, ACTUALLY. HIS NAME IS LEON. I'M TRYING TO TAME HIM.
I THOUGHT YOU WEREN'T INTERESTED IN MUTTS AND STRAYS.
THIS CASE JUST KEEPS GETTING WIERDER.
HEY! KNOCK IT OFF WITH THE CHINESE!
YOU LOOKIN' TO GET ARREST-ED, D?

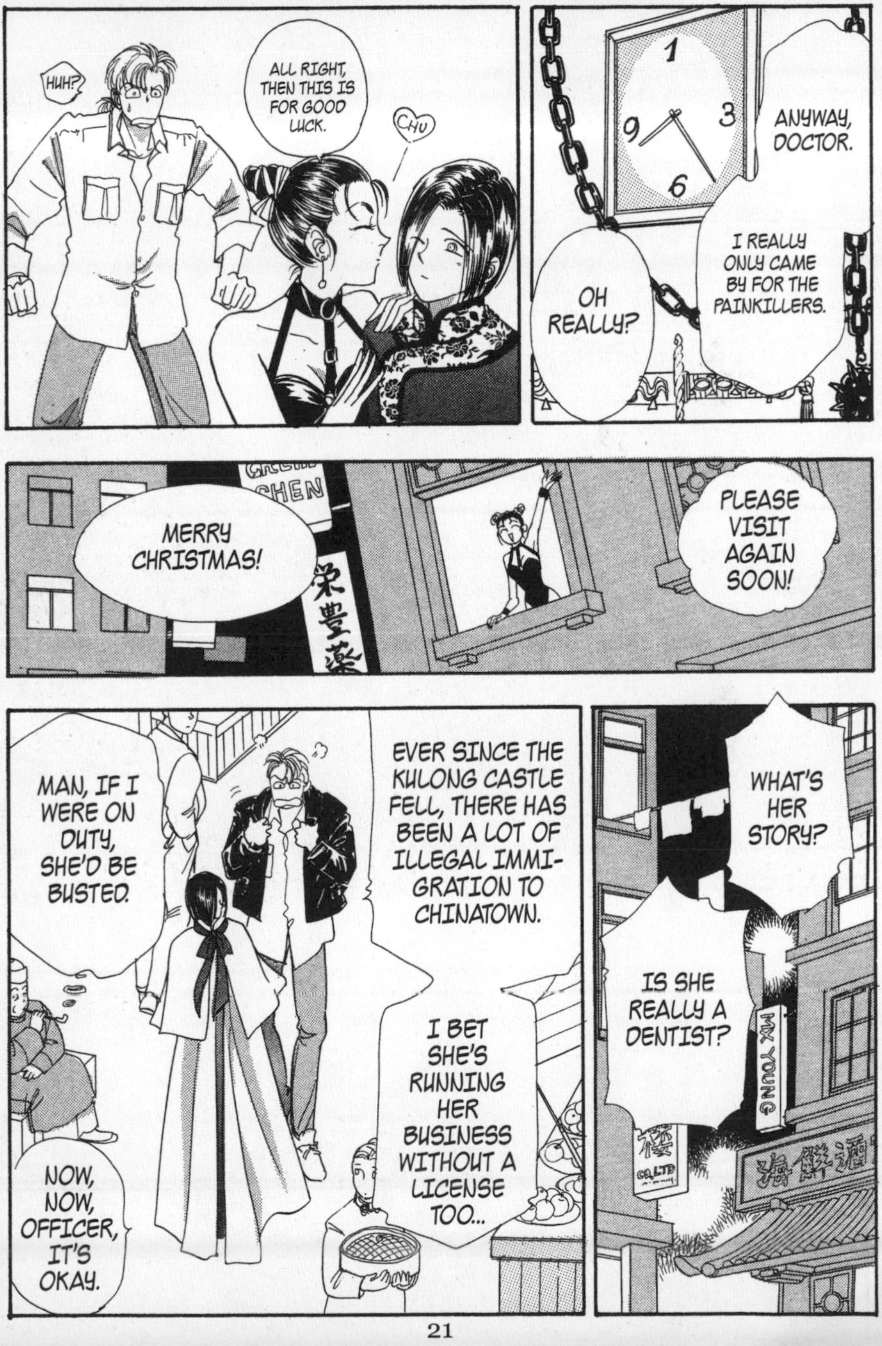
ANYWAY, DOCTOR.
I REALLY ONLY CAME BY FOR THE PAINKILLERS.
OH REALLY?
ALL RIGHT, THEN THIS IS FOR GOOD LUCK.
CHU
HUH?
PLEASE VISIT AGAIN SOON!
CHEN
MERRY CHRISTMAS!
WHAT'S HER STORY?
IS SHE REALLY A DENTIST?
MX YOUNG
CO.,LTD
EVER SINCE THE KULONG CASTLE FELL, THERE HAS BEEN A LOT OF ILLEGAL IMMIGRATION TO CHINATOWN.
MAN, IF I WERE ON DUTY, SHE'D BE BUSTED.
I BET SHE'S RUNNING HER BUSINESS WITHOUT A LICENSE TOO...
NOW, NOW, OFFICER, IT'S OKAY.

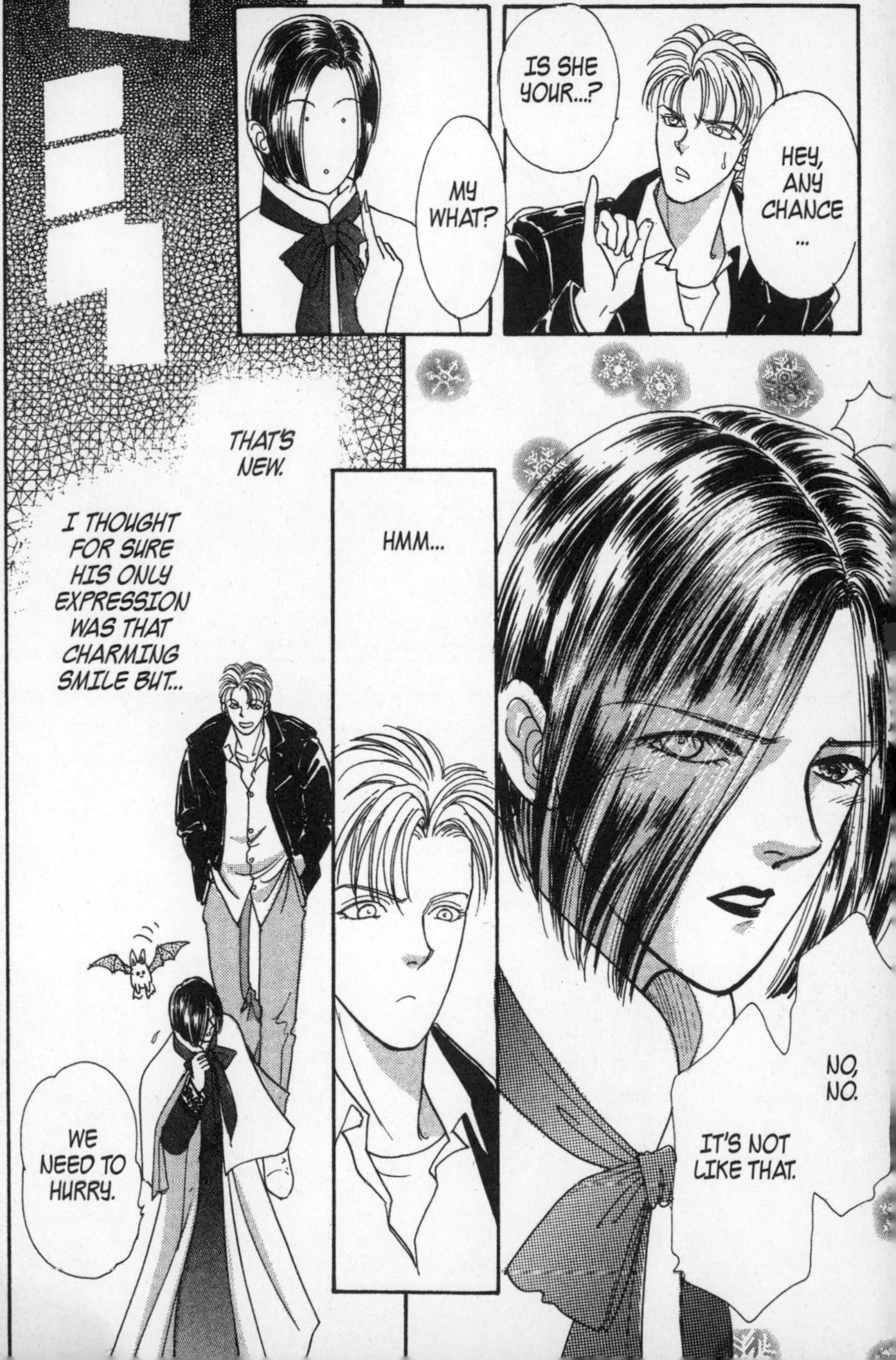
HEY, ANY CHANCE ...
IS SHE YOUR...?
MY WHAT?
NO, NO.
IT'S NOT LIKE THAT.
HMM...
THAT'S NEW.
I THOUGHT FOR SURE HIS ONLY EXPRESSION WAS THAT CHARMING SMILE BUT...
WE NEED TO HURRY.

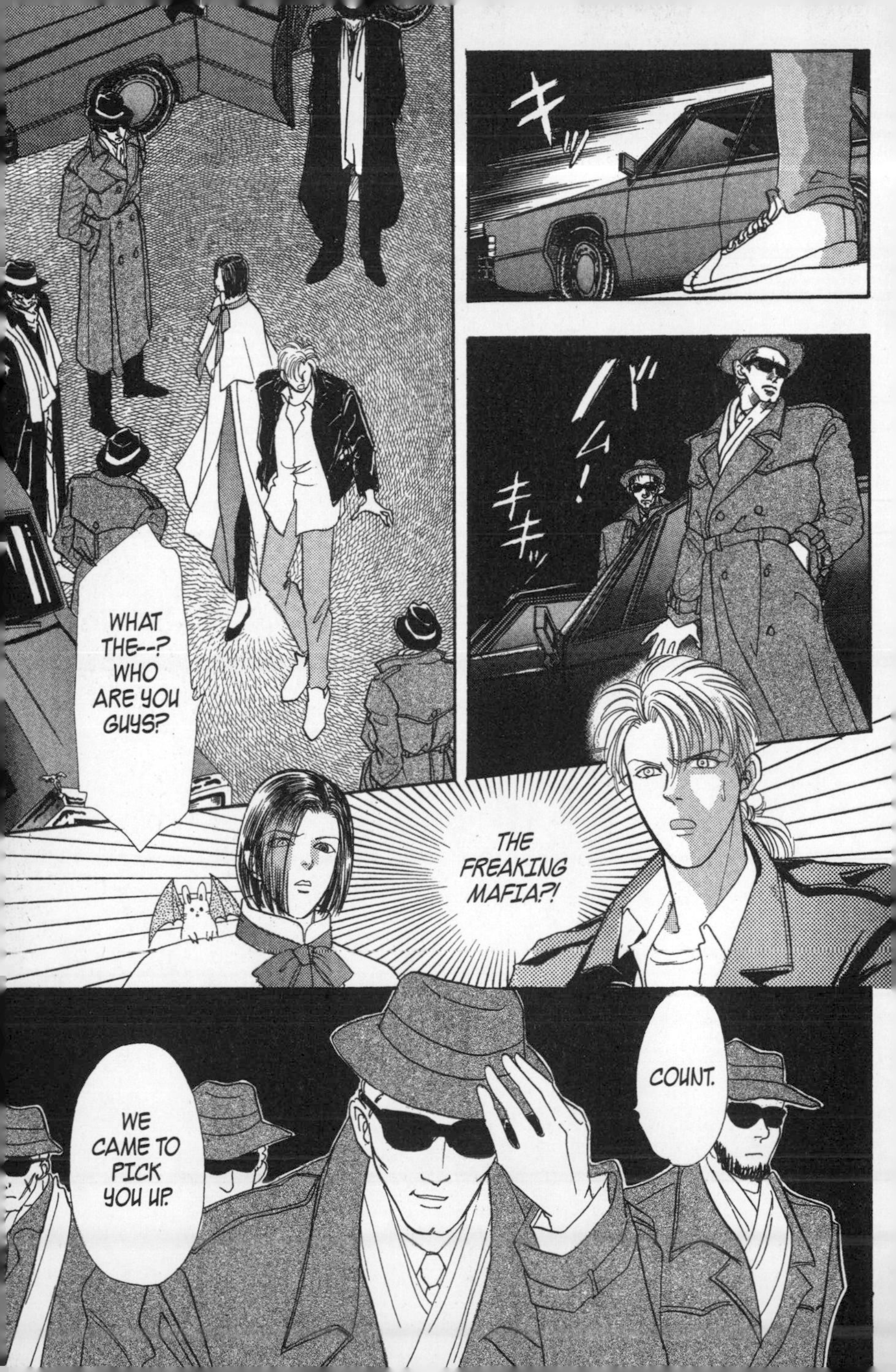
キッ
バム!
キキッ
WHAT THE--? WHO ARE YOU GUYS?
THE FREAKING MAFIA?!
COUNT.
WE CAME TO PICK YOU UP.

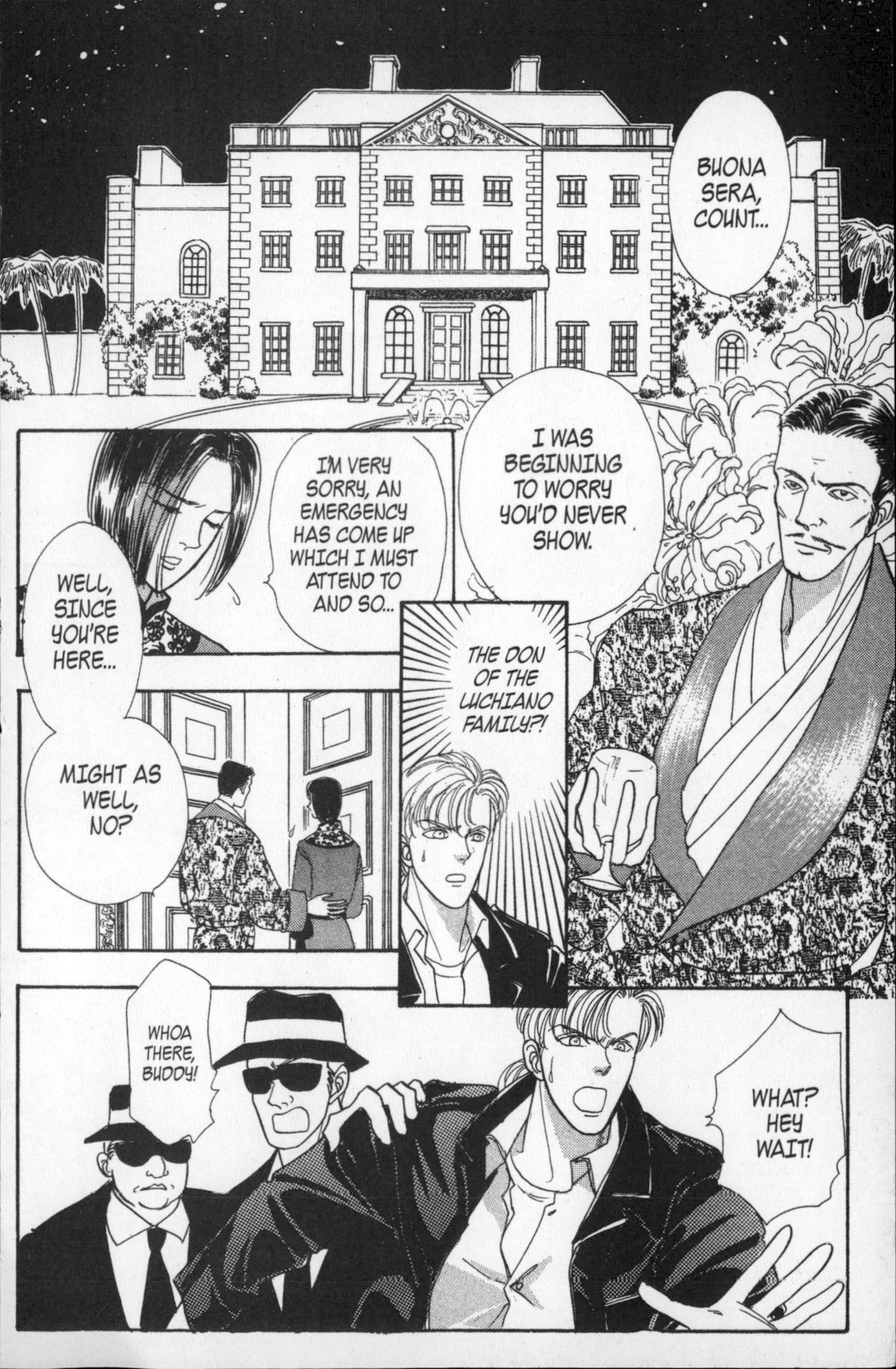

BUONA SERA, COUNT...
I WAS BEGINNING TO WORRY YOU'D NEVER SHOW.
I'M VERY SORRY, AN EMERGENCY HAS COME UP WHICH I MUST ATTEND TO AND SO...
WELL, SINCE YOU'RE HERE...
MIGHT AS WELL, NO?
THE DON OF THE LUCHIANO FAMILY?!
WHAT? HEY WAIT!
WHOA THERE, BUDDY!

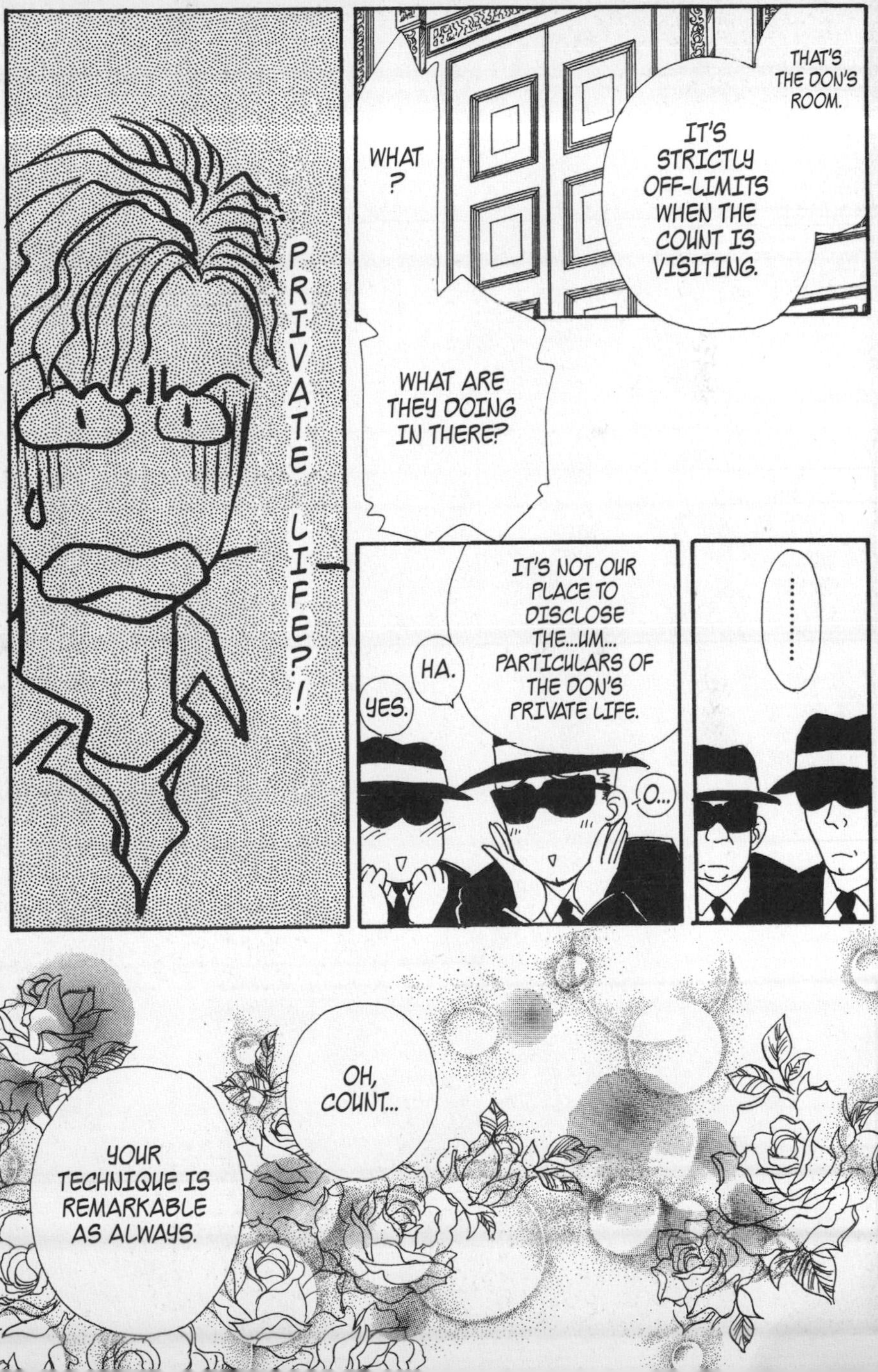
THAT'S THE DON'S ROOM.
IT'S STRICTLY OFF-LIMITS WHEN THE COUNT IS VISITING.
WHAT ?
WHAT ARE THEY DOING IN THERE?
......
IT'S NOT OUR PLACE TO DISCLOSE THE...UM... PARTICULARS OF THE DON'S PRIVATE LIFE.
HA.
YES.
O...
PRIVATE LIFE?!
OH, COUNT...
YOUR TECHNIQUE IS REMARKABLE AS ALWAYS.

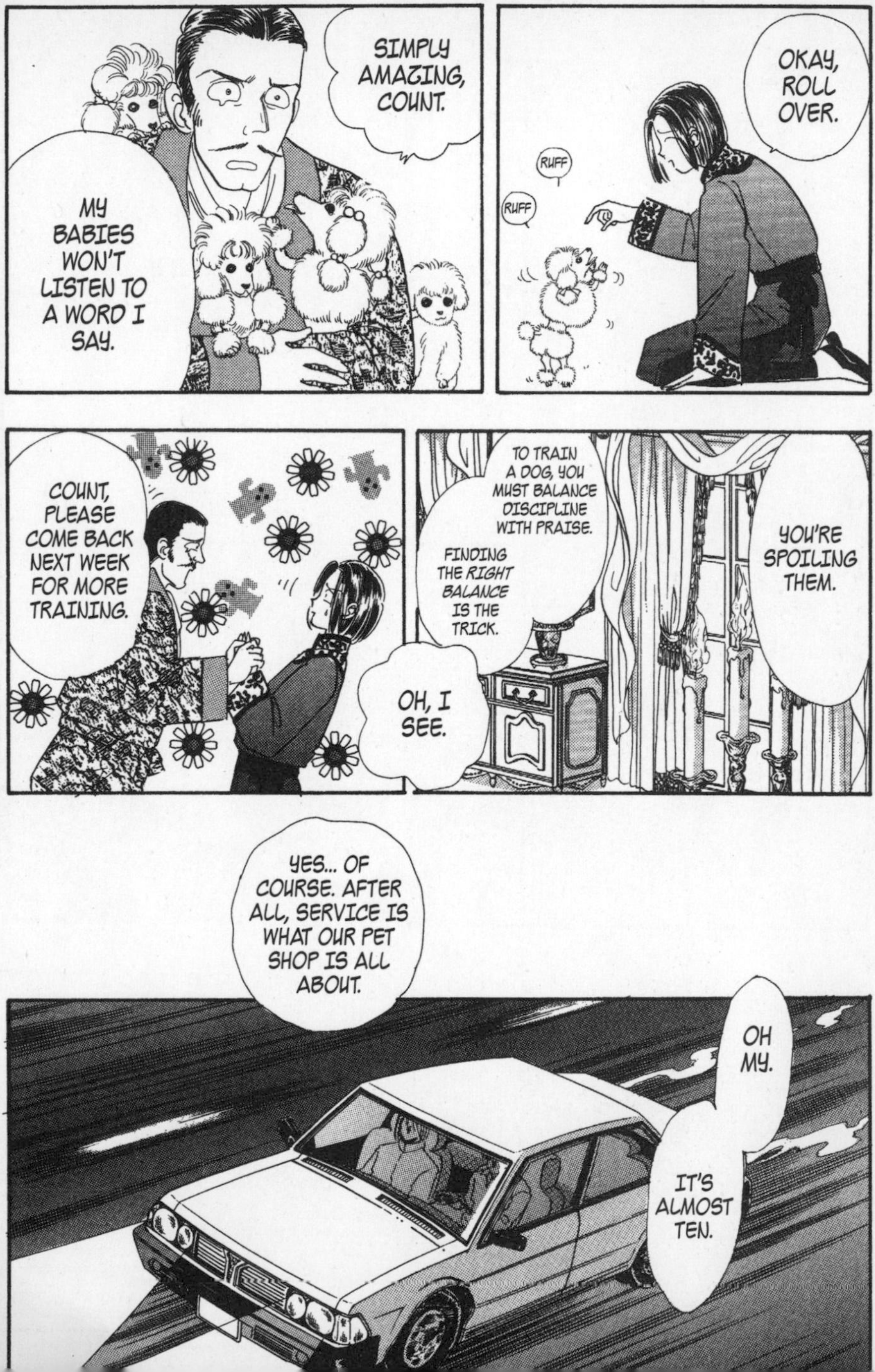
OKAY, ROLL OVER.
RUFF
RUFF
SIMPLY AMAZING, COUNT.
MY BABIES WON'T LISTEN TO A WORD I SAY.
YOU'RE SPOILING THEM.
TO TRAIN A DOG, YOU MUST BALANCE DISCIPLINE WITH PRAISE.
FINDING THE *RIGHT BALANCE* IS THE TRICK.
OH, I SEE.
COUNT, PLEASE COME BACK NEXT WEEK FOR MORE TRAINING.
YES... OF COURSE. AFTER ALL, SERVICE IS WHAT OUR PET SHOP IS ALL ABOUT.
OH MY.
IT'S ALMOST TEN.

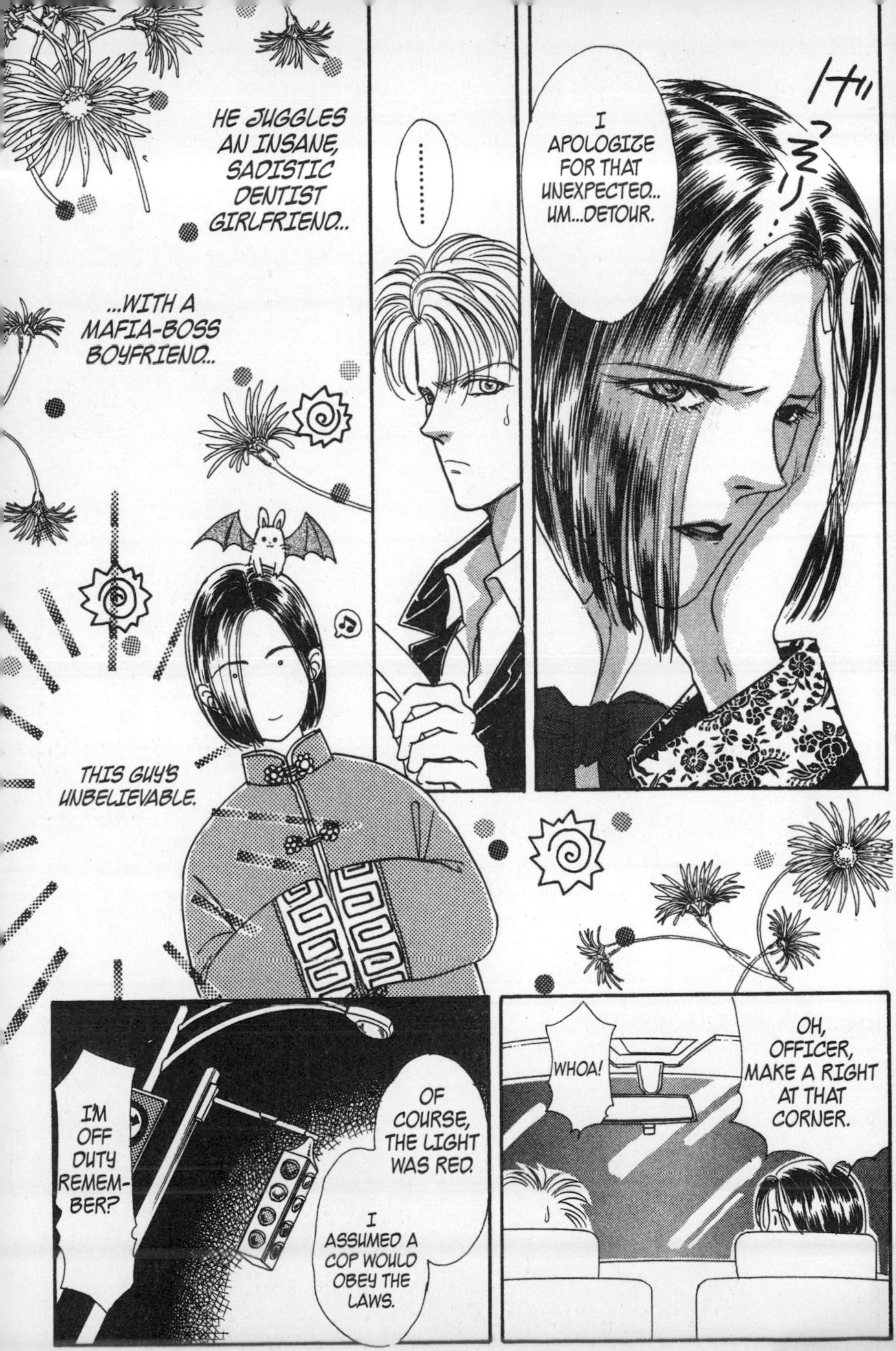
I APOLOGIZE FOR THAT UNEXPECTED... UM...DETOUR.
......
HE JUGGLES AN INSANE, SADISTIC DENTIST GIRLFRIEND...
...WITH A MAFIA-BOSS BOYFRIEND...
THIS GUY'S UNBELIEVABLE.
OH, OFFICER, MAKE A RIGHT AT THAT CORNER.
WHOA!
OF COURSE, THE LIGHT WAS RED.
I ASSUMED A COP WOULD OBEY THE LAWS.
I'M OFF DUTY REMEMBER?

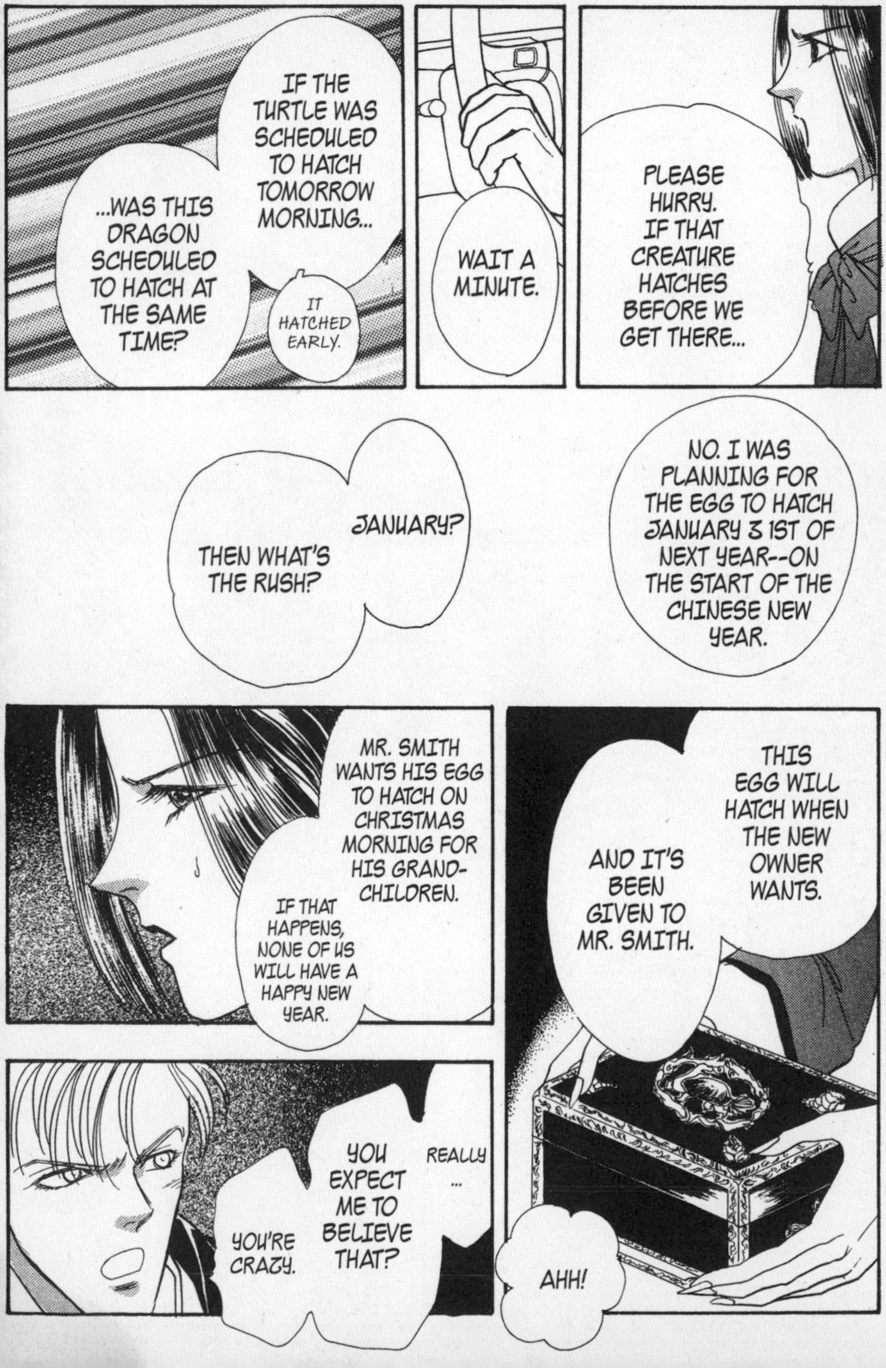
PLEASE HURRY. IF THAT CREATURE HATCHES BEFORE WE GET THERE...
WAIT A MINUTE.
IF THE TURTLE WAS SCHEDULED TO HATCH TOMORROW MORNING...
...WAS THIS DRAGON SCHEDULED TO HATCH AT THE SAME TIME?
IT HATCHED EARLY.
NO. I WAS PLANNING FOR THE EGG TO HATCH JANUARY 31ST OF NEXT YEAR--ON THE START OF THE CHINESE NEW YEAR.
JANUARY?
THEN WHAT'S THE RUSH?
THIS EGG WILL HATCH WHEN THE NEW OWNER WANTS.
AND IT'S BEEN GIVEN TO MR. SMITH.
AHH!
MR. SMITH WANTS HIS EGG TO HATCH ON CHRISTMAS MORNING FOR HIS GRAND-CHILDREN.
IF THAT HAPPENS, NONE OF US WILL HAVE A HAPPY NEW YEAR.
REALLY...
YOU EXPECT ME TO BELIEVE THAT?
YOU'RE CRAZY.

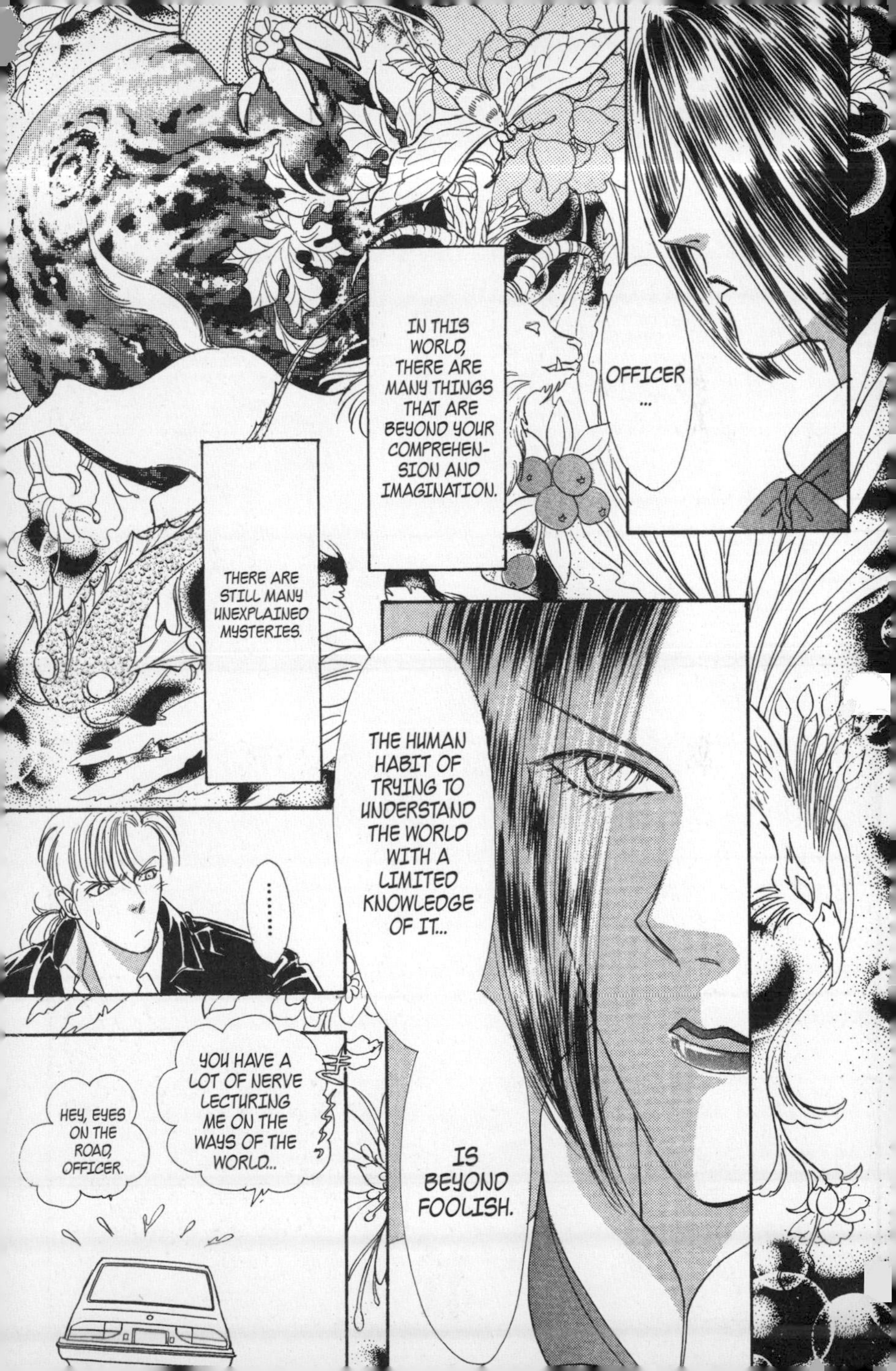
OFFICER ...
IN THIS WORLD, THERE ARE MANY THINGS THAT ARE BEYOND YOUR COMPREHEN-SION AND IMAGINATION.
THERE ARE STILL MANY UNEXPLAINED MYSTERIES.
THE HUMAN HABIT OF TRYING TO UNDERSTAND THE WORLD WITH A LIMITED KNOWLEDGE OF IT...
IS BEYOND FOOLISH.
......
YOU HAVE A LOT OF NERVE LECTURING ME ON THE WAYS OF THE WORLD...
HEY, EYES ON THE ROAD, OFFICER.

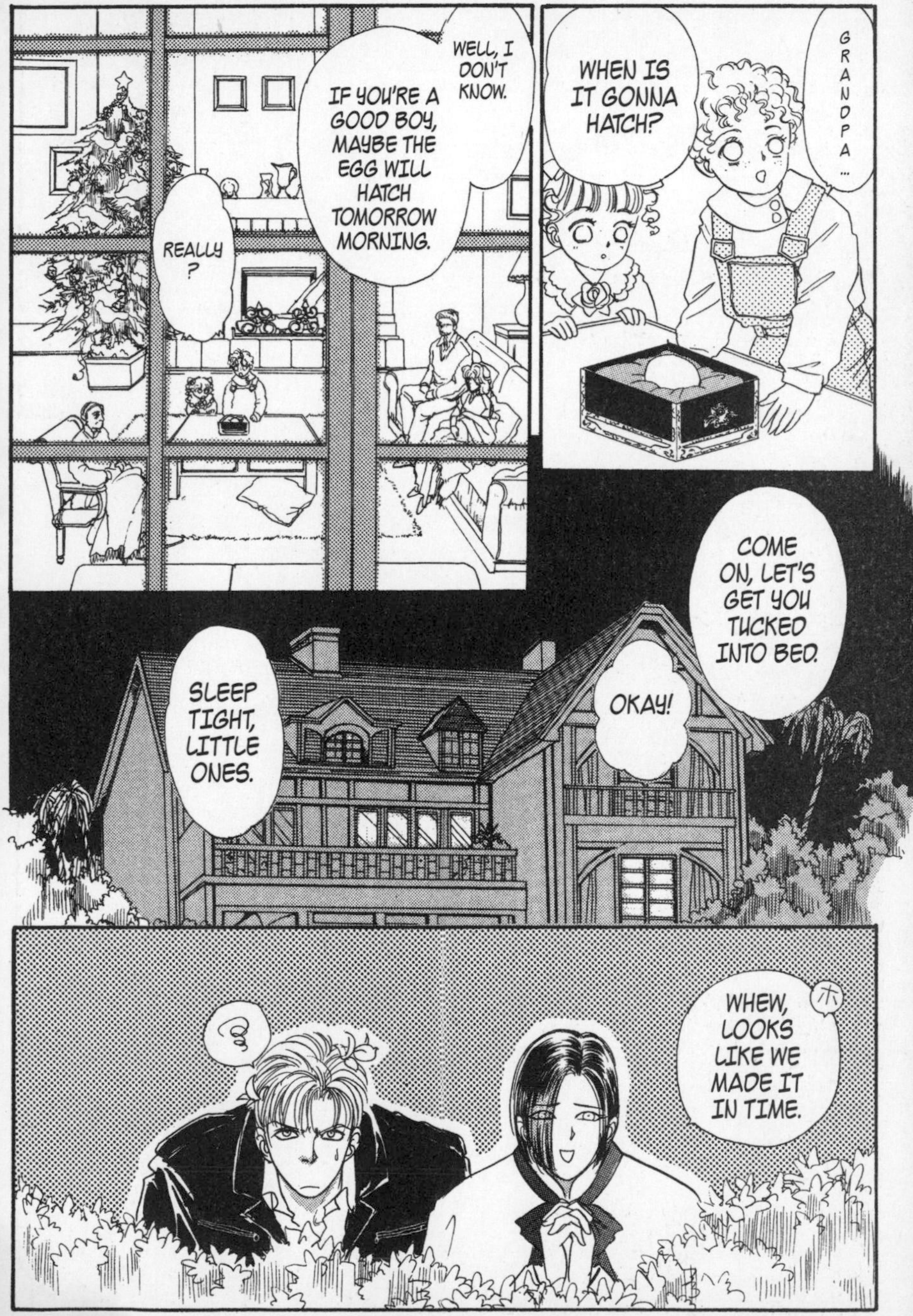
GRANDPA...
WHEN IS IT GONNA HATCH?
WELL, I DON'T KNOW.
IF YOU'RE A GOOD BOY, MAYBE THE EGG WILL HATCH TOMORROW MORNING.
REALLY?
COME ON, LET'S GET YOU TUCKED INTO BED.
OKAY!
SLEEP TIGHT, LITTLE ONES.
ホ
WHEW, LOOKS LIKE WE MADE IT IN TIME.

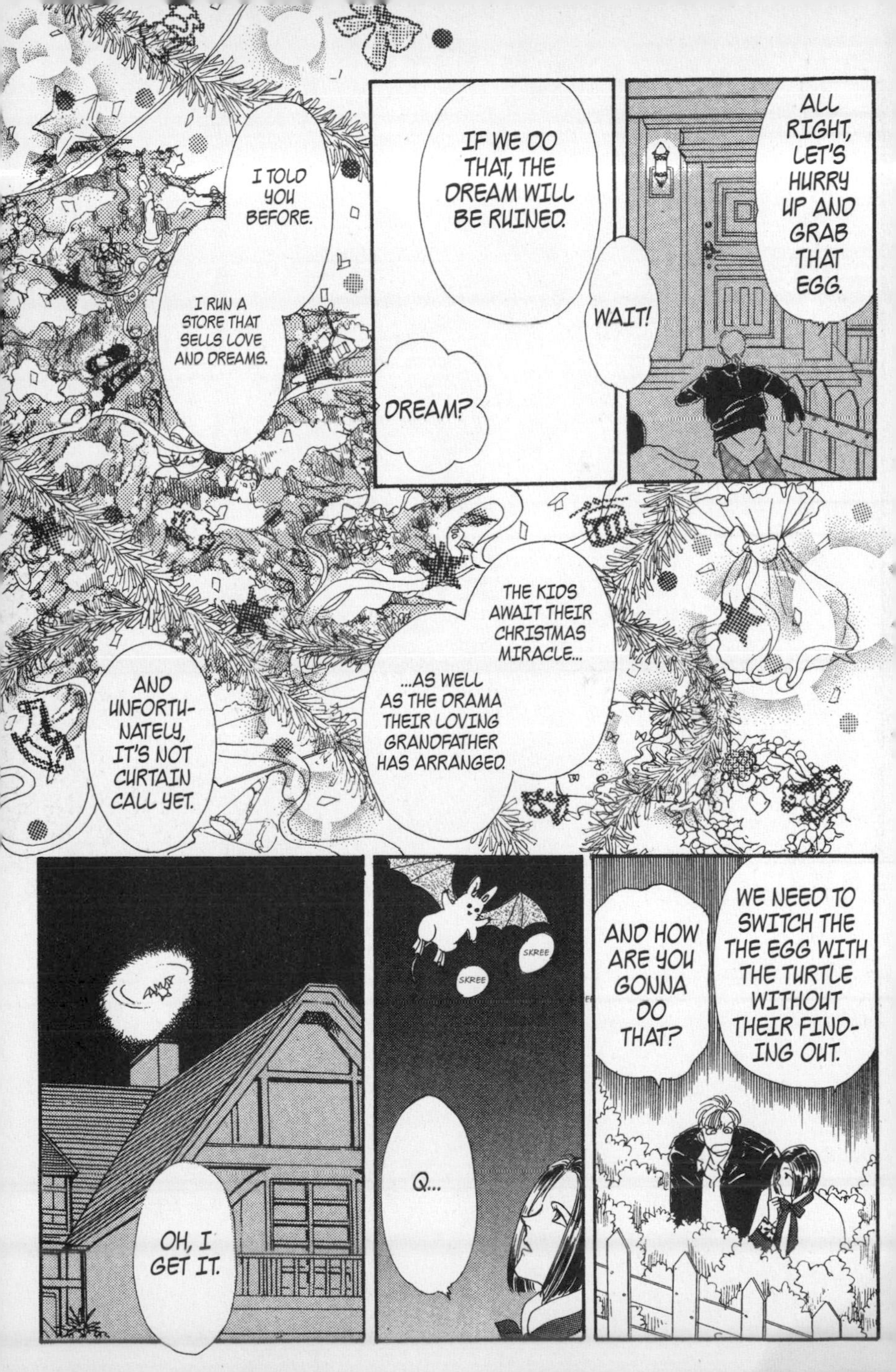
ALL RIGHT, LET'S HURRY UP AND GRAB THAT EGG.
WAIT!
IF WE DO THAT, THE DREAM WILL BE RUINED.
DREAM?
I TOLD YOU BEFORE.
I RUN A STORE THAT SELLS LOVE AND DREAMS.
THE KIDS AWAIT THEIR CHRISTMAS MIRACLE...
...AS WELL AS THE DRAMA THEIR LOVING GRANDFATHER HAS ARRANGED.
AND UNFORTU-NATELY, IT'S NOT CURTAIN CALL YET.
WE NEED TO SWITCH THE THE EGG WITH THE TURTLE WITHOUT THEIR FIND-ING OUT.
AND HOW ARE YOU GONNA DO THAT?
SKREE
SKREE
Q...
OH, I GET IT.

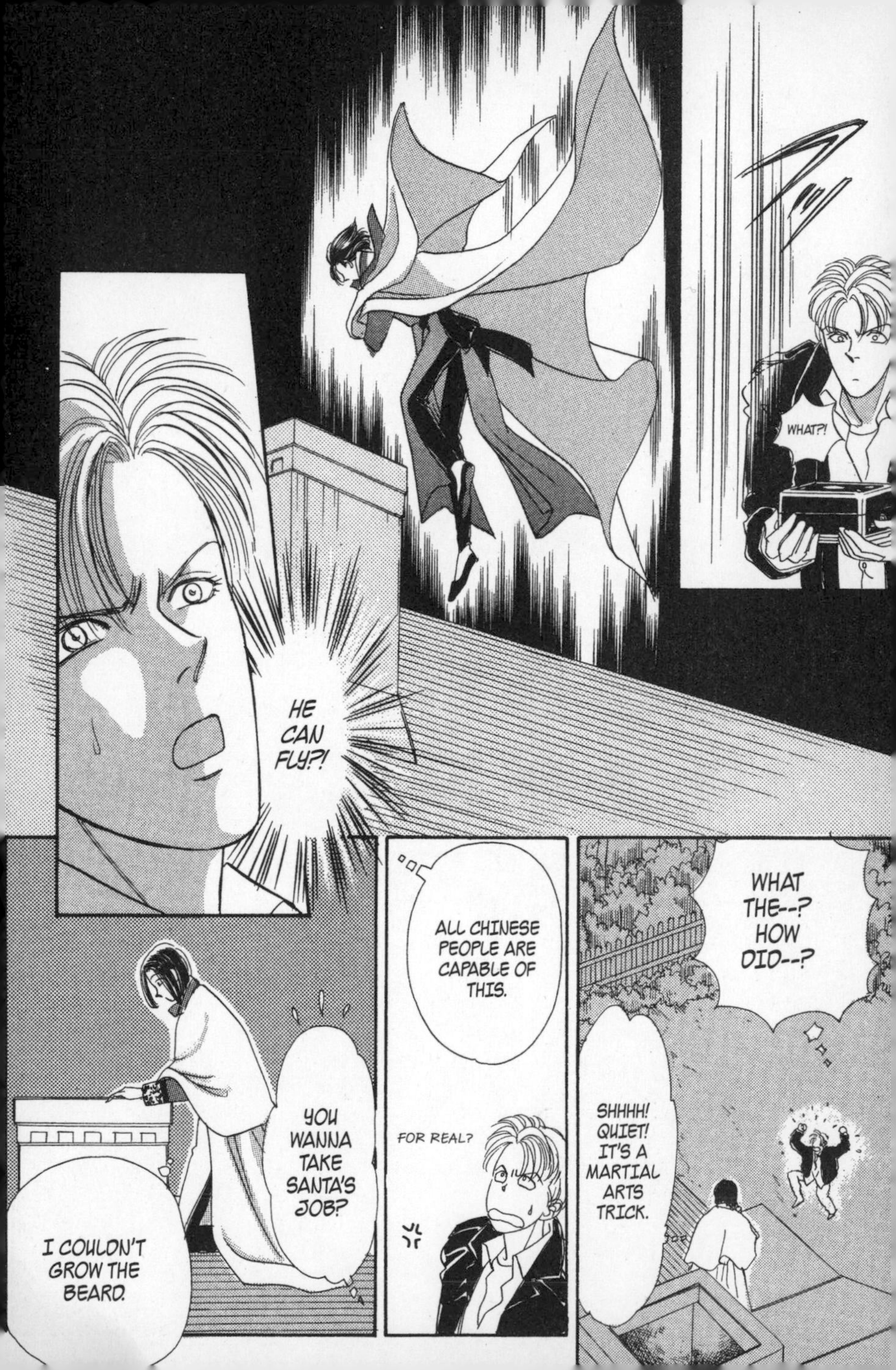
WHAT?!
HE CAN FLY?!
WHAT THE--? HOW DID--?
SHHHH! QUIET! IT'S A MARTIAL ARTS TRICK.
ALL CHINESE PEOPLE ARE CAPABLE OF THIS.
FOR REAL?
YOU WANNA TAKE SANTA'S JOB?
I COULDN'T GROW THE BEARD.

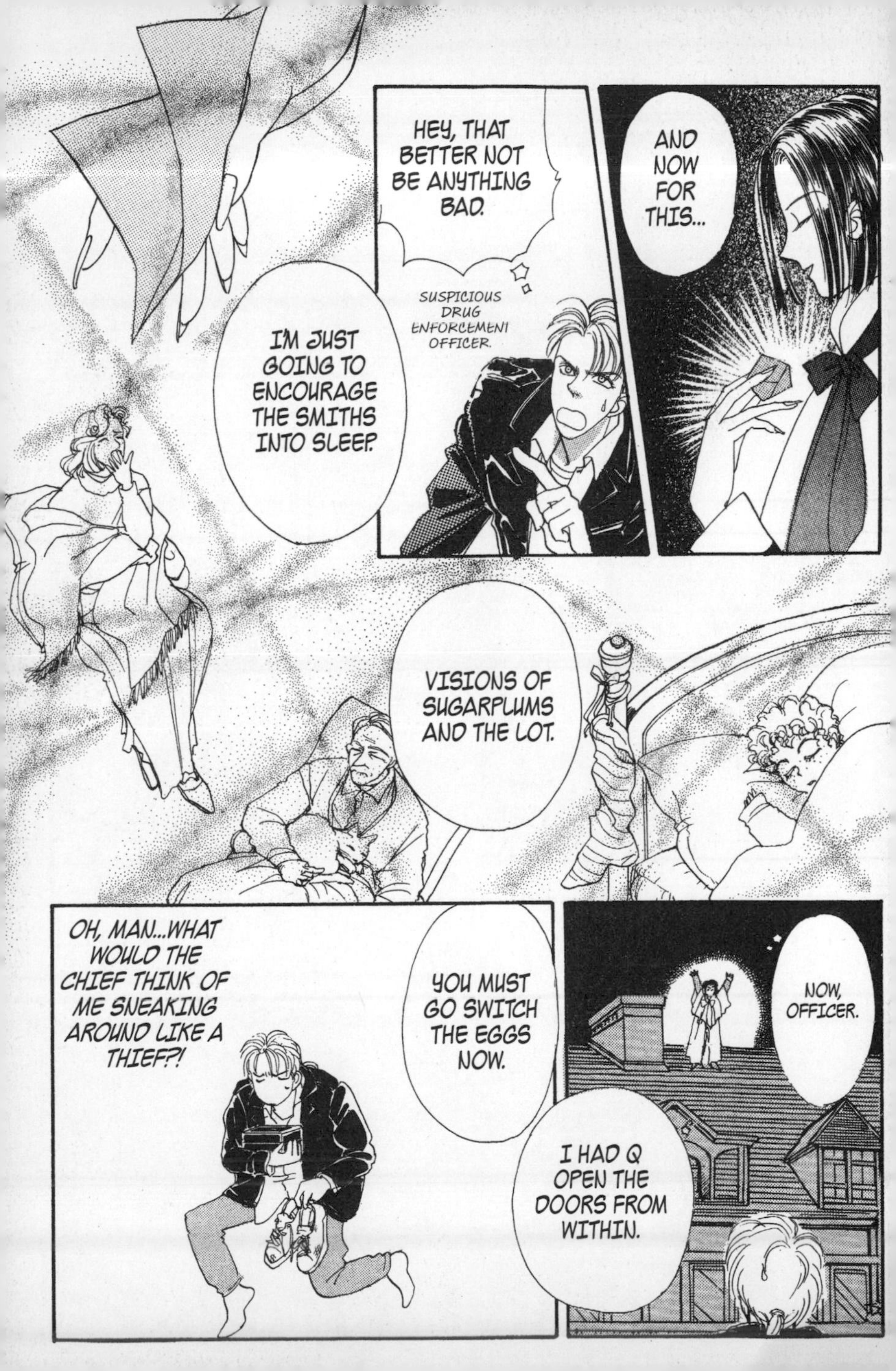
AND NOW FOR THIS...
HEY, THAT BETTER NOT BE ANYTHING BAD.
SUSPICIOUS DRUG ENFORCEMENI OFFICER.
I'M JUST GOING TO ENCOURAGE THE SMITHS INTO SLEEP.
VISIONS OF SUGARPLUMS AND THE LOT.
NOW, OFFICER.
I HAD Q OPEN THE DOORS FROM WITHIN.
YOU MUST GO SWITCH THE EGGS NOW.
OH, MAN...WHAT WOULD THE CHIEF THINK OF ME SNEAKING AROUND LIKE A THIEF?!

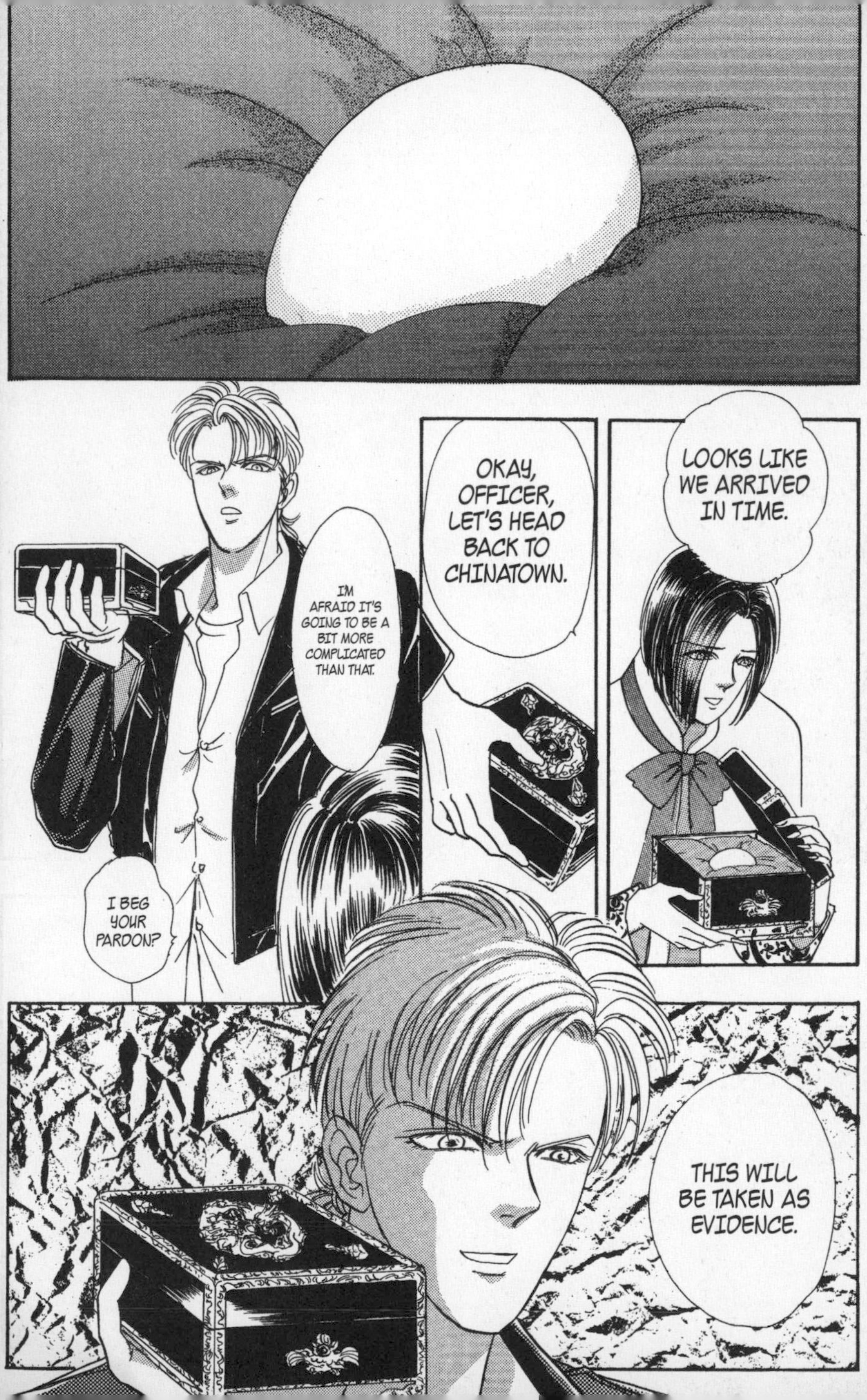
LOOKS LIKE WE ARRIVED IN TIME.
OKAY, OFFICER, LET'S HEAD BACK TO CHINATOWN.
I'M AFRAID IT'S GOING TO BE A BIT MORE COMPLICATED THAN THAT.
I BEG YOUR PARDON?
THIS WILL BE TAKEN AS EVIDENCE.

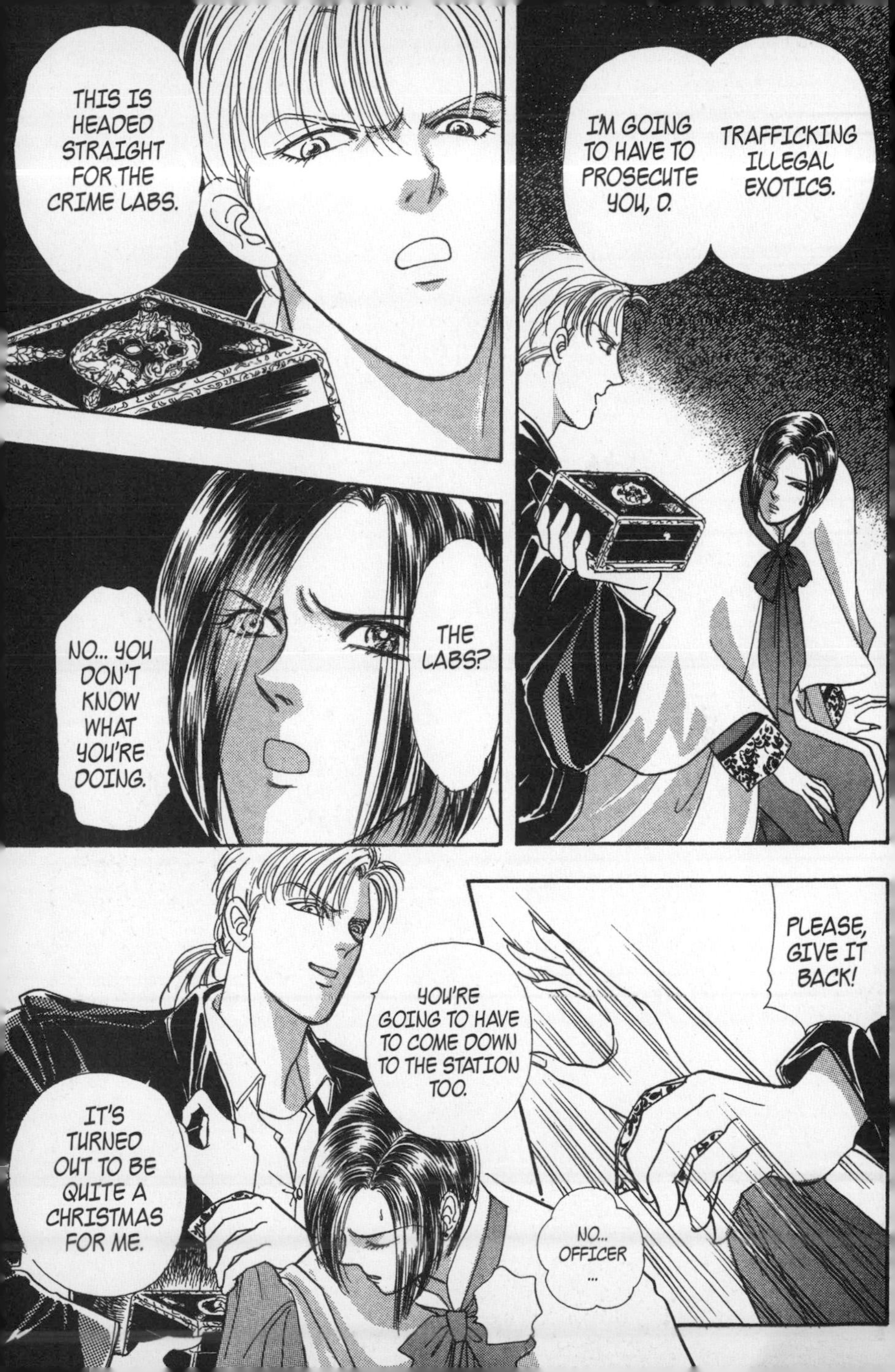
TRAFFICKING ILLEGAL EXOTICS.
I'M GOING TO HAVE TO PROSECUTE YOU, D.
THIS IS HEADED STRAIGHT FOR THE CRIME LABS.
THE LABS?
NO... YOU DON'T KNOW WHAT YOU'RE DOING.
PLEASE, GIVE IT BACK!
NO... OFFICER ...
YOU'RE GOING TO HAVE TO COME DOWN TO THE STATION TOO.
IT'S TURNED OUT TO BE QUITE A CHRISTMAS FOR ME.

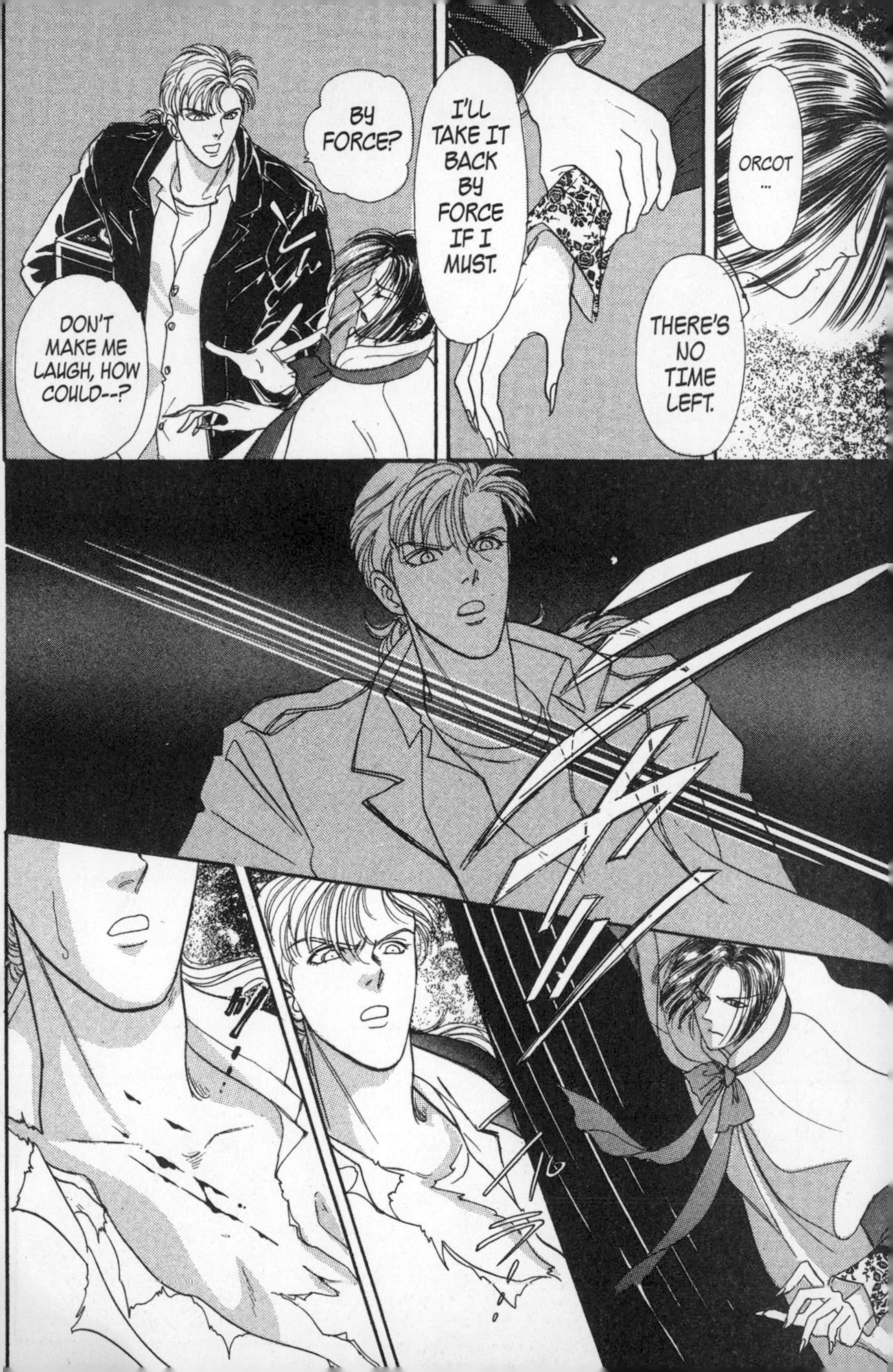
ORCOT ...
THERE'S NO TIME LEFT.
I'LL TAKE IT BACK BY FORCE IF I MUST.
BY FORCE?
DON'T MAKE ME LAUGH, HOW COULD--?

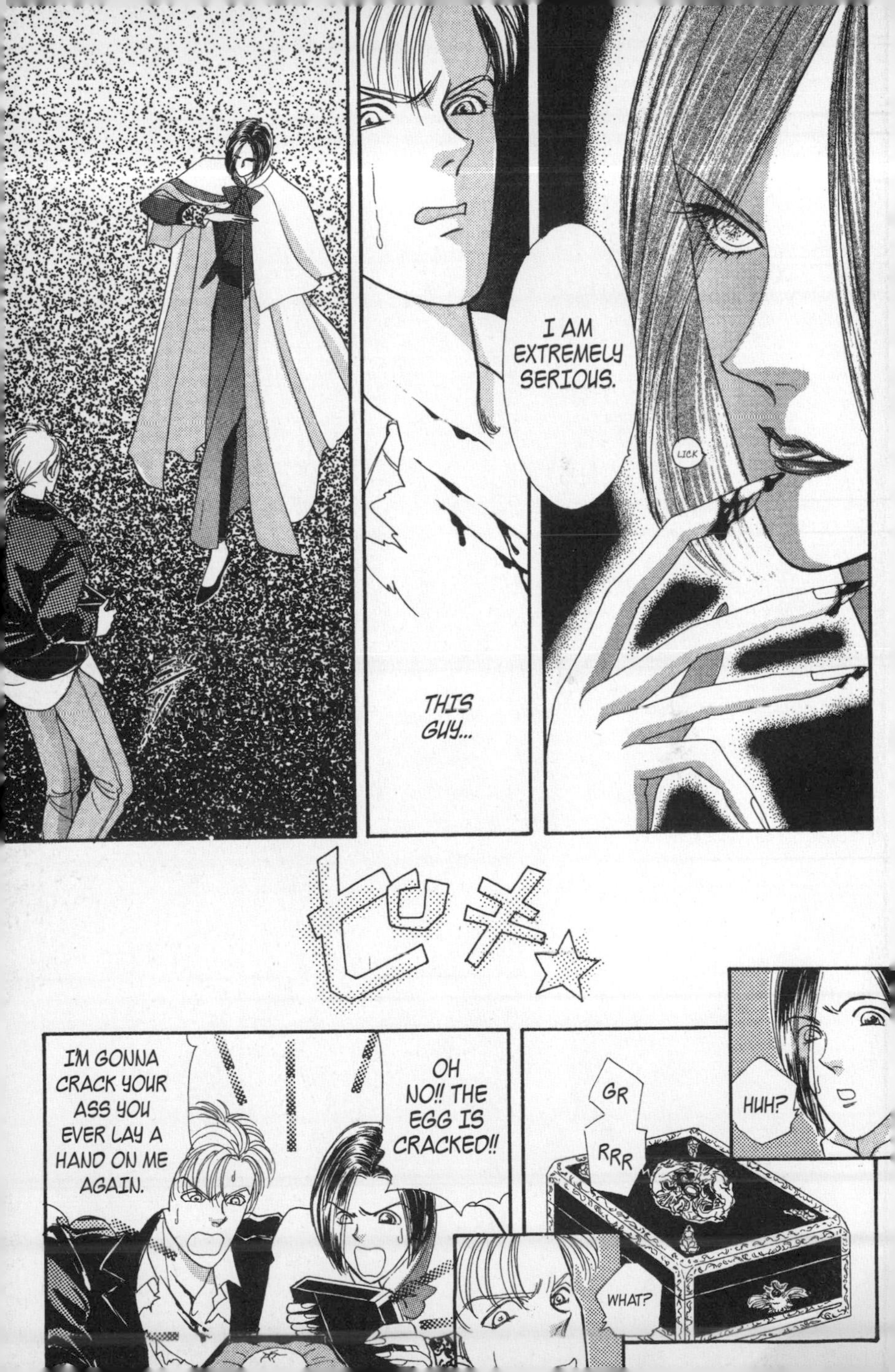
LICK
I AM EXTREMELY SERIOUS.
THIS GUY...
HUH?
GR
RRR
WHAT?
OH NO!! THE EGG IS CRACKED!!
I'M GONNA CRACK YOUR ASS YOU EVER LAY A HAND ON ME AGAIN.

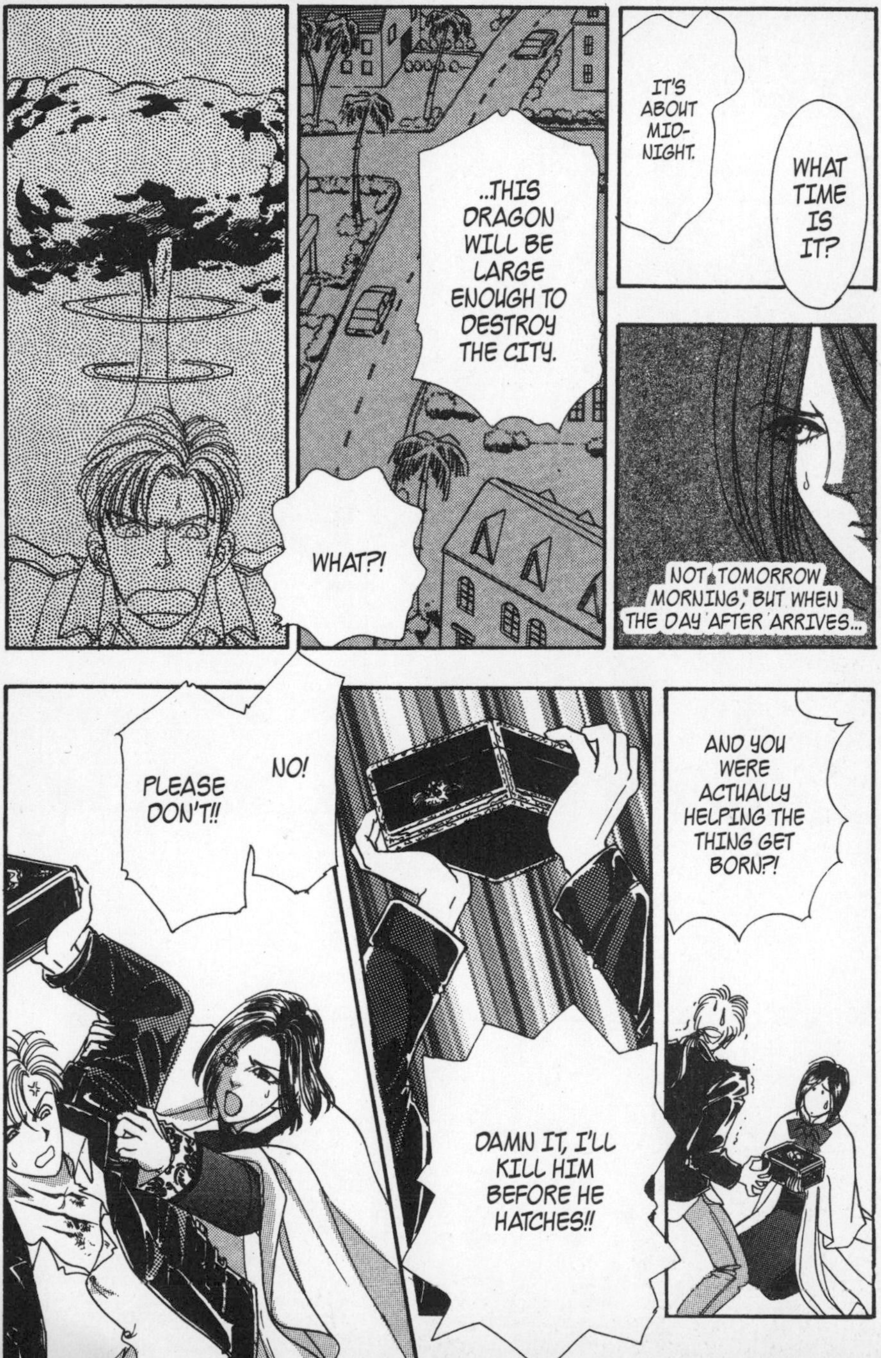
WHAT TIME IS IT?
IT'S ABOUT MID-NIGHT.
NOT TOMORROW MORNING, BUT WHEN THE DAY AFTER ARRIVES...
...THIS DRAGON WILL BE LARGE ENOUGH TO DESTROY THE CITY.
WHAT?!
AND YOU WERE ACTUALLY HELPING THE THING GET BORN?!
DAMN IT, I'LL KILL HIM BEFORE HE HATCHES!!
NO!
PLEASE DON'T!!

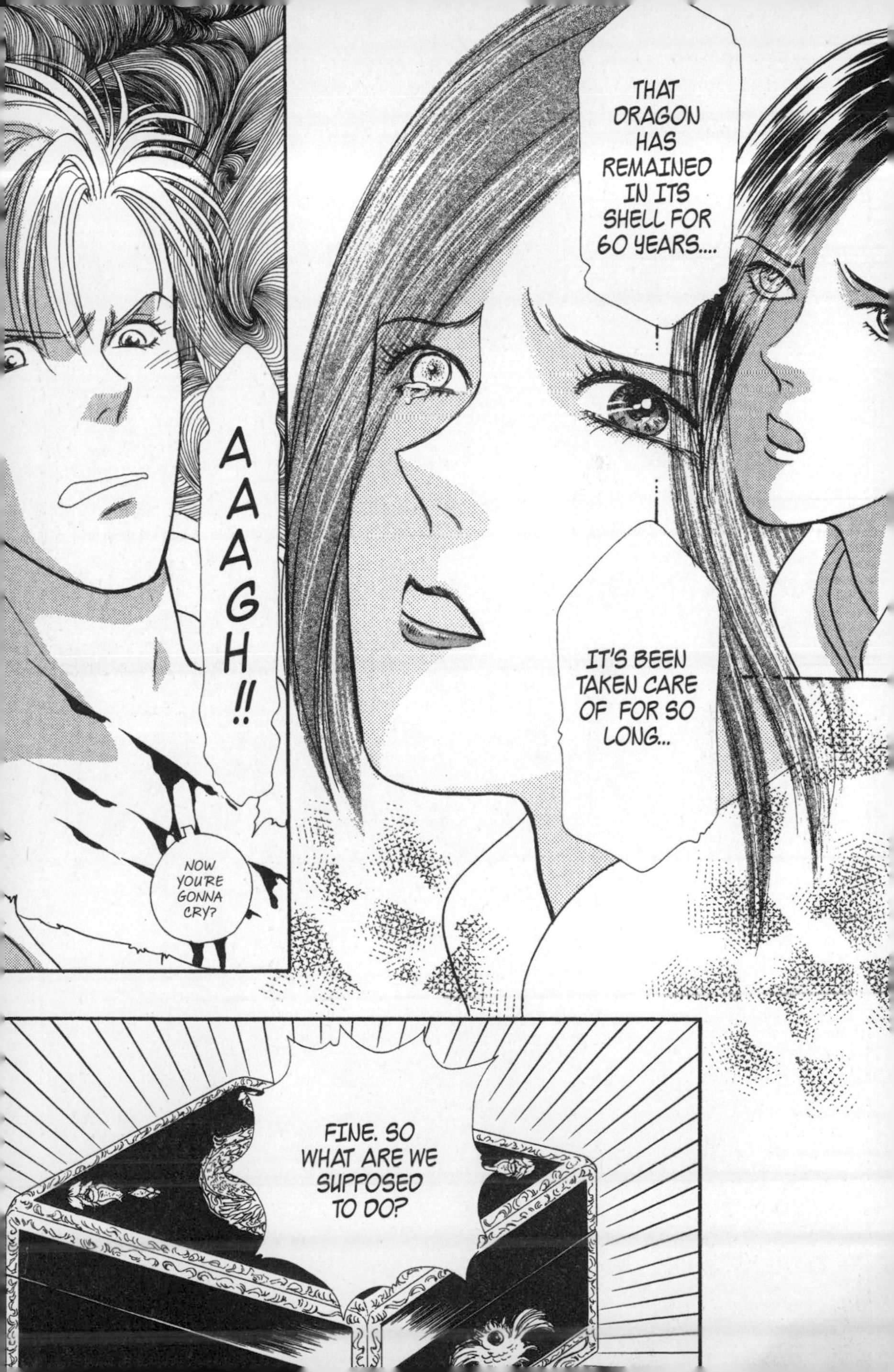
THAT DRAGON HAS REMAINED IN ITS SHELL FOR 60 YEARS....
IT'S BEEN TAKEN CARE OF FOR SO LONG...
AAAGH!!
NOW YOU'RE GONNA CRY?
FINE. SO WHAT ARE WE SUPPOSED TO DO?

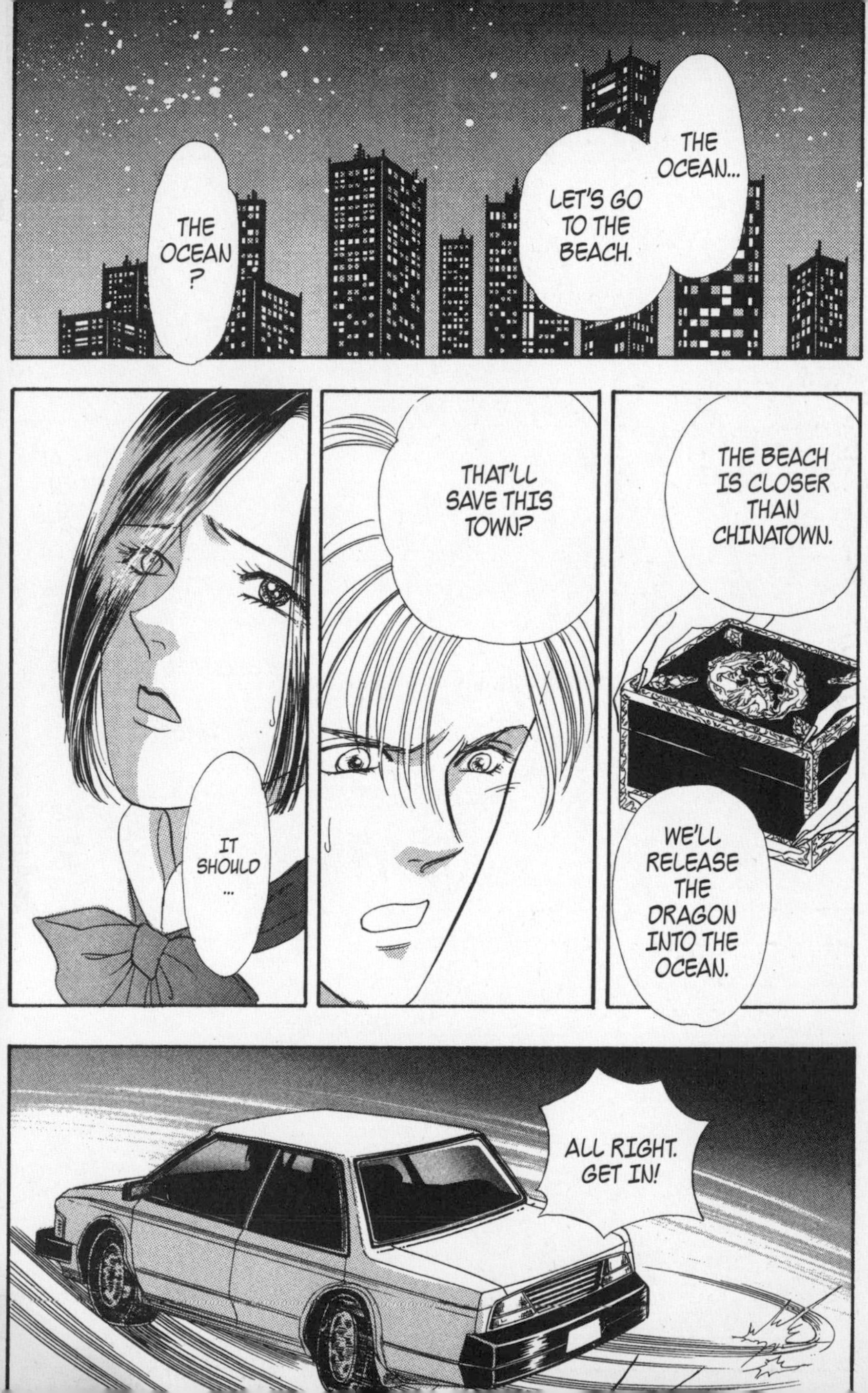
THE OCEAN...
LET'S GO TO THE BEACH.
THE OCEAN ?
THE BEACH IS CLOSER THAN CHINATOWN.
WE'LL RELEASE THE DRAGON INTO THE OCEAN.
THAT'LL SAVE THIS TOWN?
IT SHOULD ...
ALL RIGHT. GET IN!

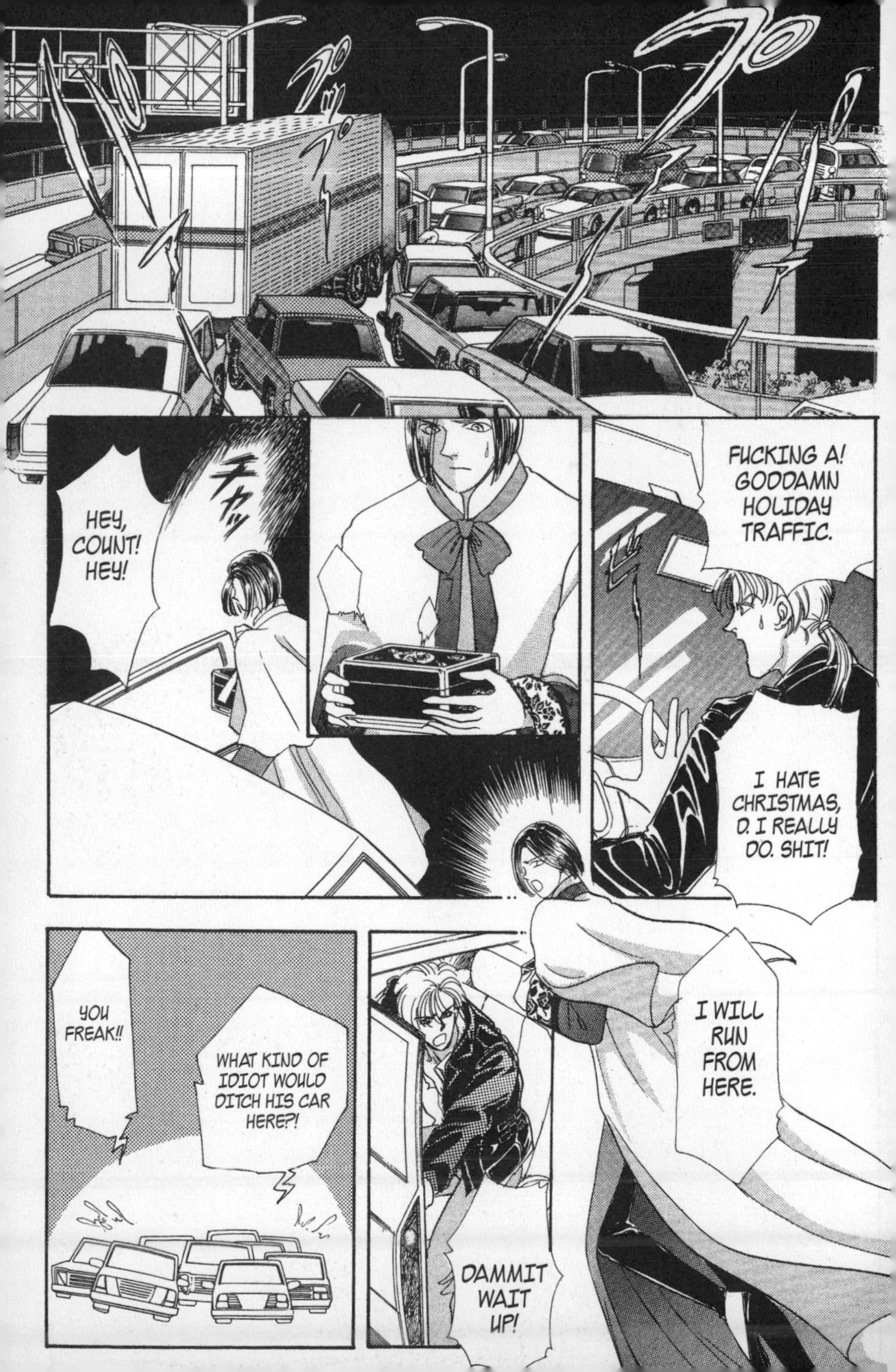
FUCKING A! GODDAMN HOLIDAY TRAFFIC.
I HATE CHRISTMAS, D. I REALLY DO. SHIT!
HEY, COUNT! HEY!
I WILL RUN FROM HERE.
DAMMIT WAIT UP!
YOU FREAK!!
WHAT KIND OF IDIOT WOULD DITCH HIS CAR HERE?!

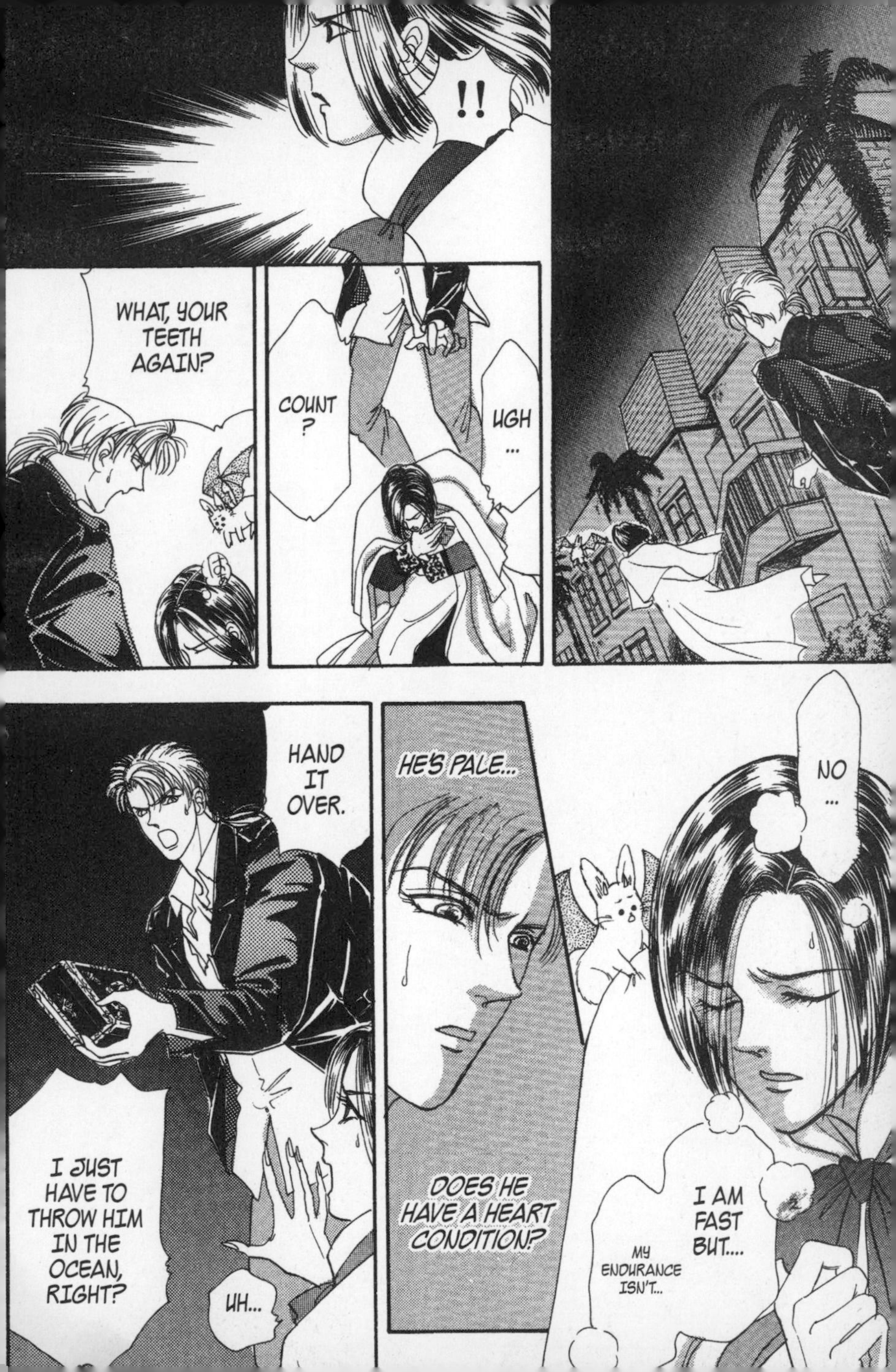
!!
UGH ...
COUNT ?
WHAT, YOUR TEETH AGAIN?
NO ...
I AM FAST BUT....
MY ENDURANCE ISN'T...
HE'S PALE...
DOES HE HAVE A HEART CONDITION?
HAND IT OVER.
I JUST HAVE TO THROW HIM IN THE OCEAN, RIGHT?
UH...

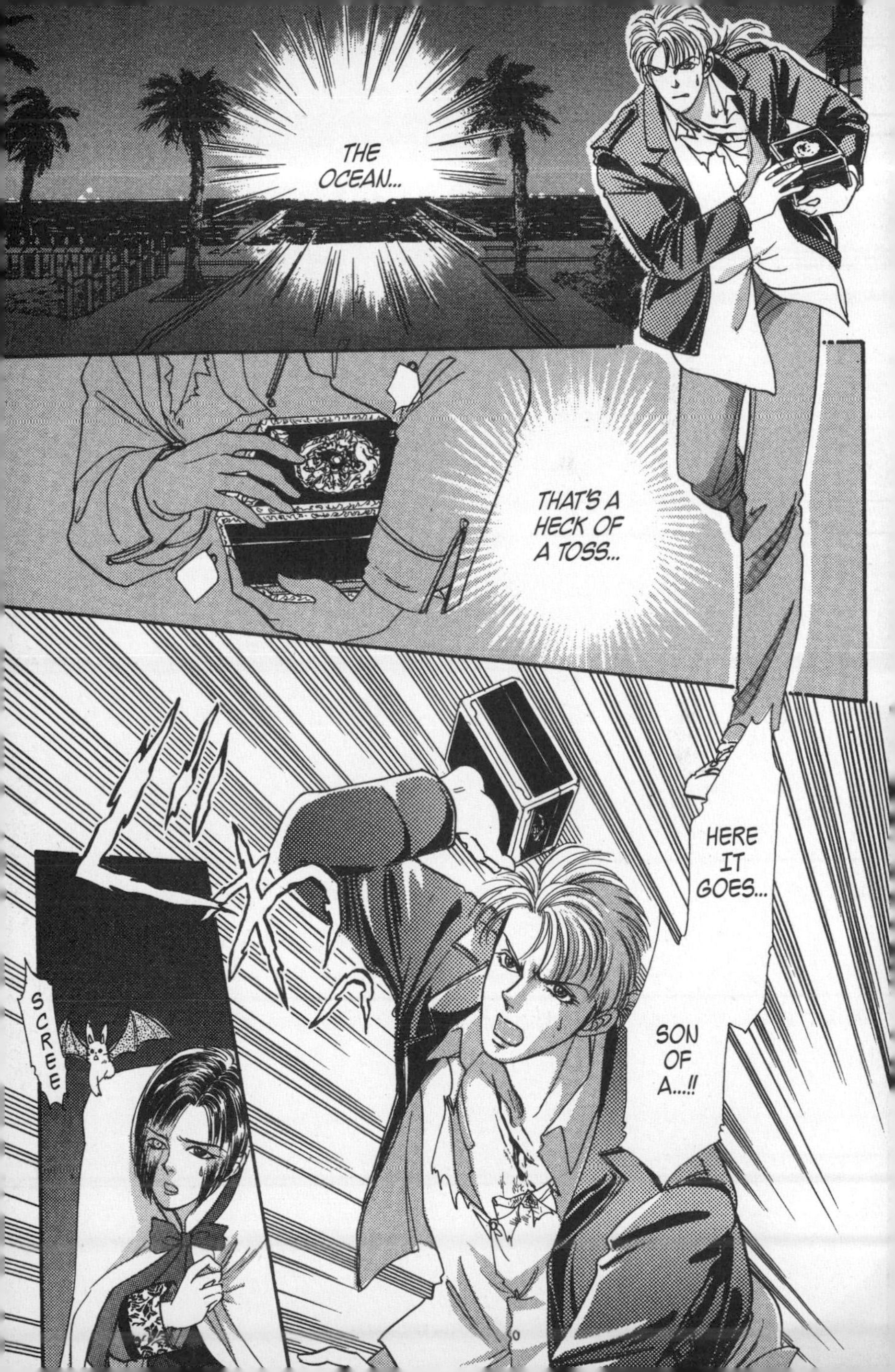
THE OCEAN...
THAT'S A HECK OF A TOSS...
HERE IT GOES...
SON OF A...!!
SCREE

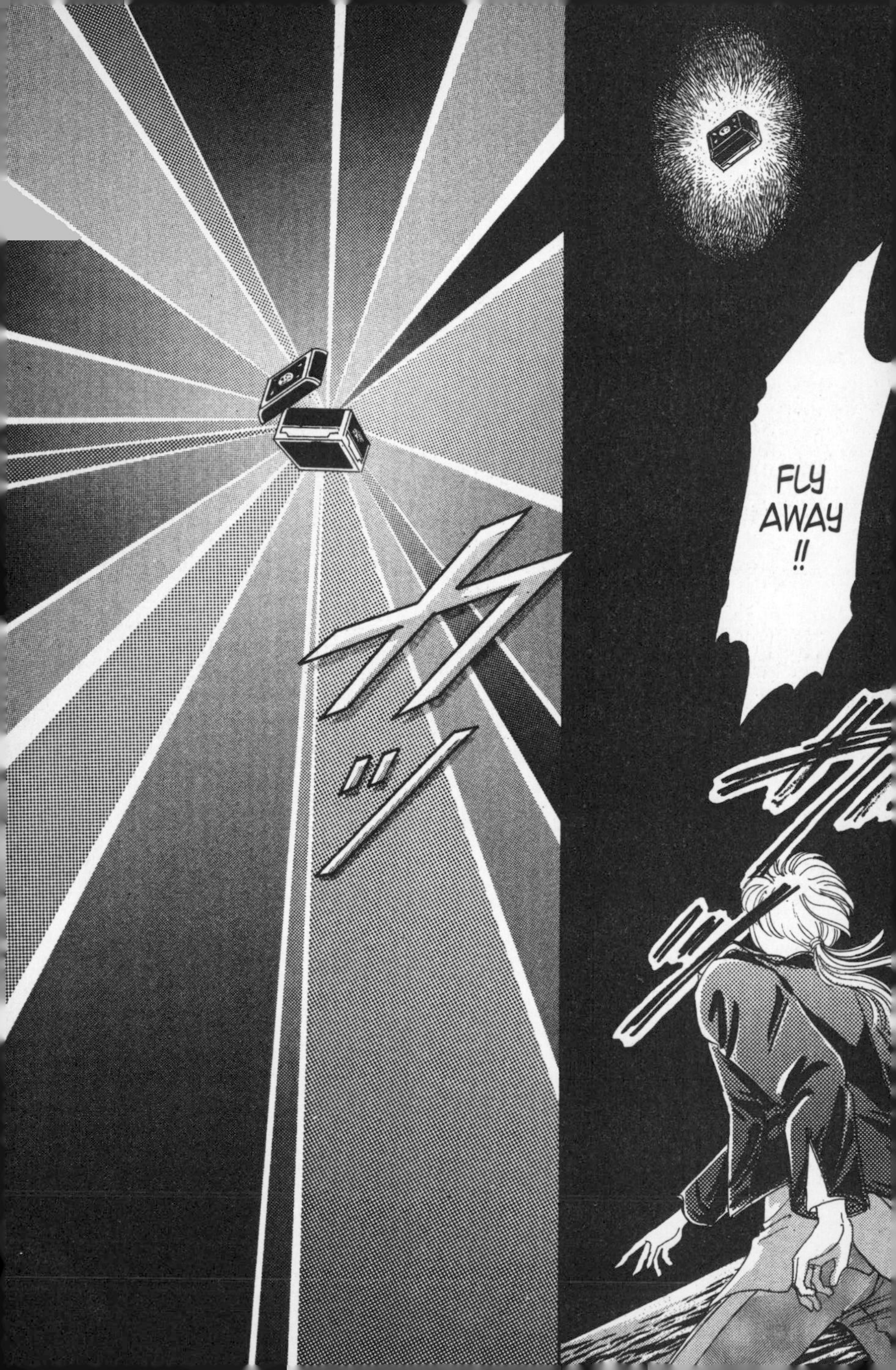
FLY AWAY !!

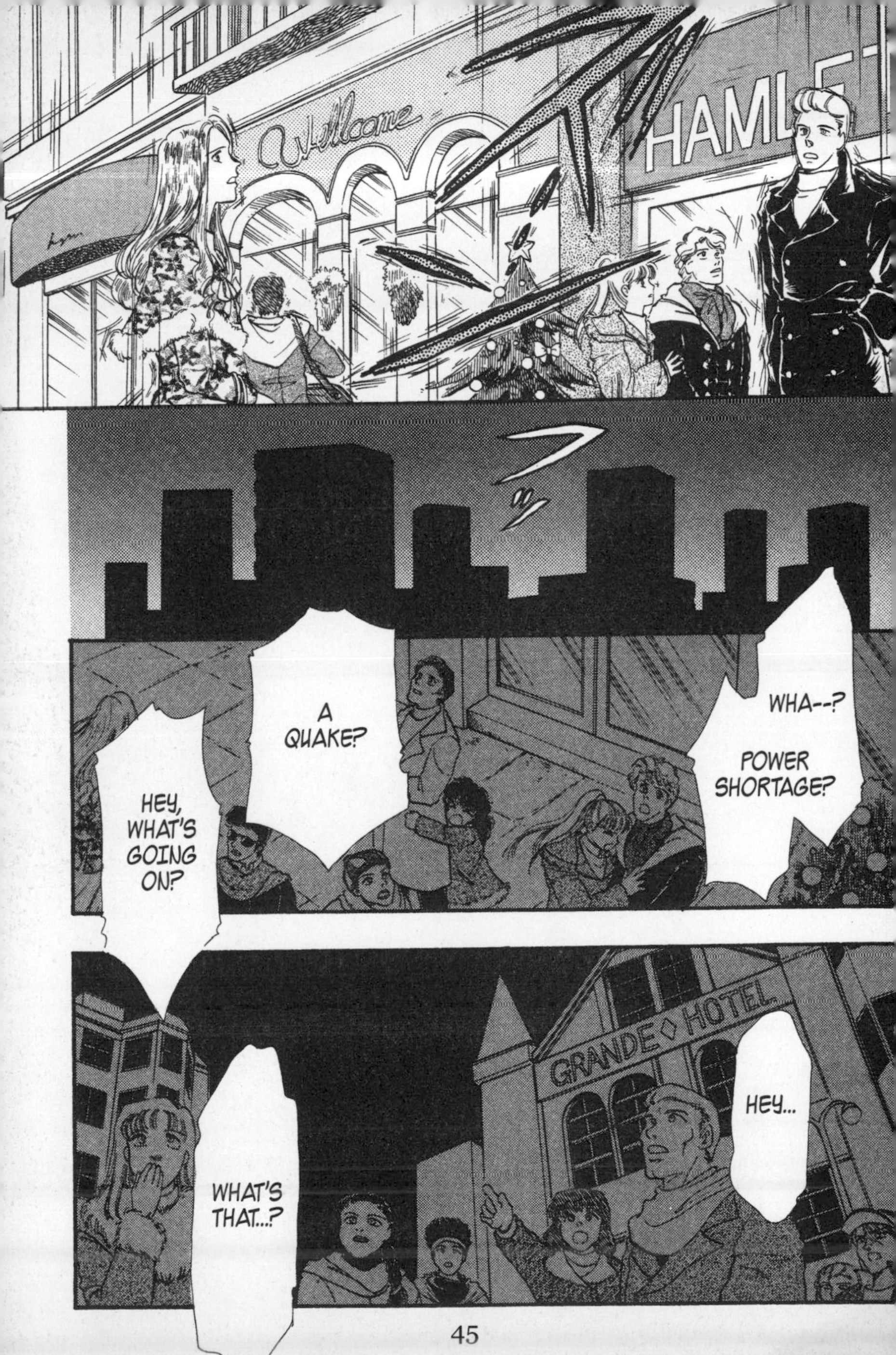
HAMLE
Wellcome
フッ
WHA--?
POWER SHORTAGE?
A QUAKE?
HEY, WHAT'S GOING ON?
GRANDE HOTEL
HEY...
WHAT'S THAT...?

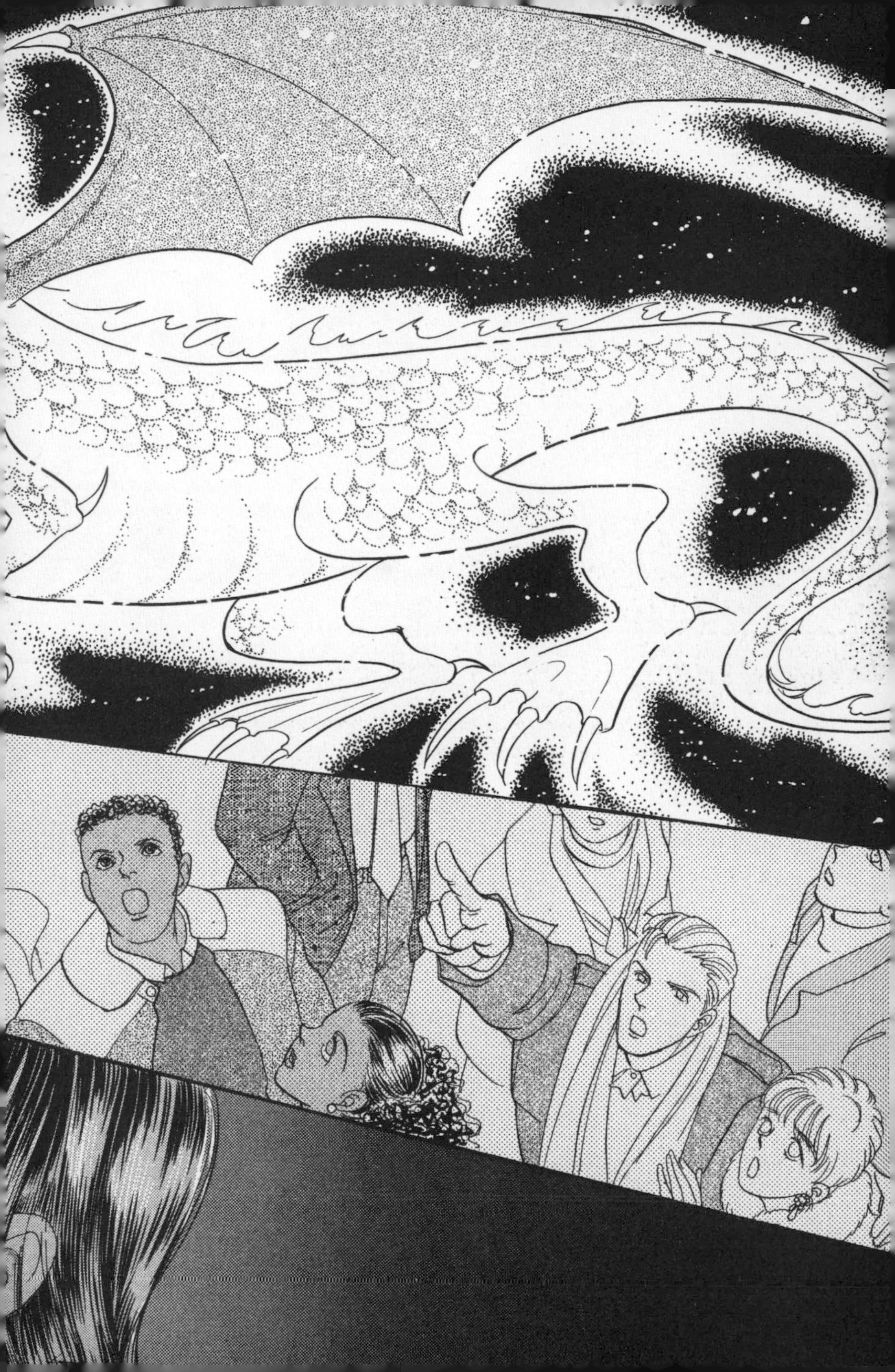

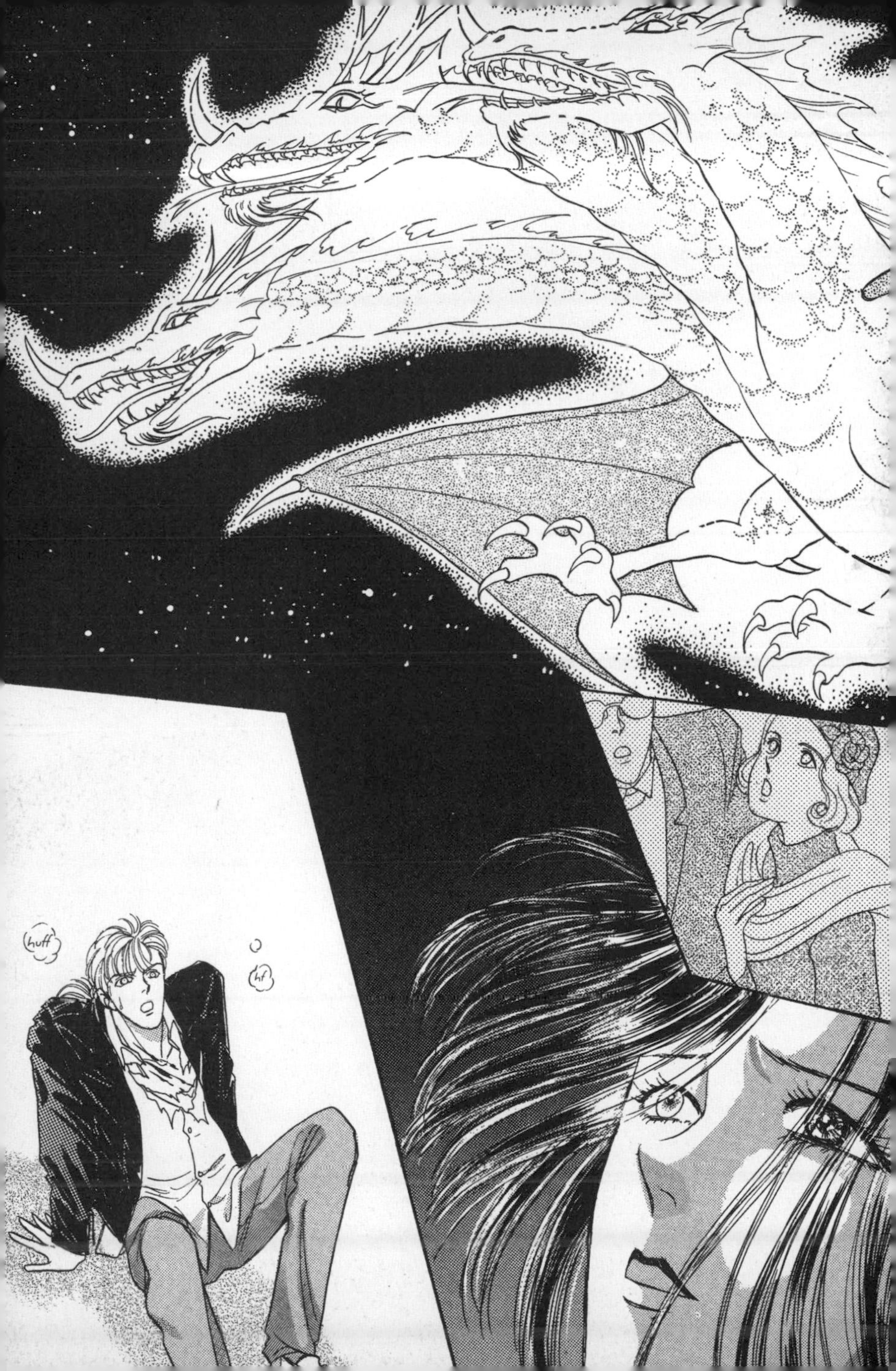
huff
hf

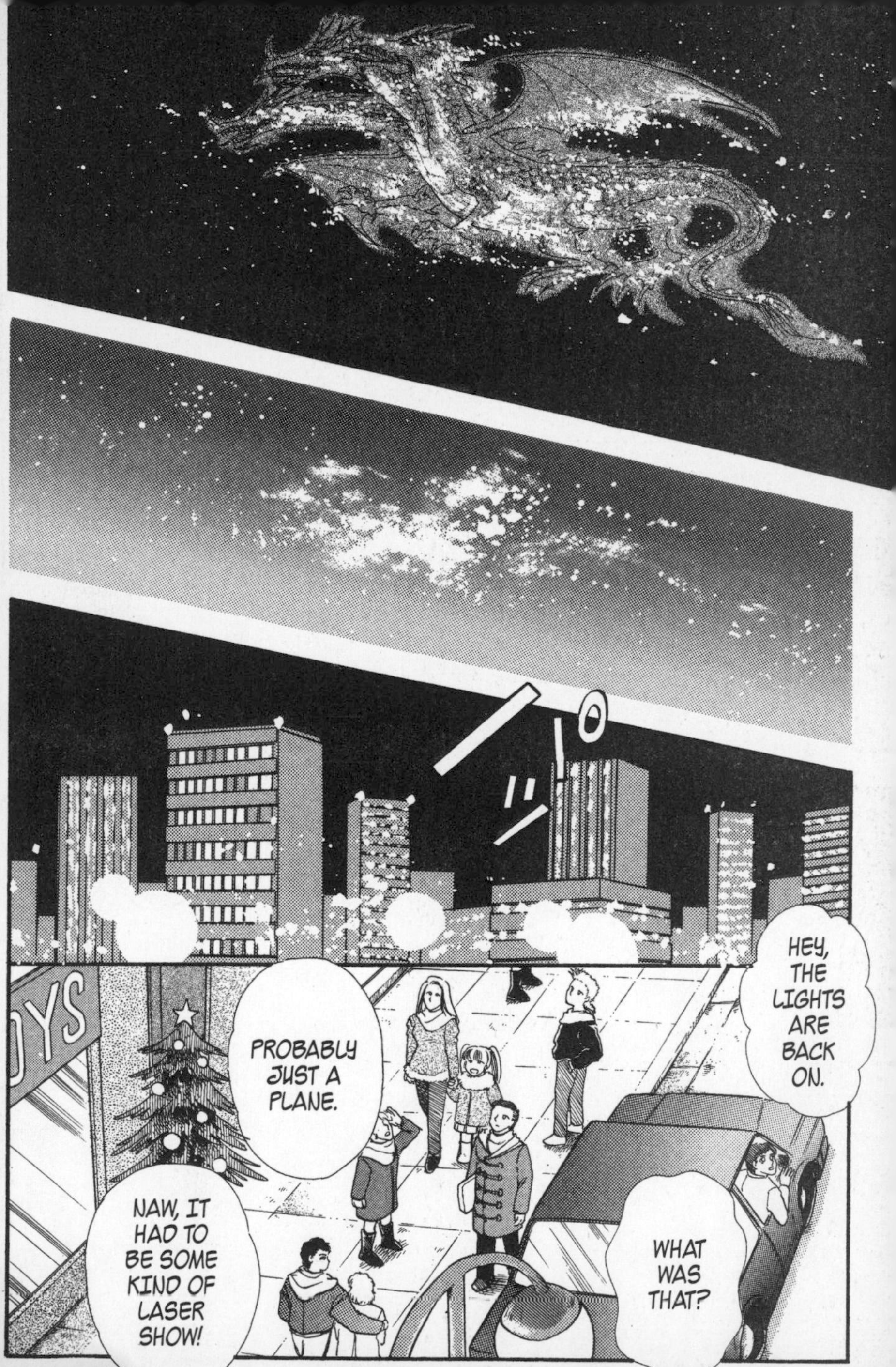

OYS
HEY, THE LIGHTS ARE BACK ON.
WHAT WAS THAT?
PROBABLY JUST A PLANE.
NAW, IT HAD TO BE SOME KIND OF LASER SHOW!

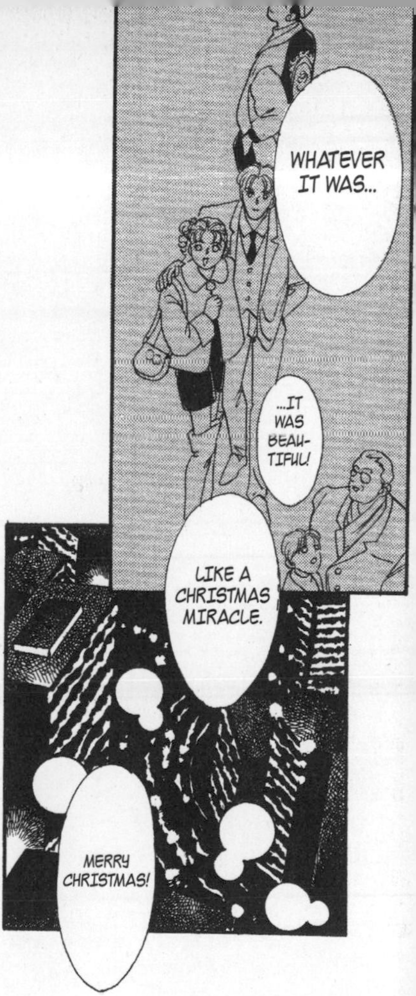
WHATEVER IT WAS...
...IT WAS BEAU-TIFUL!
LIKE A CHRISTMAS MIRACLE.
MERRY CHRISTMAS!

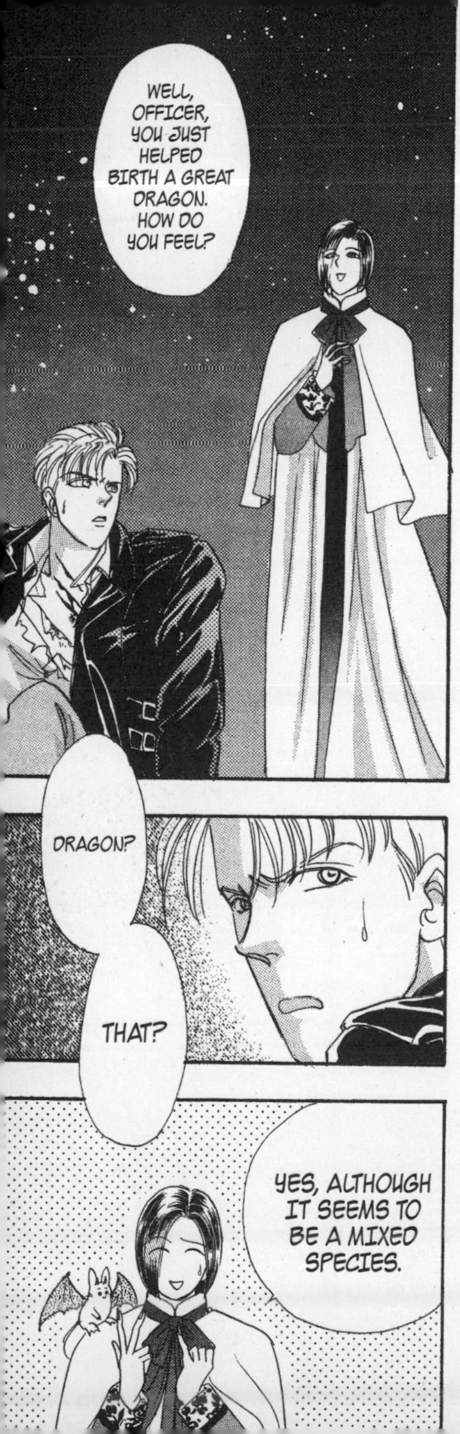
WELL, OFFICER, YOU JUST HELPED BIRTH A GREAT DRAGON. HOW DO YOU FEEL?
DRAGON?
THAT?
YES, ALTHOUGH IT SEEMS TO BE A MIXED SPECIES.

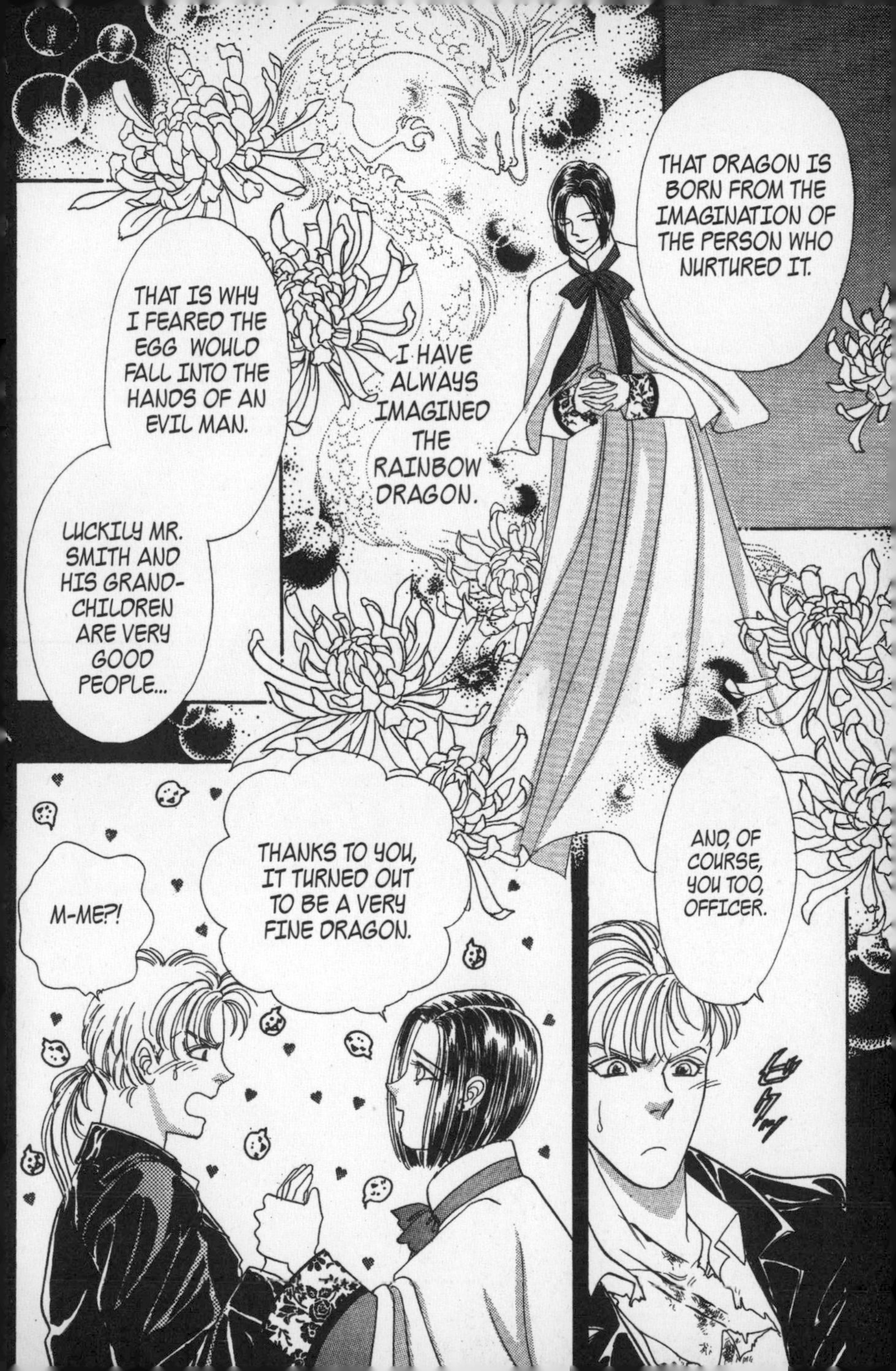
THAT DRAGON IS BORN FROM THE IMAGINATION OF THE PERSON WHO NURTURED IT.
I HAVE ALWAYS IMAGINED THE RAINBOW DRAGON.
THAT IS WHY I FEARED THE EGG WOULD FALL INTO THE HANDS OF AN EVIL MAN.
LUCKILY MR. SMITH AND HIS GRAND-CHILDREN ARE VERY GOOD PEOPLE...
AND, OF COURSE, YOU TOO, OFFICER.
THANKS TO YOU, IT TURNED OUT TO BE A VERY FINE DRAGON.
M-ME?!

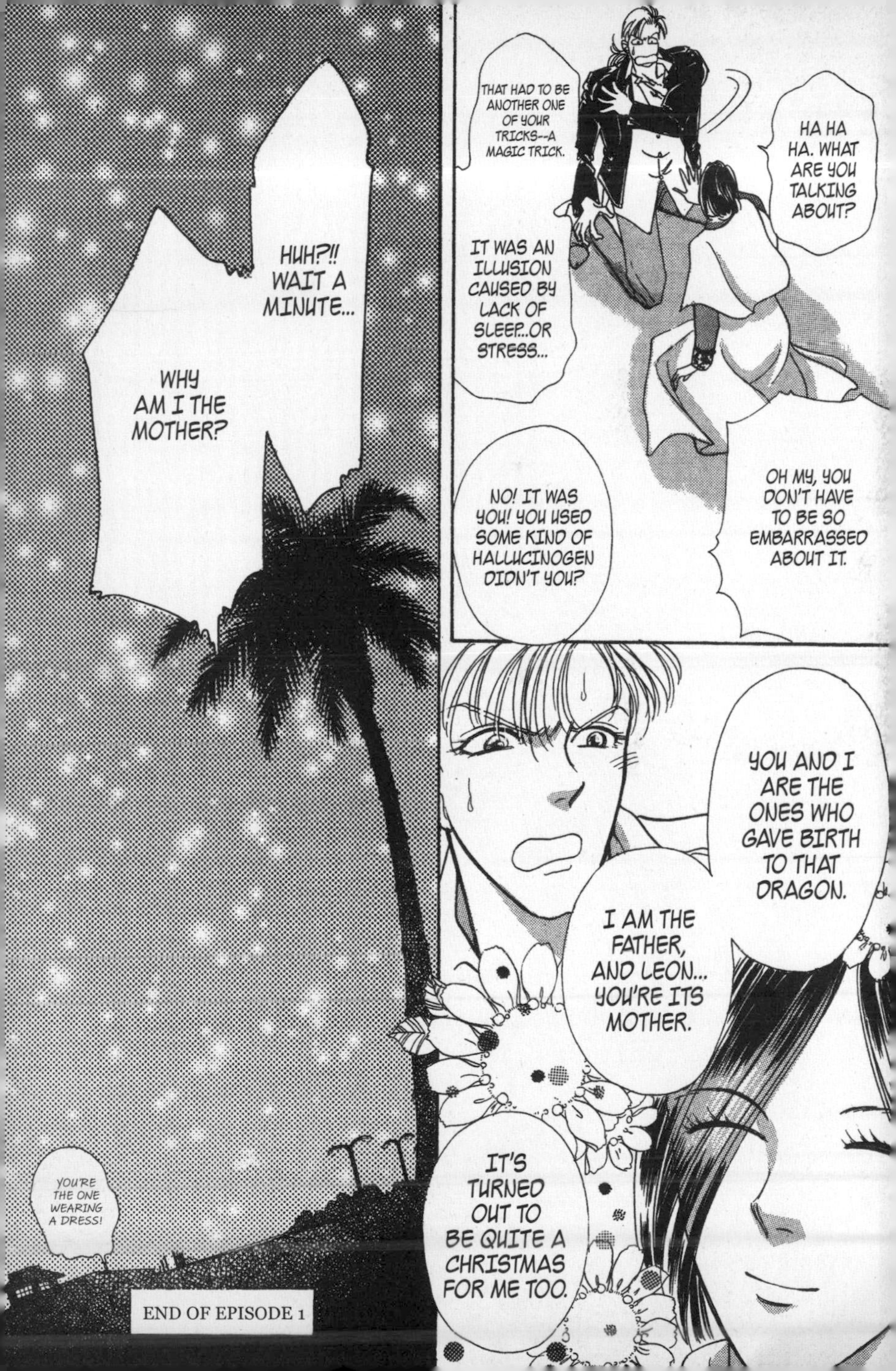
HA HA. WHAT ARE YOU TALKING ABOUT?
THAT HAD TO BE ANOTHER ONE OF YOUR TRICKS--A MAGIC TRICK.
IT WAS AN ILLUSION CAUSED BY LACK OF SLEEP...OR STRESS...
OH MY, YOU DON'T HAVE TO BE SO EMBARRASSED ABOUT IT.
NO! IT WAS YOU! YOU USED SOME KIND OF HALLUCINOGEN DIDN'T YOU?
YOU AND I ARE THE ONES WHO GAVE BIRTH TO THAT DRAGON.
I AM THE FATHER, AND LEON... YOU'RE ITS MOTHER.
IT'S TURNED OUT TO BE QUITE A CHRISTMAS FOR ME TOO.
HUH?!! WAIT A MINUTE...
WHY AM I THE MOTHER?
YOU'RE THE ONE WEARING A DRESS!
END OF EPISODE 1

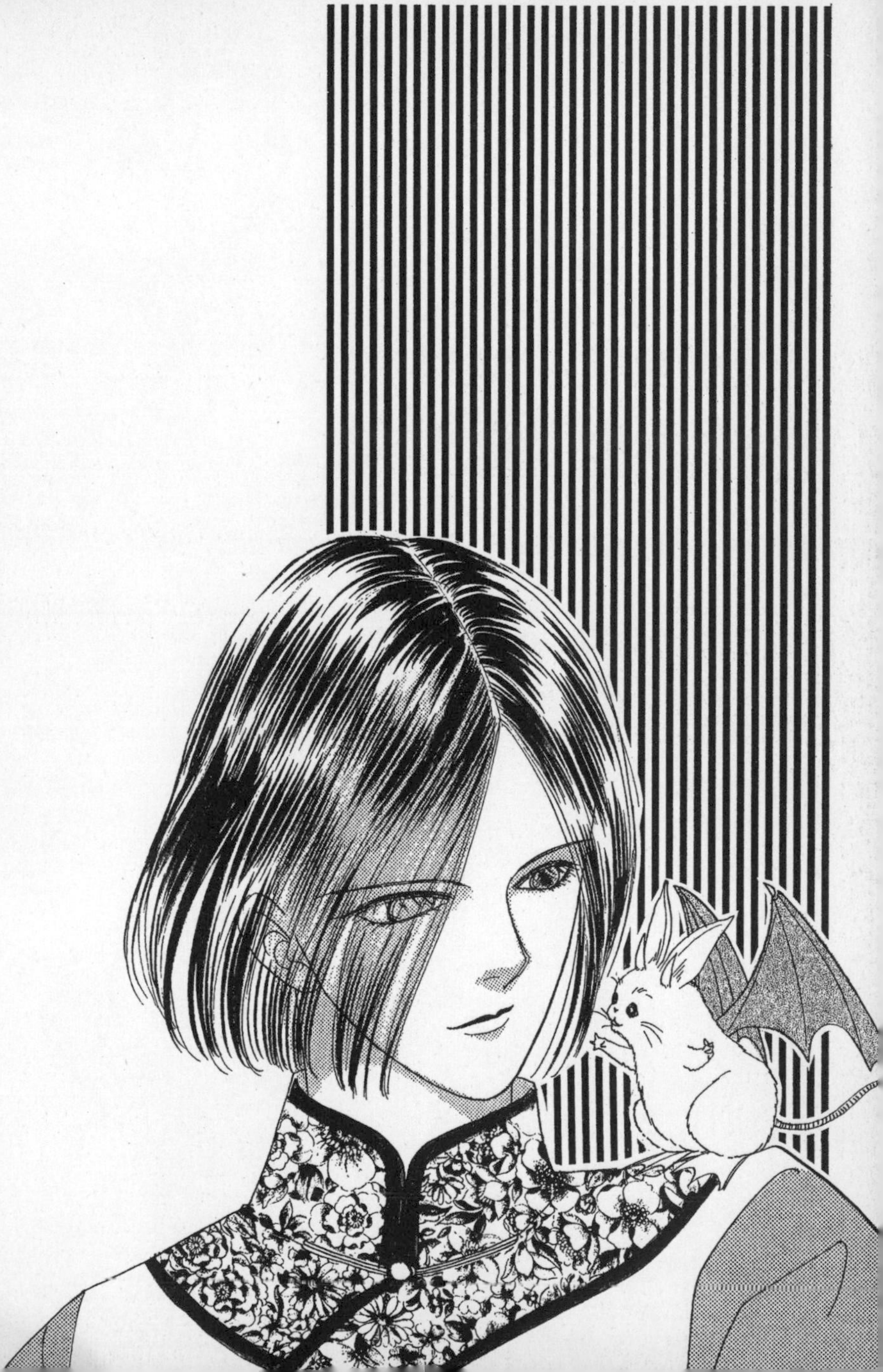

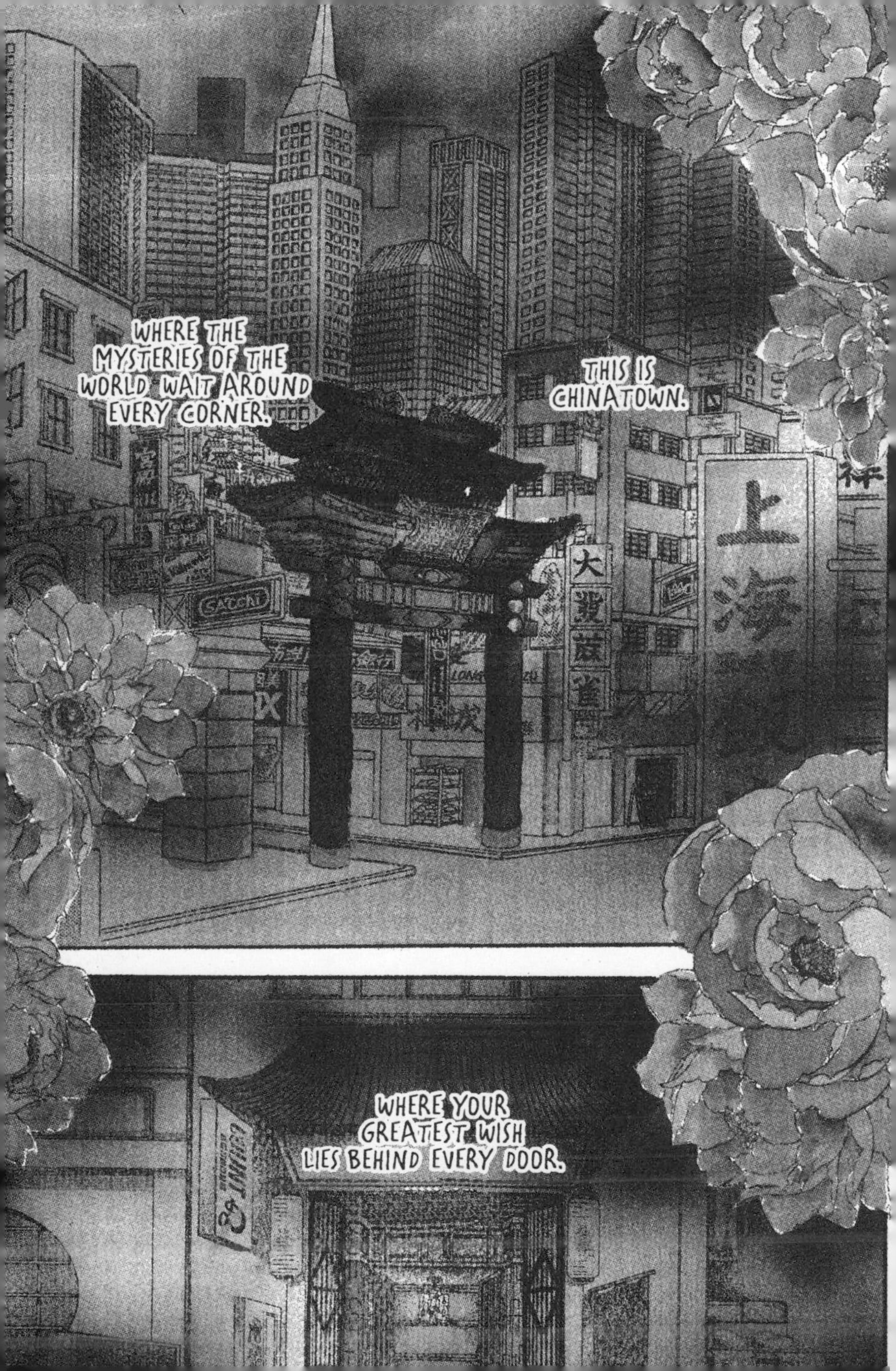
THIS IS CHINATOWN.
WHERE THE MYSTERIES OF THE WORLD WAIT AROUND EVERY CORNER.
WHERE YOUR GREATEST WISH LIES BEHIND EVERY DOOR.

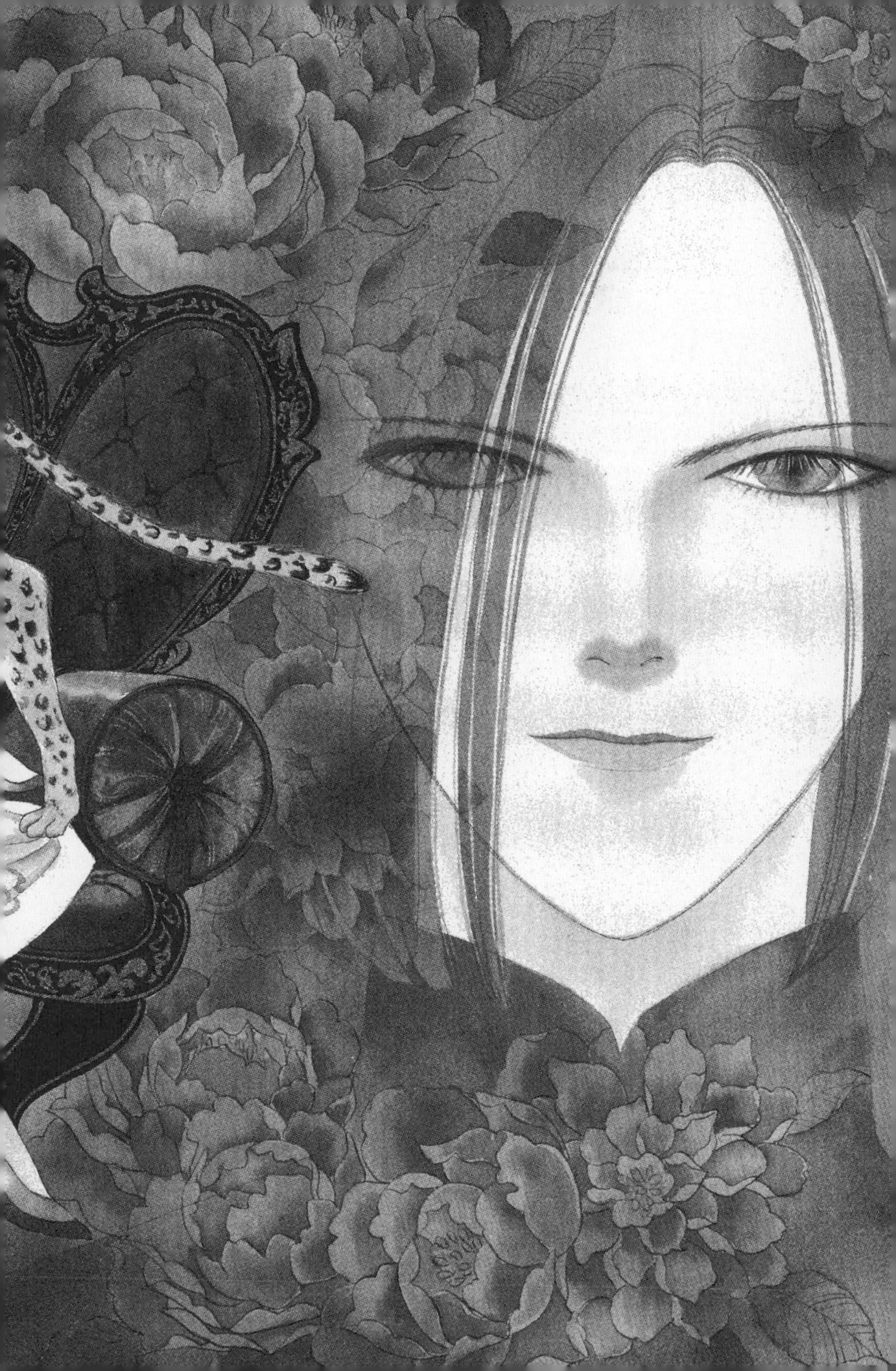

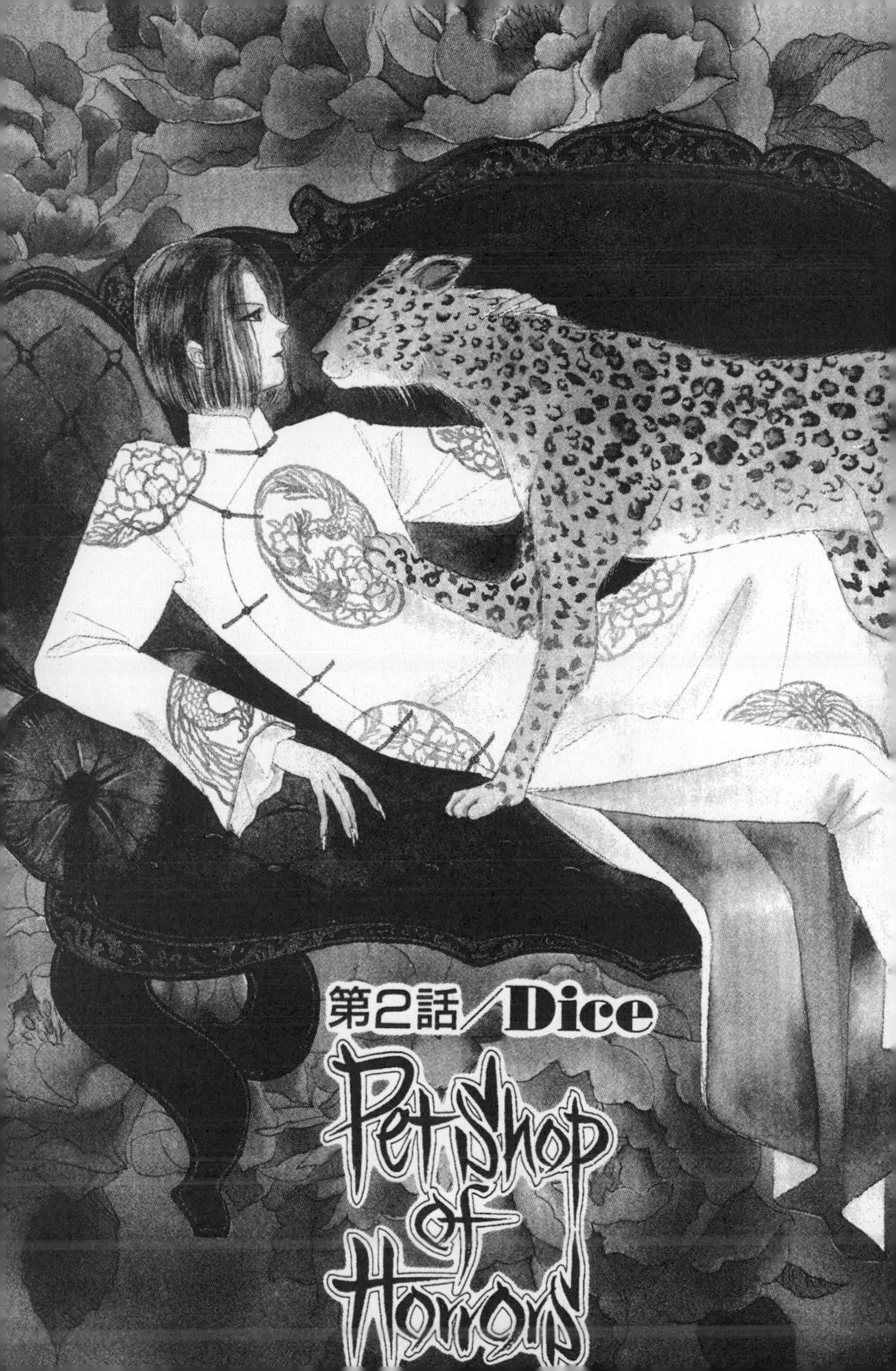
第2話／Dice
Pet Shop of Horrors

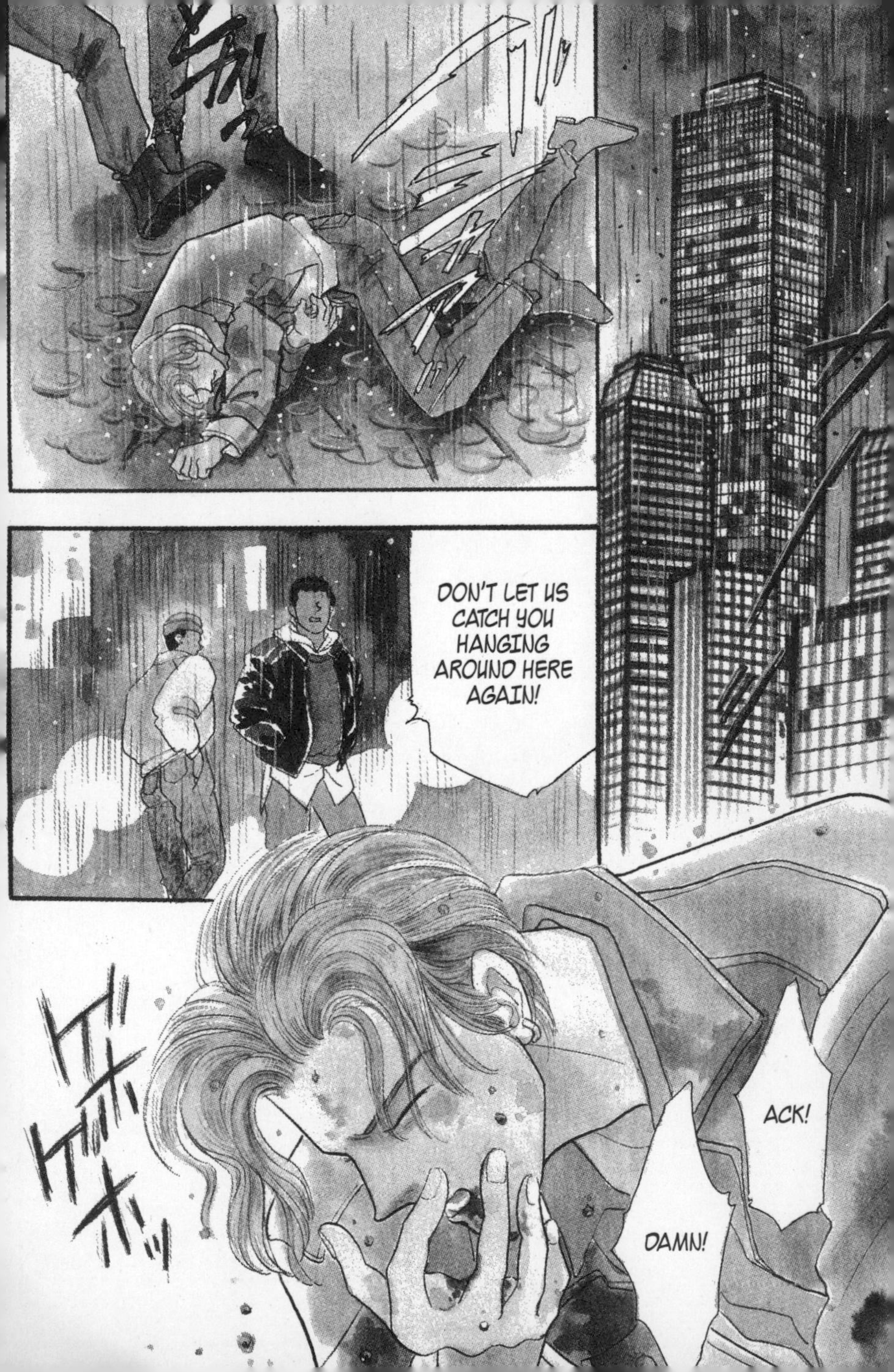
DON'T LET US CATCH YOU HANGING AROUND HERE AGAIN!
ACK!
DAMN!

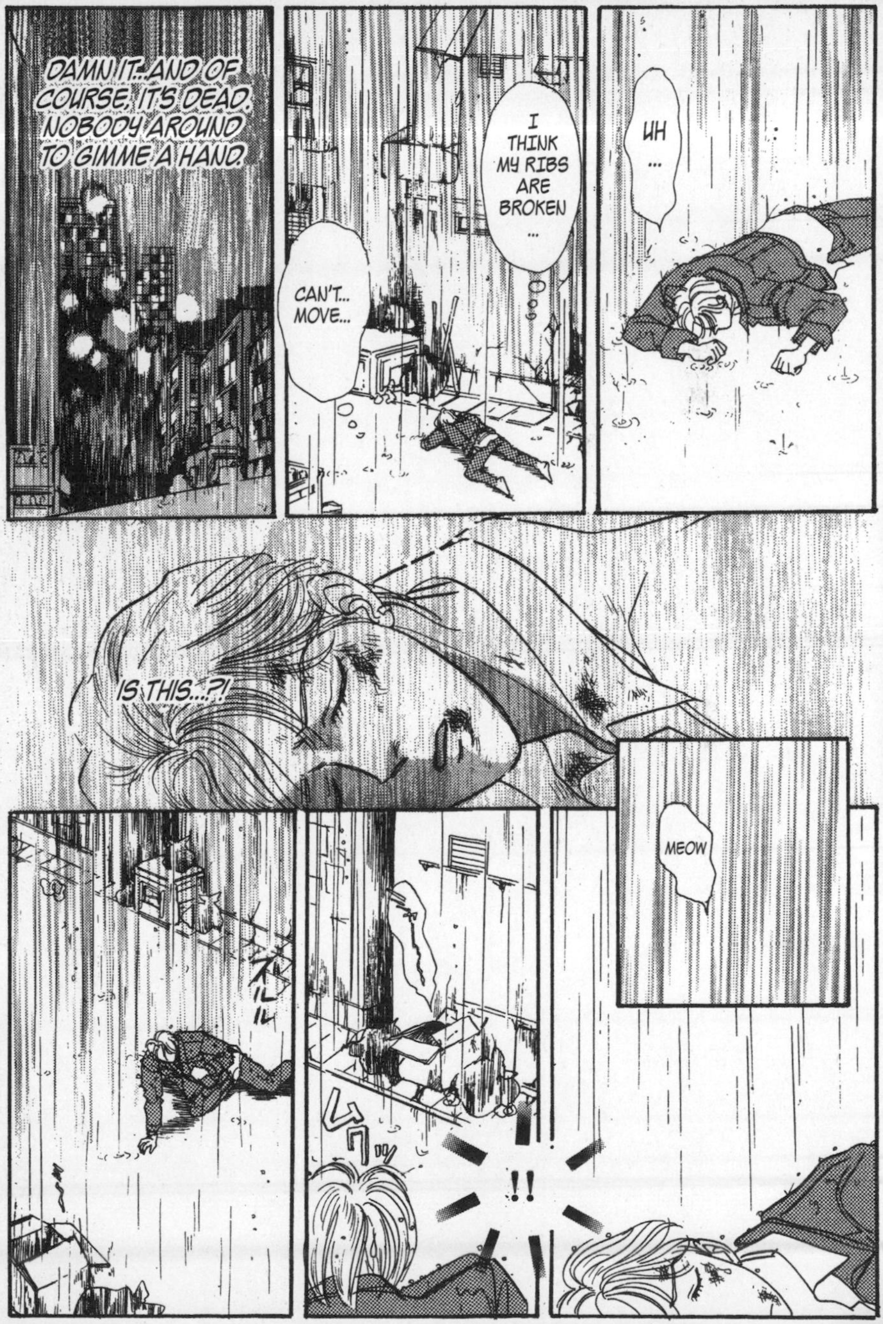
UH ...
I THINK MY RIBS ARE BROKEN ...
CAN'T... MOVE...
DAMN IT...AND OF COURSE, IT'S DEAD. NOBODY AROUND TO GIMME A HAND.
IS THIS...?!
MEOW
!!

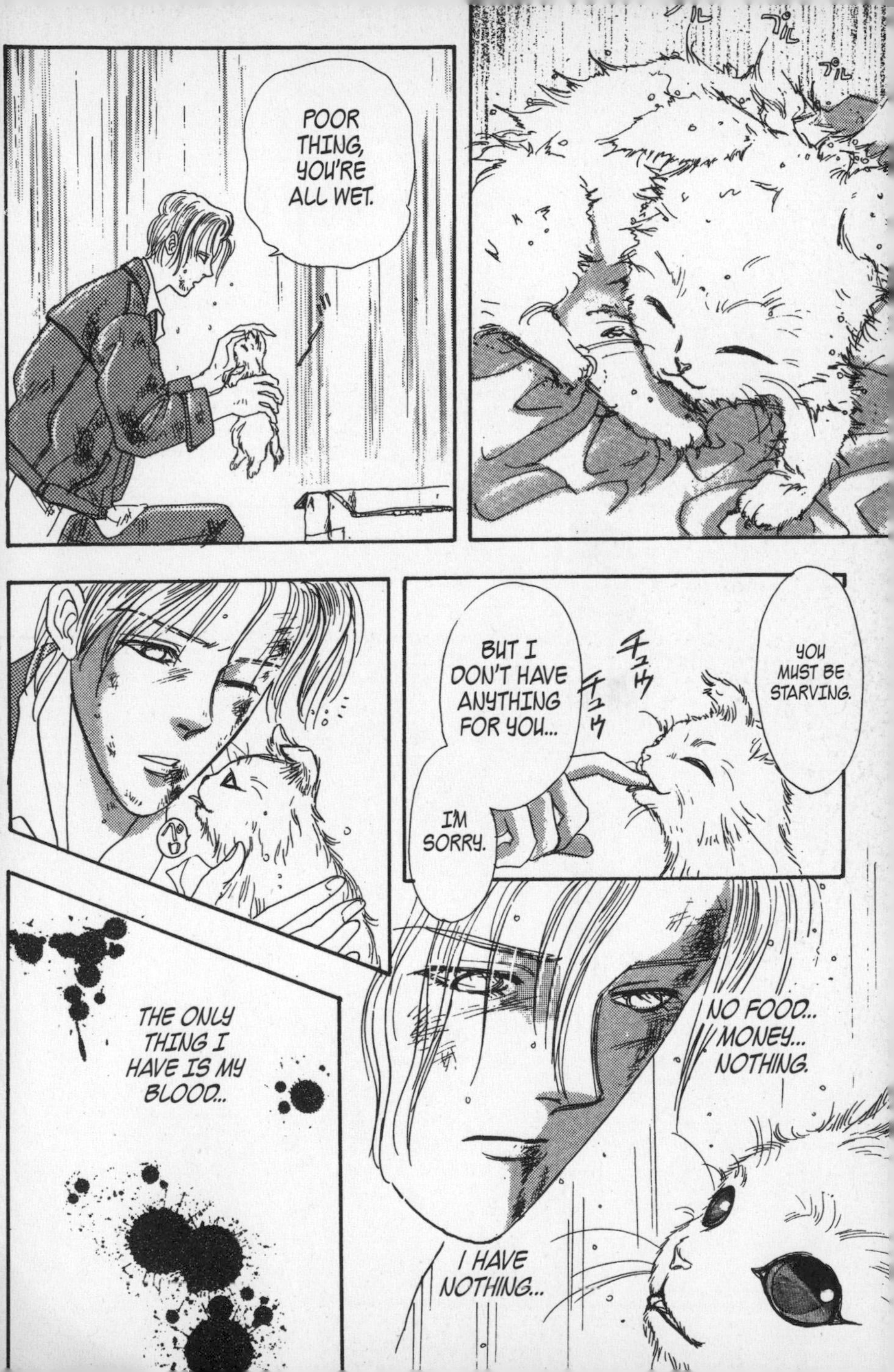
POOR THING, YOU'RE ALL WET.
YOU MUST BE STARVING.
チュウ チュウ
BUT I DON'T HAVE ANYTHING FOR YOU...
I'M SORRY.
NO FOOD... MONEY... NOTHING.
I HAVE NOTHING...
THE ONLY THING I HAVE IS MY BLOOD...

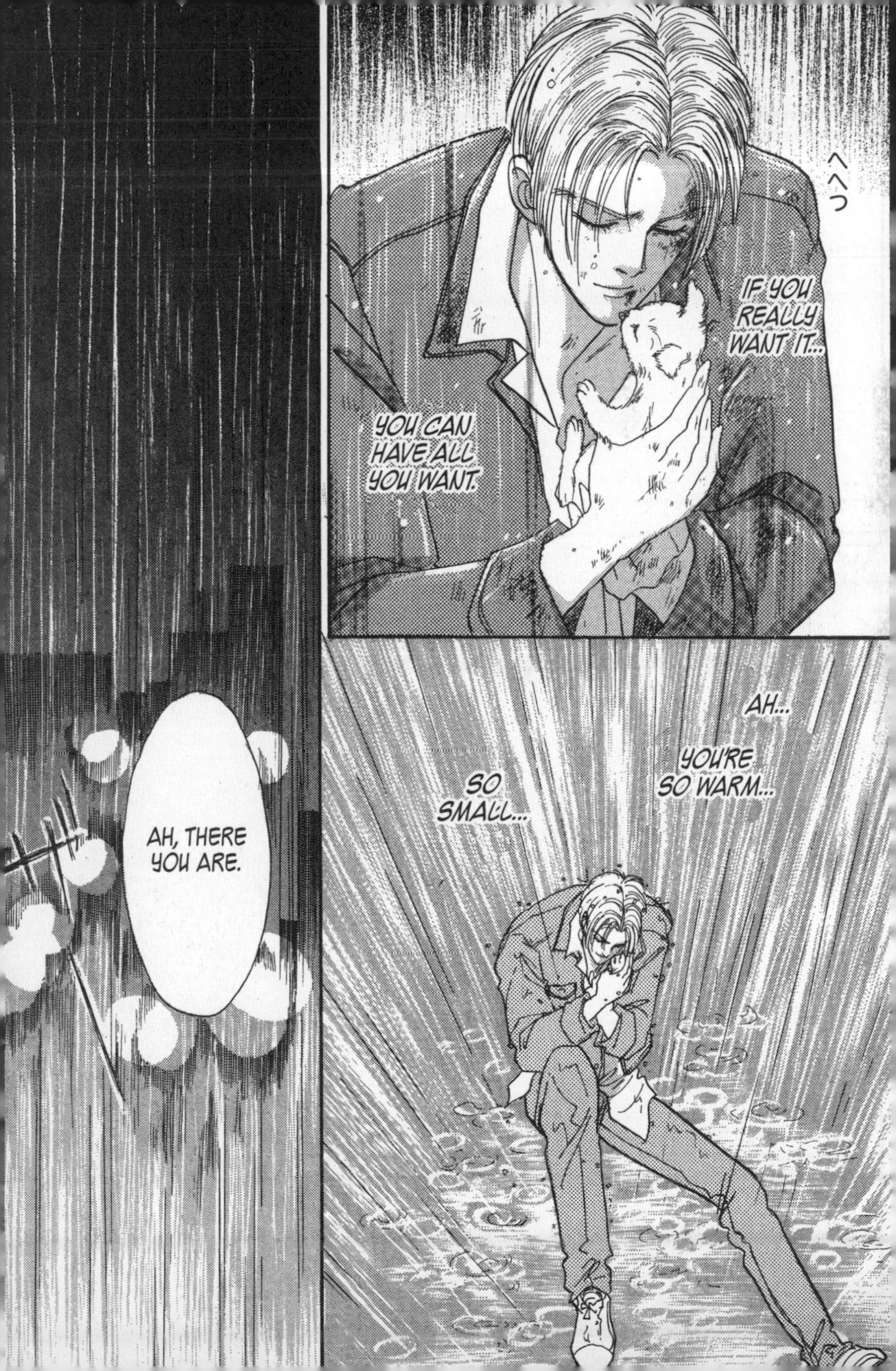
へへっ
IF YOU REALLY WANT IT...
YOU CAN HAVE ALL YOU WANT.
AH...
YOU'RE SO WARM...
SO SMALL...
AH, THERE YOU ARE.

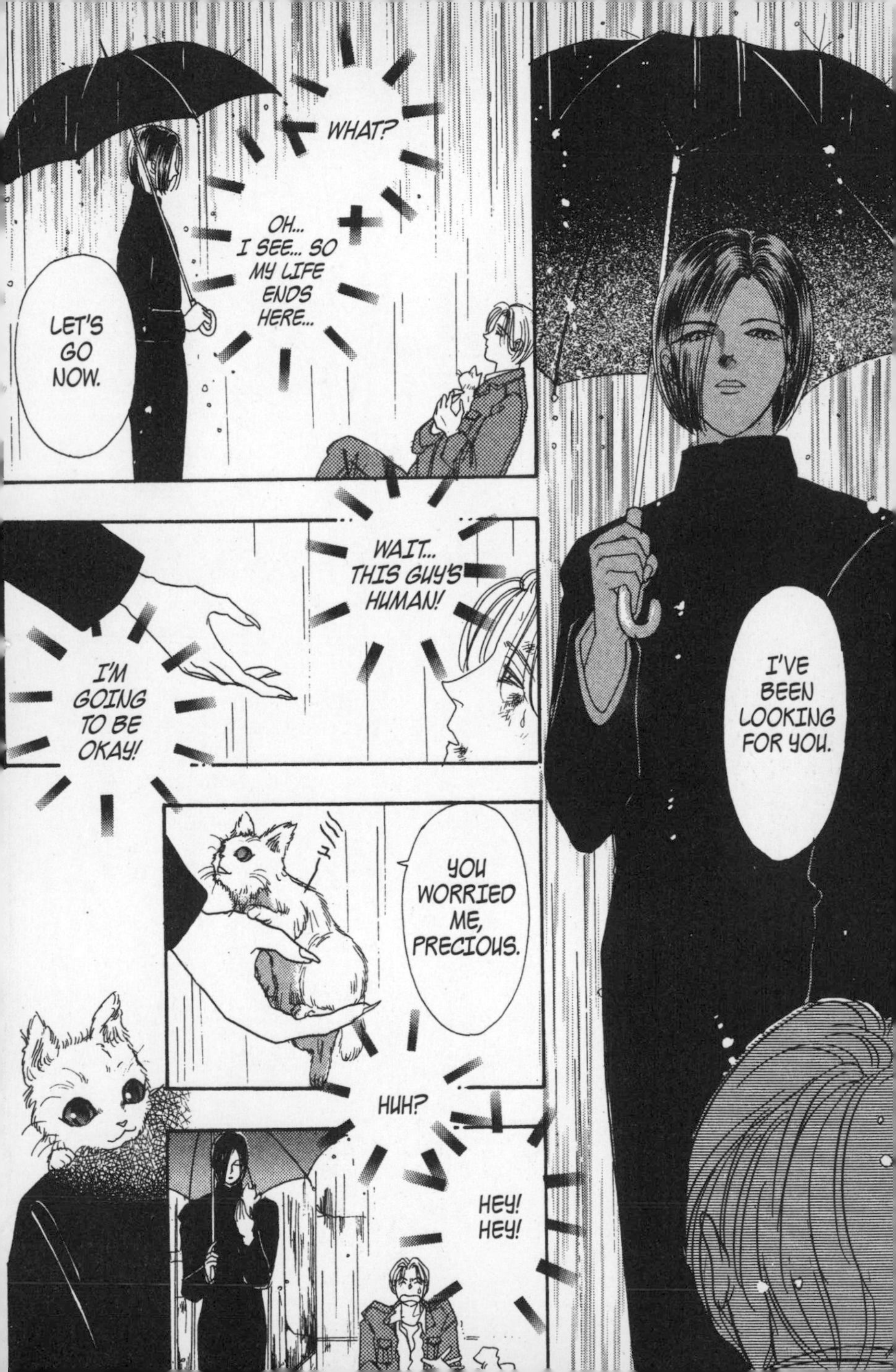
I'VE BEEN LOOKING FOR YOU.
WHAT?
OH... I SEE... SO MY LIFE ENDS HERE...
LET'S GO NOW.
WAIT... THIS GUY'S HUMAN!
I'M GOING TO BE OKAY!
YOU WORRIED ME, PRECIOUS.
HUH?
HEY! HEY!

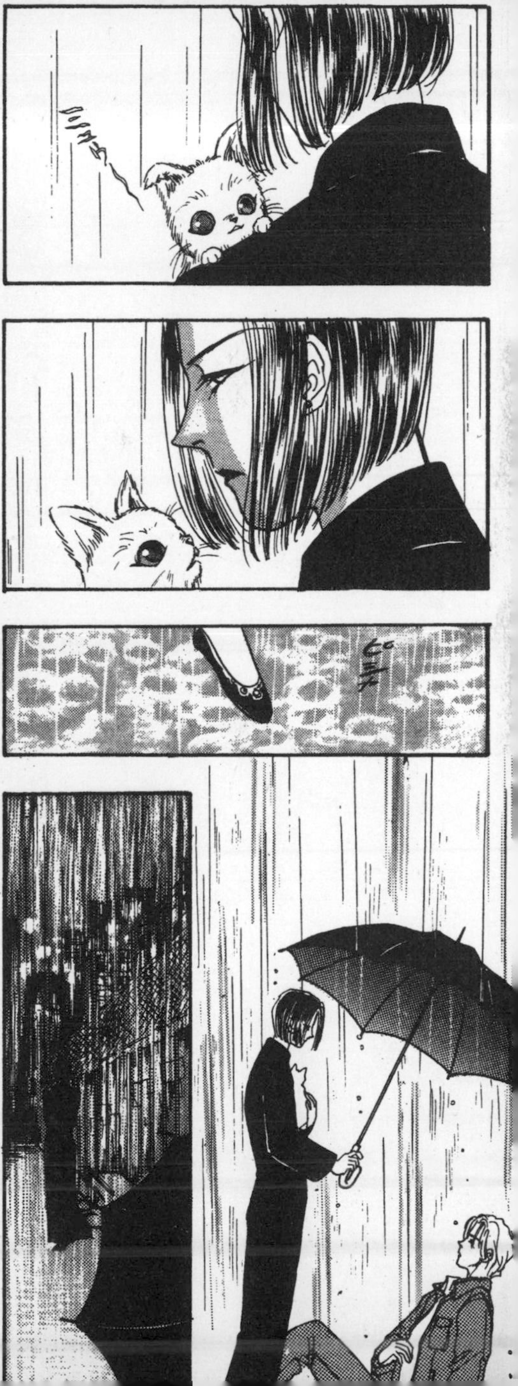

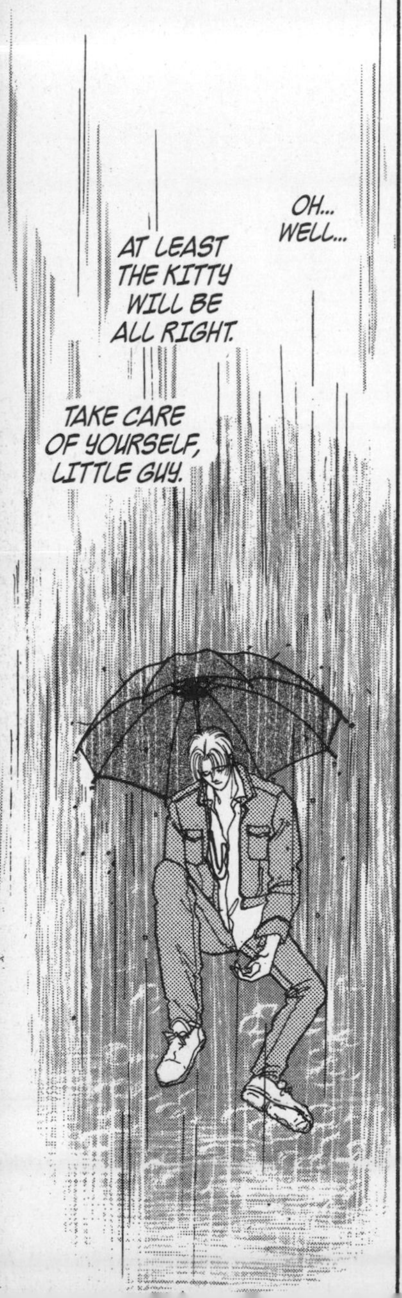
OH... WELL...
AT LEAST THE KITTY WILL BE ALL RIGHT.
TAKE CARE OF YOURSELF, LITTLE GUY.

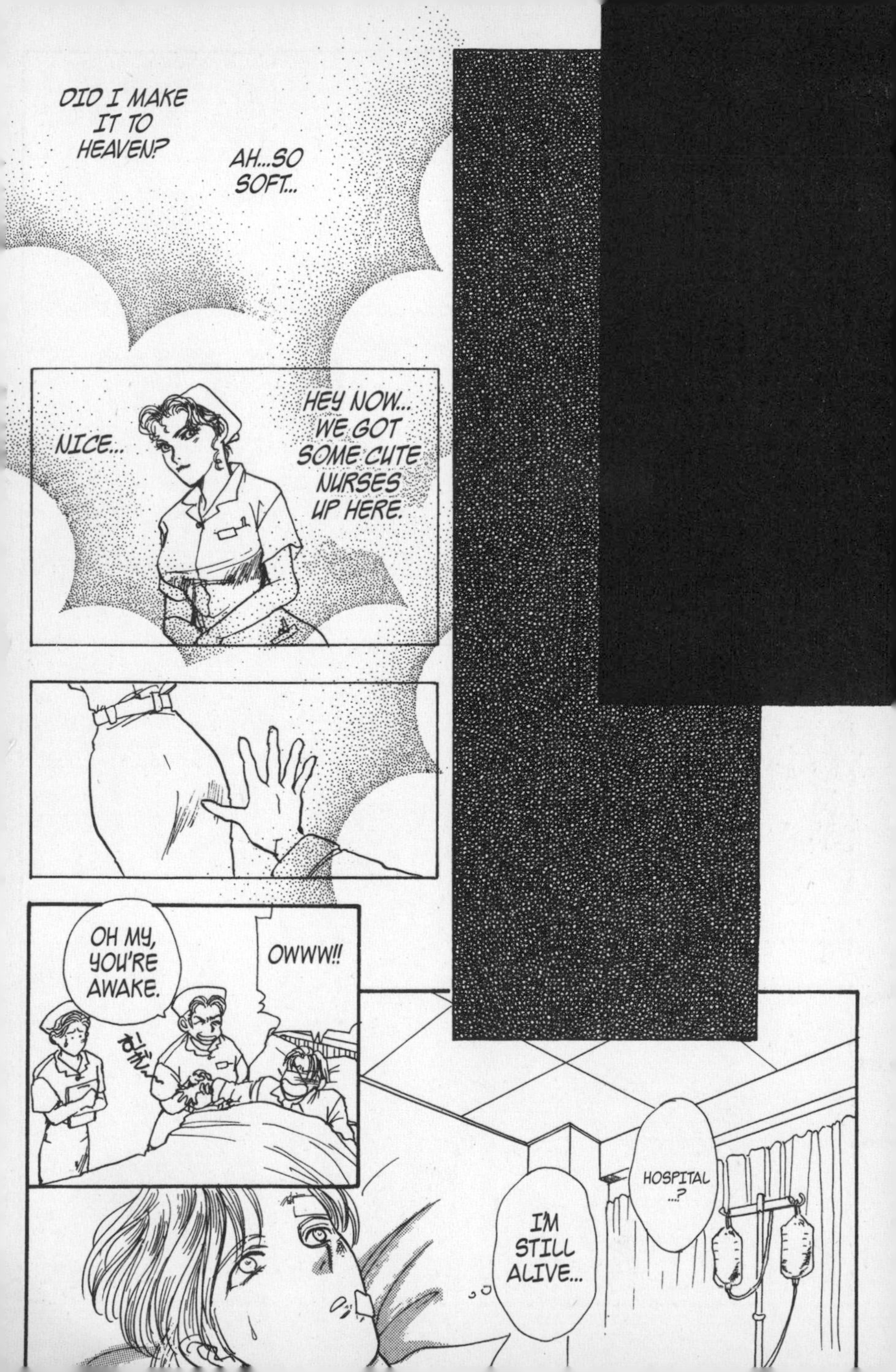
AH...SO SOFT...
DID I MAKE IT TO HEAVEN?
HEY NOW... WE GOT SOME CUTE NURSES UP HERE.
NICE...
OWWW!!
OH MY, YOU'RE AWAKE.
I'M STILL ALIVE...
HOSPITAL ...?

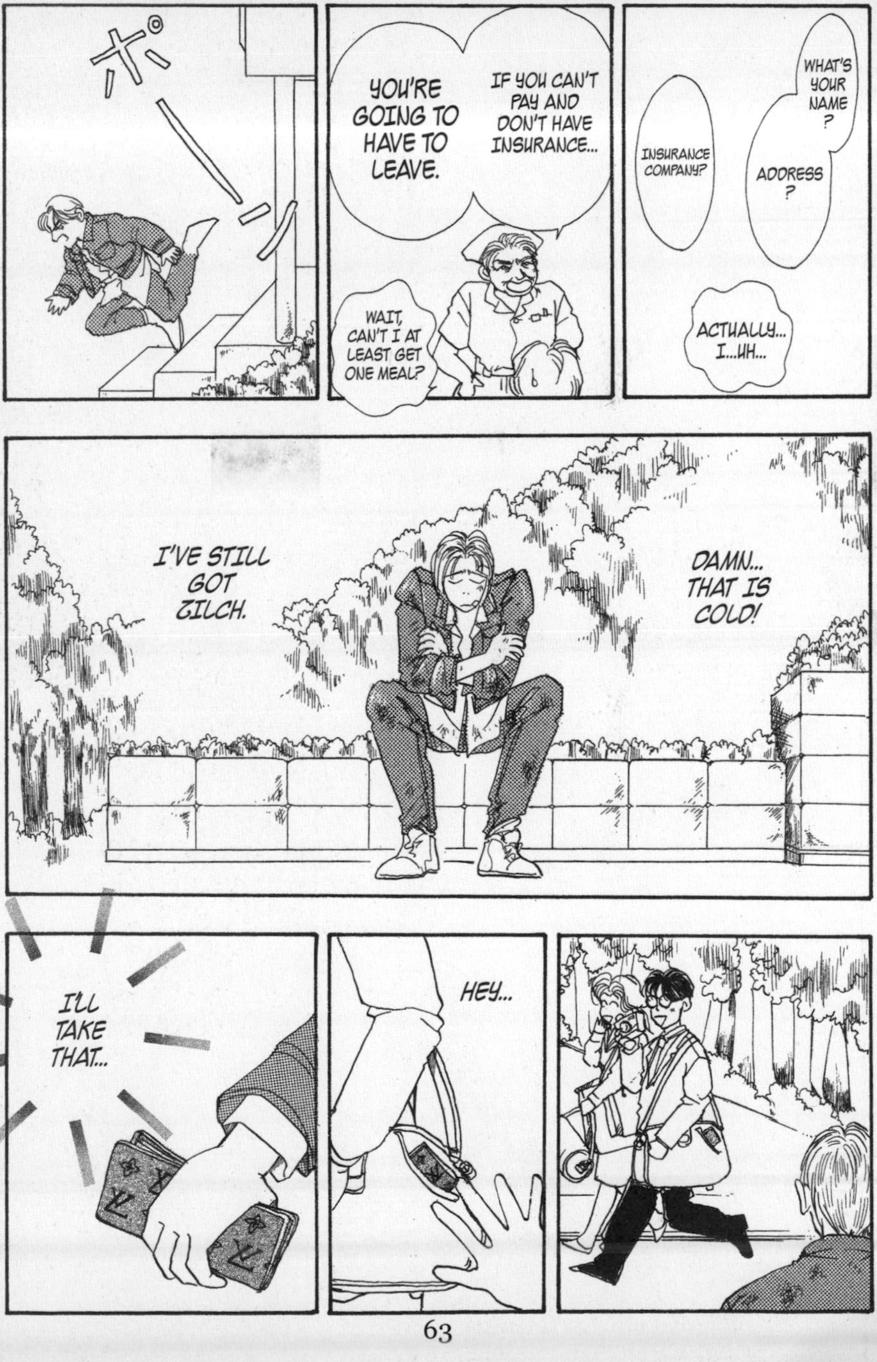
WHAT'S YOUR NAME?
ADDRESS?
INSURANCE COMPANY?
ACTUALLY... I...UH...
IF YOU CAN'T PAY AND DON'T HAVE INSURANCE...
YOU'RE GOING TO HAVE TO LEAVE.
WAIT, CAN'T I AT LEAST GET ONE MEAL?
DAMN... THAT IS COLD!
I'VE STILL GOT ZILCH.
HEY...
I'LL TAKE THAT...

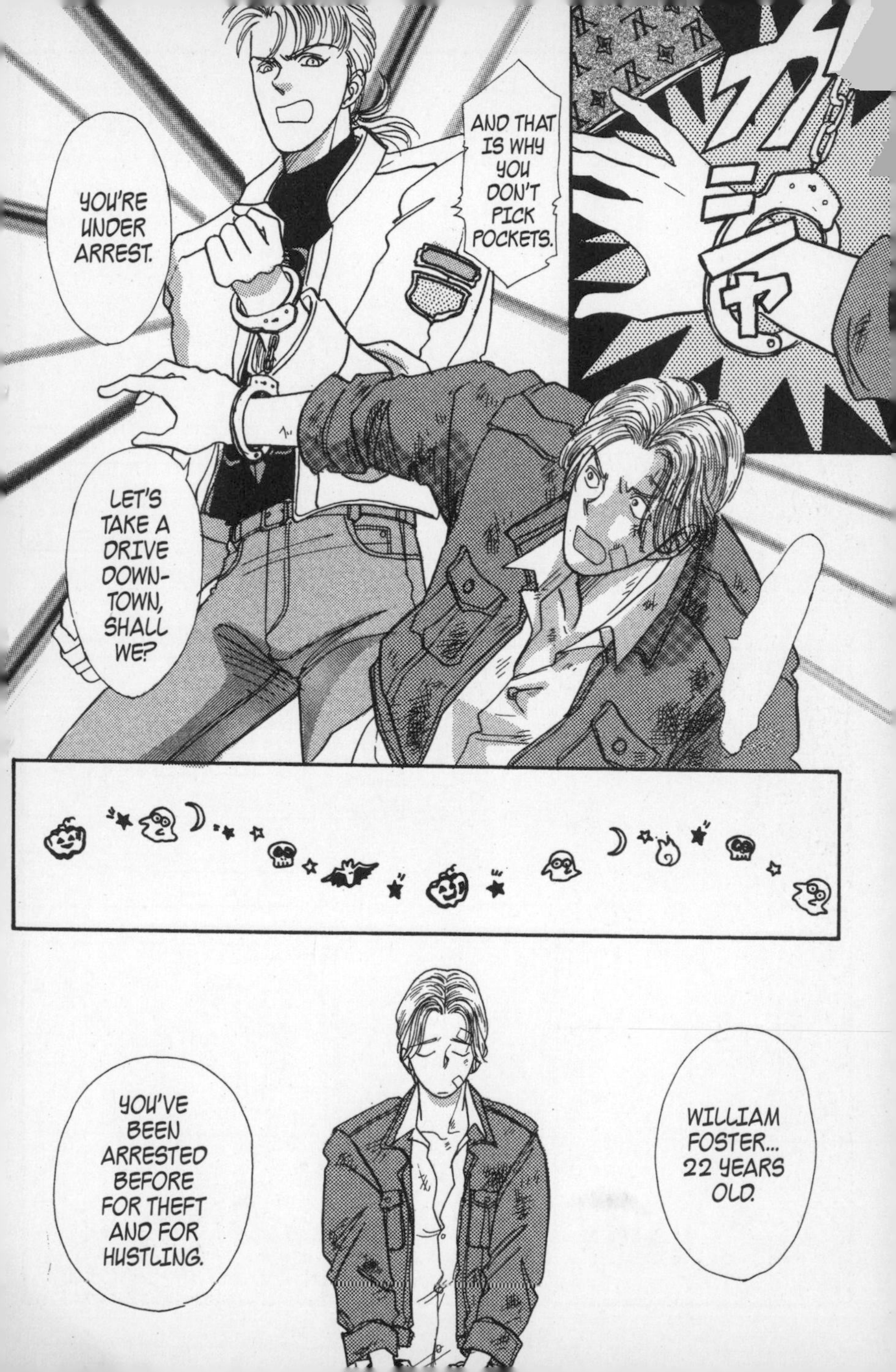
AND THAT IS WHY YOU DON'T PICK POCKETS.
YOU'RE UNDER ARREST.
LET'S TAKE A DRIVE DOWN-TOWN, SHALL WE?
WILLIAM FOSTER... 22 YEARS OLD.
YOU'VE BEEN ARRESTED BEFORE FOR THEFT AND FOR HUSTLING.

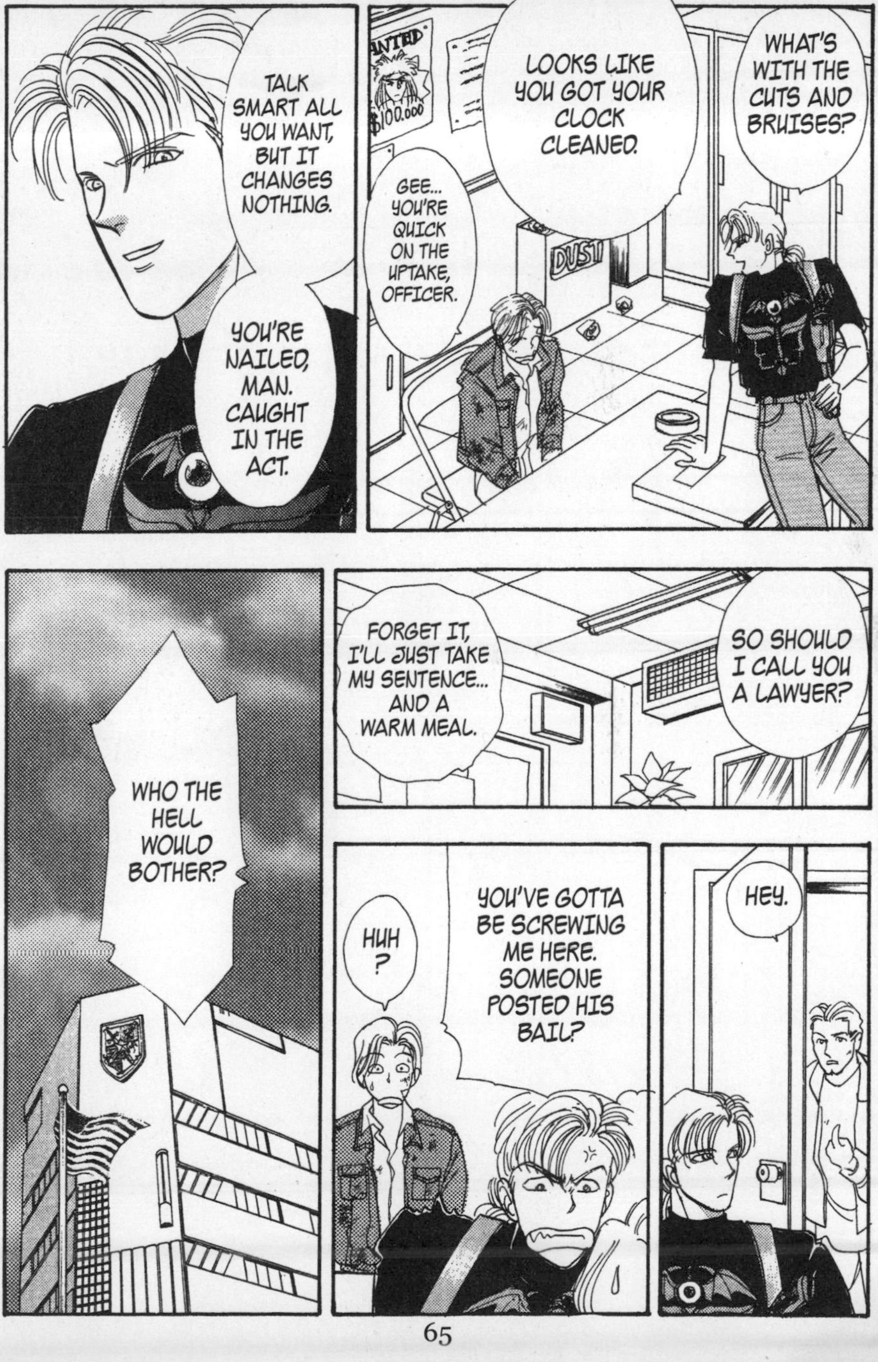

WHAT'S WITH THE CUTS AND BRUISES?
LOOKS LIKE YOU GOT YOUR CLOCK CLEANED.
ANTED
$100.000
DUST
GEE... YOU'RE QUICK ON THE UPTAKE, OFFICER.
TALK SMART ALL YOU WANT, BUT IT CHANGES NOTHING.
YOU'RE NAILED, MAN. CAUGHT IN THE ACT.
SO SHOULD I CALL YOU A LAWYER?
FORGET IT, I'LL JUST TAKE MY SENTENCE... AND A WARM MEAL.
HEY.
YOU'VE GOTTA BE SCREWING ME HERE. SOMEONE POSTED HIS BAIL?
HUH ?
WHO THE HELL WOULD BOTHER?

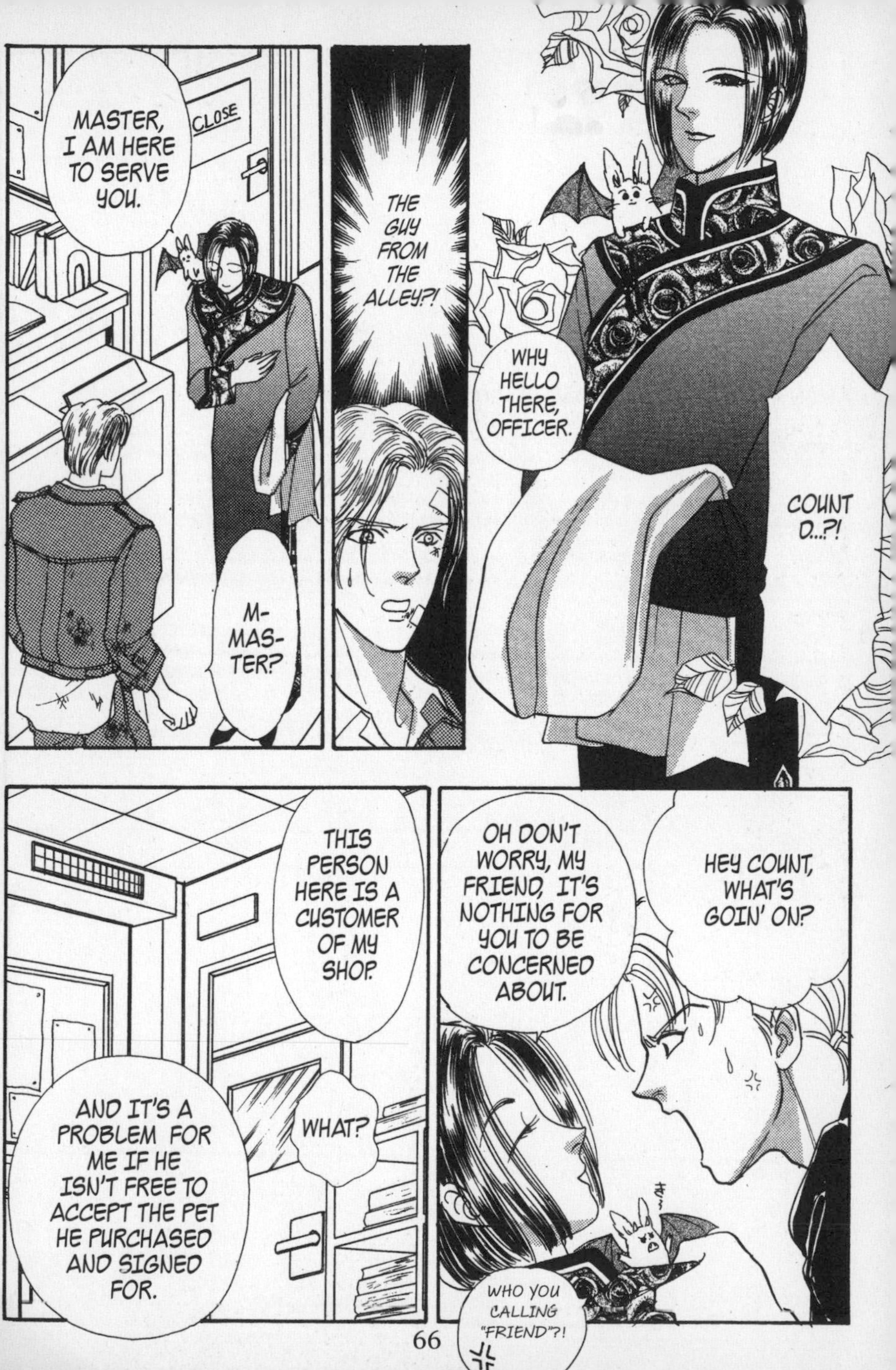

WHY HELLO THERE, OFFICER.
COUNT D..?!
THE GUY FROM THE ALLEY?!
MASTER, I AM HERE TO SERVE YOU.
CLOSE
M-MAS-TER?
HEY COUNT, WHAT'S GOIN' ON?
OH DON'T WORRY, MY FRIEND, IT'S NOTHING FOR YOU TO BE CONCERNED ABOUT.
WHO YOU CALLING "FRIEND"?!
THIS PERSON HERE IS A CUSTOMER OF MY SHOP.
WHAT?
AND IT'S A PROBLEM FOR ME IF HE ISN'T FREE TO ACCEPT THE PET HE PURCHASED AND SIGNED FOR.

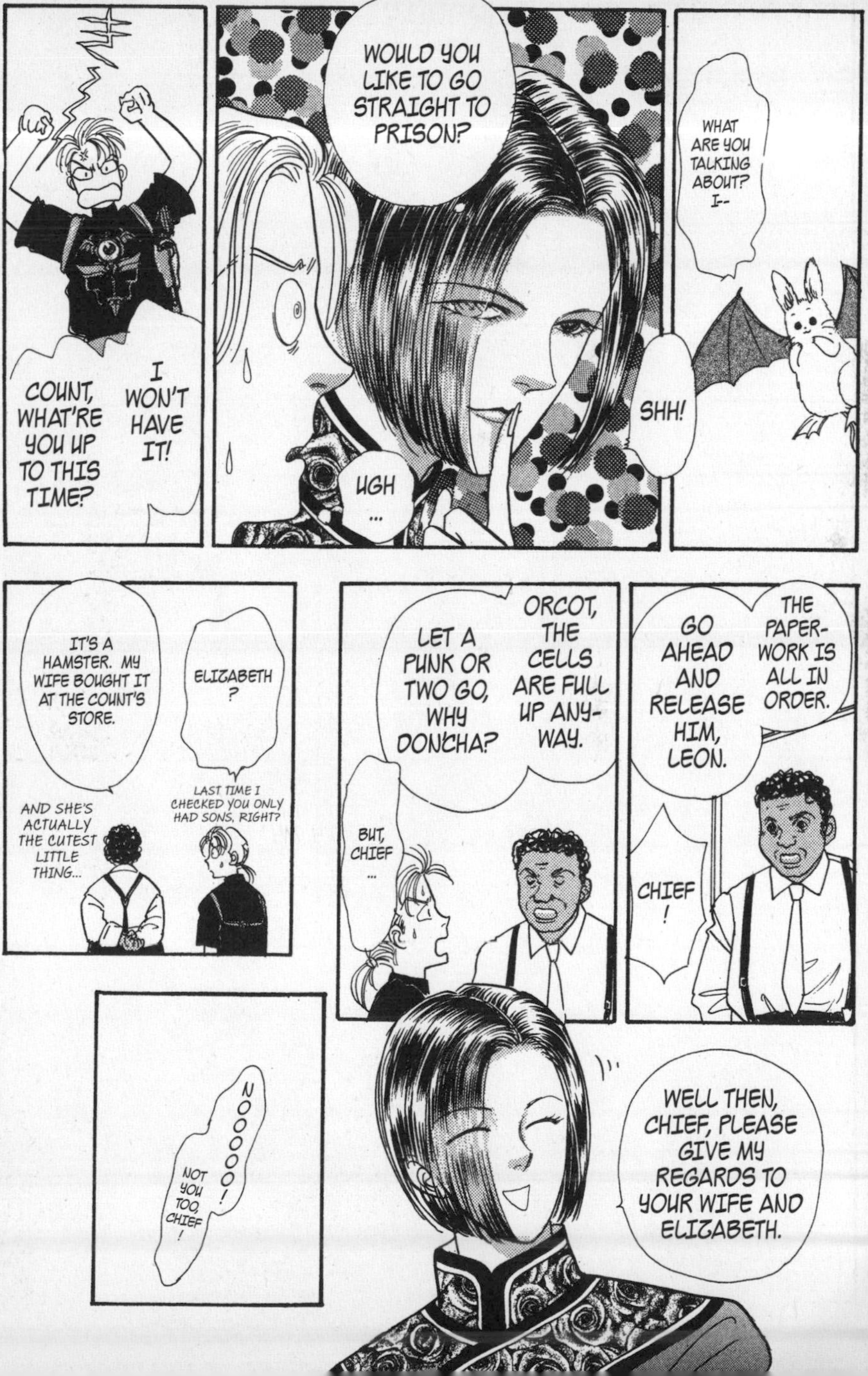
WHAT ARE YOU TALKING ABOUT? I--
SHH!
WOULD YOU LIKE TO GO STRAIGHT TO PRISON?
UGH ...
I WON'T HAVE IT!
COUNT, WHAT'RE YOU UP TO THIS TIME?
THE PAPER-WORK IS ALL IN ORDER.
GO AHEAD AND RELEASE HIM, LEON.
CHIEF!
ORCOT, THE CELLS ARE FULL UP ANY-WAY.
LET A PUNK OR TWO GO, WHY DONCHA?
BUT, CHIEF ...
ELIZABETH?
LAST TIME I CHECKED YOU ONLY HAD SONS, RIGHT?
IT'S A HAMSTER. MY WIFE BOUGHT IT AT THE COUNT'S STORE.
AND SHE'S ACTUALLY THE CUTEST LITTLE THING...
WELL THEN, CHIEF, PLEASE GIVE MY REGARDS TO YOUR WIFE AND ELIZABETH.
NOOOOOO!
NOT YOU TOO, CHIEF!

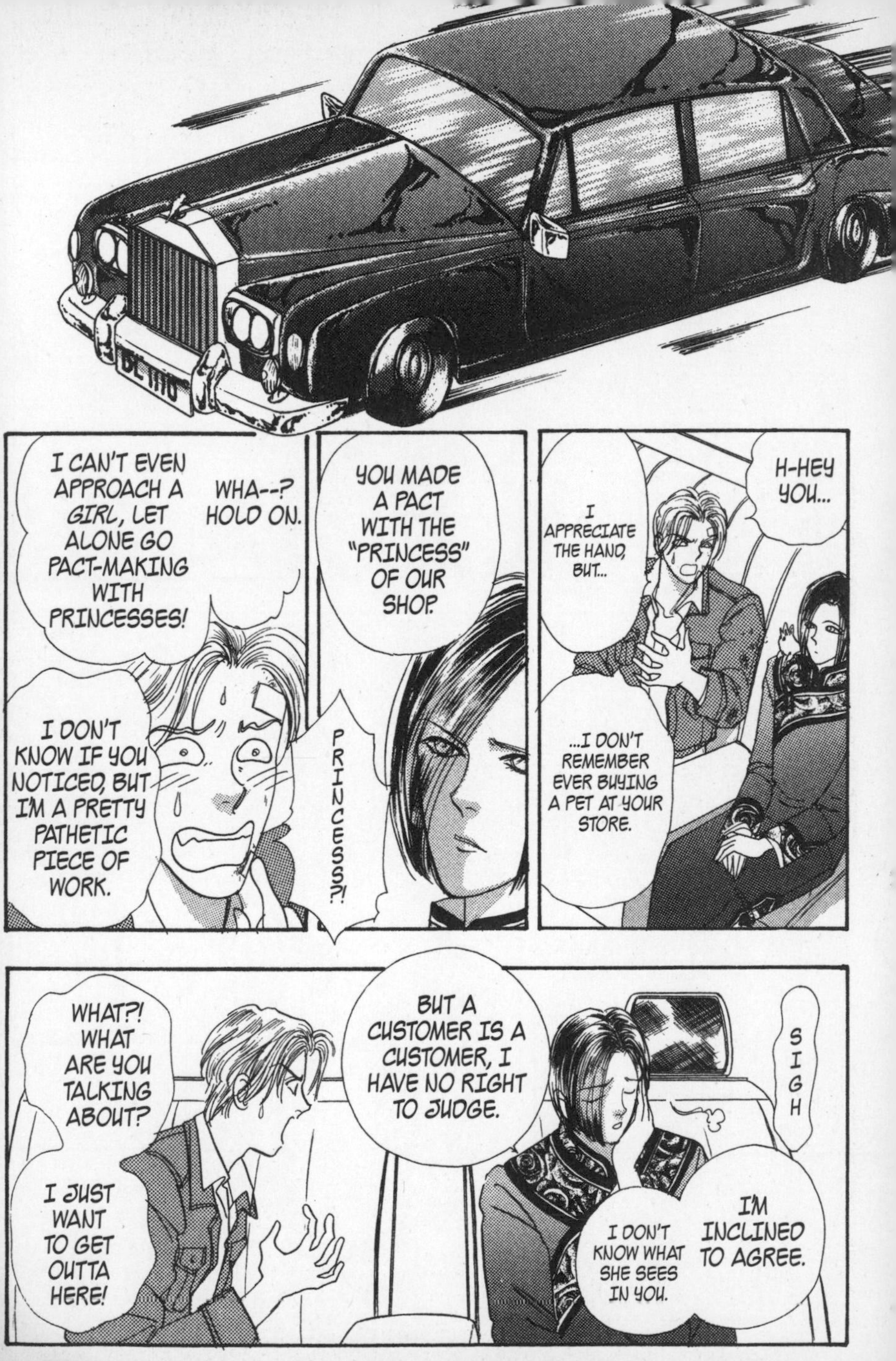
BL 1110
H-HEY YOU...
I APPRECIATE THE HAND, BUT...
...I DON'T REMEMBER EVER BUYING A PET AT YOUR STORE.
YOU MADE A PACT WITH THE "PRINCESS" OF OUR SHOP.
PRINCESS?!
WHA--? HOLD ON.
I CAN'T EVEN APPROACH A GIRL, LET ALONE GO PACT-MAKING WITH PRINCESSES!
I DON'T KNOW IF YOU NOTICED, BUT I'M A PRETTY PATHETIC PIECE OF WORK.
SIGH
I'M INCLINED TO AGREE.
I DON'T KNOW WHAT SHE SEES IN YOU.
BUT A CUSTOMER IS A CUSTOMER, I HAVE NO RIGHT TO JUDGE.
WHAT?! WHAT ARE YOU TALKING ABOUT?
I JUST WANT TO GET OUTTA HERE!

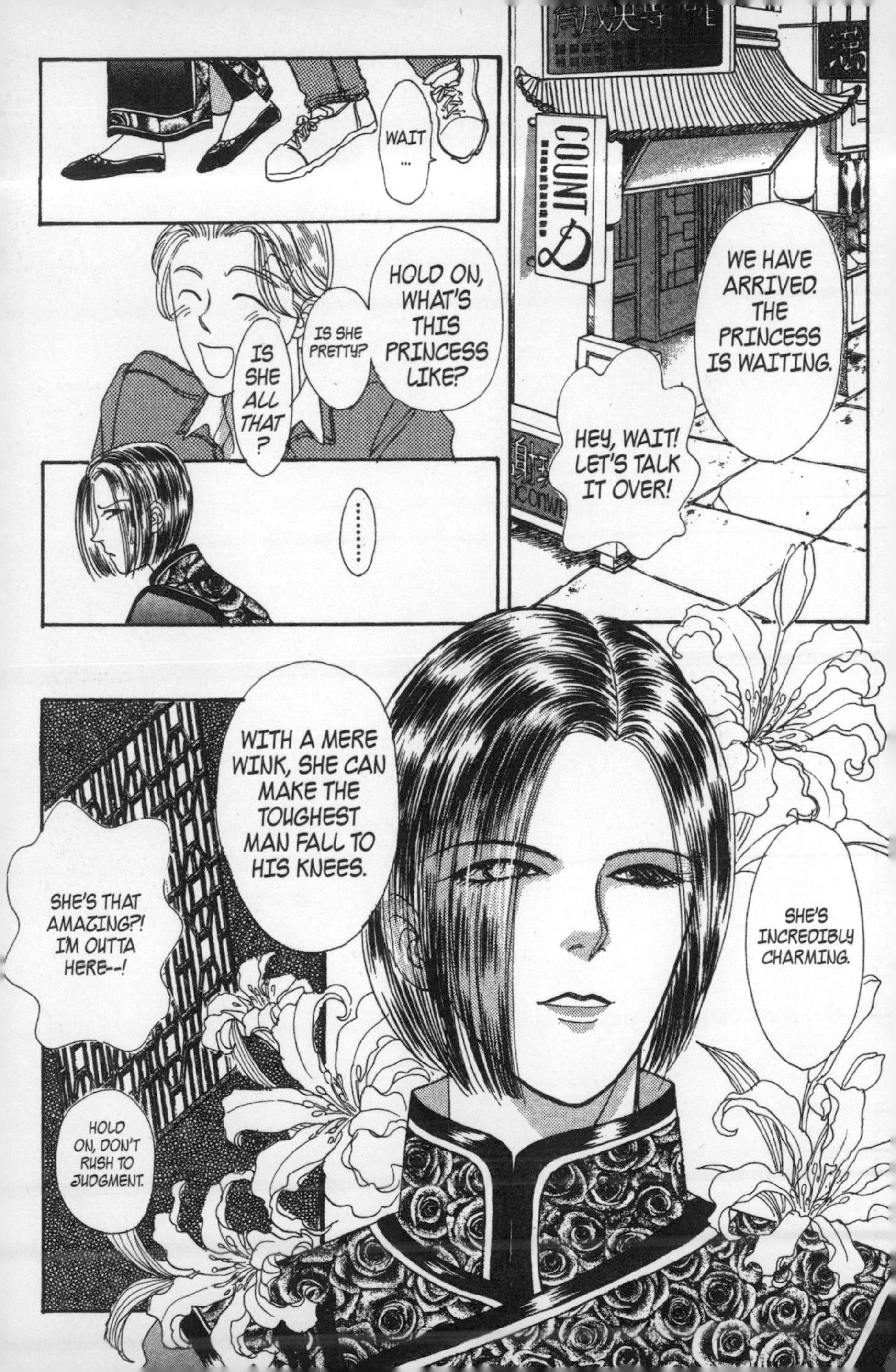
COUNT D
WE HAVE ARRIVED. THE PRINCESS IS WAITING.
HEY, WAIT! LET'S TALK IT OVER!
WAIT ...
HOLD ON, WHAT'S THIS PRINCESS LIKE?
IS SHE PRETTY?
IS SHE ALL THAT?
....
SHE'S INCREDIBLY CHARMING.
WITH A MERE WINK, SHE CAN MAKE THE TOUGHEST MAN FALL TO HIS KNEES.
SHE'S THAT AMAZING?! I'M OUTTA HERE--!
HOLD ON, DON'T RUSH TO JUDGMENT.

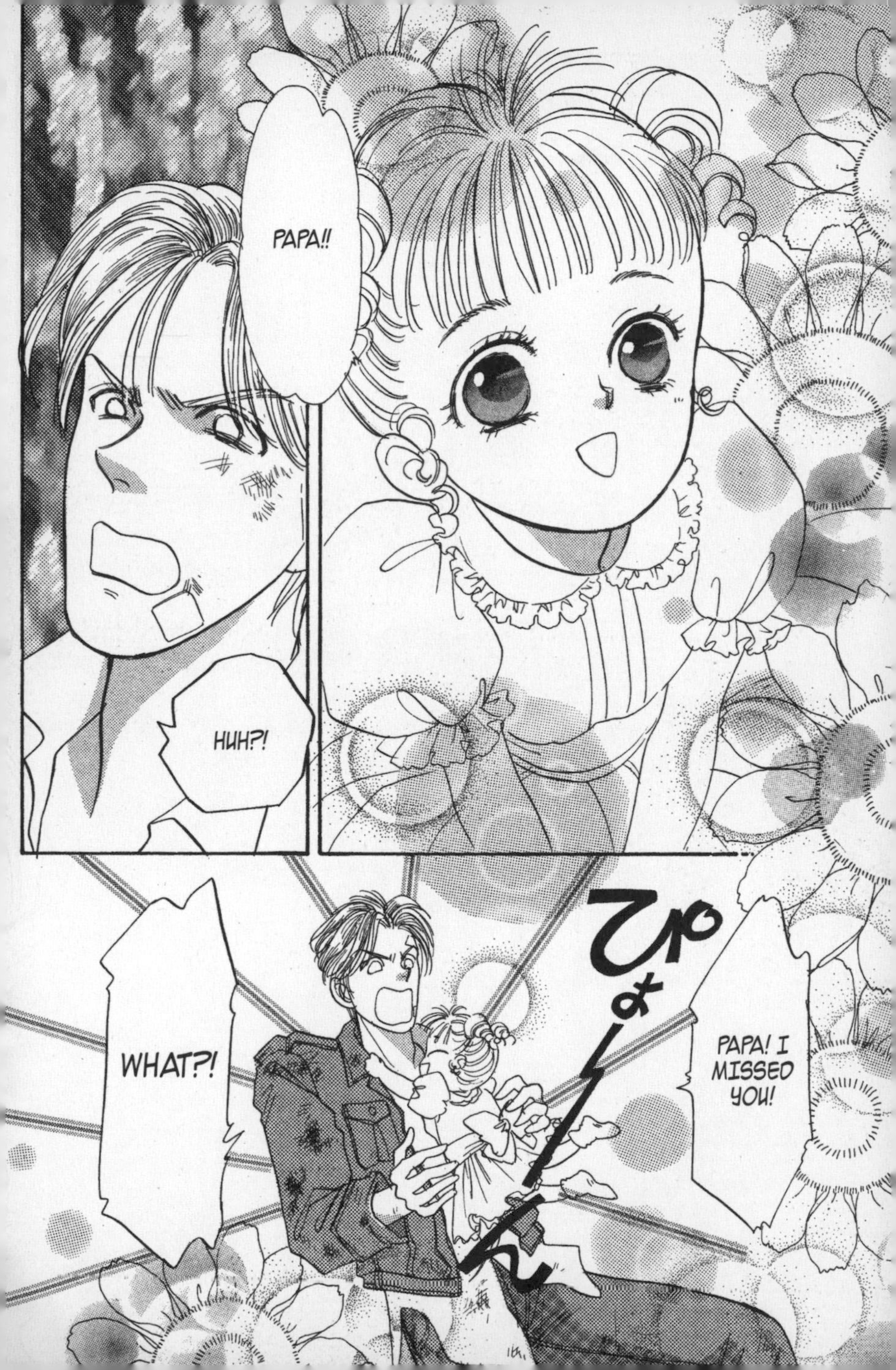

PAPA!!
HUH?!
PAPA! I MISSED YOU!
ぴょーん
WHAT?!

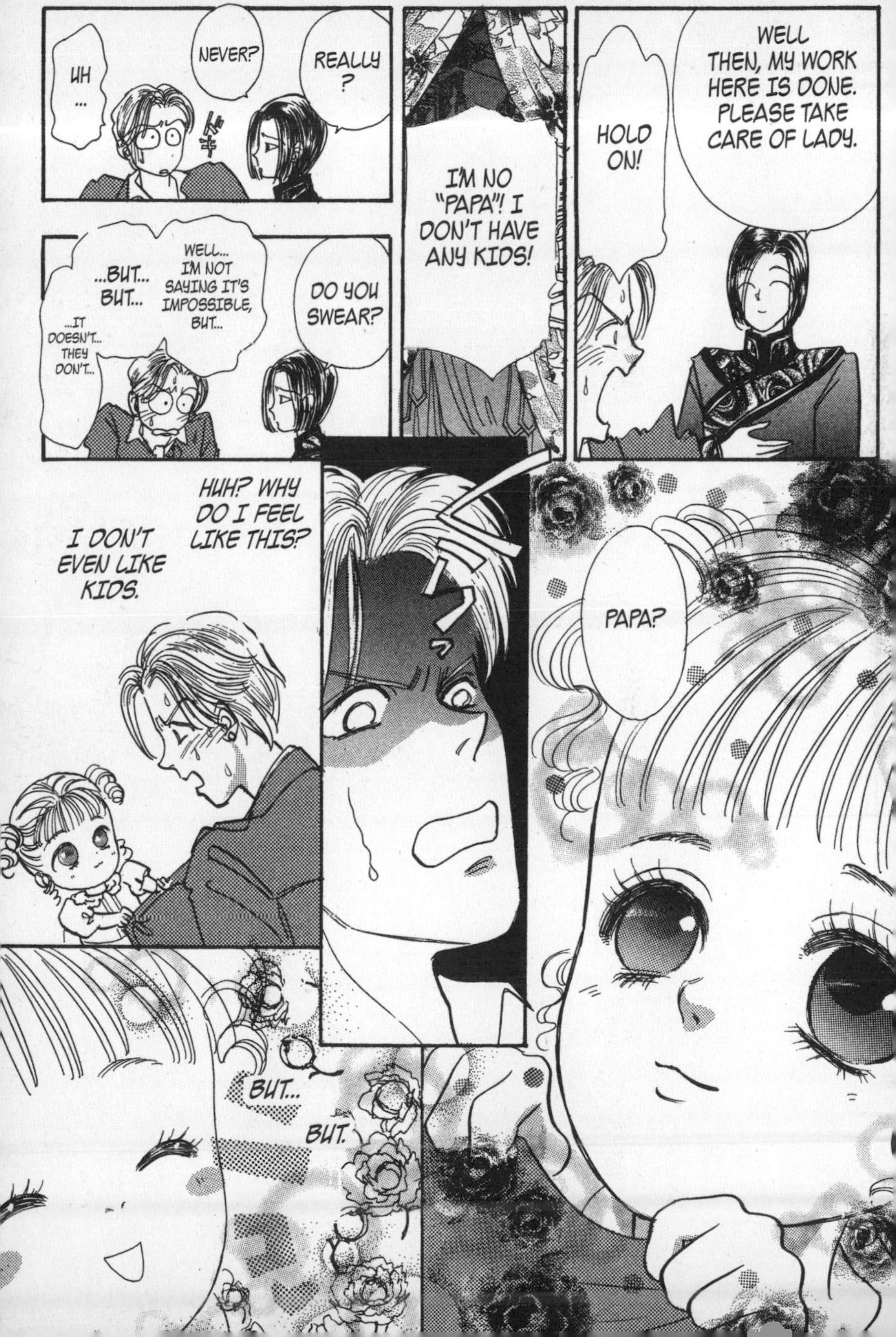
WELL THEN, MY WORK HERE IS DONE. PLEASE TAKE CARE OF LADY.
HOLD ON!
I'M NO "PAPA"! I DON'T HAVE ANY KIDS!
REALLY?
NEVER?
UH...
DO YOU SWEAR?
WELL... I'M NOT SAYING IT'S IMPOSSIBLE, BUT...
...BUT... BUT...
...IT DOESN'T... THEY DON'T...
PAPA?
HUH? WHY DO I FEEL LIKE THIS?
I DON'T EVEN LIKE KIDS.
BUT...
BUT.

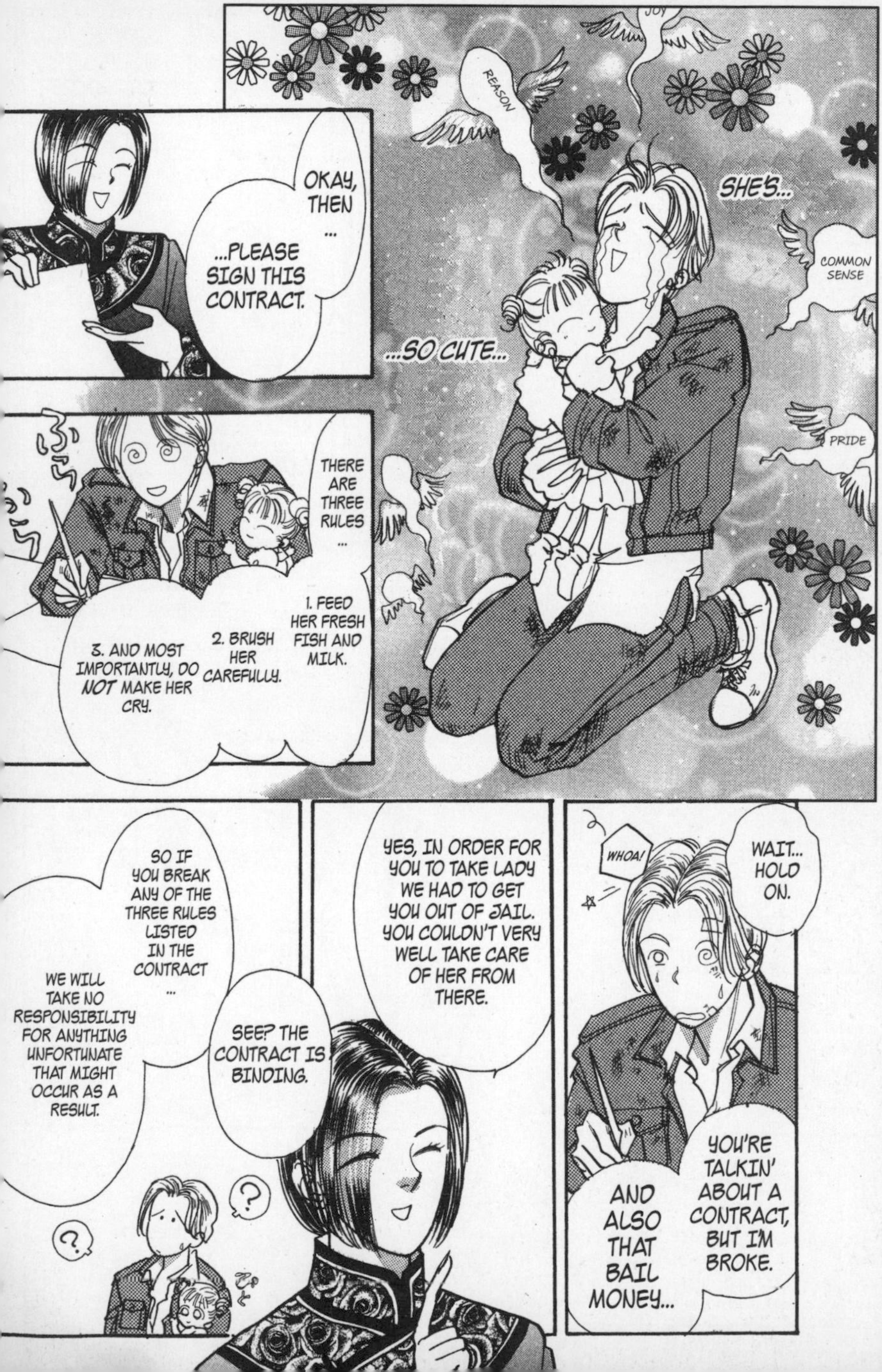
JOY
SHE'S...
COMMON SENSE
REASON
...SO CUTE...
PRIDE
OKAY, THEN ...
...PLEASE SIGN THIS CONTRACT.
THERE ARE THREE RULES ...
1. FEED HER FRESH FISH AND MILK.
2. BRUSH HER CAREFULLY.
3. AND MOST IMPORTANTLY, DO *NOT* MAKE HER CRY.
WHOA!
WAIT... HOLD ON.
YOU'RE TALKIN' ABOUT A CONTRACT, BUT I'M BROKE.
AND ALSO THAT BAIL MONEY...
YES, IN ORDER FOR YOU TO TAKE LADY WE HAD TO GET YOU OUT OF JAIL. YOU COULDN'T VERY WELL TAKE CARE OF HER FROM THERE.
SEE? THE CONTRACT IS BINDING.
SO IF YOU BREAK ANY OF THE THREE RULES LISTED IN THE CONTRACT ...
WE WILL TAKE NO RESPONSIBILITY FOR ANYTHING UNFORTUNATE THAT MIGHT OCCUR AS A RESULT.

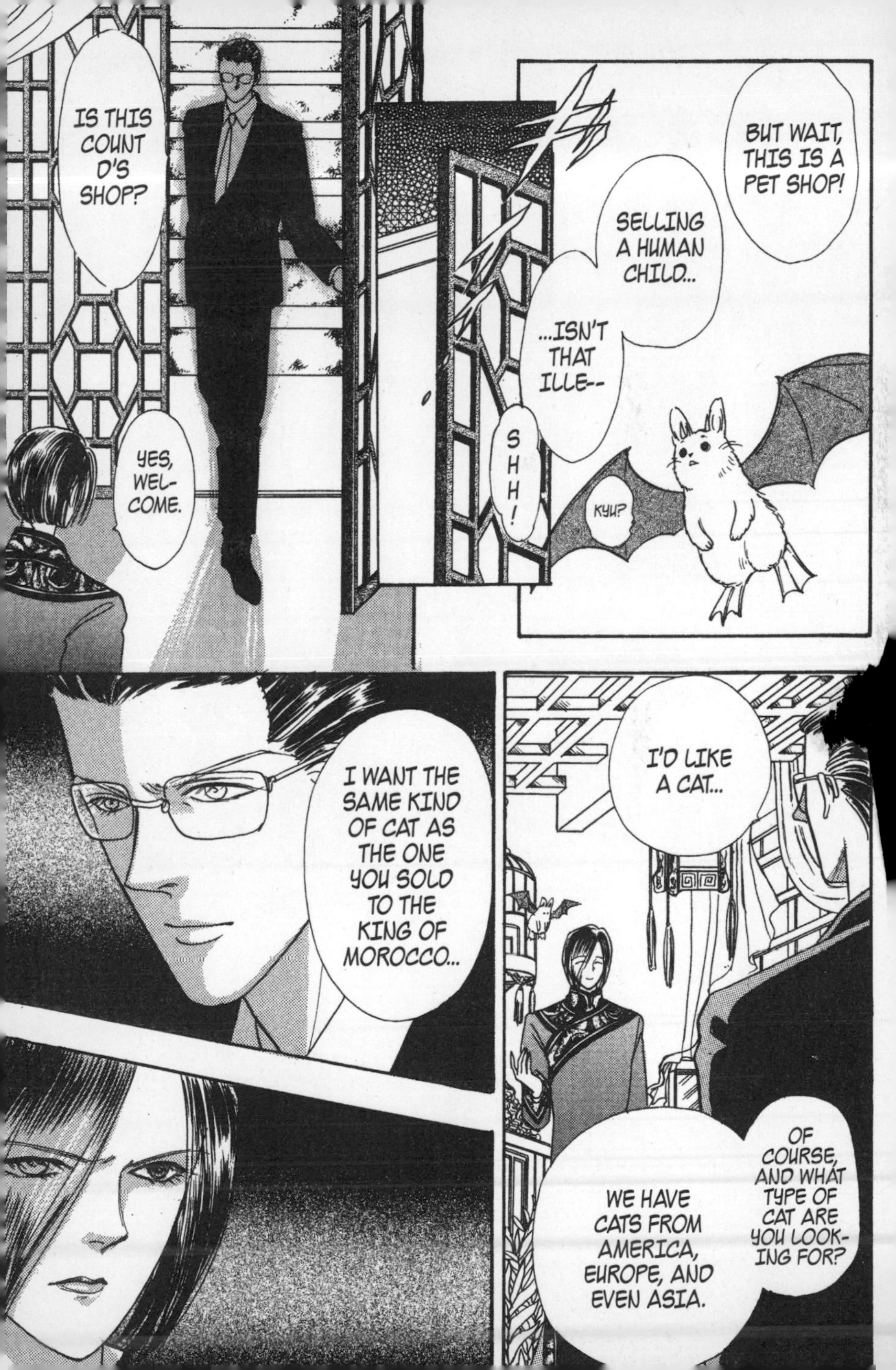
BUT WAIT, THIS IS A PET SHOP!
SELLING A HUMAN CHILD...
...ISN'T THAT ILLE--
SHH!
KYU?
IS THIS COUNT D'S SHOP?
YES, WEL-COME.
I'D LIKE A CAT...
OF COURSE, AND WHAT TYPE OF CAT ARE YOU LOOK-ING FOR?
WE HAVE CATS FROM AMERICA, EUROPE, AND EVEN ASIA.
I WANT THE SAME KIND OF CAT AS THE ONE YOU SOLD TO THE KING OF MOROCCO...

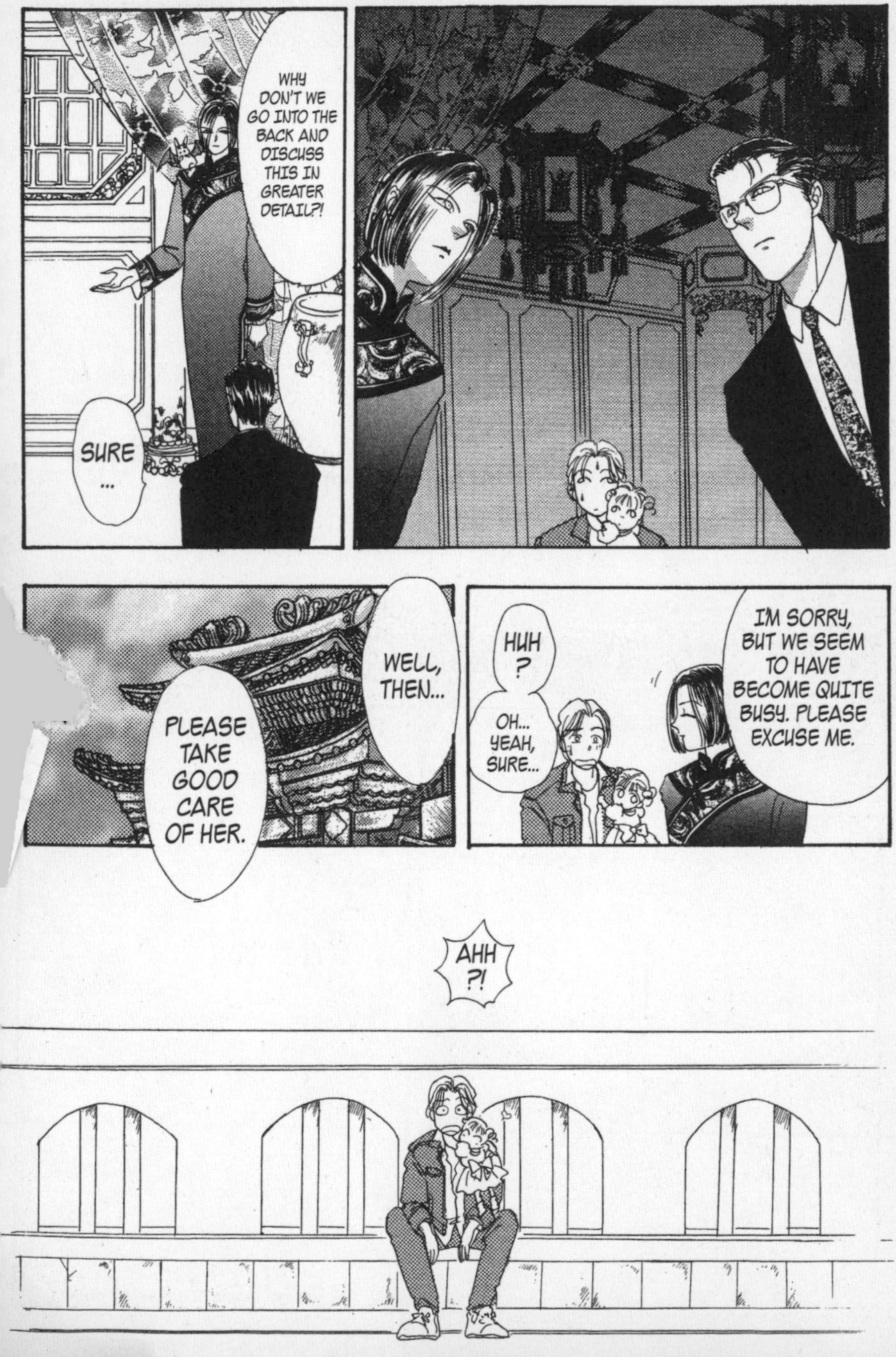
WHY DON'T WE GO INTO THE BACK AND DISCUSS THIS IN GREATER DETAIL?!
SURE ...
I'M SORRY, BUT WE SEEM TO HAVE BECOME QUITE BUSY. PLEASE EXCUSE ME.
HUH ?
OH... YEAH, SURE...
WELL, THEN...
PLEASE TAKE GOOD CARE OF HER.
AHH ?!

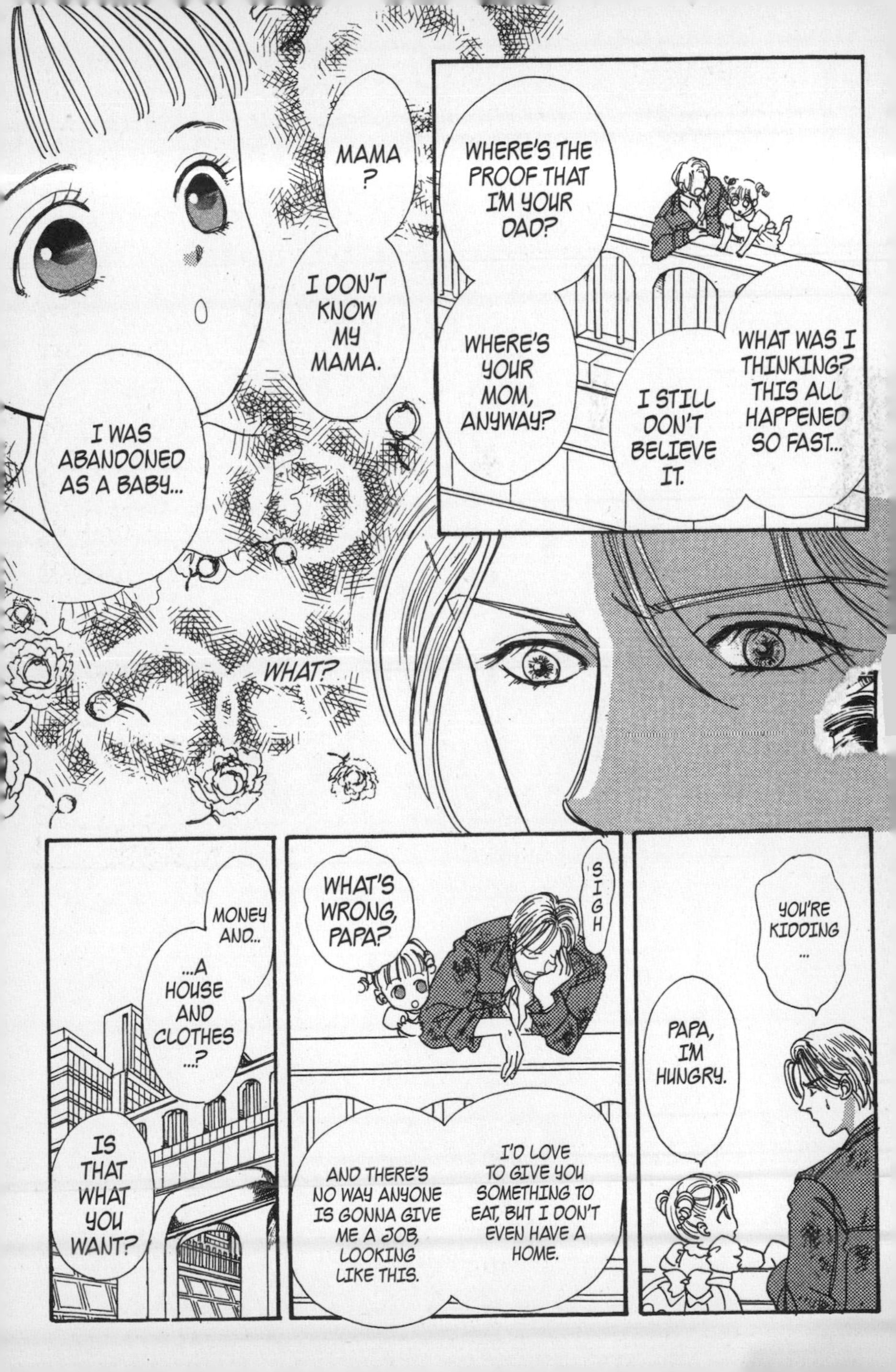
WHAT WAS I THINKING? THIS ALL HAPPENED SO FAST...
I STILL DON'T BELIEVE IT.
WHERE'S THE PROOF THAT I'M YOUR DAD?
WHERE'S YOUR MOM, ANYWAY?
MAMA ?
I DON'T KNOW MY MAMA.
I WAS ABANDONED AS A BABY...
WHAT?
YOU'RE KIDDING ...
PAPA, I'M HUNGRY.
SIGH
WHAT'S WRONG, PAPA?
I'D LOVE TO GIVE YOU SOMETHING TO EAT, BUT I DON'T EVEN HAVE A HOME.
AND THERE'S NO WAY ANYONE IS GONNA GIVE ME A JOB, LOOKING LIKE THIS.
MONEY AND...
...A HOUSE AND CLOTHES ...?
IS THAT WHAT YOU WANT?

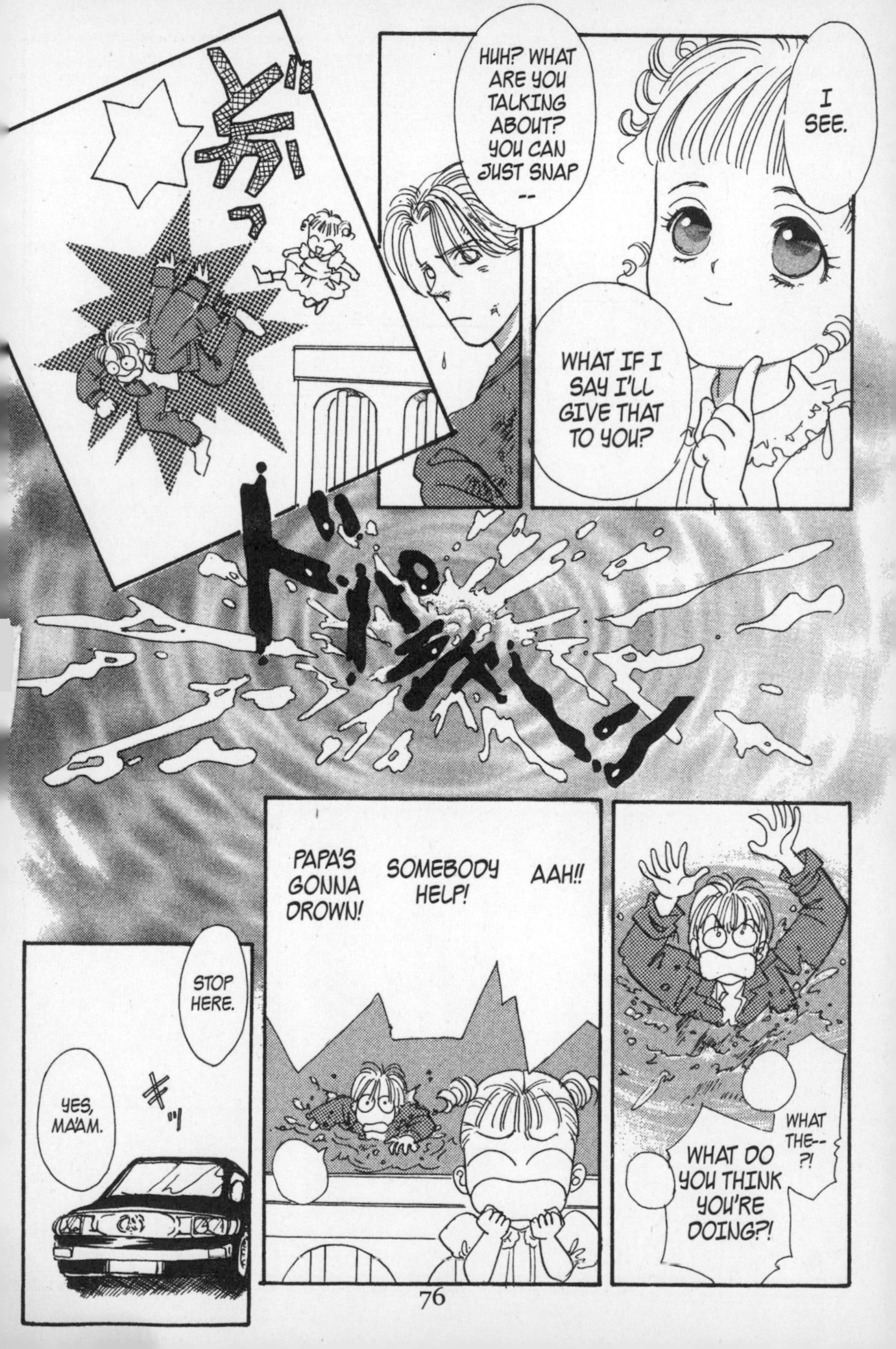
I SEE.
WHAT IF I SAY I'LL GIVE THAT TO YOU?
HUH? WHAT ARE YOU TALKING ABOUT? YOU CAN JUST SNAP --
WHAT THE--?!
WHAT DO YOU THINK YOU'RE DOING?!
AAH!!
SOMEBODY HELP!
PAPA'S GONNA DROWN!
STOP HERE.
YES, MA'AM.

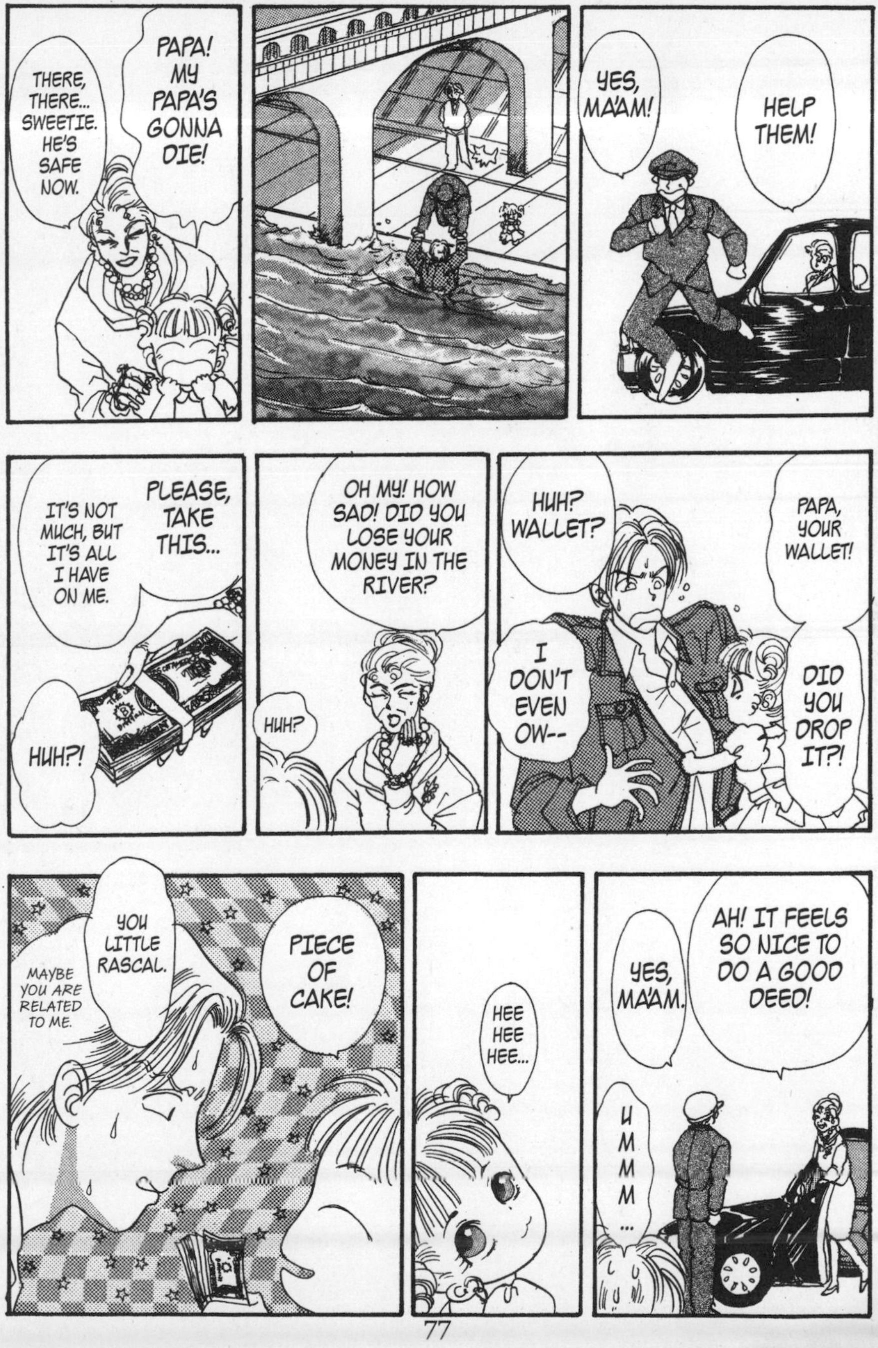
HELP THEM!
YES, MA'AM!
PAPA! MY PAPA'S GONNA DIE!
THERE, THERE... SWEETIE. HE'S SAFE NOW.
PAPA, YOUR WALLET!
HUH? WALLET?
DID YOU DROP IT?!
I DON'T EVEN OW--
OH MY! HOW SAD! DID YOU LOSE YOUR MONEY IN THE RIVER?
HUH?
PLEASE, TAKE THIS...
IT'S NOT MUCH, BUT IT'S ALL I HAVE ON ME.
HUH?!
AH! IT FEELS SO NICE TO DO A GOOD DEED!
YES, MA'AM.
UMMMM...
HEE HEE HEE...
PIECE OF CAKE!
YOU LITTLE RASCAL.
MAYBE YOU ARE RELATED TO ME.

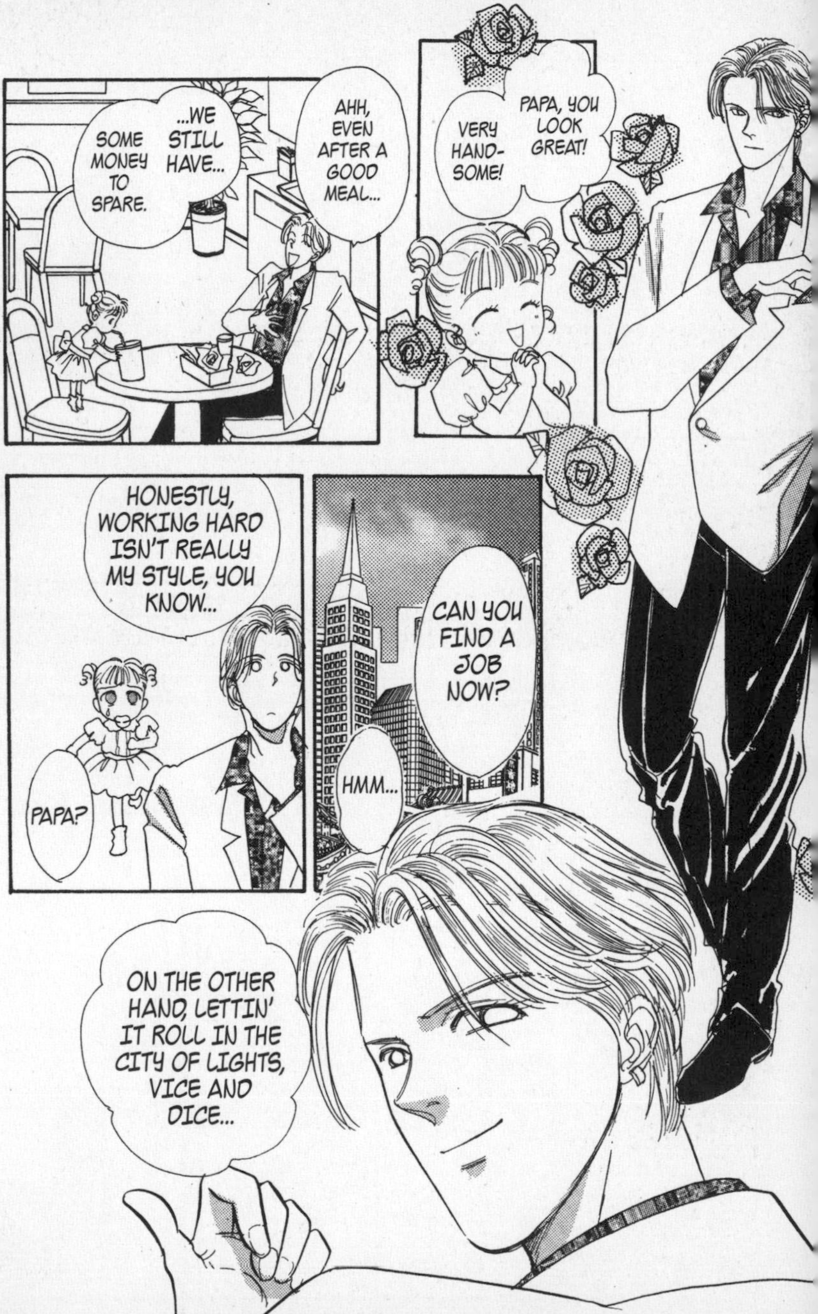
PAPA, YOU LOOK GREAT!
VERY HAND-SOME!
AHH, EVEN AFTER A GOOD MEAL...
...WE STILL HAVE...
SOME MONEY TO SPARE.
CAN YOU FIND A JOB NOW?
HMM...
HONESTLY, WORKING HARD ISN'T REALLY MY STYLE, YOU KNOW...
PAPA?
ON THE OTHER HAND, LETTIN' IT ROLL IN THE CITY OF LIGHTS, VICE AND DICE...

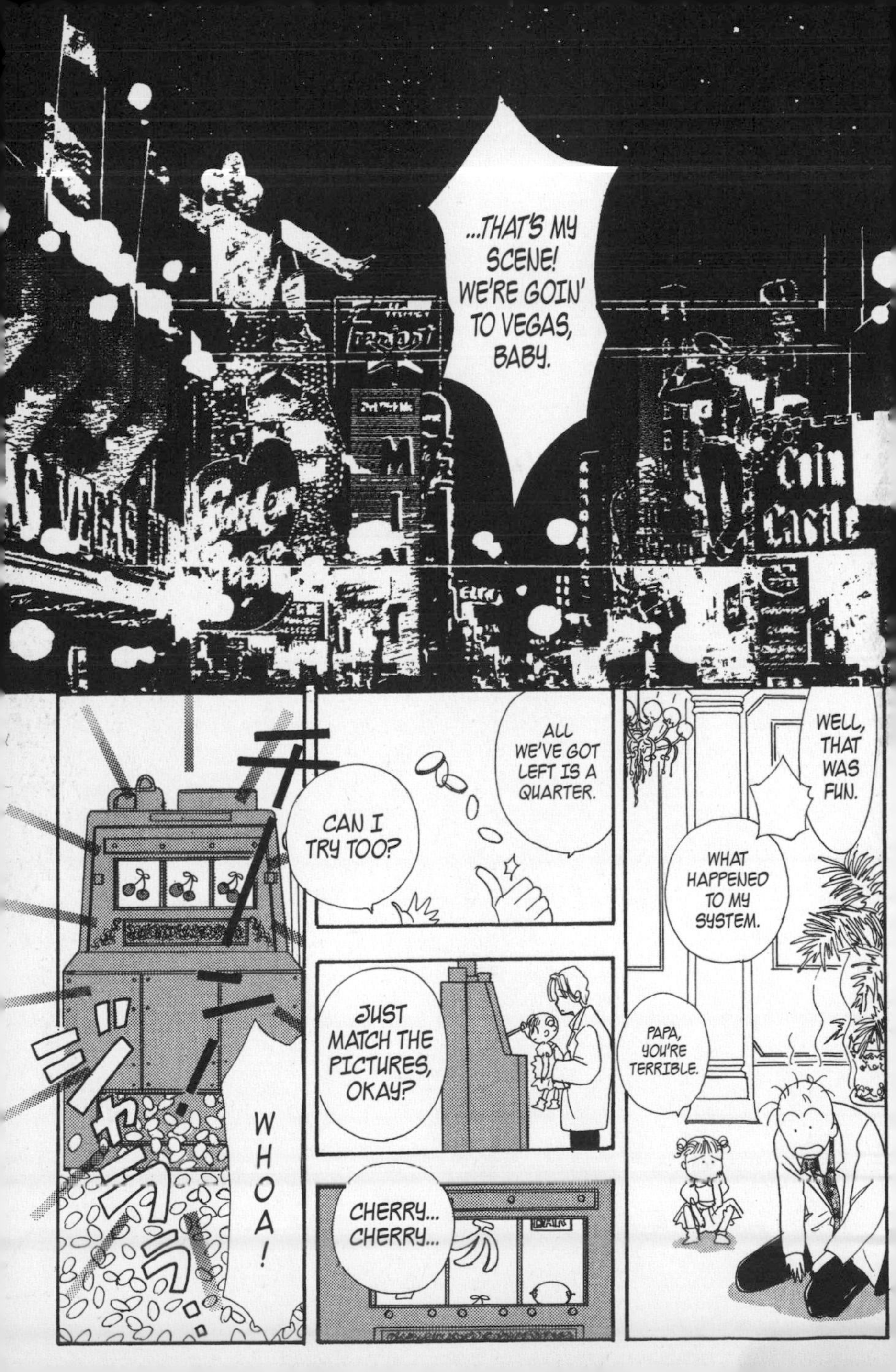
...THAT'S MY SCENE! WE'RE GOIN' TO VEGAS, BABY.
Coin Castle
WELL, THAT WAS FUN.
WHAT HAPPENED TO MY SYSTEM.
PAPA, YOU'RE TERRIBLE.
ALL WE'VE GOT LEFT IS A QUARTER.
CAN I TRY TOO?
JUST MATCH THE PICTURES, OKAY?
CHERRY... CHERRY...
WHOA!

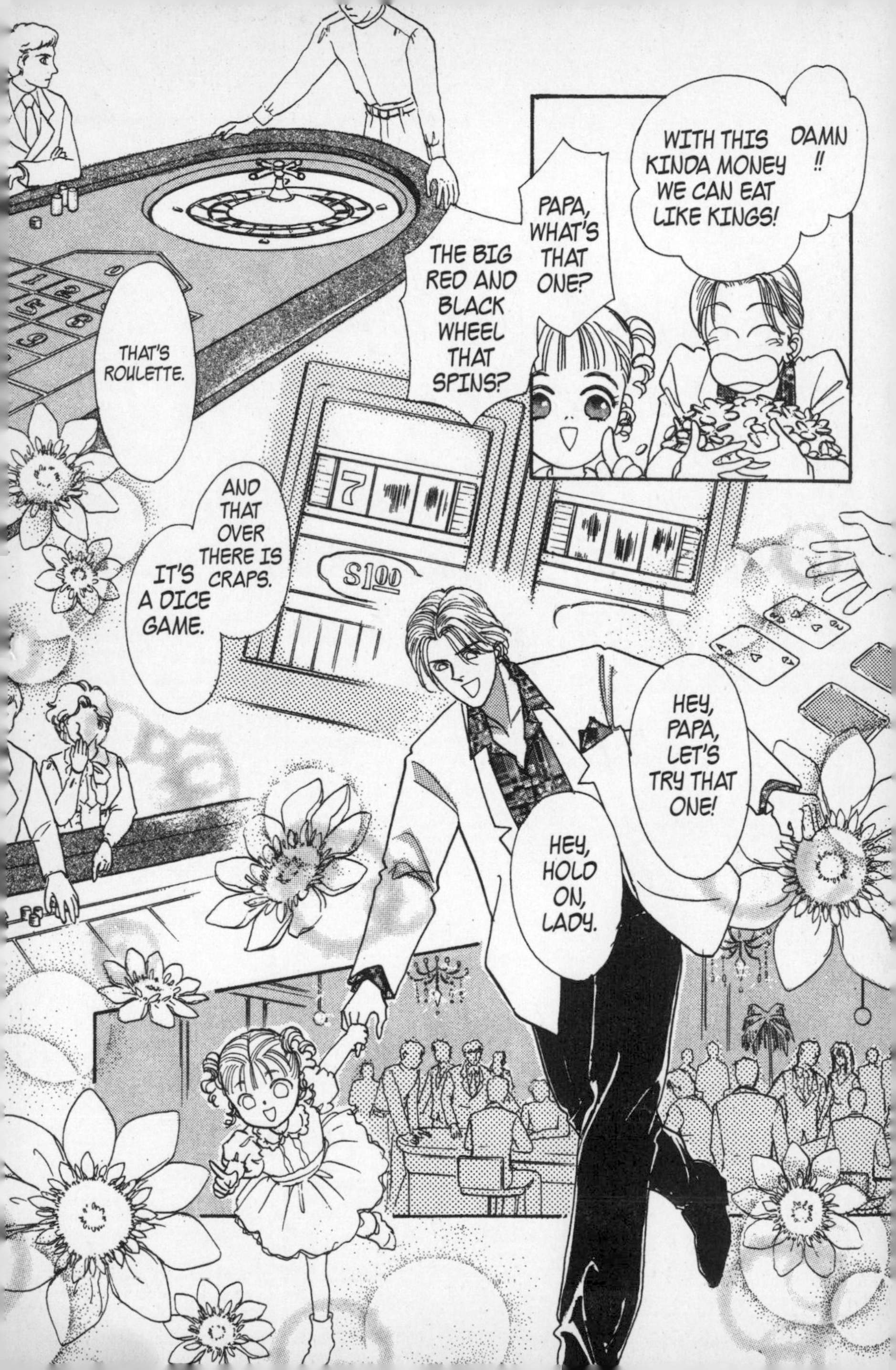

DAMN !!
WITH THIS KINDA MONEY WE CAN EAT LIKE KINGS!
PAPA, WHAT'S THAT ONE?
THE BIG RED AND BLACK WHEEL THAT SPINS?
THAT'S ROULETTE.
AND THAT OVER THERE IS CRAPS.
IT'S A DICE GAME.
HEY, PAPA, LET'S TRY THAT ONE!
HEY, HOLD ON, LADY.

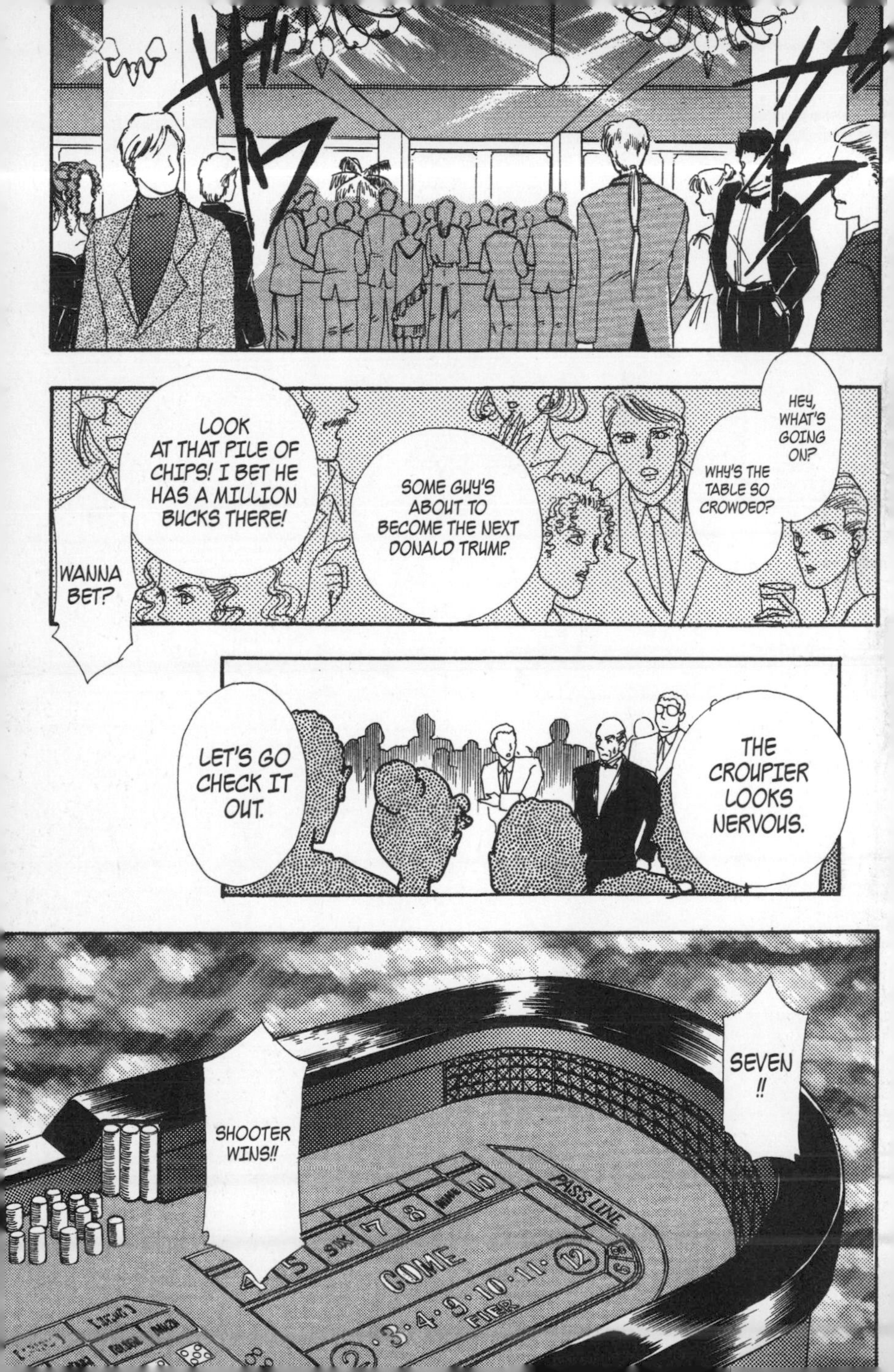

HEY, WHAT'S GOING ON?
WHY'S THE TABLE SO CROWDED?
SOME GUY'S ABOUT TO BECOME THE NEXT DONALD TRUMP.
LOOK AT THAT PILE OF CHIPS! I BET HE HAS A MILLION BUCKS THERE!
WANNA BET?
THE CROUPIER LOOKS NERVOUS.
LET'S GO CHECK IT OUT.
SEVEN !!
SHOOTER WINS!!
PASS LINE
COME

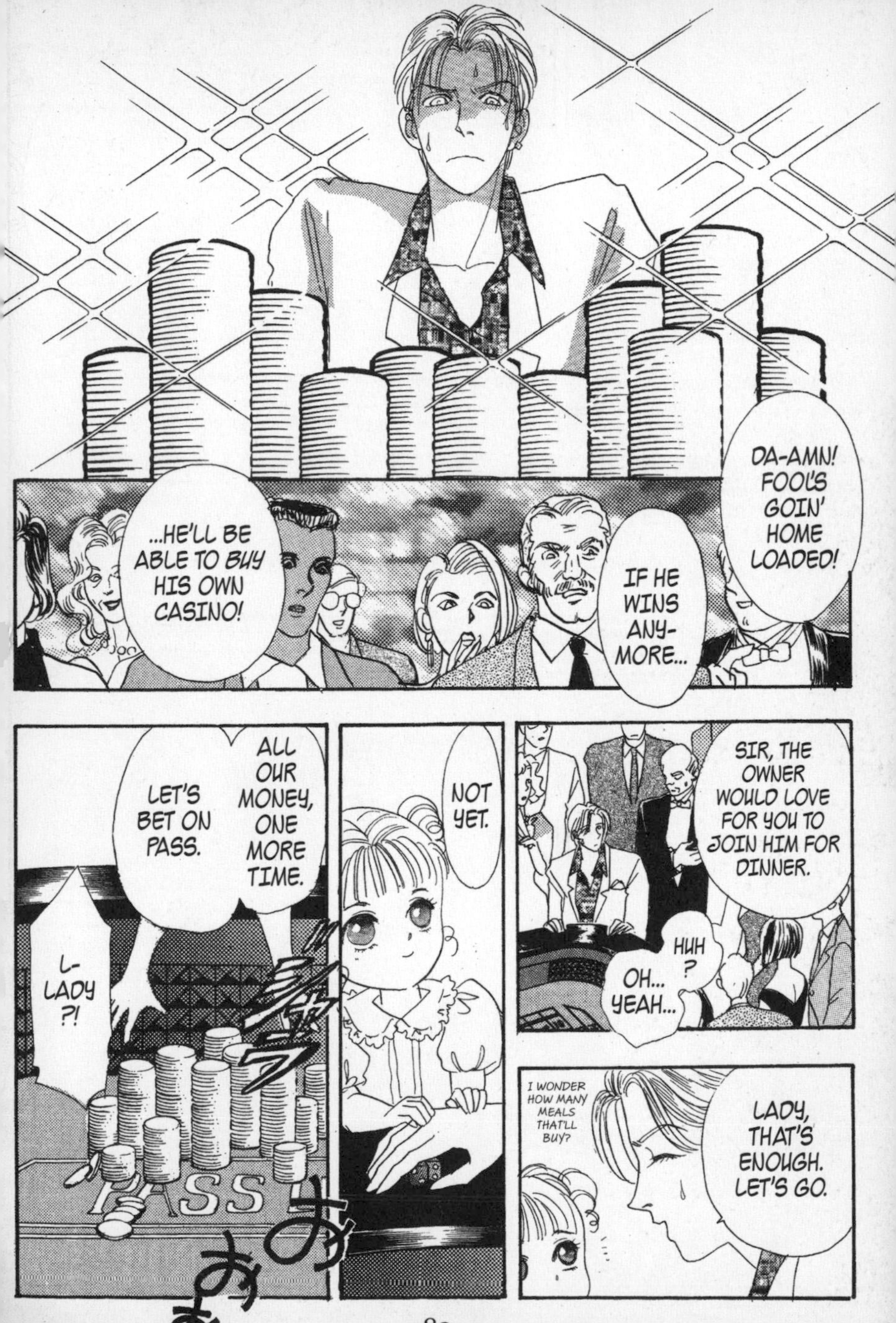
DA-AMN! FOOL'S GOIN' HOME LOADED!
IF HE WINS ANY-MORE...
...HE'LL BE ABLE TO BUY HIS OWN CASINO!
SIR, THE OWNER WOULD LOVE FOR YOU TO JOIN HIM FOR DINNER.
HUH?
OH... YEAH...
LADY, THAT'S ENOUGH. LET'S GO.
I WONDER HOW MANY MEALS THAT'LL BUY?
NOT YET.
ALL OUR MONEY, ONE MORE TIME.
LET'S BET ON PASS.
L-LADY?!
PASS

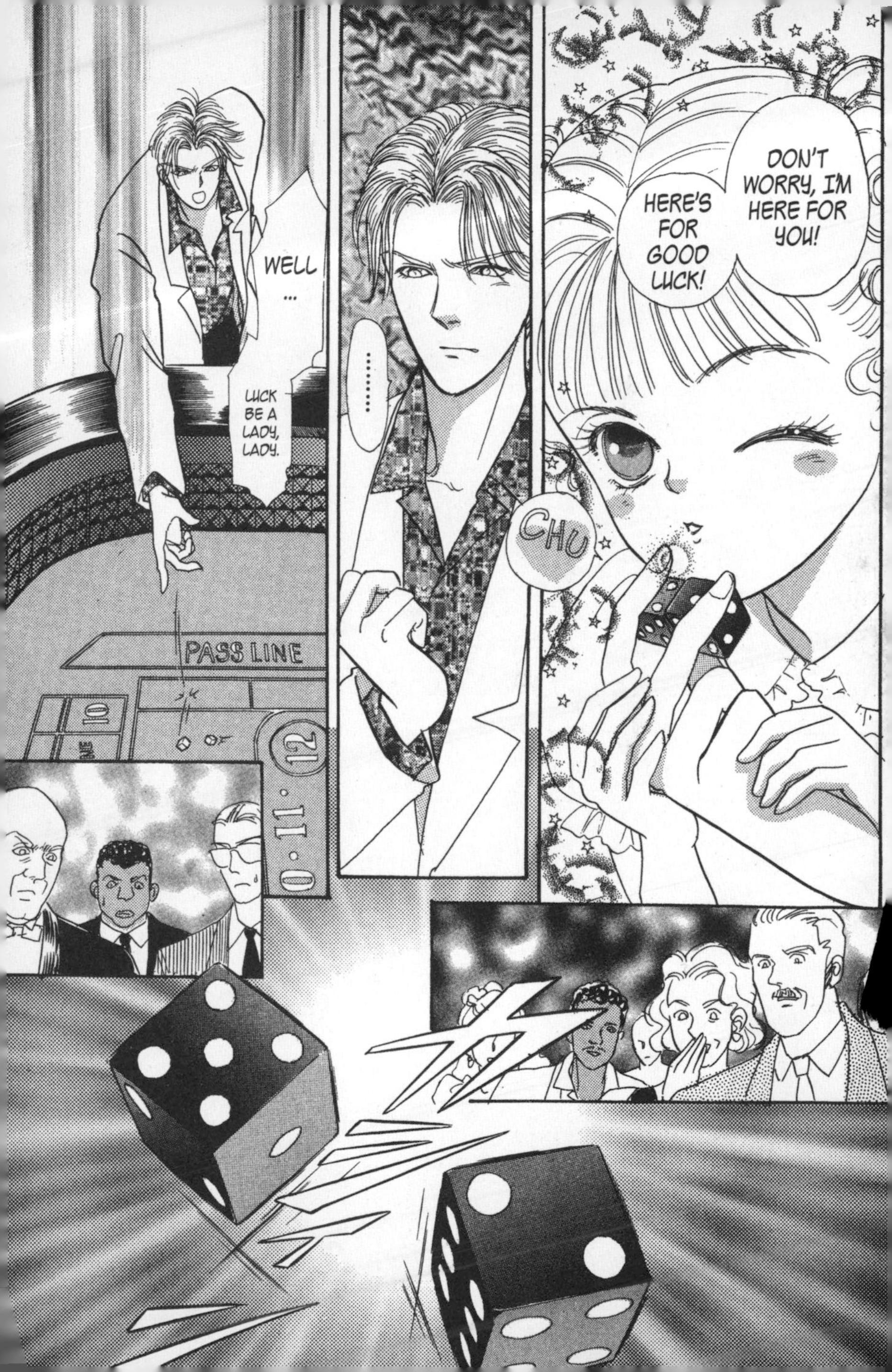
DON'T WORRY, I'M HERE FOR YOU!
HERE'S FOR GOOD LUCK!
CHU
......
WELL ...
LUCK BE A LADY, LADY.
PASS LINE

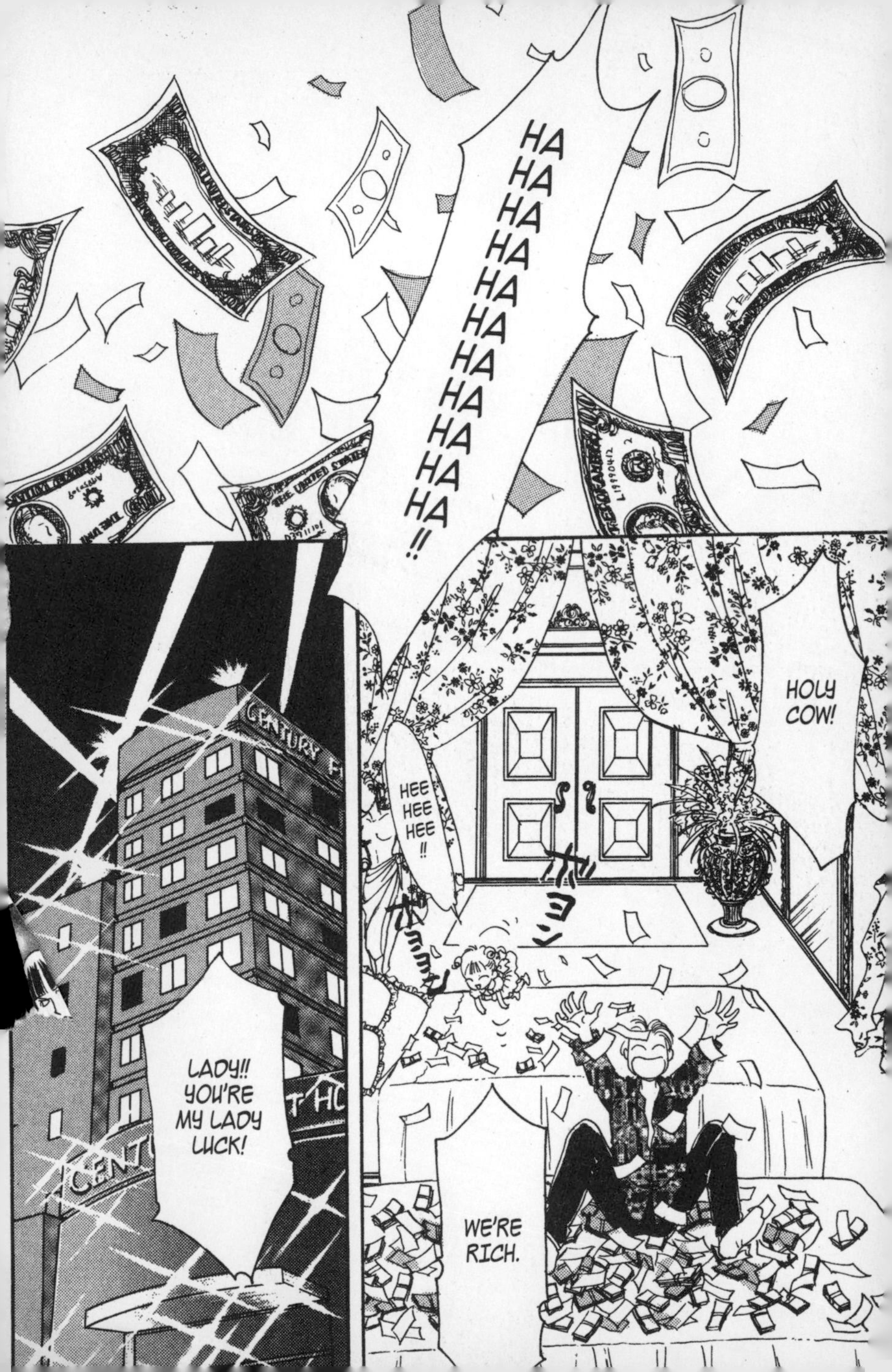
HA HA HA HA HA HA HA HA HA HA HA!!
HOLY COW!
HEE HEE HEE!!
WE'RE RICH.
LADY!! YOU'RE MY LADY LUCK!

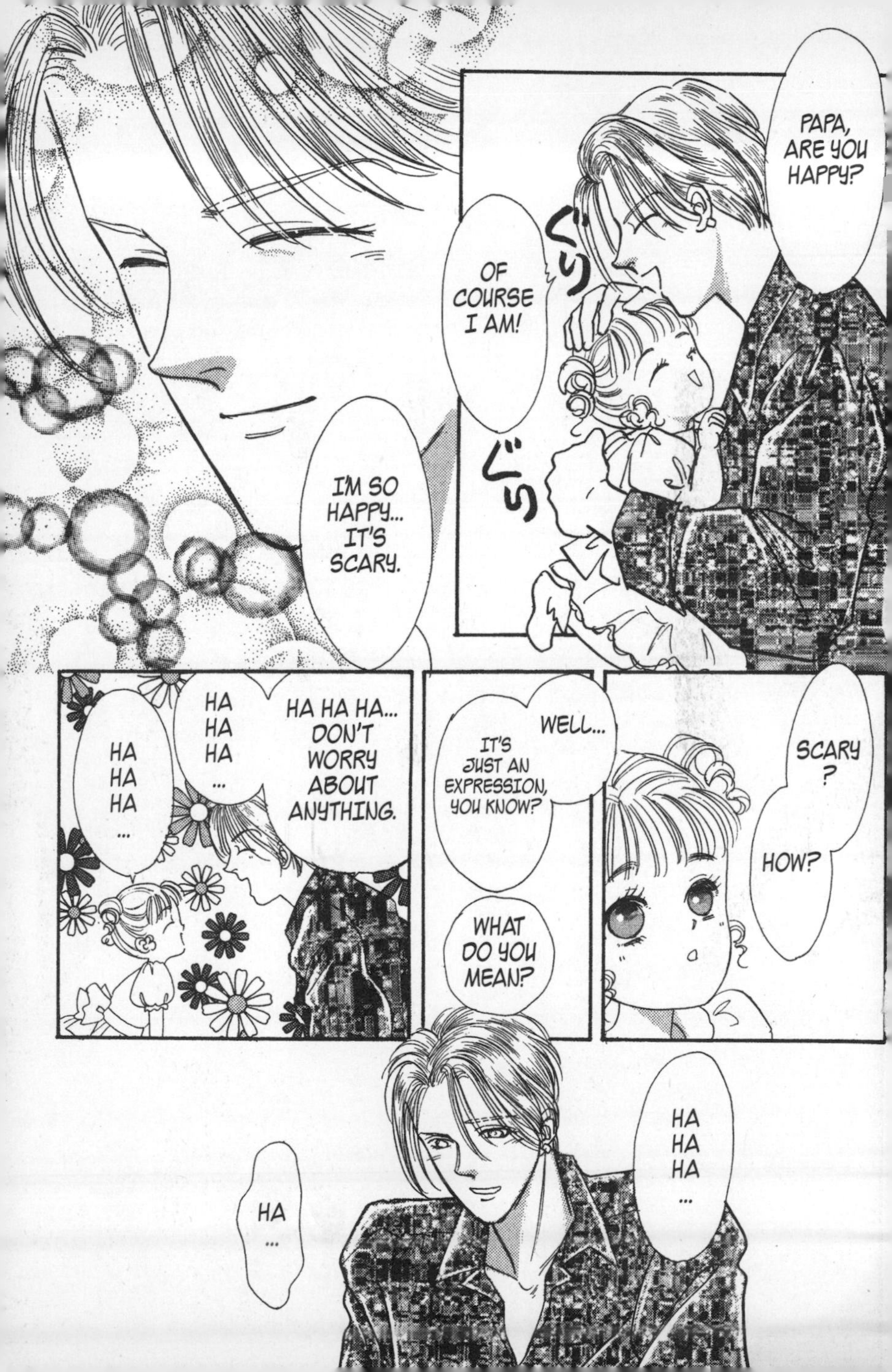
PAPA, ARE YOU HAPPY?
OF COURSE I AM!
ぐり
ぐり
I'M SO HAPPY... IT'S SCARY.
SCARY?
HOW?
WELL...
IT'S JUST AN EXPRESSION, YOU KNOW?
WHAT DO YOU MEAN?
HA HA HA... DON'T WORRY ABOUT ANYTHING.
HA HA HA ...
HA HA HA ...
HA HA HA ...
HA ...

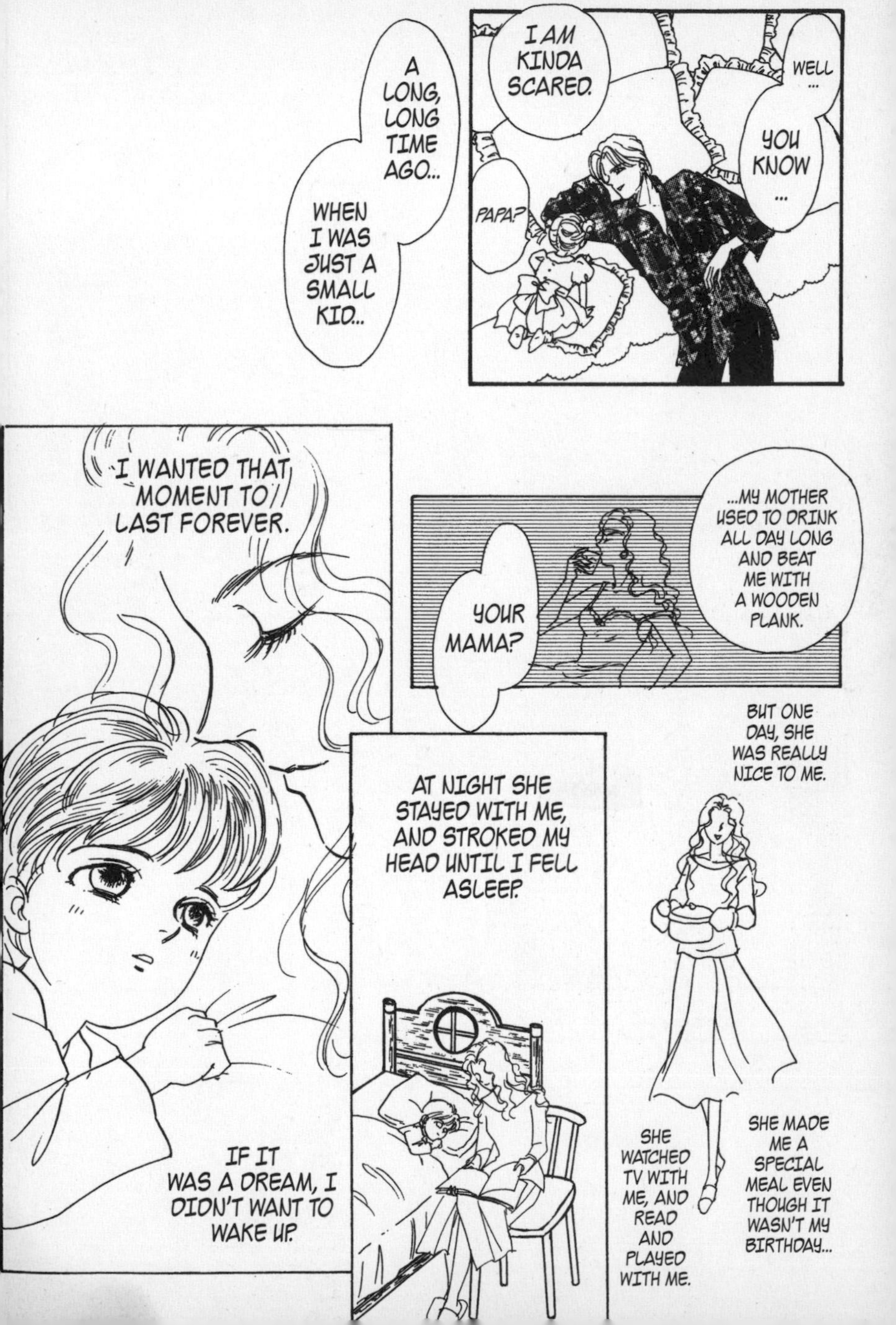
WELL ... YOU KNOW ...
I AM KINDA SCARED.
PAPA?
A LONG, LONG TIME AGO...
WHEN I WAS JUST A SMALL KID...
...MY MOTHER USED TO DRINK ALL DAY LONG AND BEAT ME WITH A WOODEN PLANK.
YOUR MAMA?
BUT ONE DAY, SHE WAS REALLY NICE TO ME.
SHE MADE ME A SPECIAL MEAL EVEN THOUGH IT WASN'T MY BIRTHDAY...
SHE WATCHED TV WITH ME, AND READ AND PLAYED WITH ME.
AT NIGHT SHE STAYED WITH ME, AND STROKED MY HEAD UNTIL I FELL ASLEEP.
I WANTED THAT MOMENT TO LAST FOREVER.
IF IT WAS A DREAM, I DIDN'T WANT TO WAKE UP.

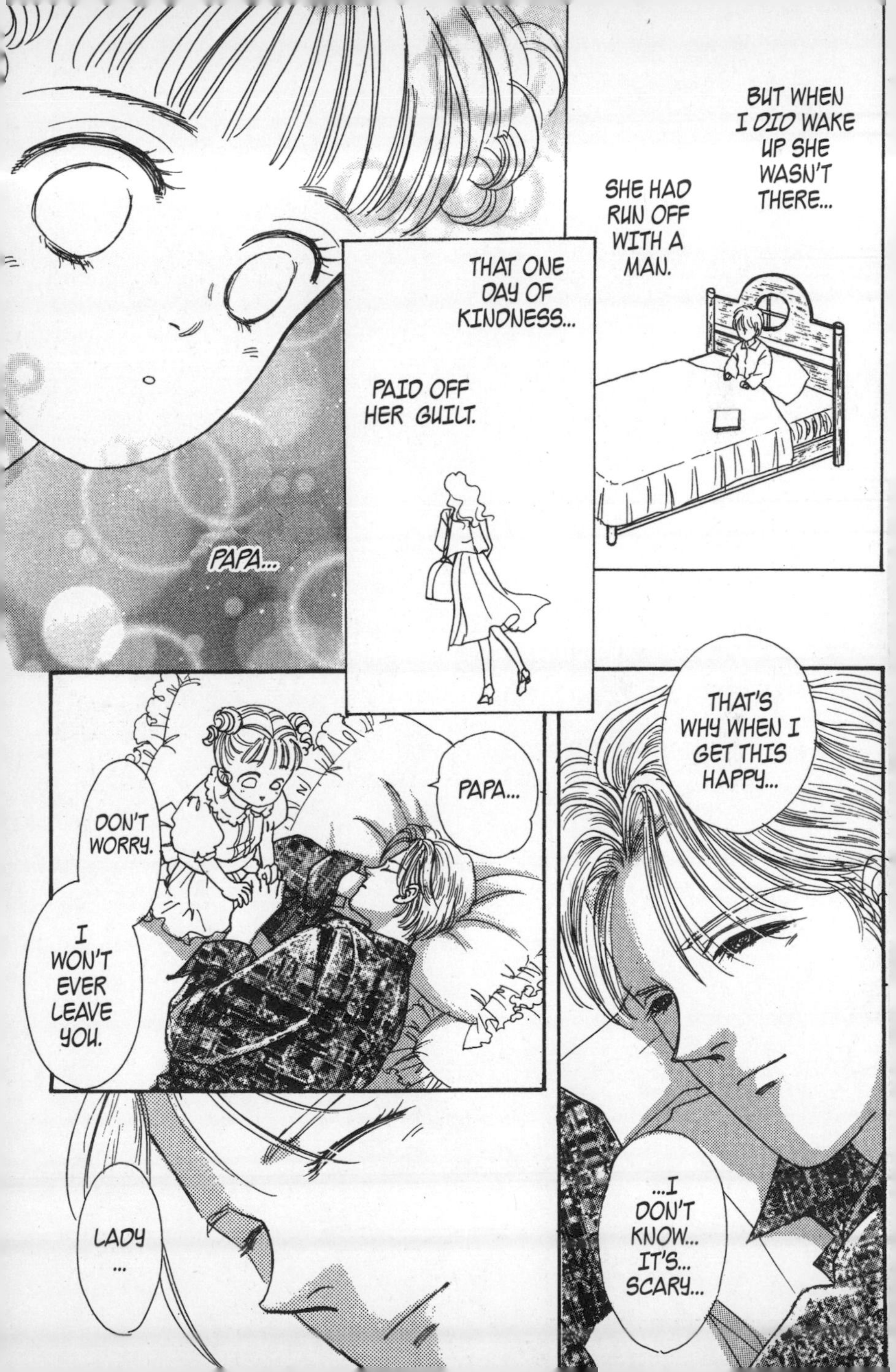
BUT WHEN I DID WAKE UP SHE WASN'T THERE...
SHE HAD RUN OFF WITH A MAN.
THAT ONE DAY OF KINDNESS...
PAID OFF HER GUILT.
PAPA...
THAT'S WHY WHEN I GET THIS HAPPY...
...I DON'T KNOW... IT'S... SCARY...
PAPA...
DON'T WORRY.
I WON'T EVER LEAVE YOU.
LADY ...

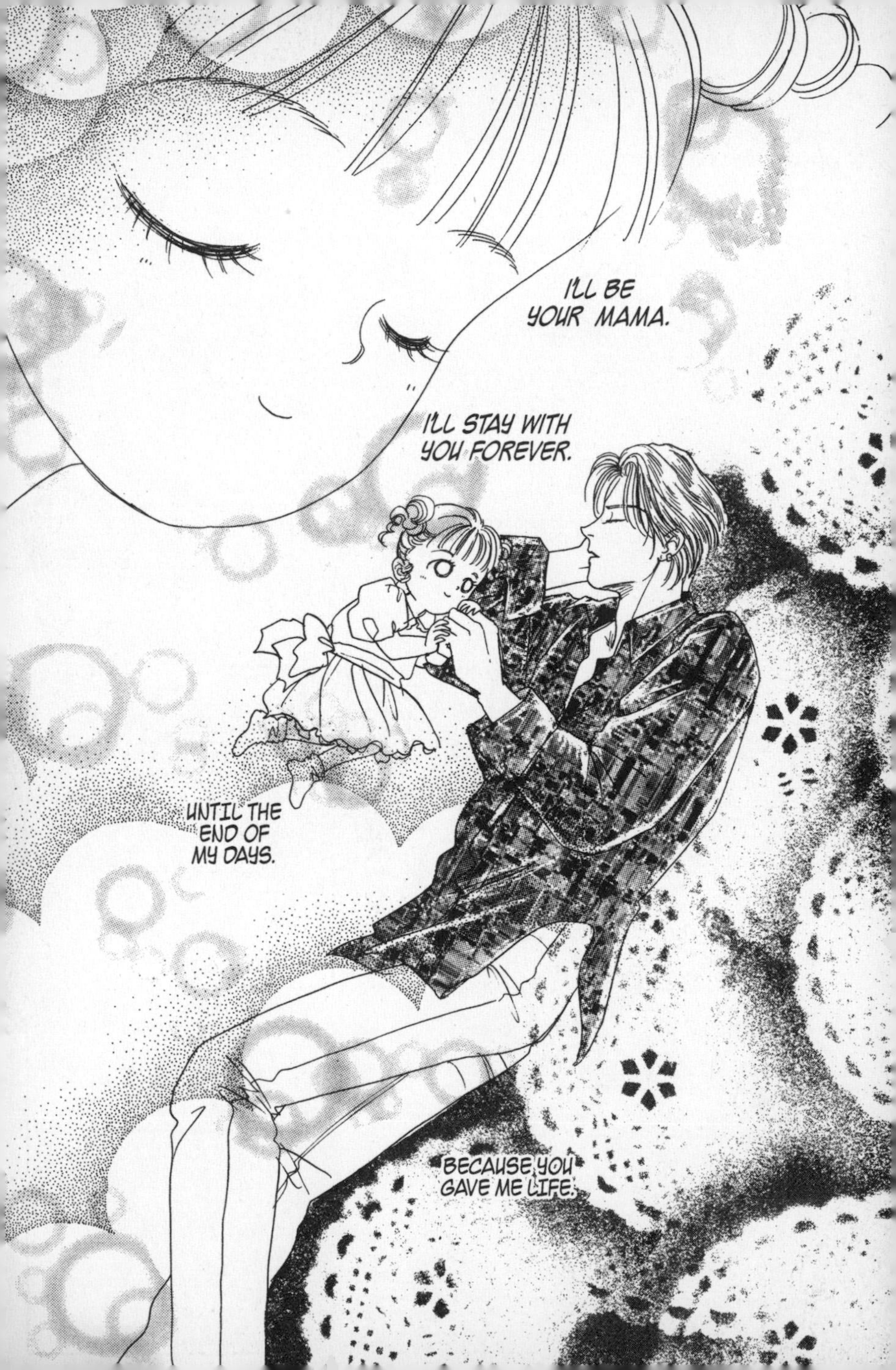
I'LL BE YOUR MAMA.
I'LL STAY WITH YOU FOREVER.
UNTIL THE END OF MY DAYS.
BECAUSE YOU GAVE ME LIFE.

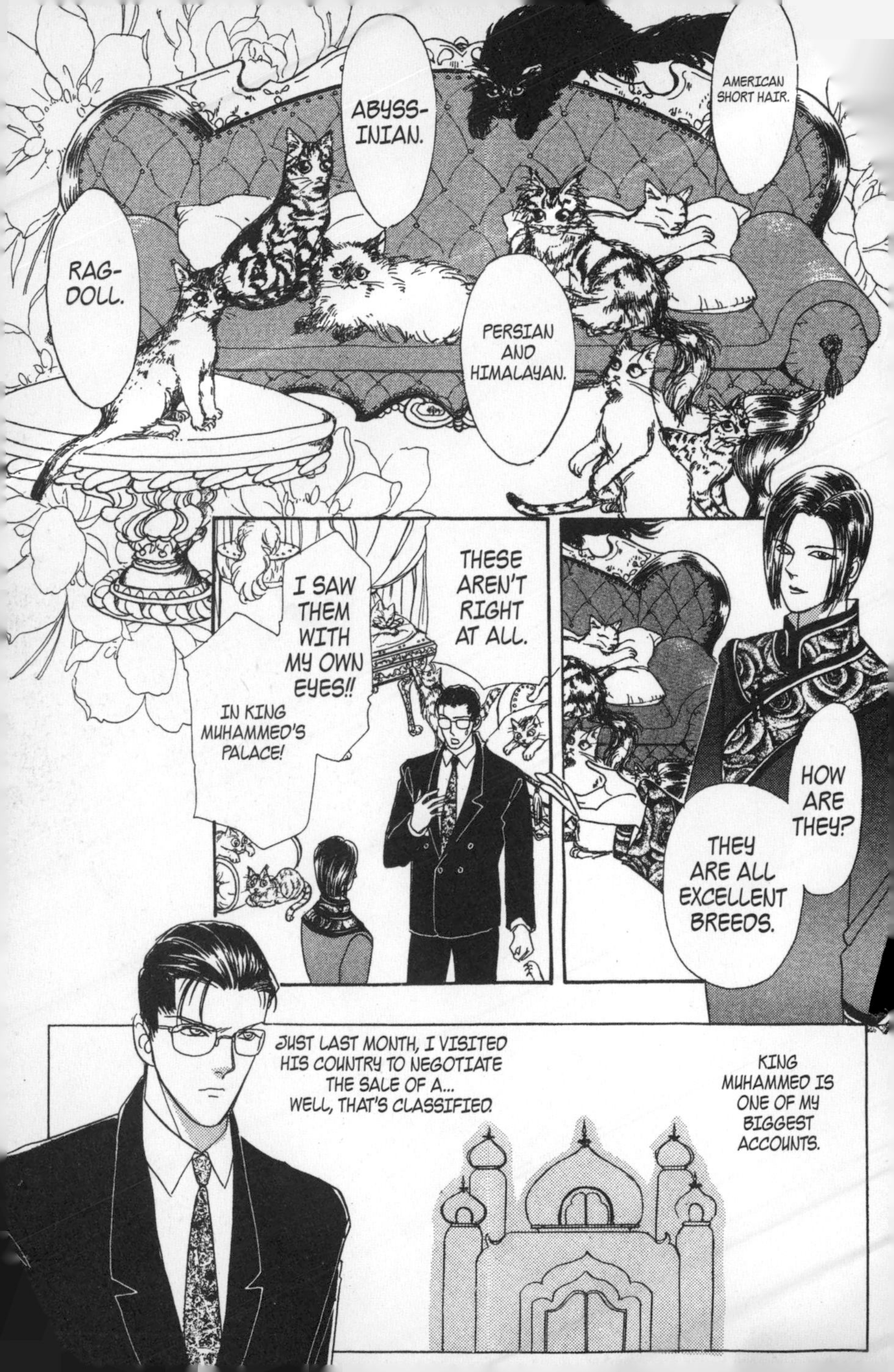
AMERICAN SHORT HAIR.
ABYSS-INIAN.
PERSIAN AND HIMALAYAN.
RAG-DOLL.
HOW ARE THEY?
THEY ARE ALL EXCELLENT BREEDS.
THESE AREN'T RIGHT AT ALL.
I SAW THEM WITH MY OWN EYES!!
IN KING MUHAMMED'S PALACE!
KING MUHAMMED IS ONE OF MY BIGGEST ACCOUNTS.
JUST LAST MONTH, I VISITED HIS COUNTRY TO NEGOTIATE THE SALE OF A... WELL, THAT'S CLASSIFIED.

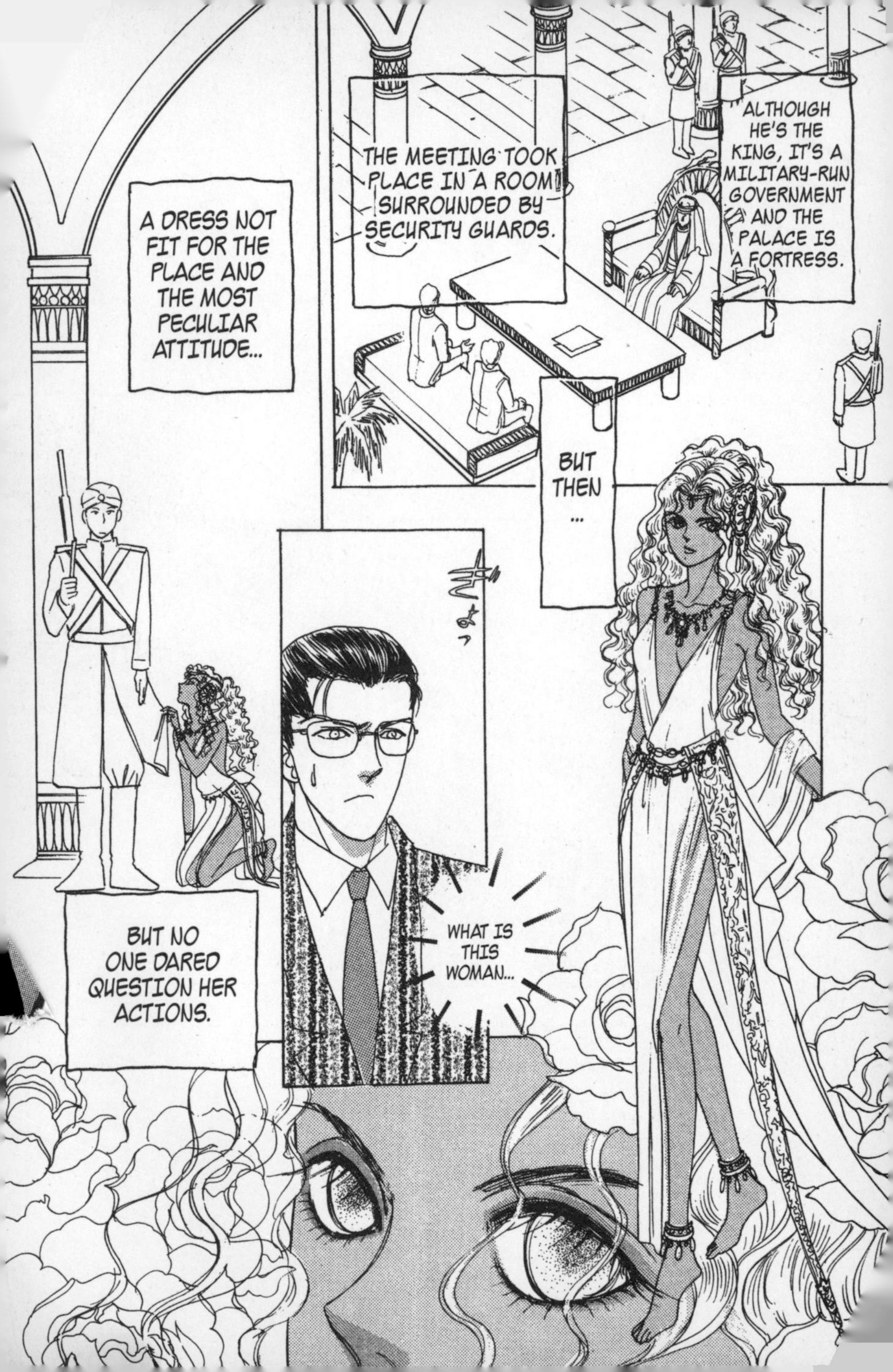
ALTHOUGH HE'S THE KING, IT'S A MILITARY-RUN GOVERNMENT AND THE PALACE IS A FORTRESS.
THE MEETING TOOK PLACE IN A ROOM SURROUNDED BY SECURITY GUARDS.
BUT THEN ...
WHAT IS THIS WOMAN...
A DRESS NOT FIT FOR THE PLACE AND THE MOST PECULIAR ATTITUDE...
BUT NO ONE DARED QUESTION HER ACTIONS.

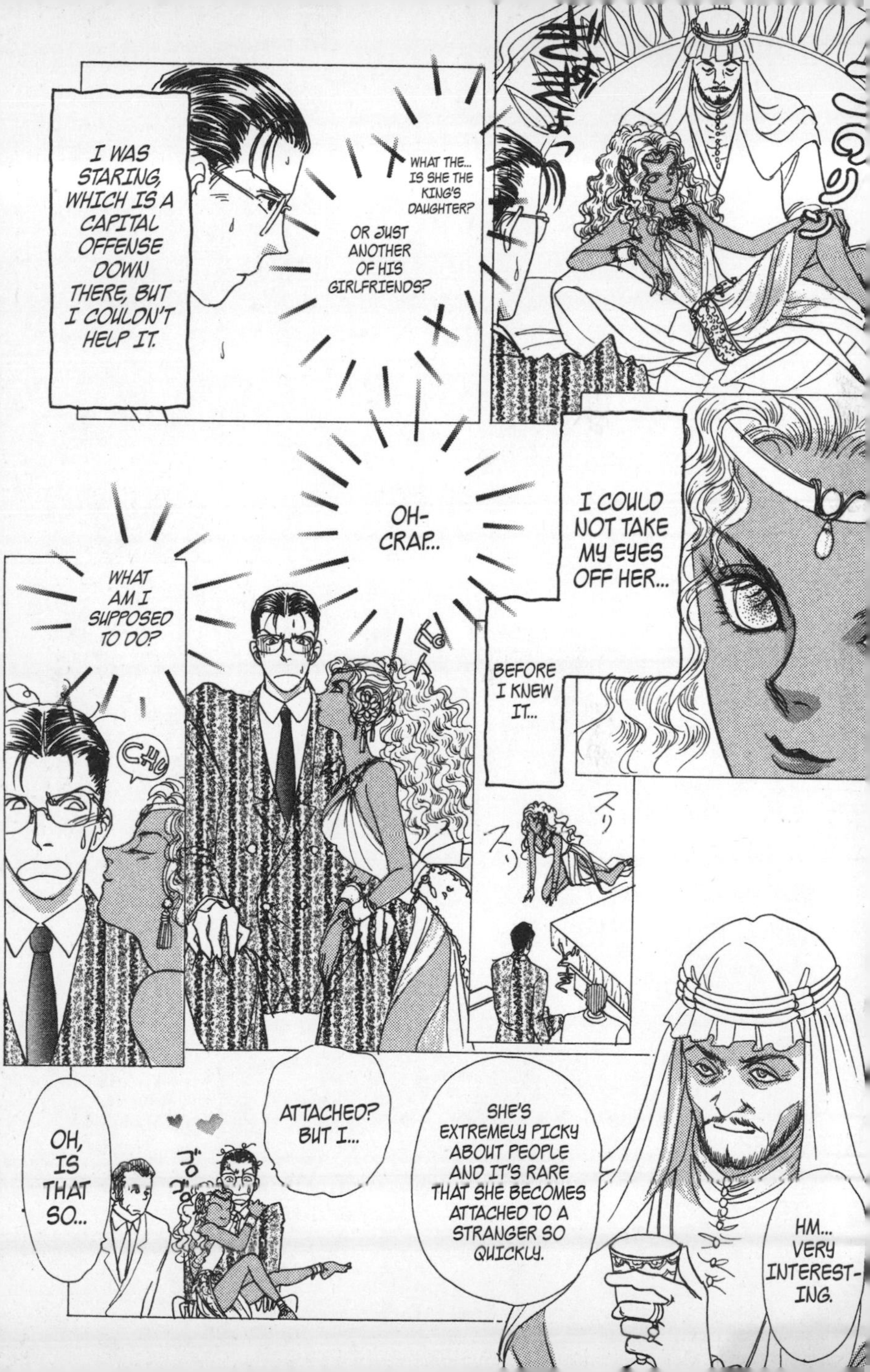
I WAS STARING, WHICH IS A CAPITAL OFFENSE DOWN THERE, BUT I COULDN'T HELP IT.
WHAT THE... IS SHE THE KING'S DAUGHTER?
OR JUST ANOTHER OF HIS GIRLFRIENDS?
I COULD NOT TAKE MY EYES OFF HER...
BEFORE I KNEW IT...
スリ
スリ
OH- CRAP...
WHAT AM I SUPPOSED TO DO?
CHU
HM... VERY INTEREST-ING.
SHE'S EXTREMELY PICKY ABOUT PEOPLE AND IT'S RARE THAT SHE BECOMES ATTACHED TO A STRANGER SO QUICKLY.
ATTACHED? BUT I...
OH, IS THAT SO...

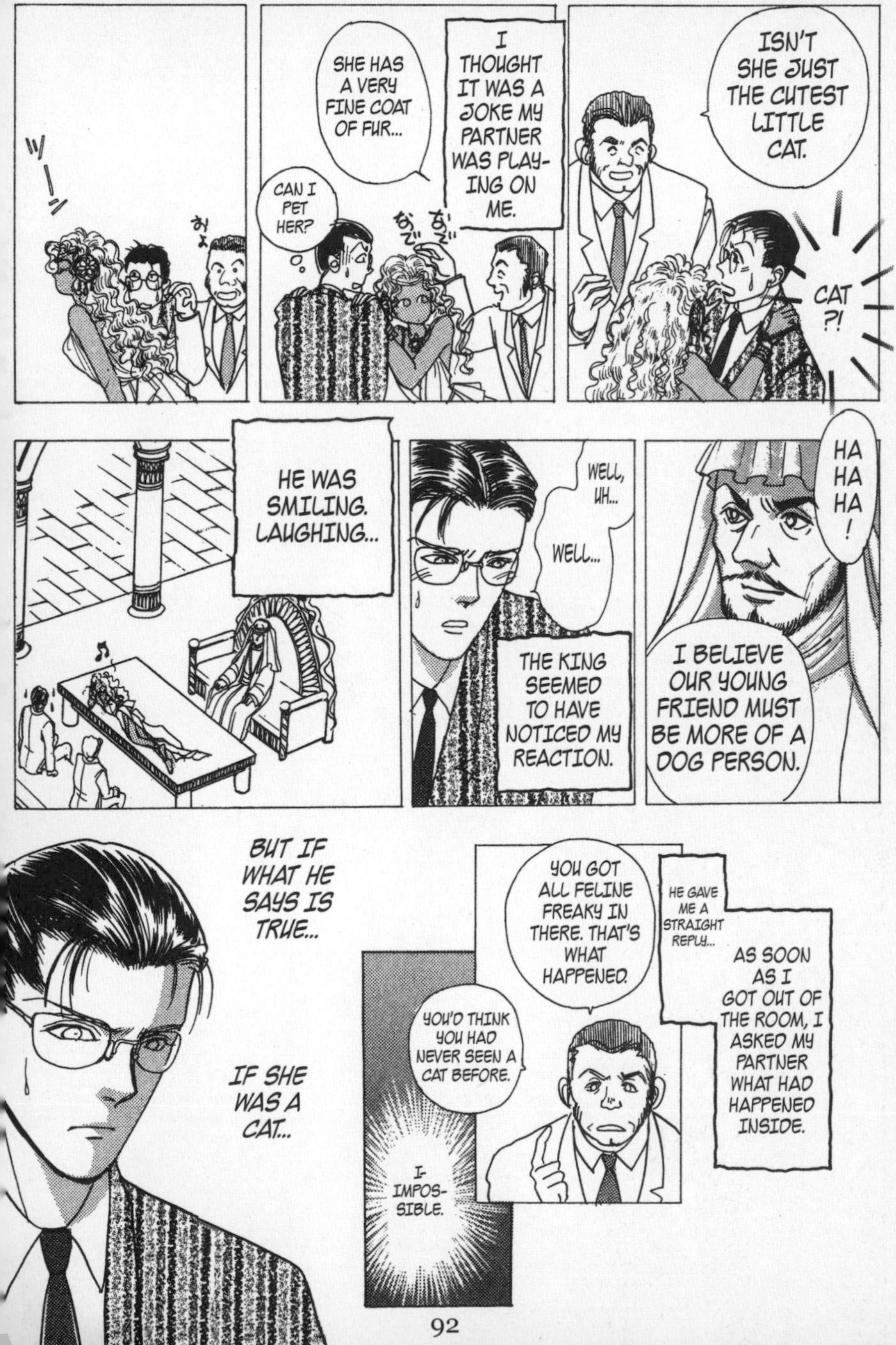
ISN'T SHE JUST THE CUTEST LITTLE CAT.
CAT ?!
I THOUGHT IT WAS A JOKE MY PARTNER WAS PLAYING ON ME.
SHE HAS A VERY FINE COAT OF FUR...
CAN I PET HER?
なで なで
ツーン
およ
HA HA HA!
I BELIEVE OUR YOUNG FRIEND MUST BE MORE OF A DOG PERSON.
WELL, UH...
WELL...
THE KING SEEMED TO HAVE NOTICED MY REACTION.
HE WAS SMILING. LAUGHING...
AS SOON AS I GOT OUT OF THE ROOM, I ASKED MY PARTNER WHAT HAD HAPPENED INSIDE.
HE GAVE ME A STRAIGHT REPLY...
YOU GOT ALL FELINE FREAKY IN THERE. THAT'S WHAT HAPPENED.
YOU'D THINK YOU HAD NEVER SEEN A CAT BEFORE.
I- IMPOSSIBLE.
BUT IF WHAT HE SAYS IS TRUE...
IF SHE WAS A CAT...

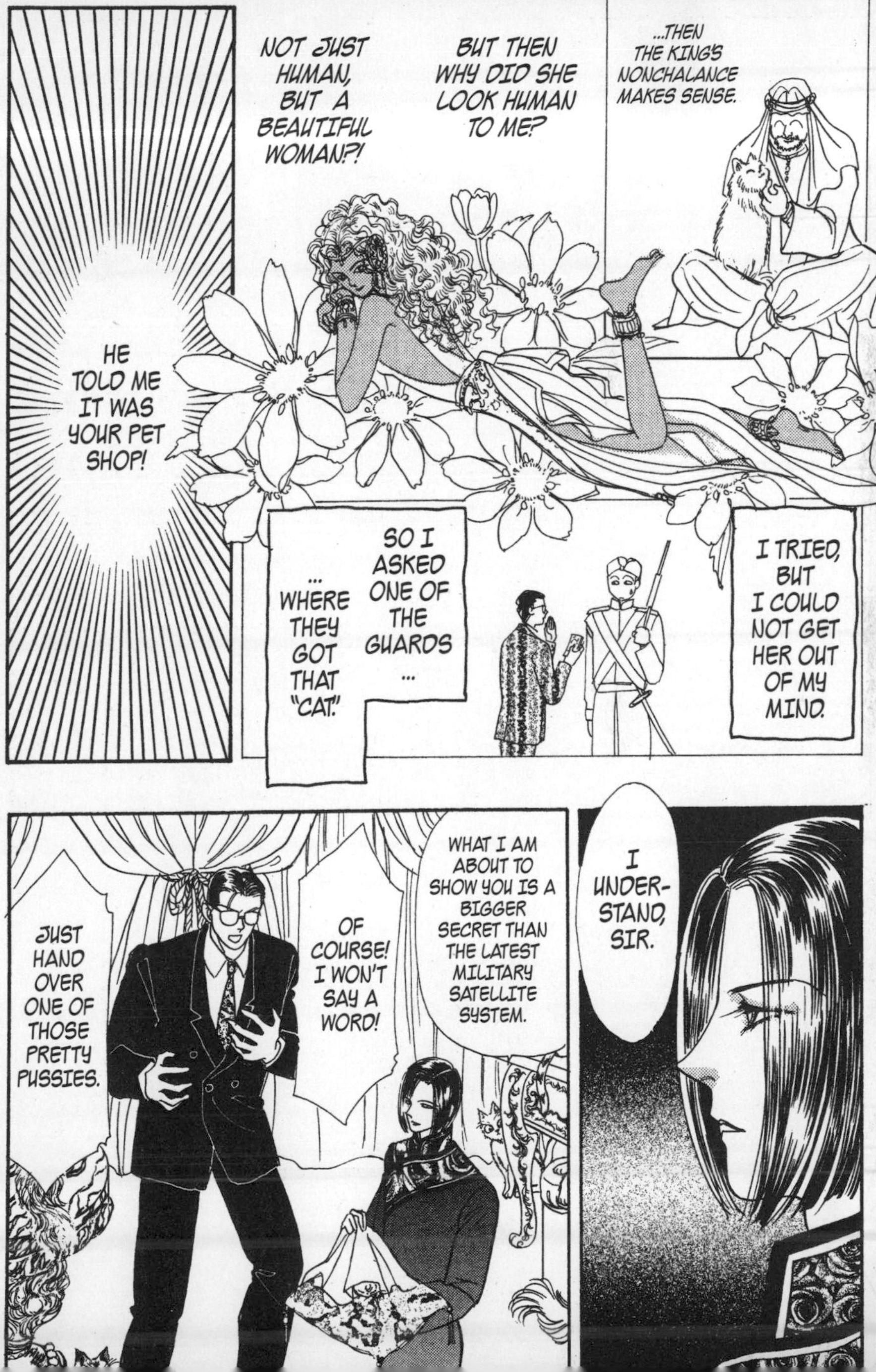
...THEN THE KING'S NONCHALANCE MAKES SENSE.
BUT THEN WHY DID SHE LOOK HUMAN TO ME?
NOT JUST HUMAN, BUT A BEAUTIFUL WOMAN?!
I TRIED, BUT I COULD NOT GET HER OUT OF MY MIND.
SO I ASKED ONE OF THE GUARDS...
...WHERE THEY GOT THAT "CAT."
HE TOLD ME IT WAS YOUR PET SHOP!
I UNDERSTAND, SIR.
WHAT I AM ABOUT TO SHOW YOU IS A BIGGER SECRET THAN THE LATEST MILITARY SATELLITE SYSTEM.
OF COURSE! I WON'T SAY A WORD!
JUST HAND OVER ONE OF THOSE PRETTY PUSSIES.

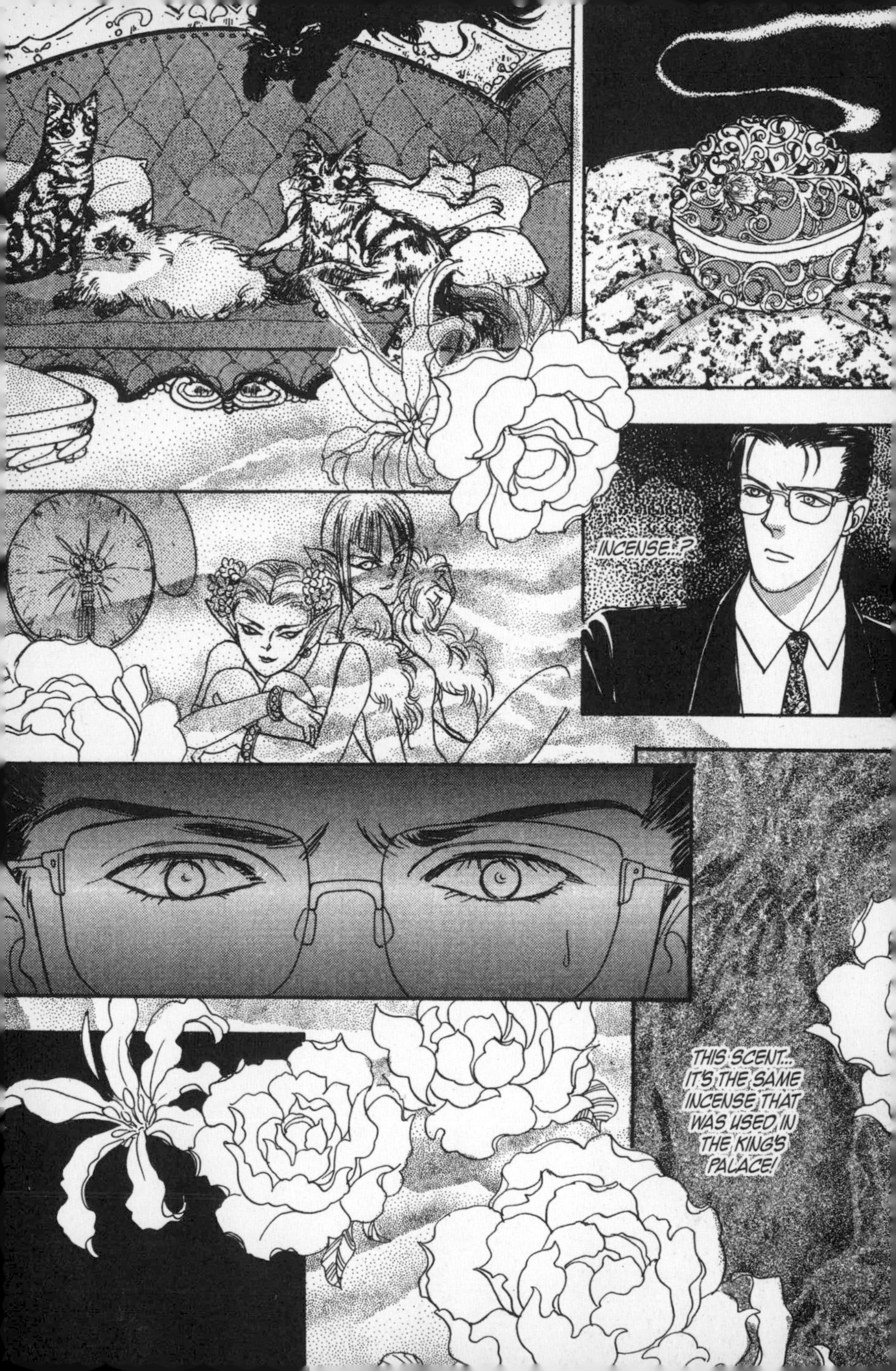
INCENSE...?
THIS SCENT... IT'S THE SAME INCENSE THAT WAS USED IN THE KING'S PALACE!

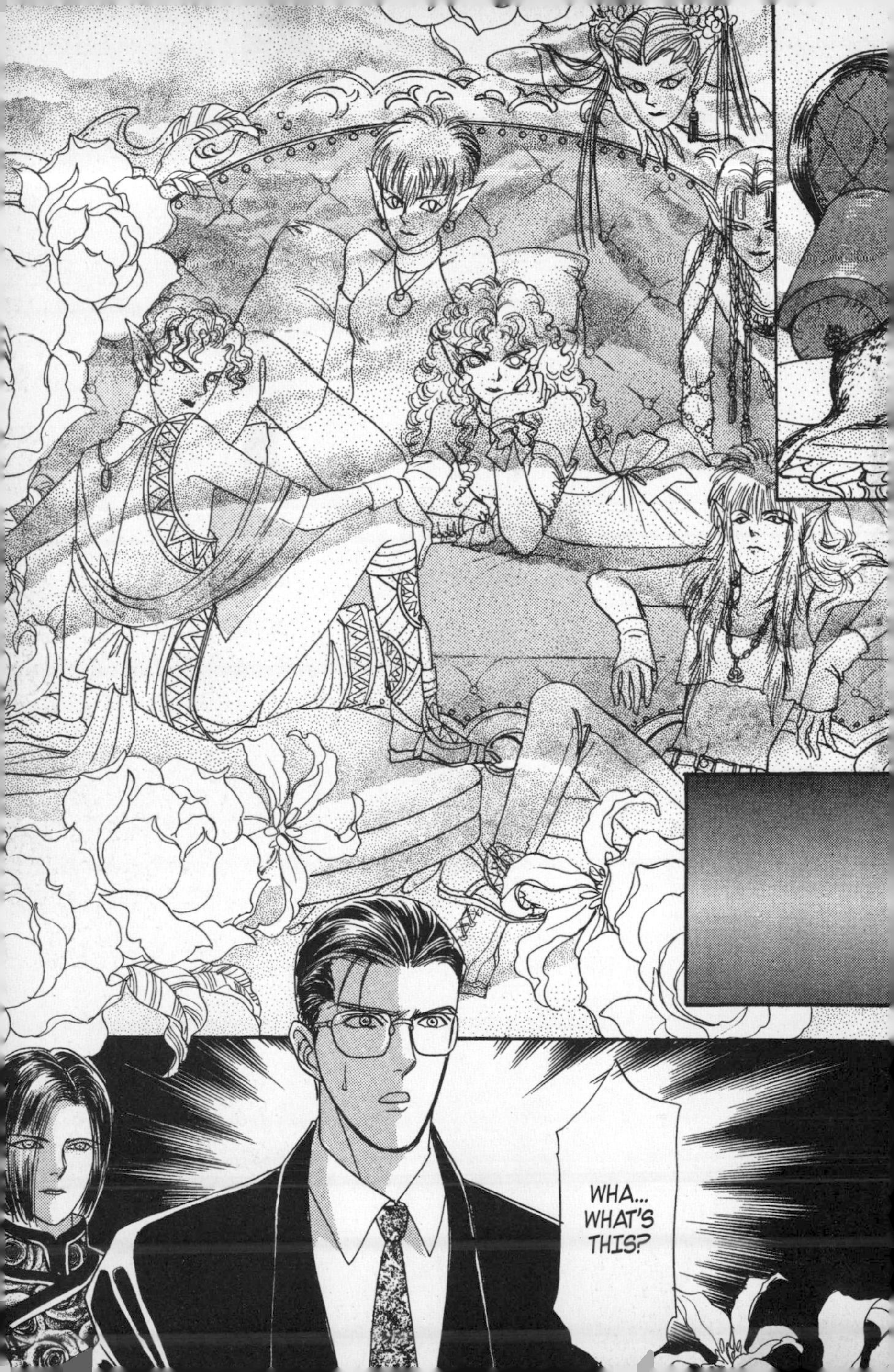
WHA...
WHAT'S
THIS?

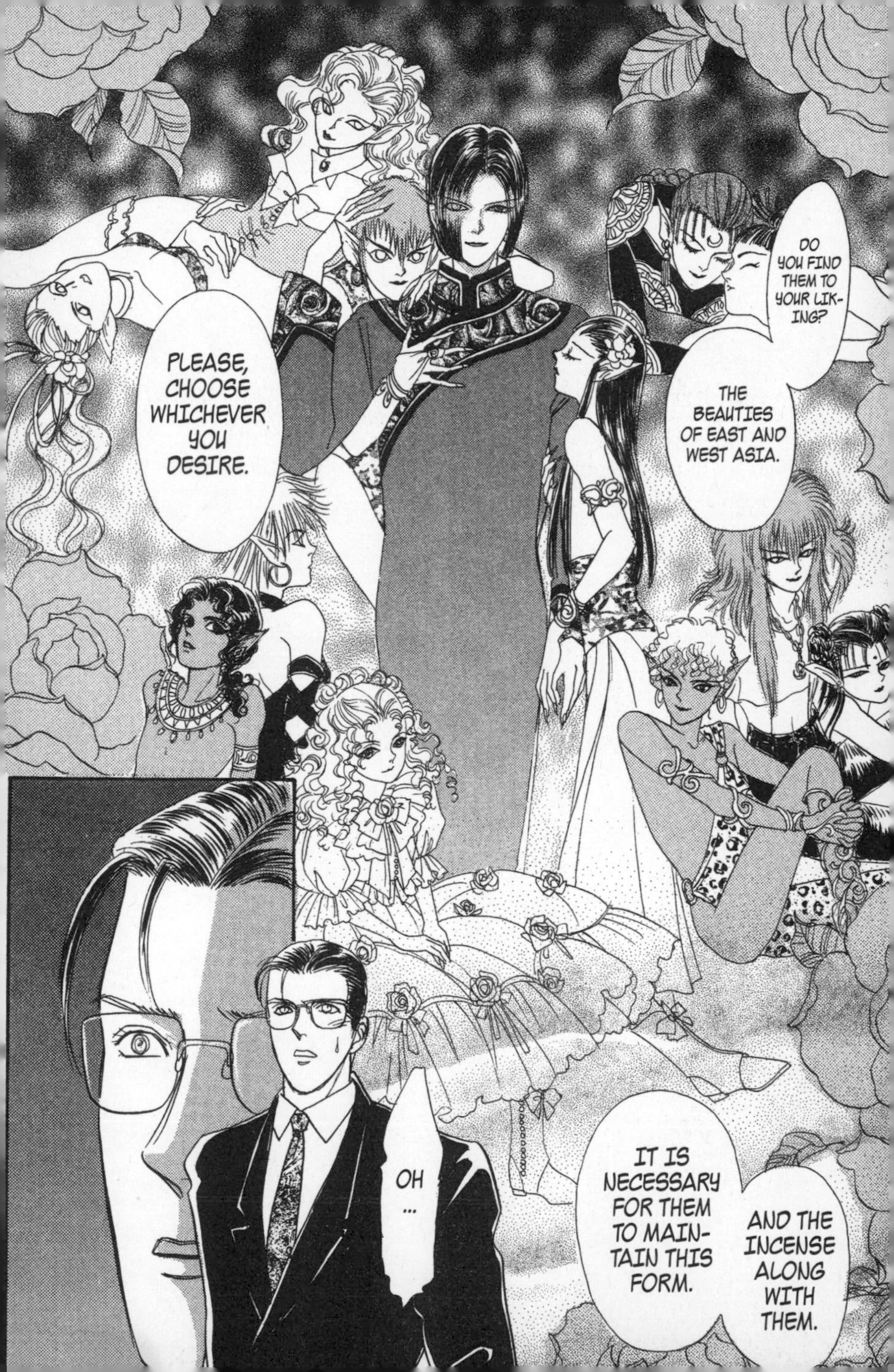
DO YOU FIND THEM TO YOUR LIK-ING?
THE BEAUTIES OF EAST AND WEST ASIA.
PLEASE, CHOOSE WHICHEVER YOU DESIRE.
IT IS NECESSARY FOR THEM TO MAIN-TAIN THIS FORM.
AND THE INCENSE ALONG WITH THEM.
OH ...

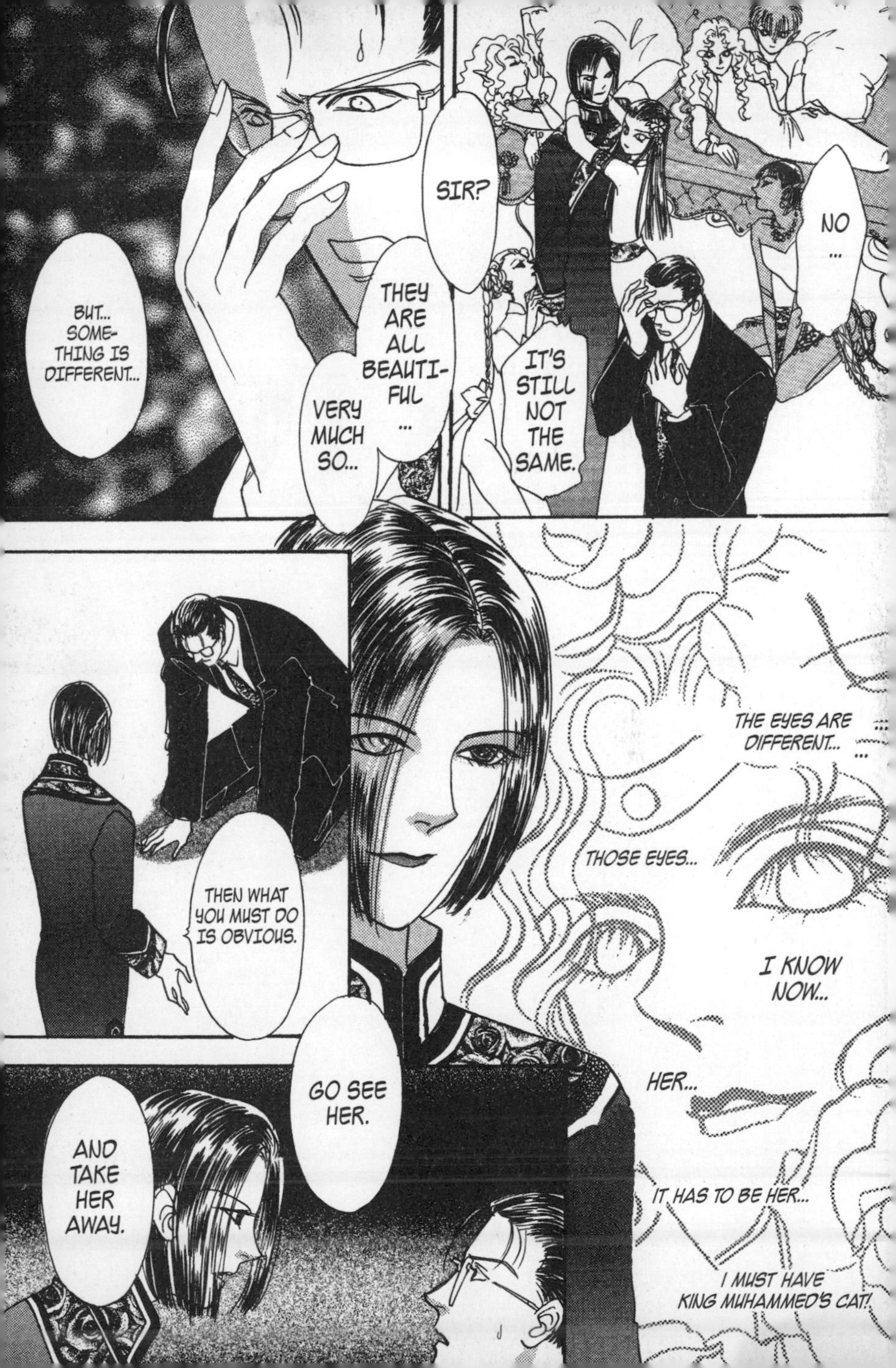
NO ...
IT'S STILL NOT THE SAME.
SIR?
THEY ARE ALL BEAUTIFUL ...
VERY MUCH SO...
BUT... SOMETHING IS DIFFERENT...
THE EYES ARE DIFFERENT... ...
THOSE EYES...
I KNOW NOW...
HER...
IT HAS TO BE HER...
I MUST HAVE KING MUHAMMED'S CAT!
THEN WHAT YOU MUST DO IS OBVIOUS.
GO SEE HER.
AND TAKE HER AWAY.

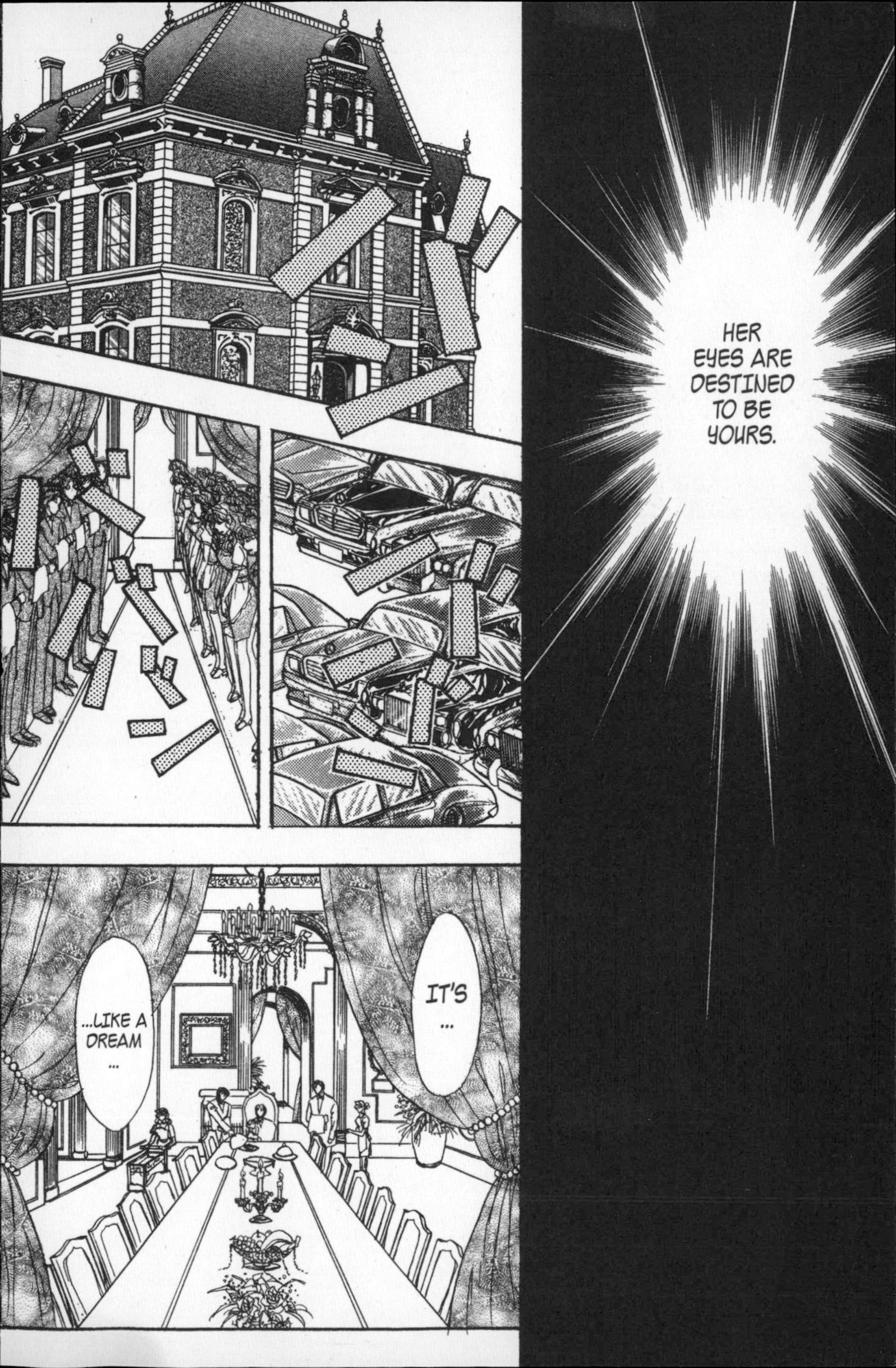
HER EYES ARE DESTINED TO BE YOURS.
IT'S ...
...LIKE A DREAM ...

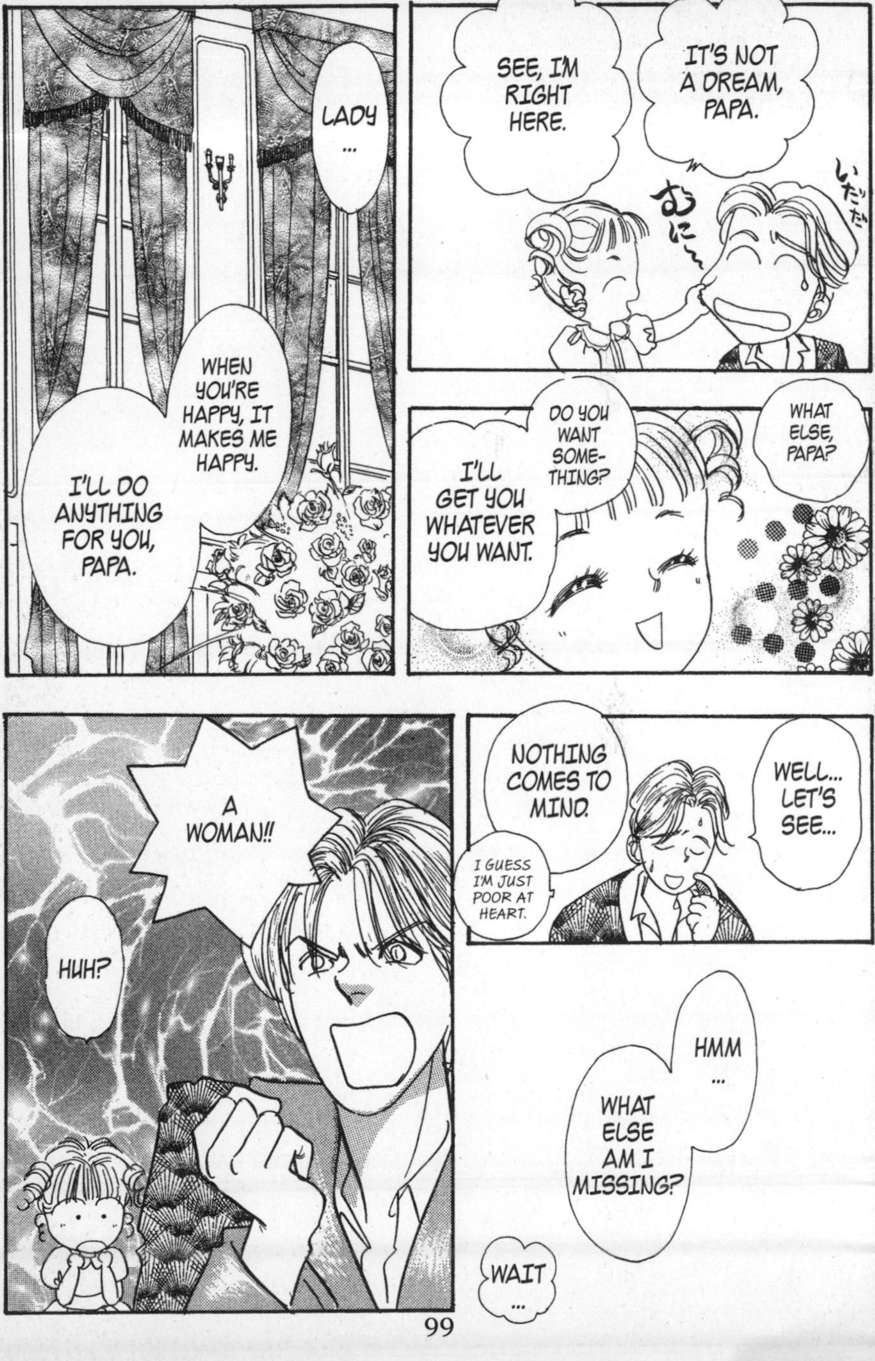
IT'S NOT A DREAM, PAPA.
SEE, I'M RIGHT HERE.
むに〜
WHAT ELSE, PAPA?
DO YOU WANT SOMETHING?
I'LL GET YOU WHATEVER YOU WANT.
LADY ...
WHEN YOU'RE HAPPY, IT MAKES ME HAPPY.
I'LL DO ANYTHING FOR YOU, PAPA.
WELL... LET'S SEE...
NOTHING COMES TO MIND.
I GUESS I'M JUST POOR AT HEART.
HMM ...
WHAT ELSE AM I MISSING?
WAIT ...
A WOMAN!!
HUH?

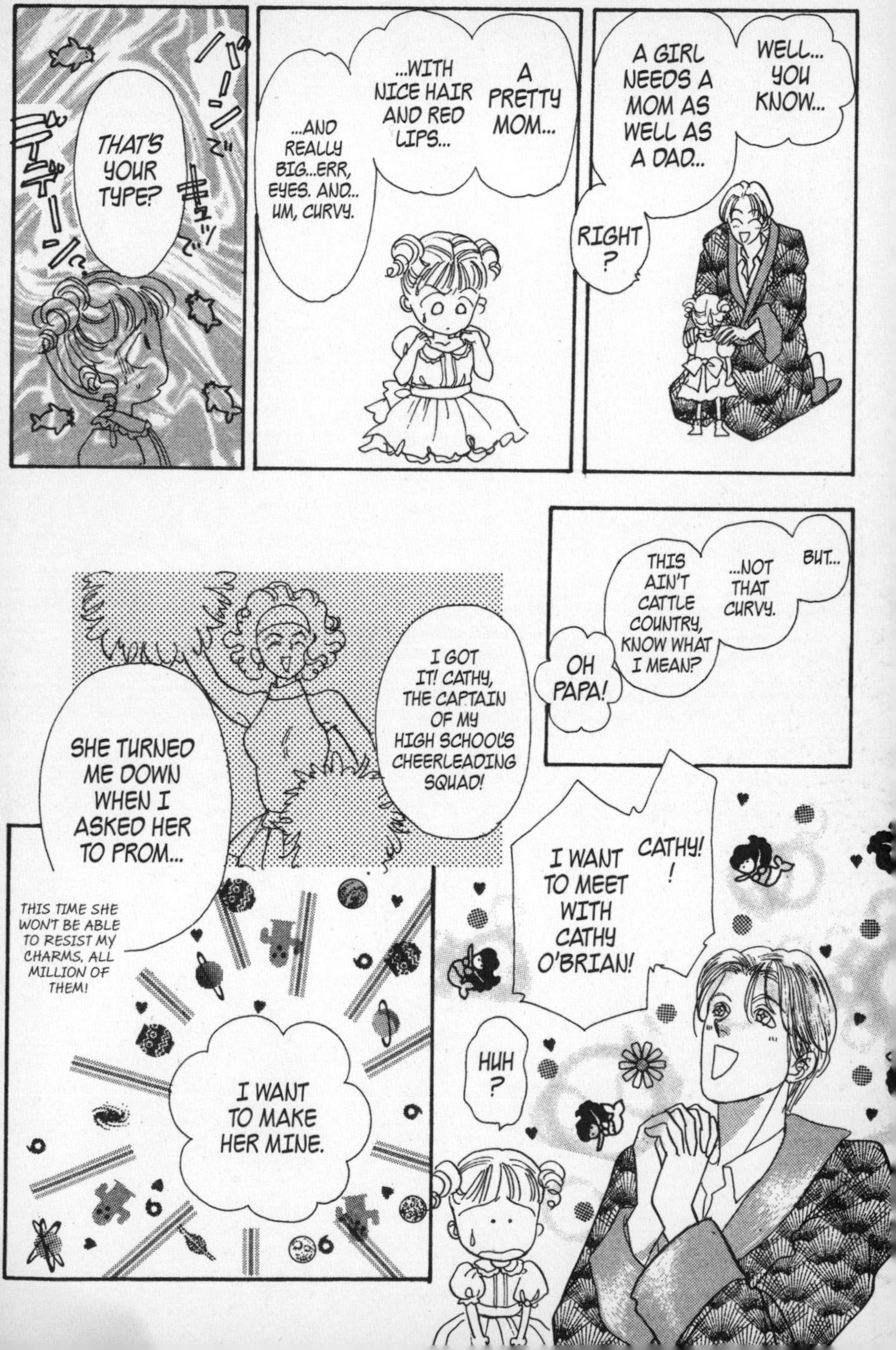
WELL... YOU KNOW...
A GIRL NEEDS A MOM AS WELL AS A DAD...
RIGHT?
A PRETTY MOM...
...WITH NICE HAIR AND RED LIPS...
...AND REALLY BIG...ERR, EYES. AND... UM, CURVY.
THAT'S YOUR TYPE?
BUT...
...NOT THAT CURVY.
THIS AIN'T CATTLE COUNTRY, KNOW WHAT I MEAN?
OH PAPA!
I GOT IT! CATHY, THE CAPTAIN OF MY HIGH SCHOOL'S CHEERLEADING SQUAD!
SHE TURNED ME DOWN WHEN I ASKED HER TO PROM...
CATHY!!
I WANT TO MEET WITH CATHY O'BRIAN!
HUH?
THIS TIME SHE WON'T BE ABLE TO RESIST MY CHARMS, ALL MILLION OF THEM!
I WANT TO MAKE HER MINE.

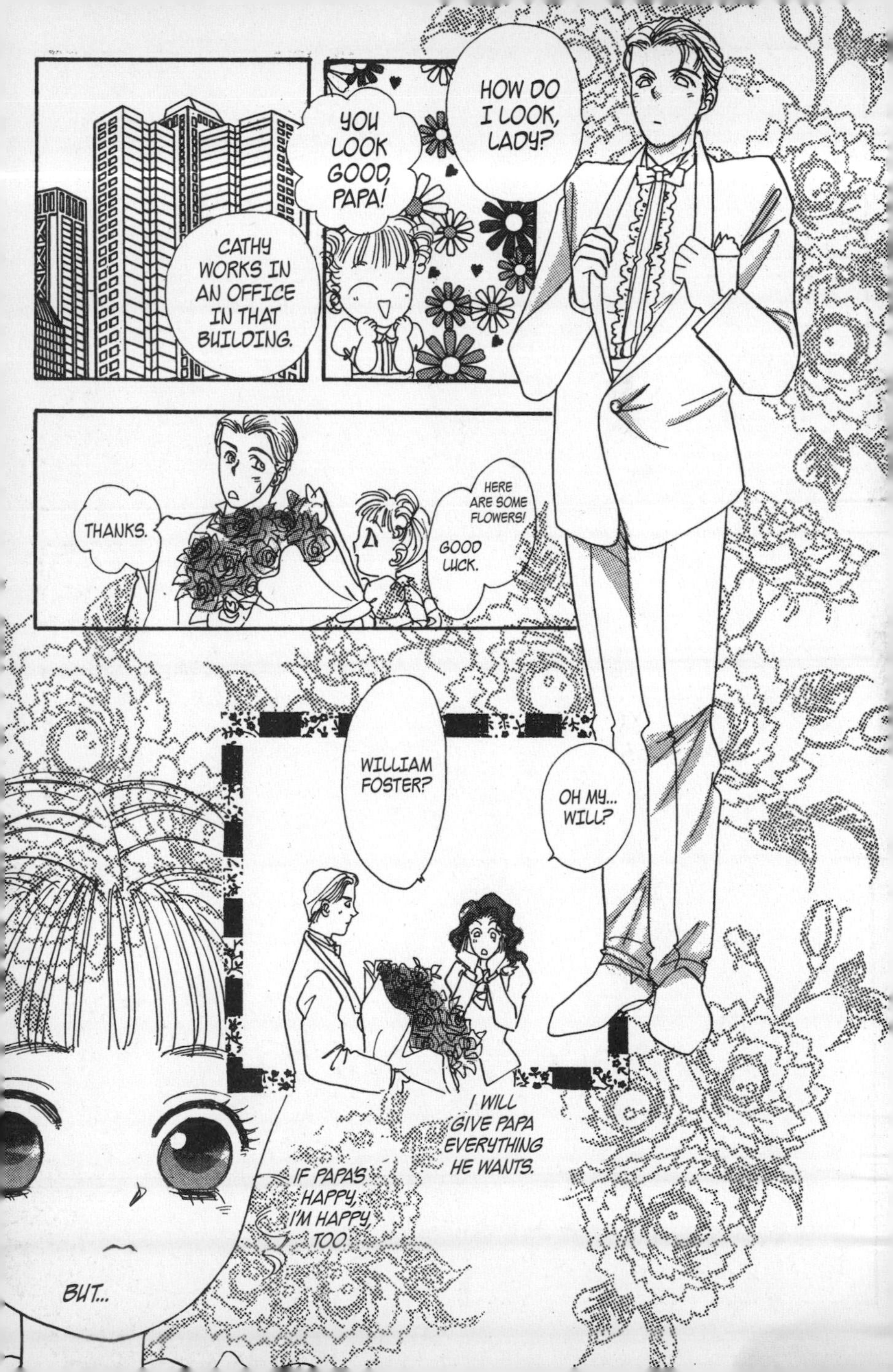
HOW DO I LOOK, LADY?
YOU LOOK GOOD, PAPA!
CATHY WORKS IN AN OFFICE IN THAT BUILDING.
HERE ARE SOME FLOWERS!
GOOD LUCK.
THANKS.
WILLIAM FOSTER?
OH MY... WILL?
I WILL GIVE PAPA EVERYTHING HE WANTS.
IF PAPA'S HAPPY, I'M HAPPY, TOO.
BUT...

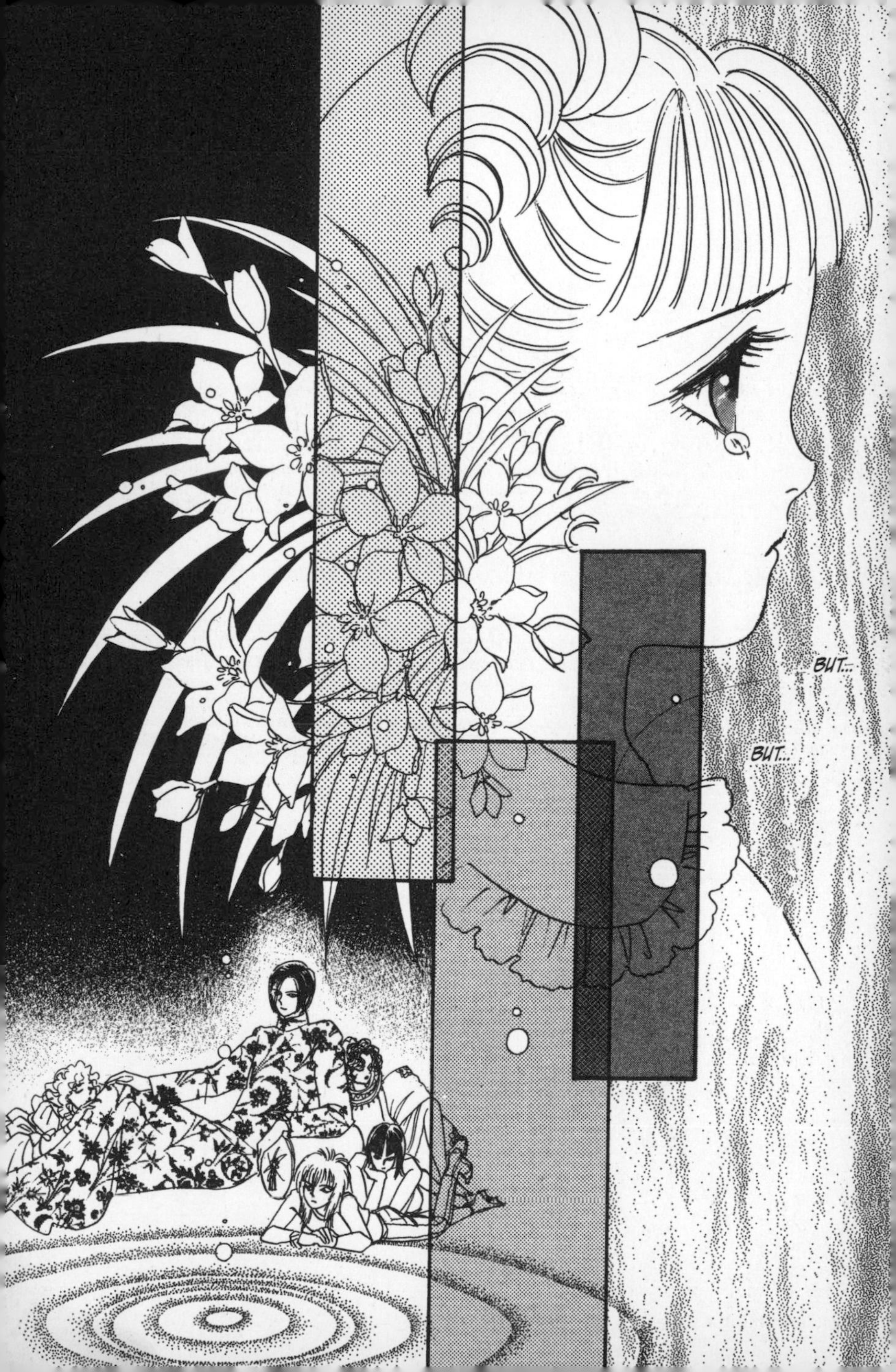
BUT...
BUT...

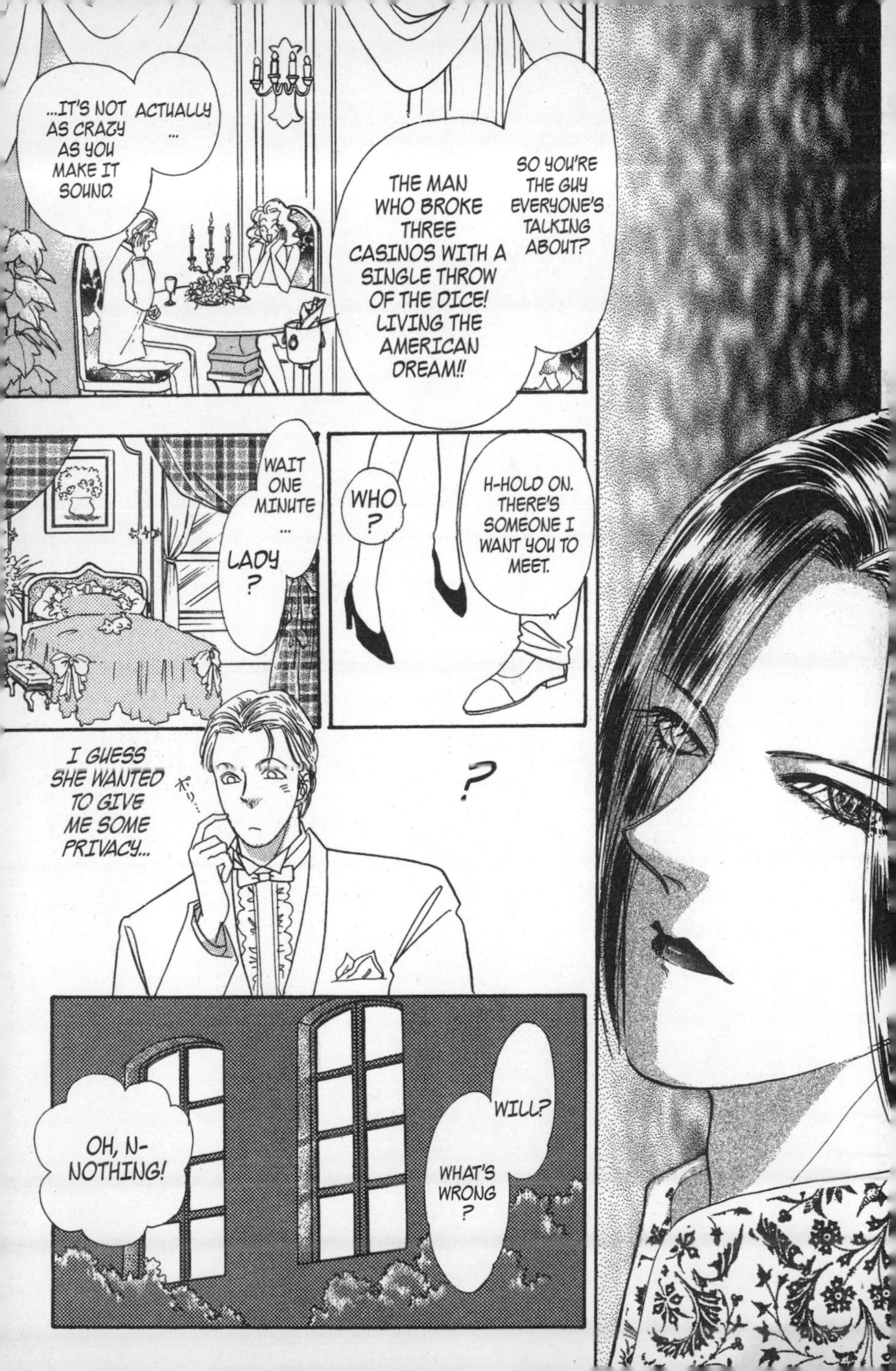
SO YOU'RE THE GUY EVERYONE'S TALKING ABOUT?
THE MAN WHO BROKE THREE CASINOS WITH A SINGLE THROW OF THE DICE! LIVING THE AMERICAN DREAM!!
ACTUALLY ...
...IT'S NOT AS CRAZY AS YOU MAKE IT SOUND.
H-HOLD ON. THERE'S SOMEONE I WANT YOU TO MEET.
WHO ?
WAIT ONE MINUTE ...
LADY ?
?
ポリ…
I GUESS SHE WANTED TO GIVE ME SOME PRIVACY...
WILL?
WHAT'S WRONG ?
OH, N-NOTHING!

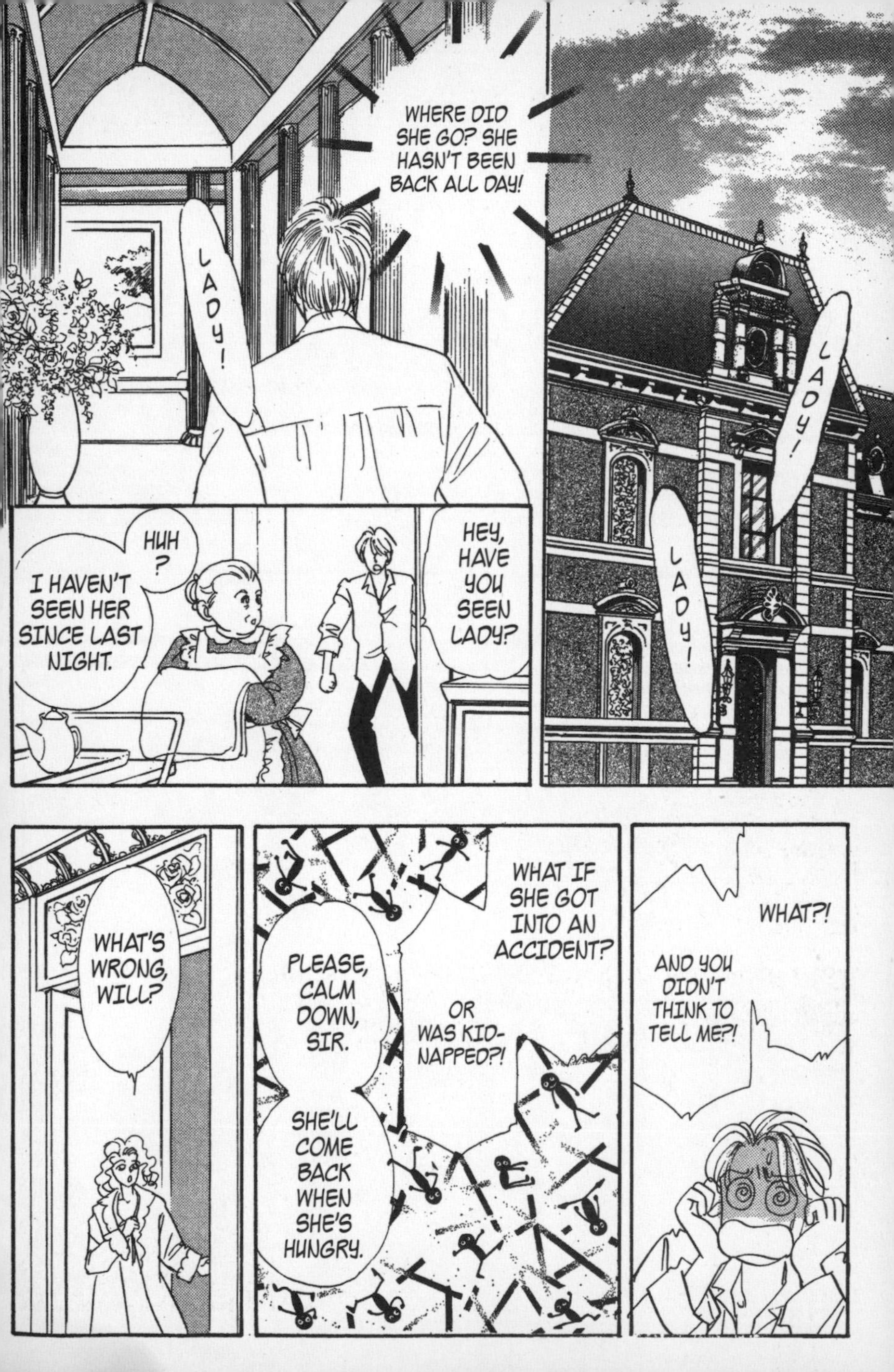
LADY!
LADY!
WHERE DID SHE GO? SHE HASN'T BEEN BACK ALL DAY!
LADY!
HEY, HAVE YOU SEEN LADY?
HUH?
I HAVEN'T SEEN HER SINCE LAST NIGHT.
WHAT?!
AND YOU DIDN'T THINK TO TELL ME?!
WHAT IF SHE GOT INTO AN ACCIDENT?
OR WAS KID-NAPPED?!
PLEASE, CALM DOWN, SIR.
SHE'LL COME BACK WHEN SHE'S HUNGRY.
WHAT'S WRONG, WILL?

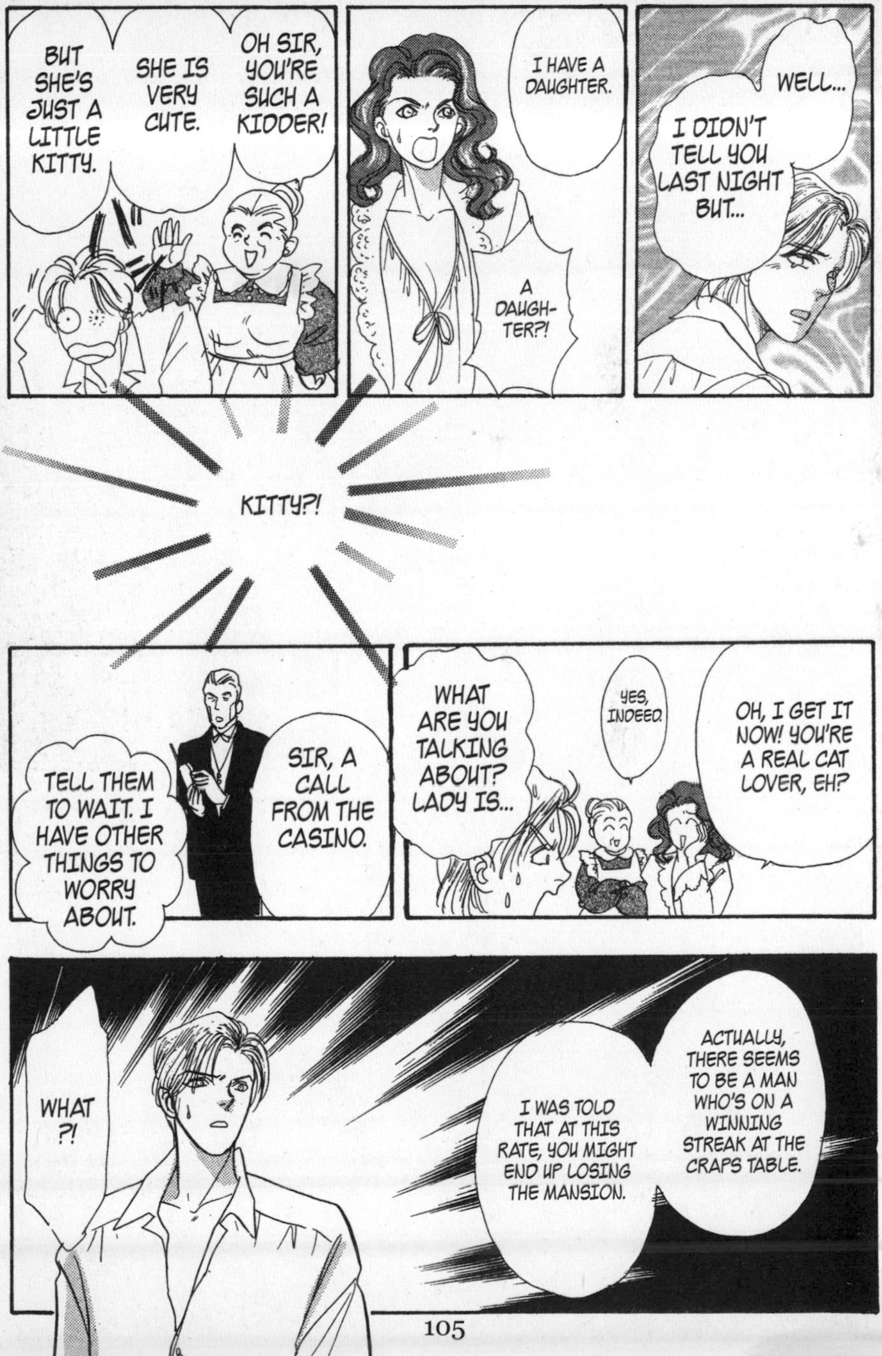
WELL...
I DIDN'T TELL YOU LAST NIGHT BUT...
I HAVE A DAUGHTER.
A DAUGHTER?!
OH SIR, YOU'RE SUCH A KIDDER!
SHE IS VERY CUTE.
BUT SHE'S JUST A LITTLE KITTY.
KITTY?!
OH, I GET IT NOW! YOU'RE A REAL CAT LOVER, EH?
YES, INDEED.
WHAT ARE YOU TALKING ABOUT? LADY IS...
SIR, A CALL FROM THE CASINO.
TELL THEM TO WAIT. I HAVE OTHER THINGS TO WORRY ABOUT.
ACTUALLY, THERE SEEMS TO BE A MAN WHO'S ON A WINNING STREAK AT THE CRAPS TABLE.
I WAS TOLD THAT AT THIS RATE, YOU MIGHT END UP LOSING THE MANSION.
WHAT ?!

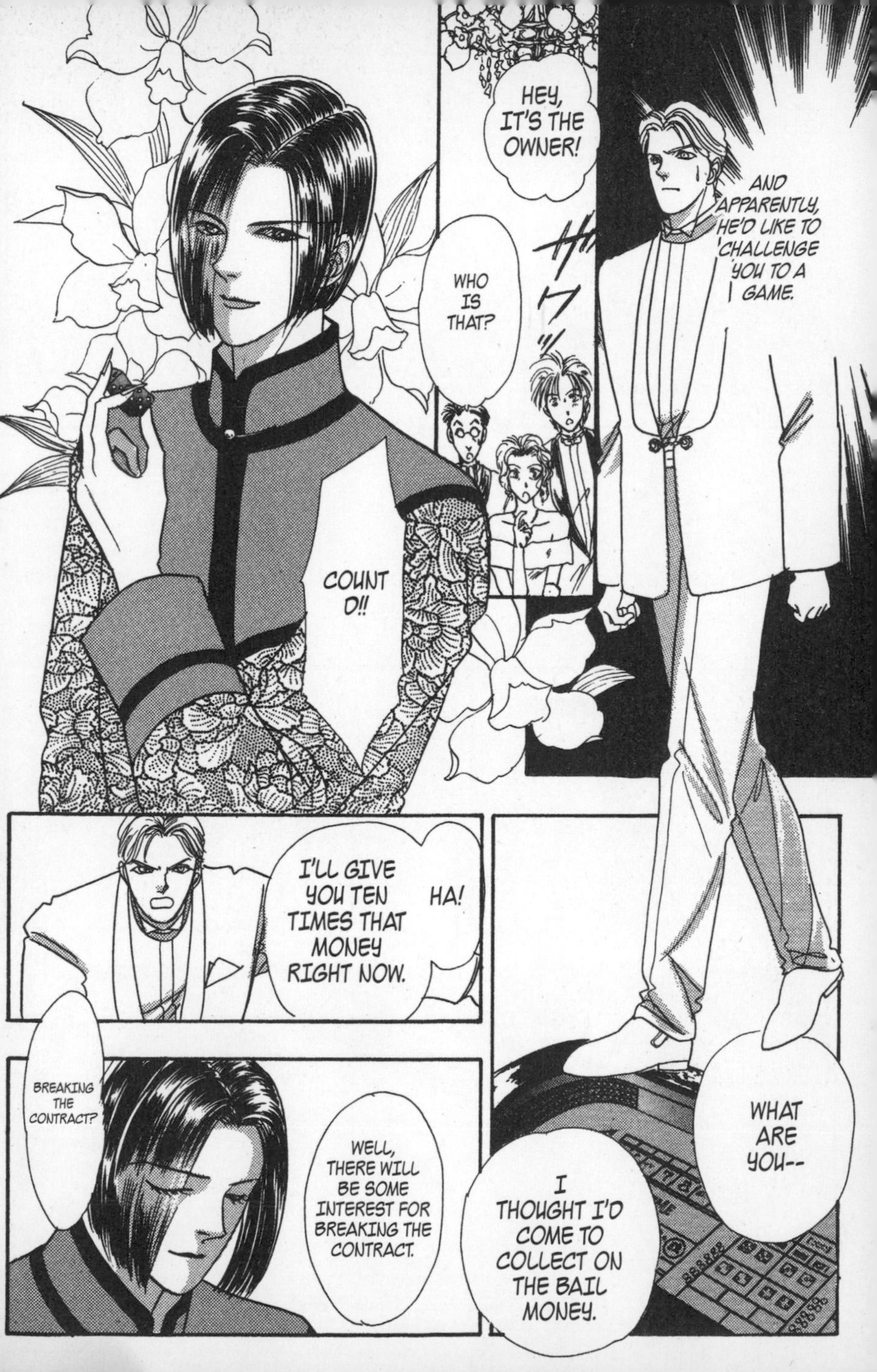

AND APPARENTLY, HE'D LIKE TO CHALLENGE YOU TO A GAME.
HEY, IT'S THE OWNER!
WHO IS THAT?
COUNT D!!
WHAT ARE YOU--
I THOUGHT I'D COME TO COLLECT ON THE BAIL MONEY.
HA!
I'LL GIVE YOU TEN TIMES THAT MONEY RIGHT NOW.
WELL, THERE WILL BE SOME INTEREST FOR BREAKING THE CONTRACT.
BREAKING THE CONTRACT?

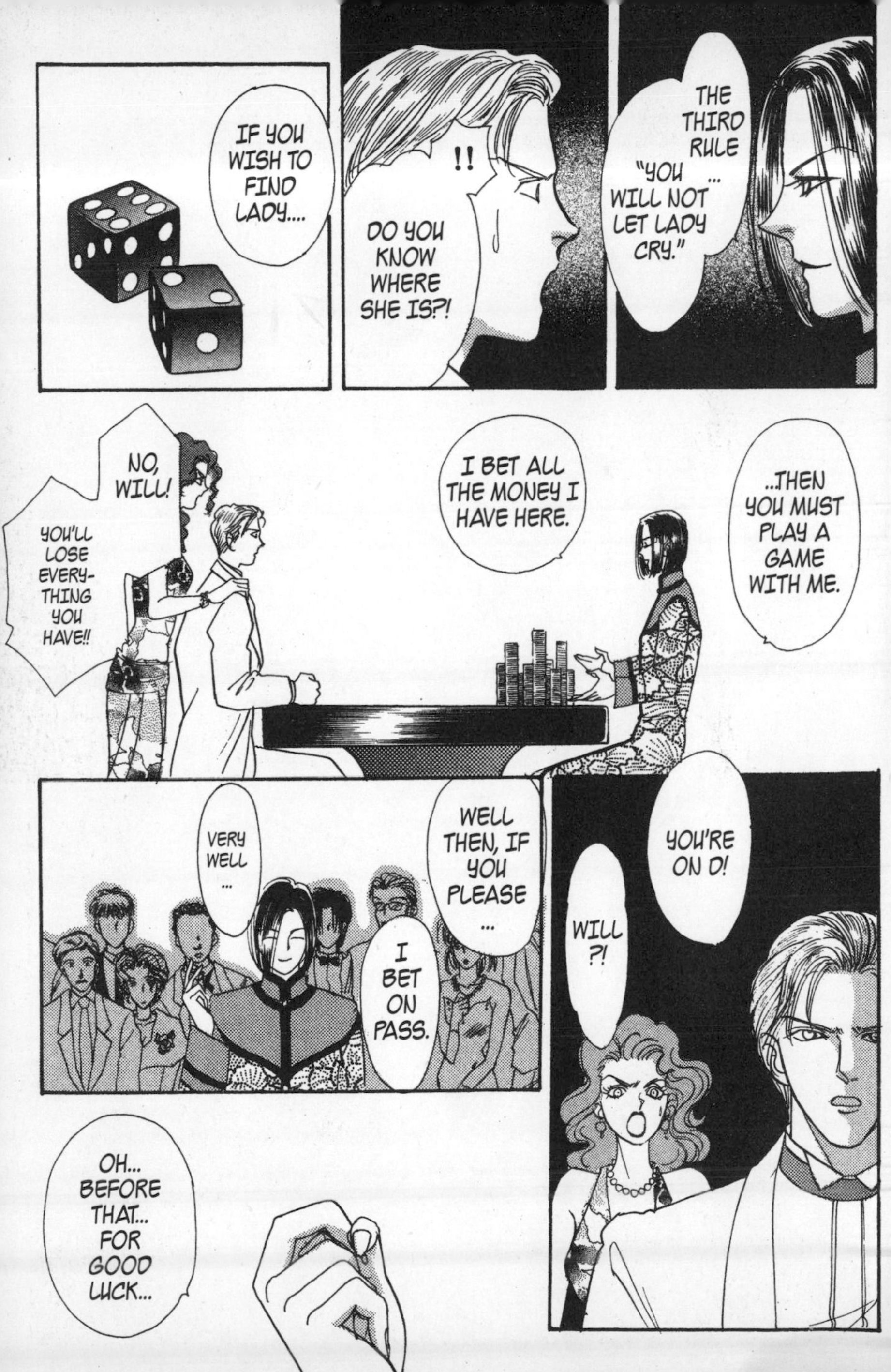
THE THIRD RULE ... "YOU WILL NOT LET LADY CRY."
!!
DO YOU KNOW WHERE SHE IS?!
IF YOU WISH TO FIND LADY....
...THEN YOU MUST PLAY A GAME WITH ME.
I BET ALL THE MONEY I HAVE HERE.
NO, WILL!
YOU'LL LOSE EVERY-THING YOU HAVE!!
YOU'RE ON D!
WILL ?!
WELL THEN, IF YOU PLEASE ...
VERY WELL ...
I BET ON PASS.
OH... BEFORE THAT... FOR GOOD LUCK...

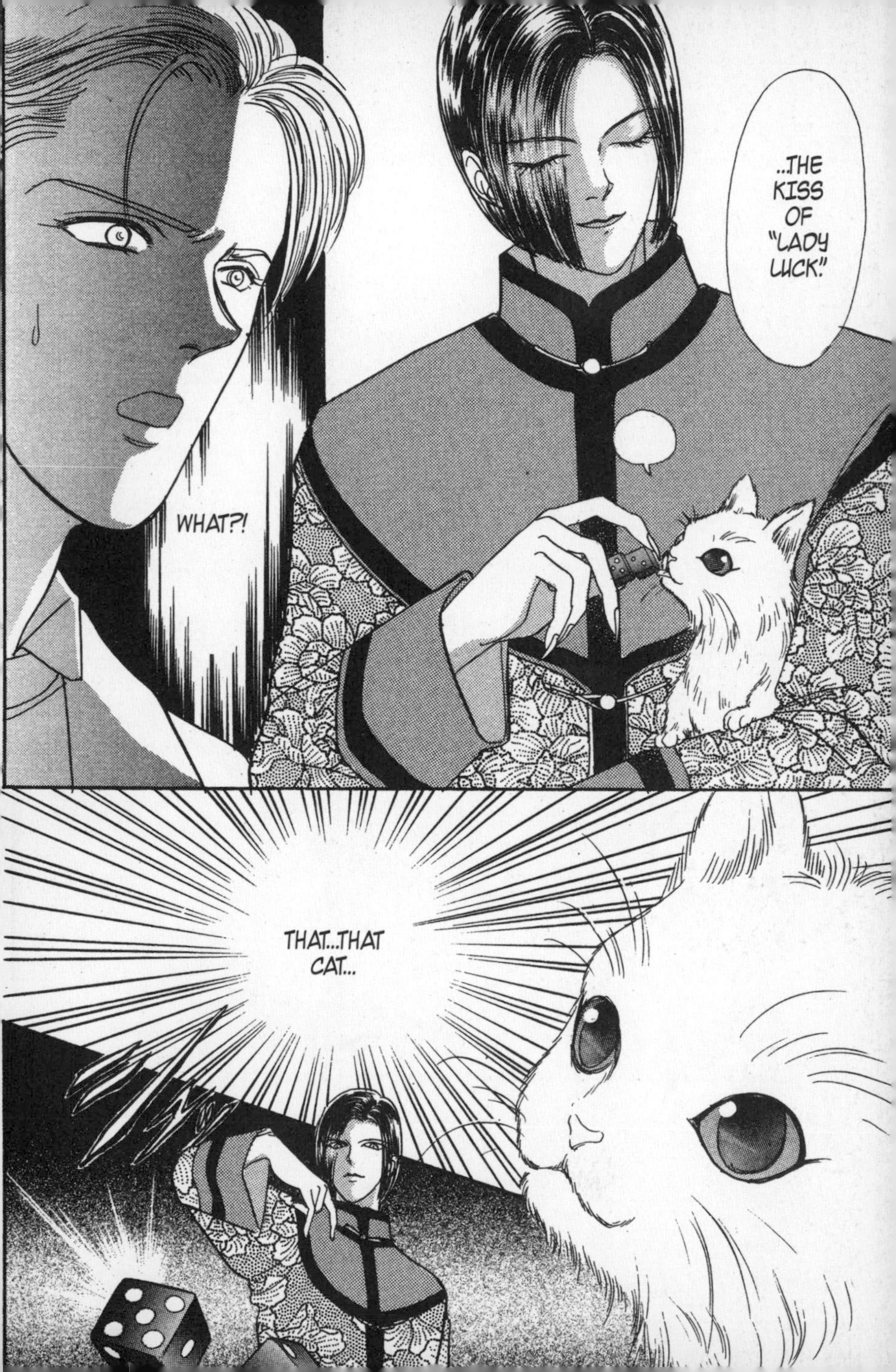
...THE KISS OF "LADY LUCK."
WHAT?!
THAT...THAT CAT...

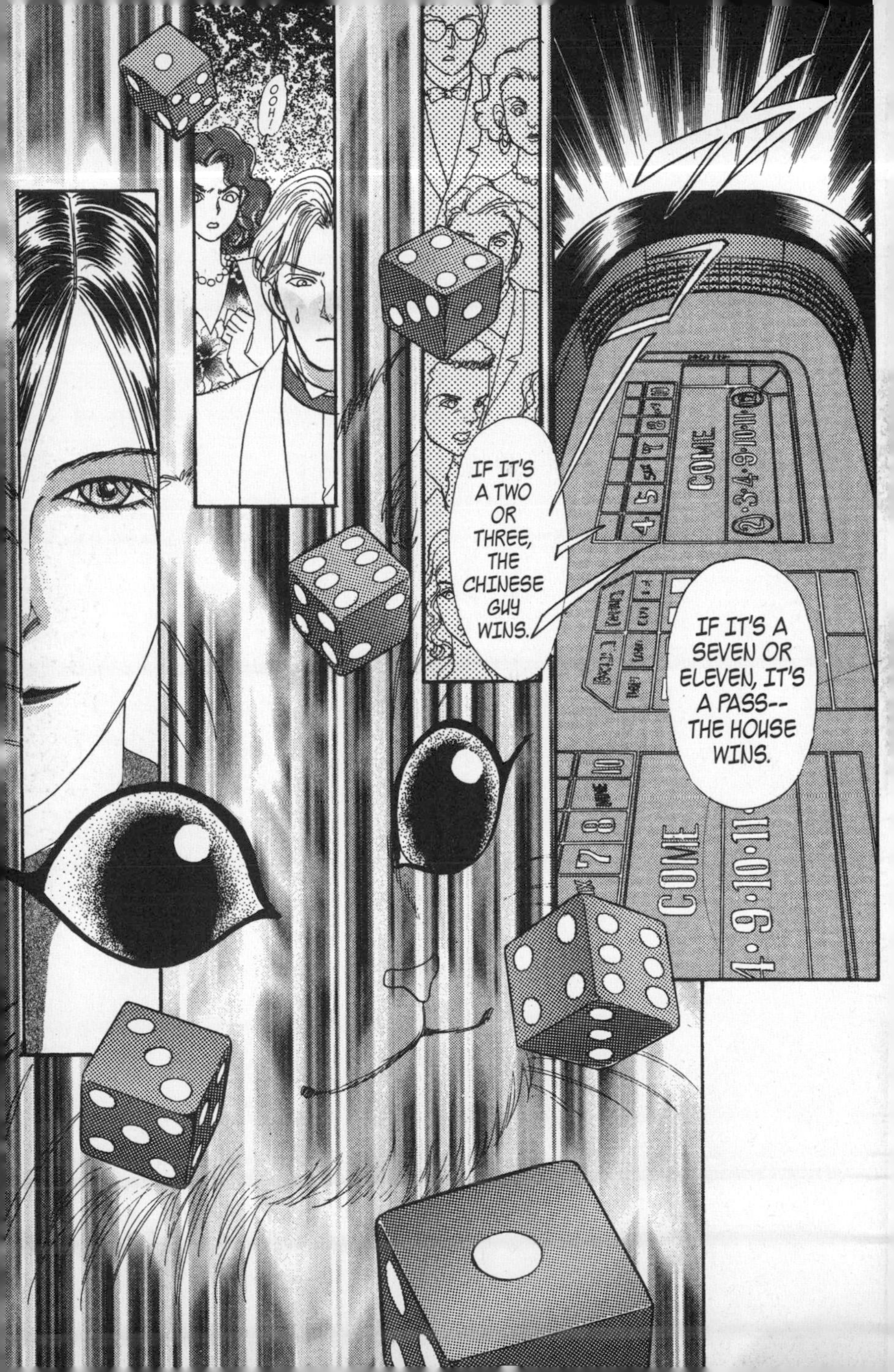
IF IT'S A TWO OR THREE, THE CHINESE GUY WINS.
IF IT'S A SEVEN OR ELEVEN, IT'S A PASS-- THE HOUSE WINS.
COME
COME
OOH!

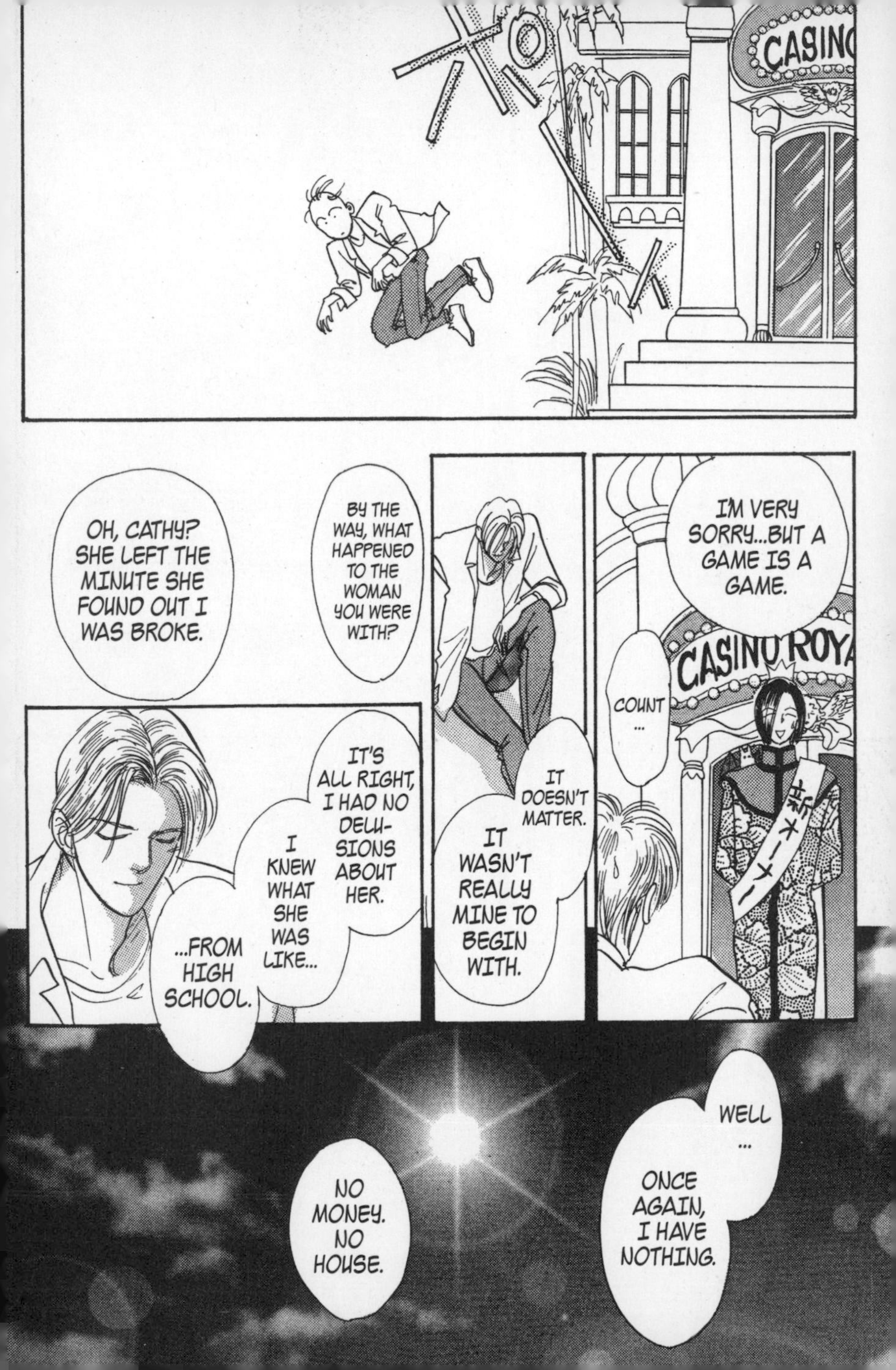
CASINO
I'M VERY SORRY...BUT A GAME IS A GAME.
COUNT ...
CASINO ROYA
新オーナー
IT DOESN'T MATTER.
IT WASN'T REALLY MINE TO BEGIN WITH.
BY THE WAY, WHAT HAPPENED TO THE WOMAN YOU WERE WITH?
OH, CATHY? SHE LEFT THE MINUTE SHE FOUND OUT I WAS BROKE.
IT'S ALL RIGHT, I HAD NO DELU-SIONS ABOUT HER.
I KNEW WHAT SHE WAS LIKE...
...FROM HIGH SCHOOL.
WELL ...
ONCE AGAIN, I HAVE NOTHING.
NO MONEY. NO HOUSE.

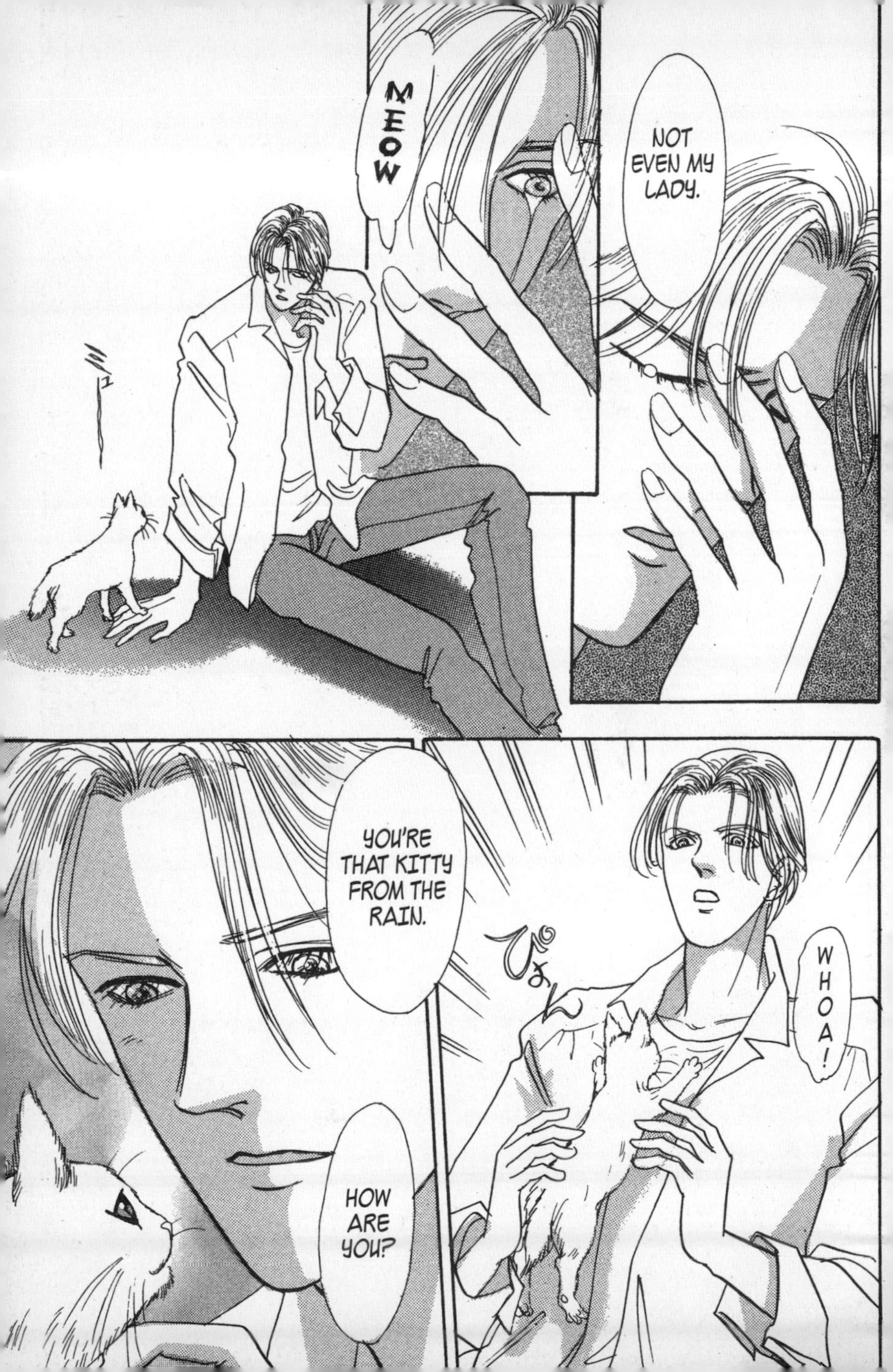

NOT EVEN MY LADY.
MEOW
WHOA!
ぴょん
YOU'RE THAT KITTY FROM THE RAIN.
HOW ARE YOU?

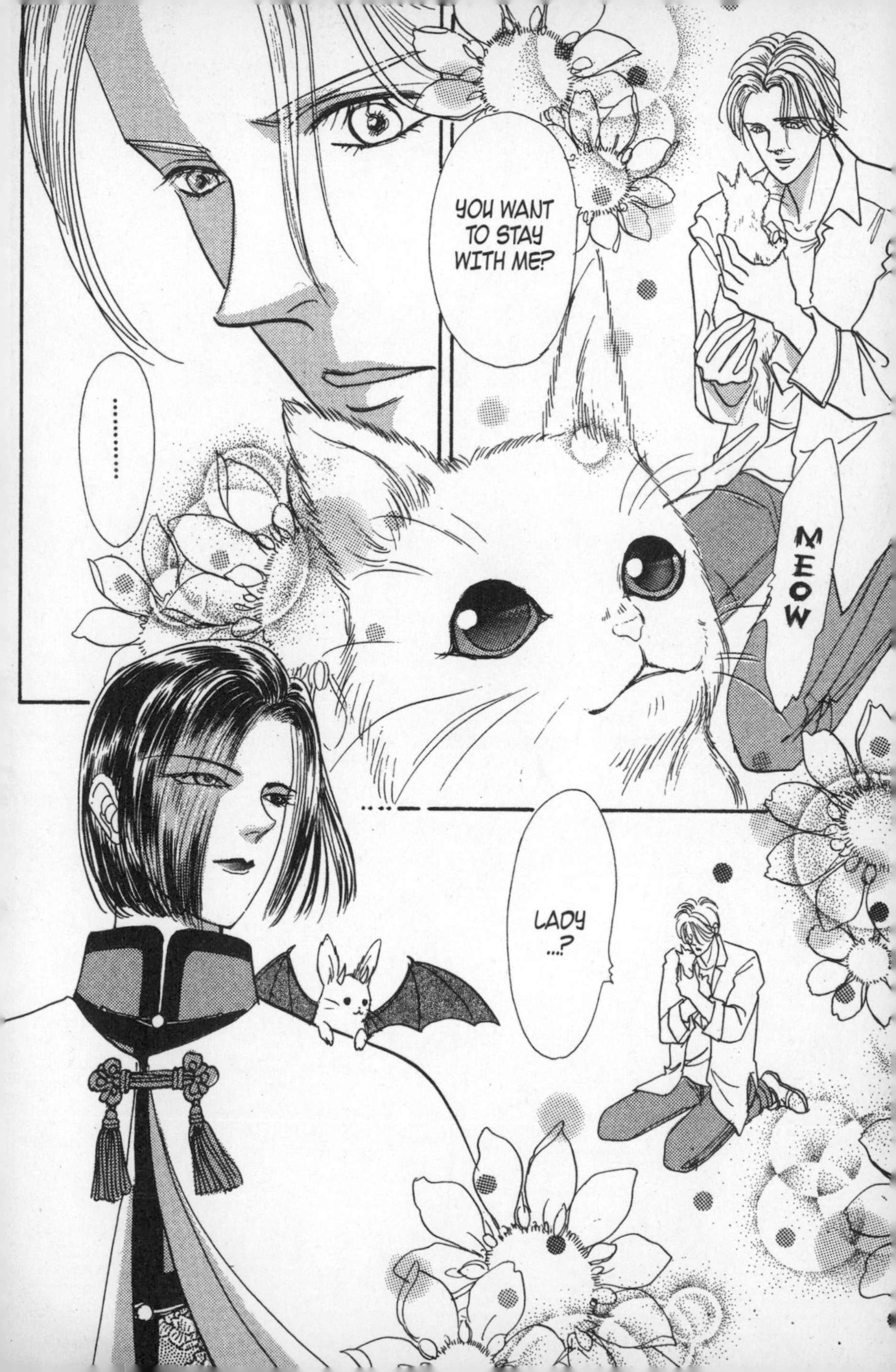
YOU WANT TO STAY WITH ME?
......
MEOW
LADY ...?

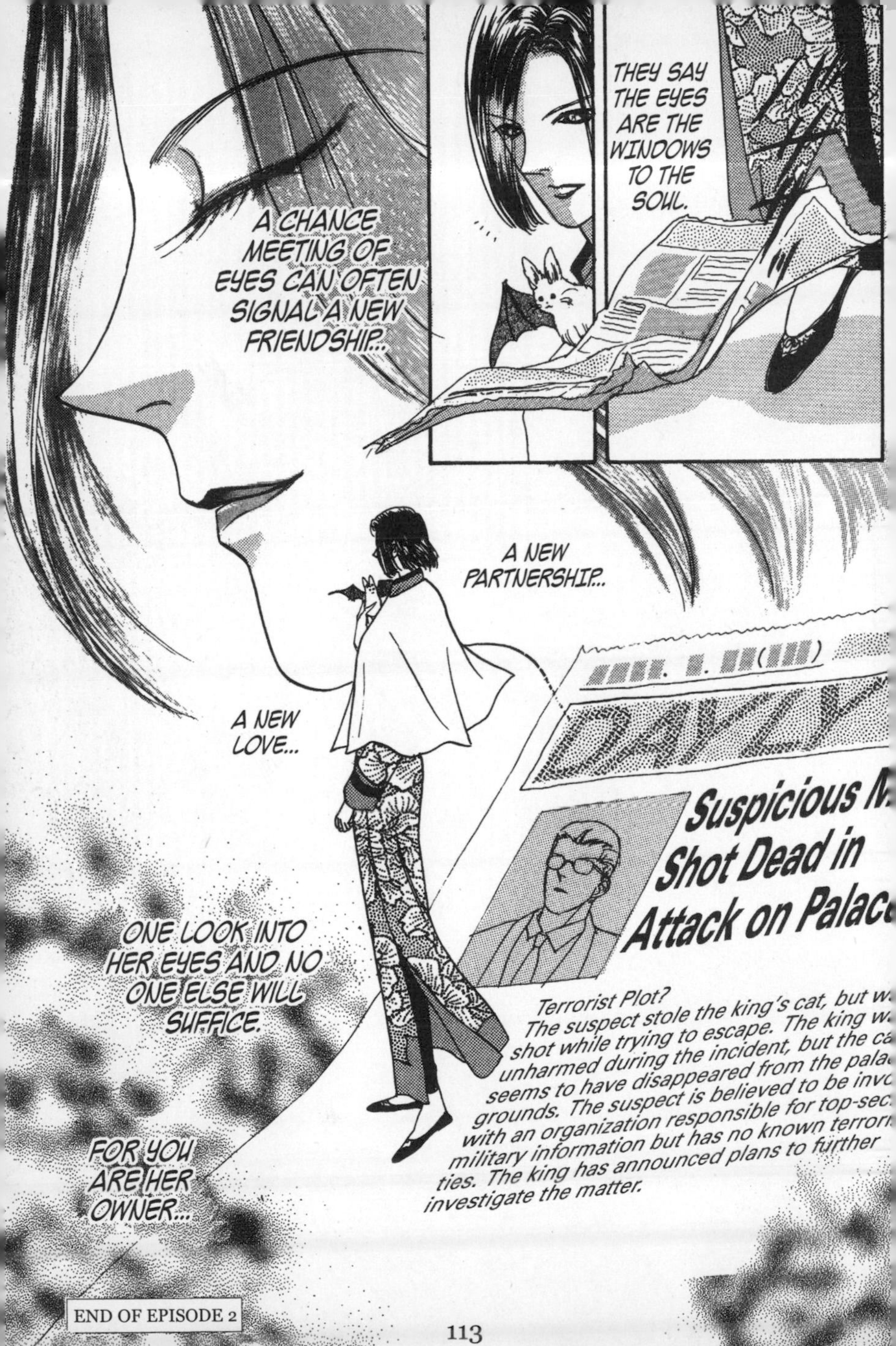
THEY SAY THE EYES ARE THE WINDOWS TO THE SOUL.
A CHANCE MEETING OF EYES CAN OFTEN SIGNAL A NEW FRIENDSHIP...
A NEW PARTNERSHIP...
A NEW LOVE...
Suspicious M
Shot Dead in
Attack on Palac
Terrorist Plot?
The suspect stole the king's cat, but w
shot while trying to escape. The king w
unharmed during the incident, but the ca
seems to have disappeared from the pala
grounds. The suspect is believed to be inv
with an organization responsible for top-se
military information but has no known terror
ties. The king has announced plans to further
investigate the matter.
ONE LOOK INTO HER EYES AND NO ONE ELSE WILL SUFFICE.
FOR YOU ARE HER OWNER...
END OF EPISODE 2

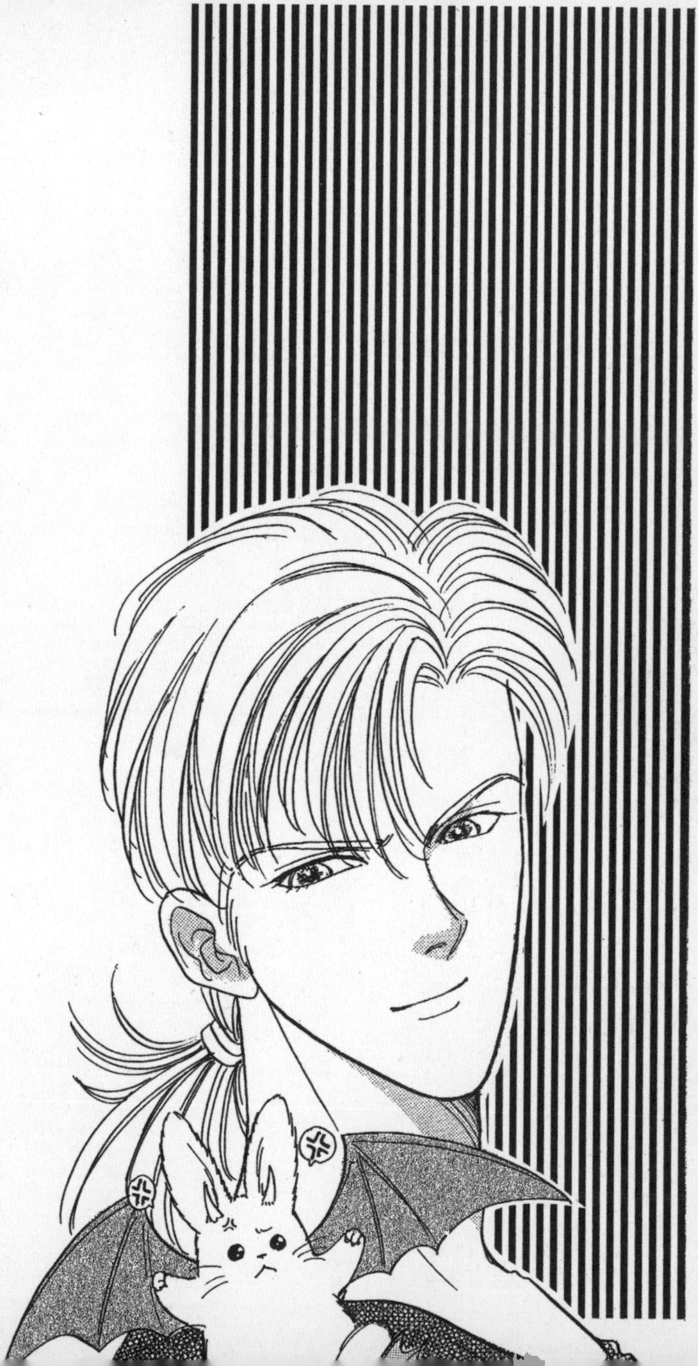

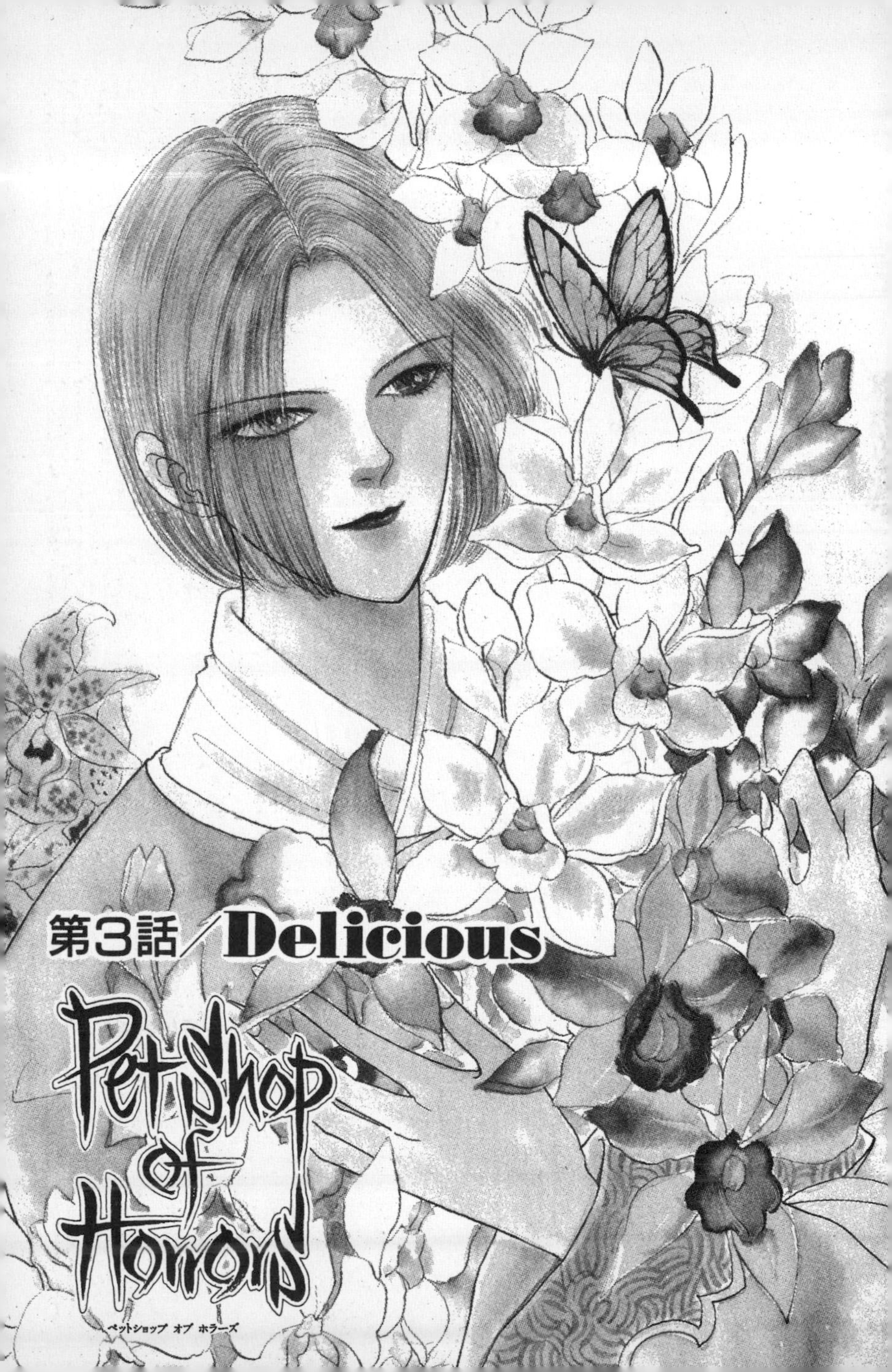
第3話／Delicious
Pet Shop of Horrors
ペットショップ オブ ホラーズ

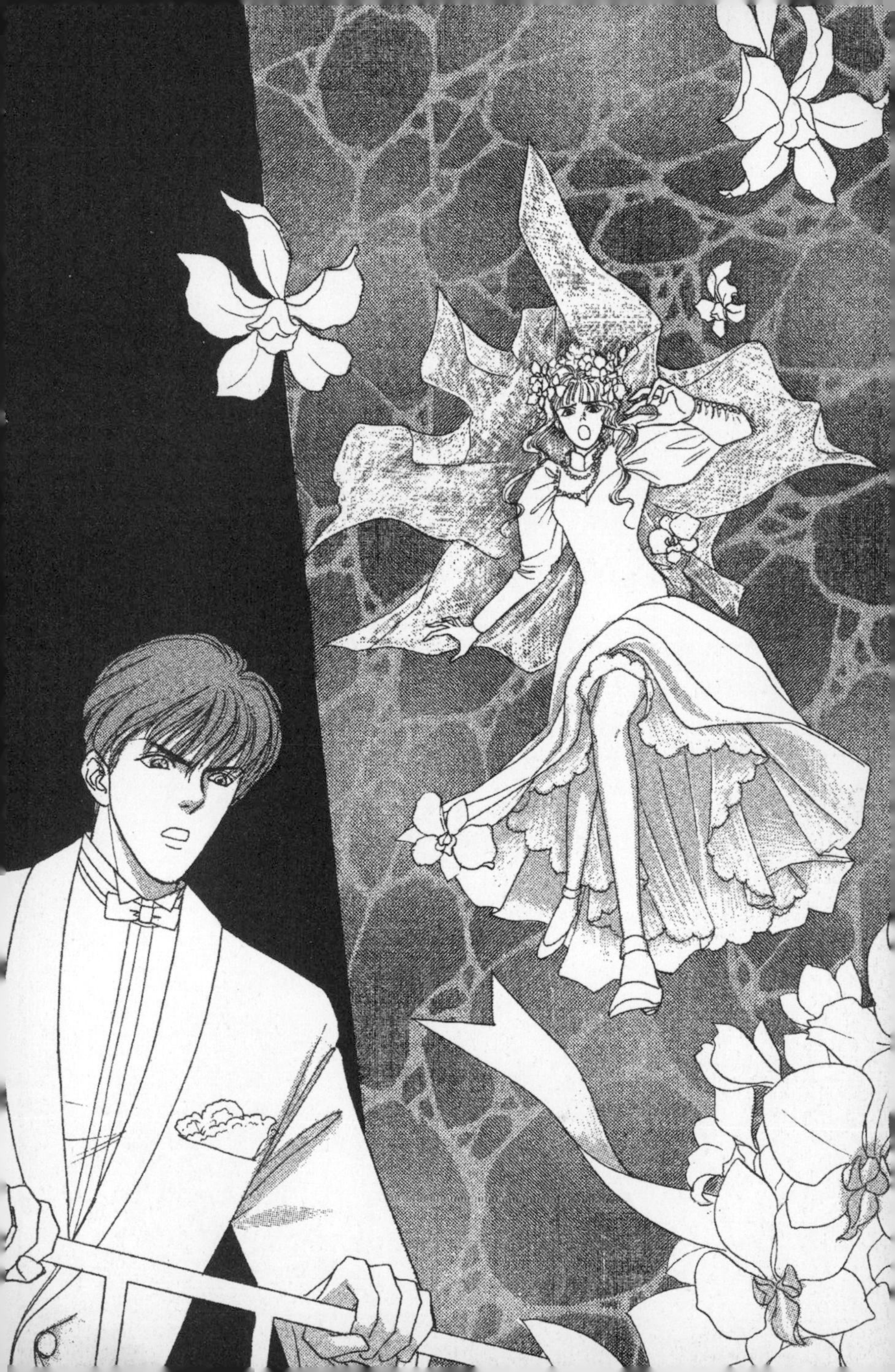

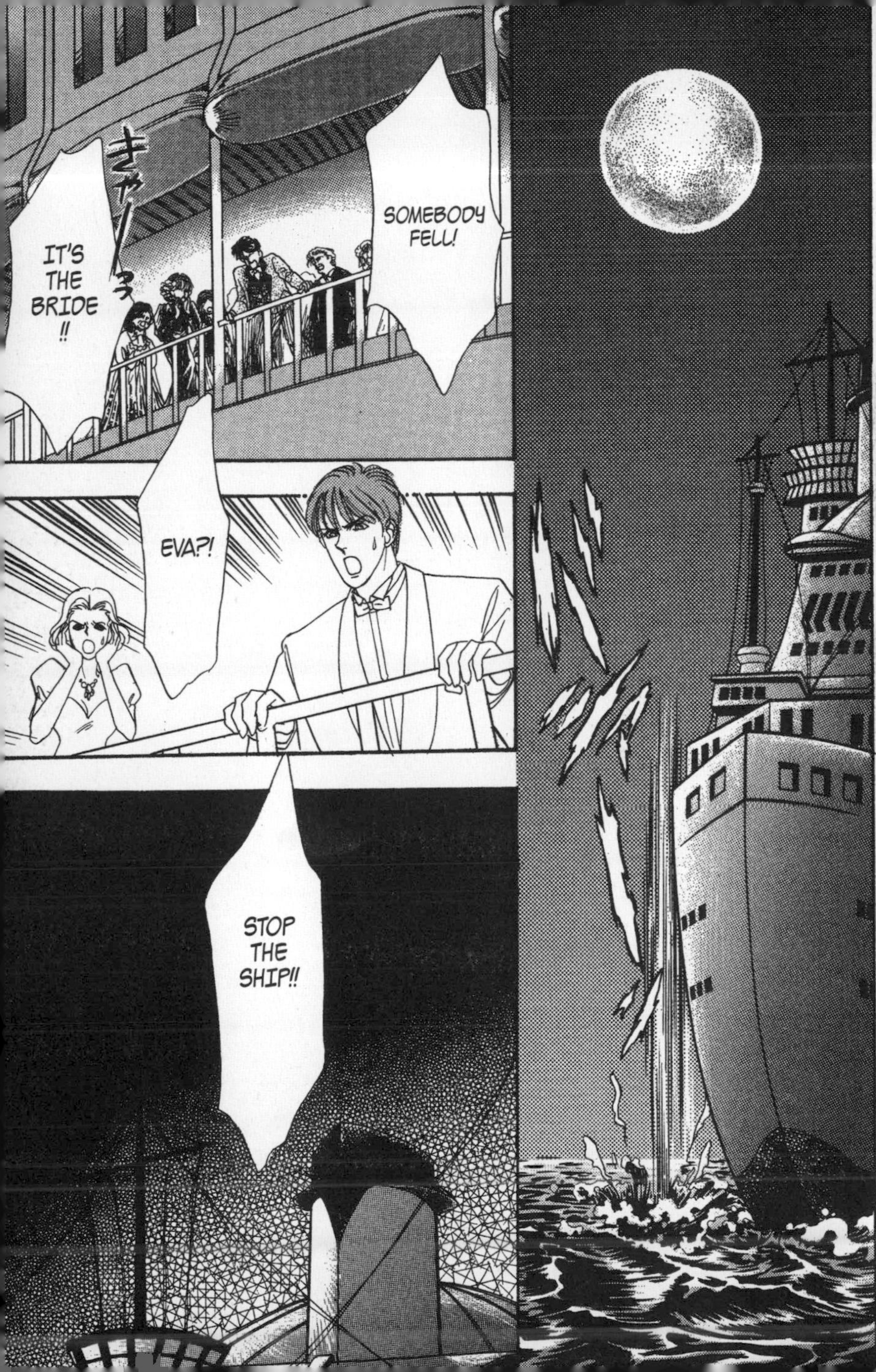

きゃーッ
SOMEBODY FELL!
IT'S THE BRIDE !!
EVA?!
STOP THE SHIP!!

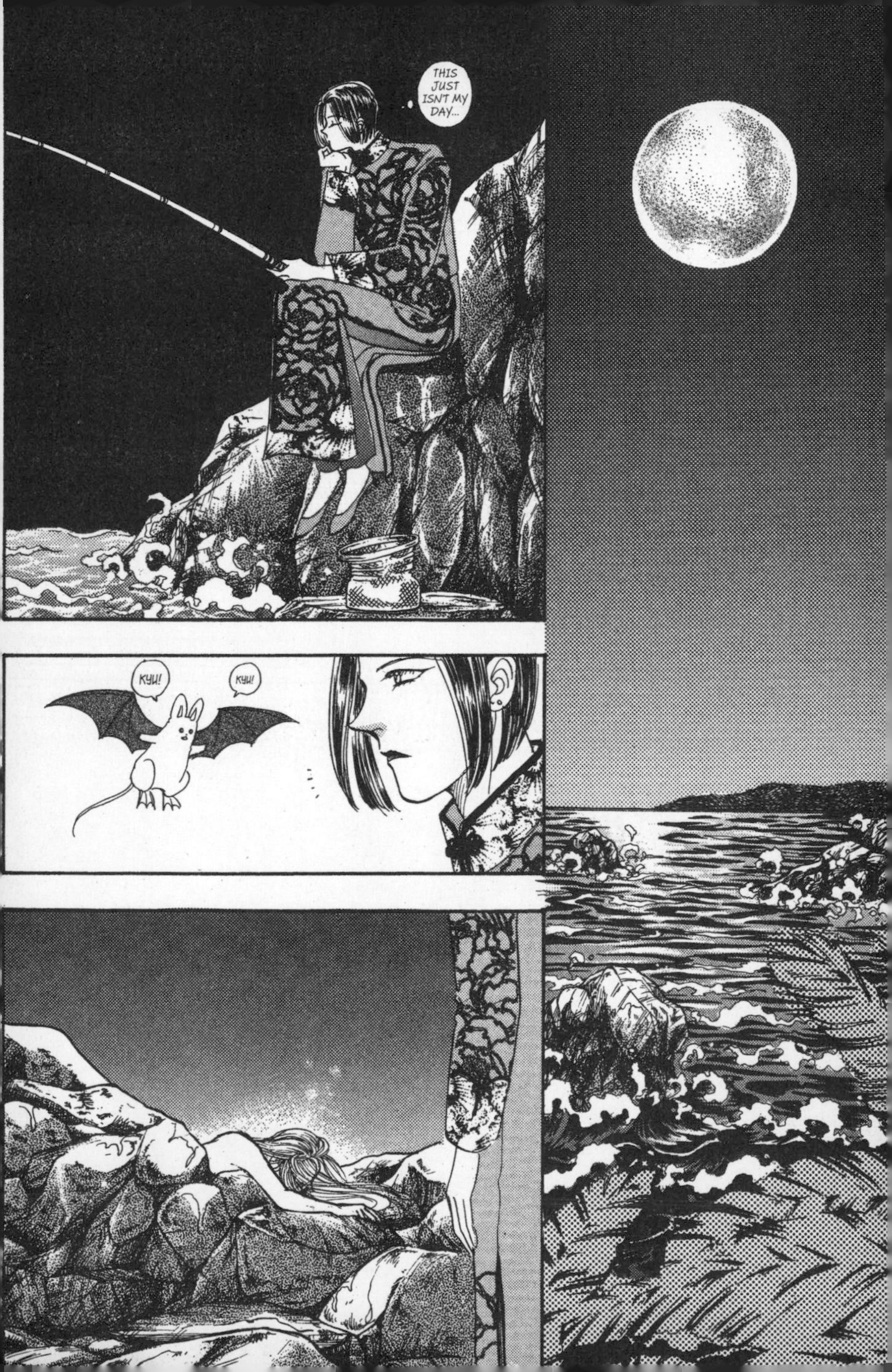
THIS JUST ISN'T MY DAY...
KYU!
KYU!

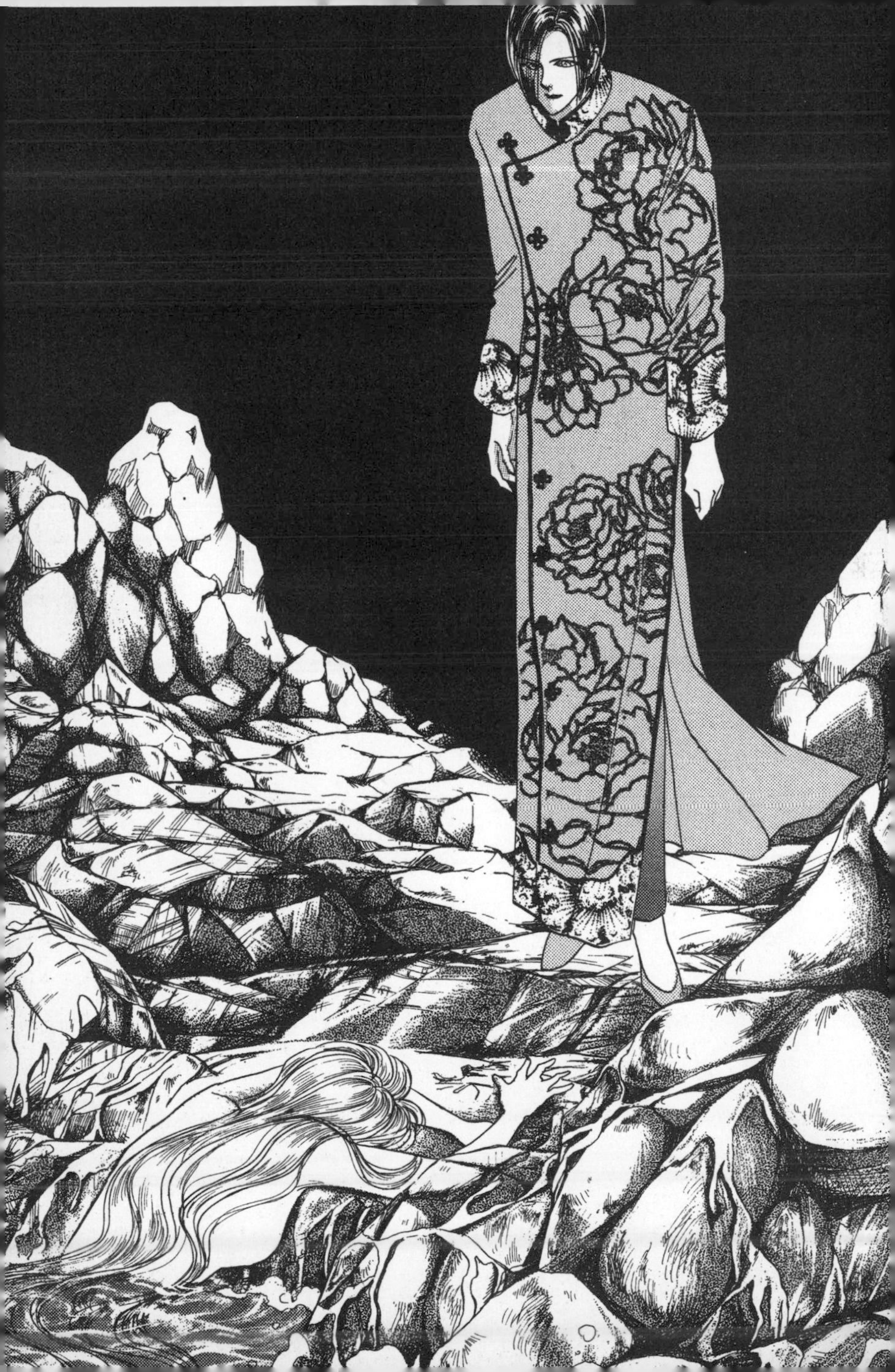

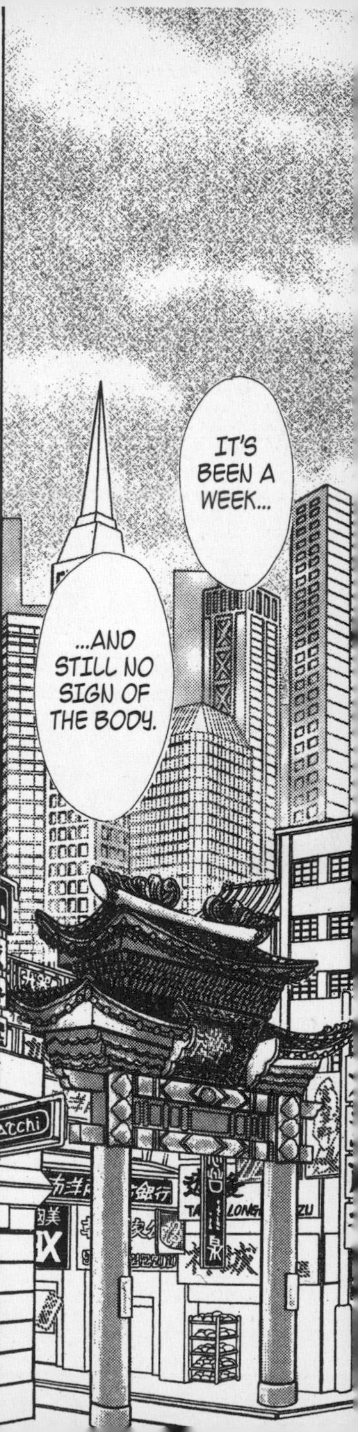
IT'S BEEN A WEEK...
...AND STILL NO SIGN OF THE BODY.

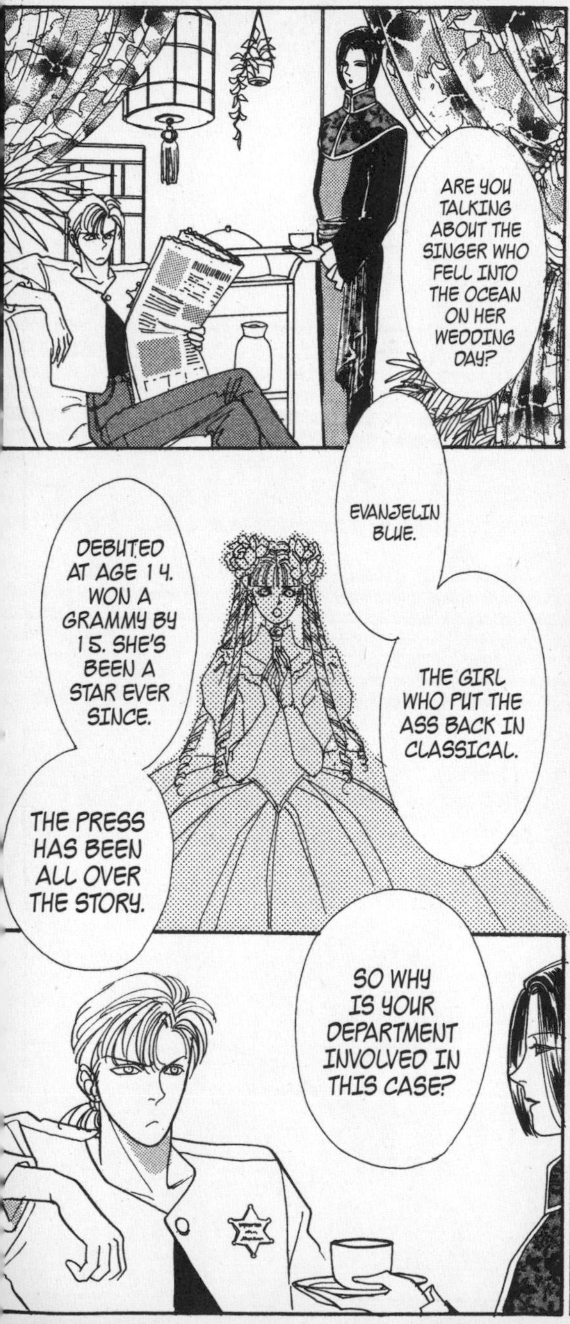
ARE YOU TALKING ABOUT THE SINGER WHO FELL INTO THE OCEAN ON HER WEDDING DAY?
EVANJELIN BLUE.
THE GIRL WHO PUT THE ASS BACK IN CLASSICAL.
DEBUTED AT AGE 14. WON A GRAMMY BY 15. SHE'S BEEN A STAR EVER SINCE.
THE PRESS HAS BEEN ALL OVER THE STORY.
SO WHY IS YOUR DEPARTMENT INVOLVED IN THIS CASE?

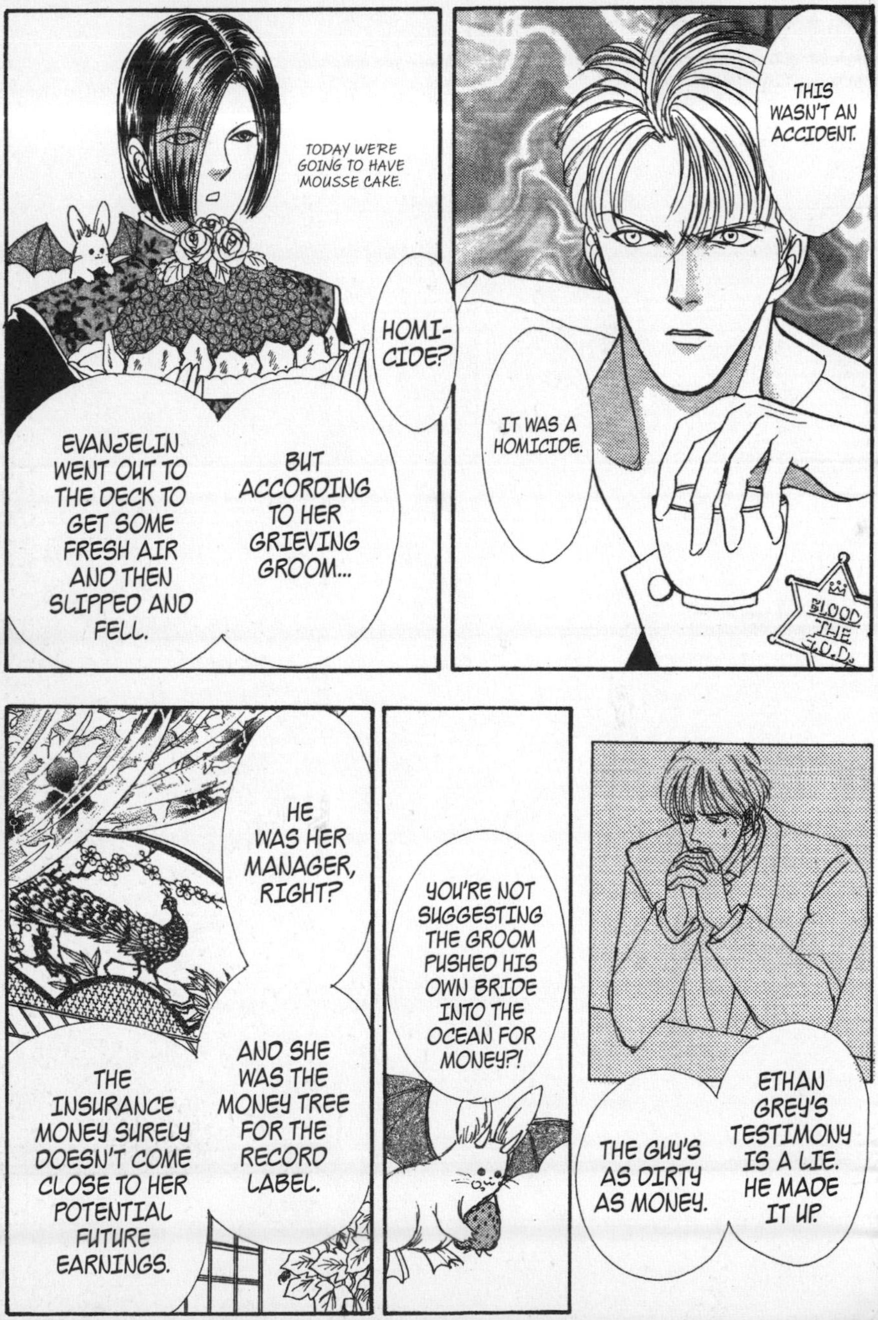
THIS WASN'T AN ACCIDENT.
IT WAS A HOMICIDE.
BLOOD THE S.O.D.
HOMI-CIDE?
TODAY WE'RE GOING TO HAVE MOUSSE CAKE.
BUT ACCORDING TO HER GRIEVING GROOM...
EVANJELIN WENT OUT TO THE DECK TO GET SOME FRESH AIR AND THEN SLIPPED AND FELL.
ETHAN GREY'S TESTIMONY IS A LIE. HE MADE IT UP.
THE GUY'S AS DIRTY AS MONEY.
YOU'RE NOT SUGGESTING THE GROOM PUSHED HIS OWN BRIDE INTO THE OCEAN FOR MONEY?!
HE WAS HER MANAGER, RIGHT?
AND SHE WAS THE MONEY TREE FOR THE RECORD LABEL.
THE INSURANCE MONEY SURELY DOESN'T COME CLOSE TO HER POTENTIAL FUTURE EARNINGS.

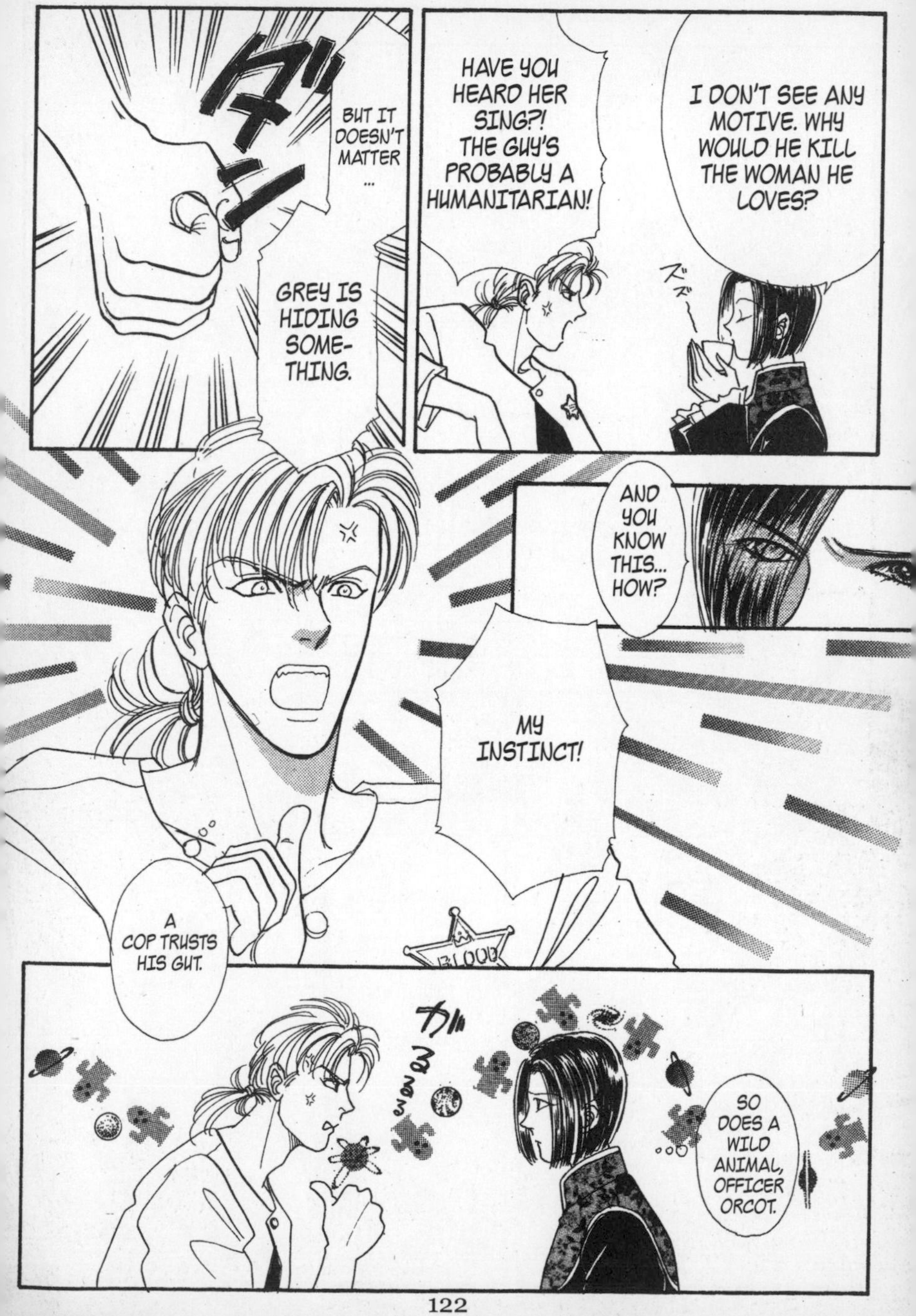
I DON'T SEE ANY MOTIVE. WHY WOULD HE KILL THE WOMAN HE LOVES?
HAVE YOU HEARD HER SING?! THE GUY'S PROBABLY A HUMANITARIAN!
BUT IT DOESN'T MATTER ...
GREY IS HIDING SOMETHING.
AND YOU KNOW THIS... HOW?
MY INSTINCT!
A COP TRUSTS HIS GUT.
SO DOES A WILD ANIMAL, OFFICER ORCOT.

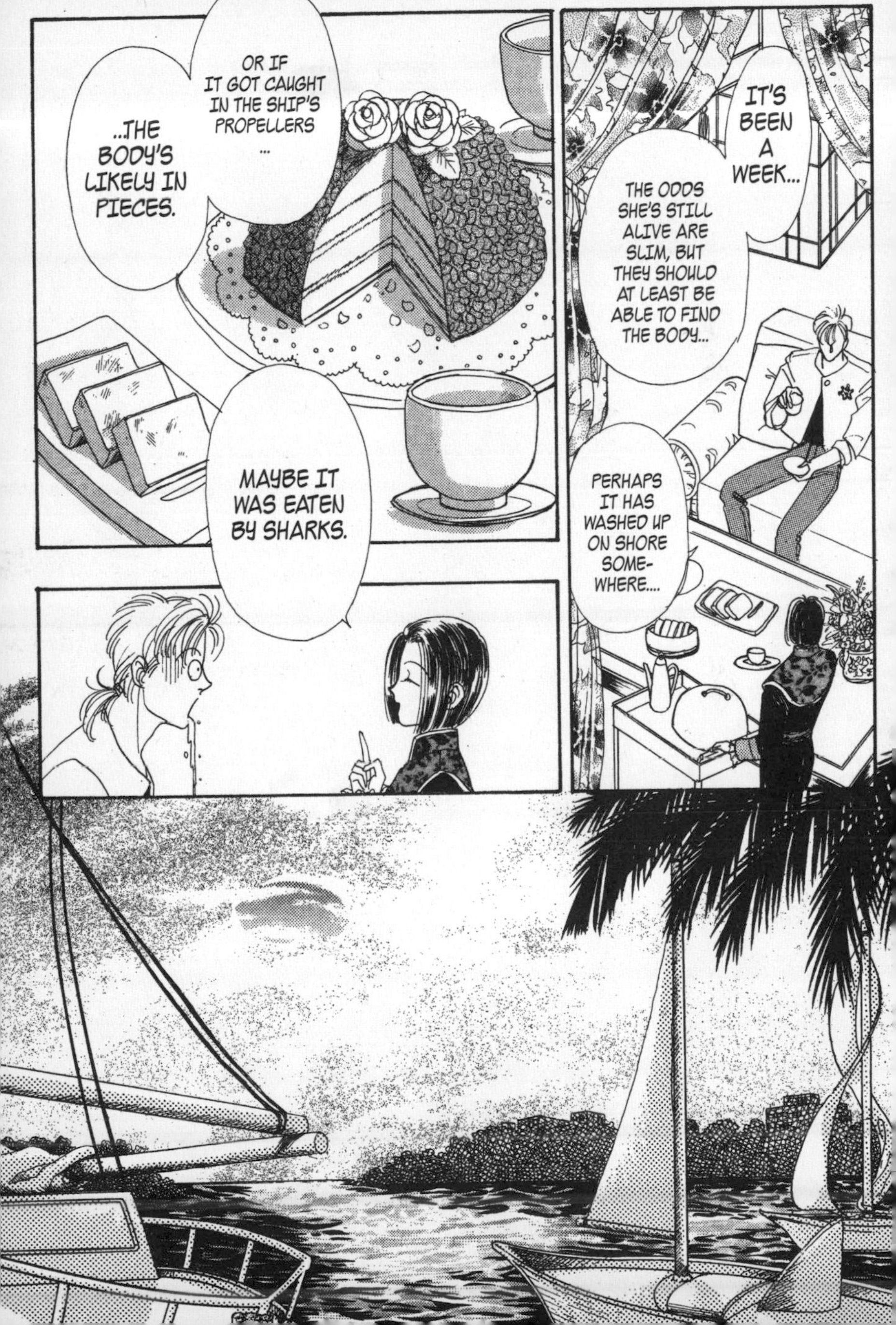
IT'S BEEN A WEEK...
THE ODDS SHE'S STILL ALIVE ARE SLIM, BUT THEY SHOULD AT LEAST BE ABLE TO FIND THE BODY...
PERHAPS IT HAS WASHED UP ON SHORE SOME-WHERE....
OR IF IT GOT CAUGHT IN THE SHIP'S PROPELLERS ...
...THE BODY'S LIKELY IN PIECES.
MAYBE IT WAS EATEN BY SHARKS.

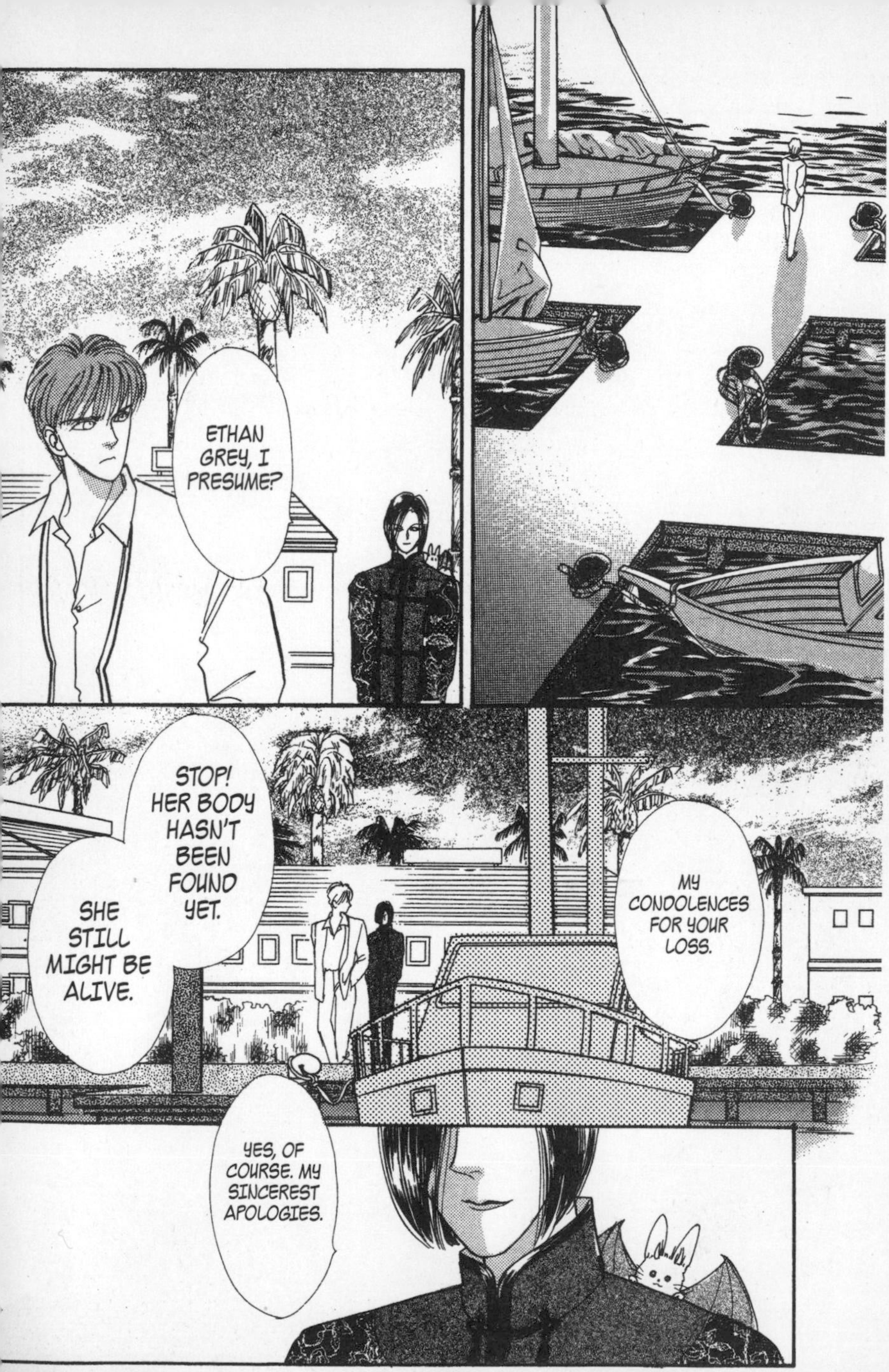
ETHAN GREY, I PRESUME?
MY CONDOLENCES FOR YOUR LOSS.
STOP! HER BODY HASN'T BEEN FOUND YET.
SHE STILL MIGHT BE ALIVE.
YES, OF COURSE. MY SINCEREST APOLOGIES.

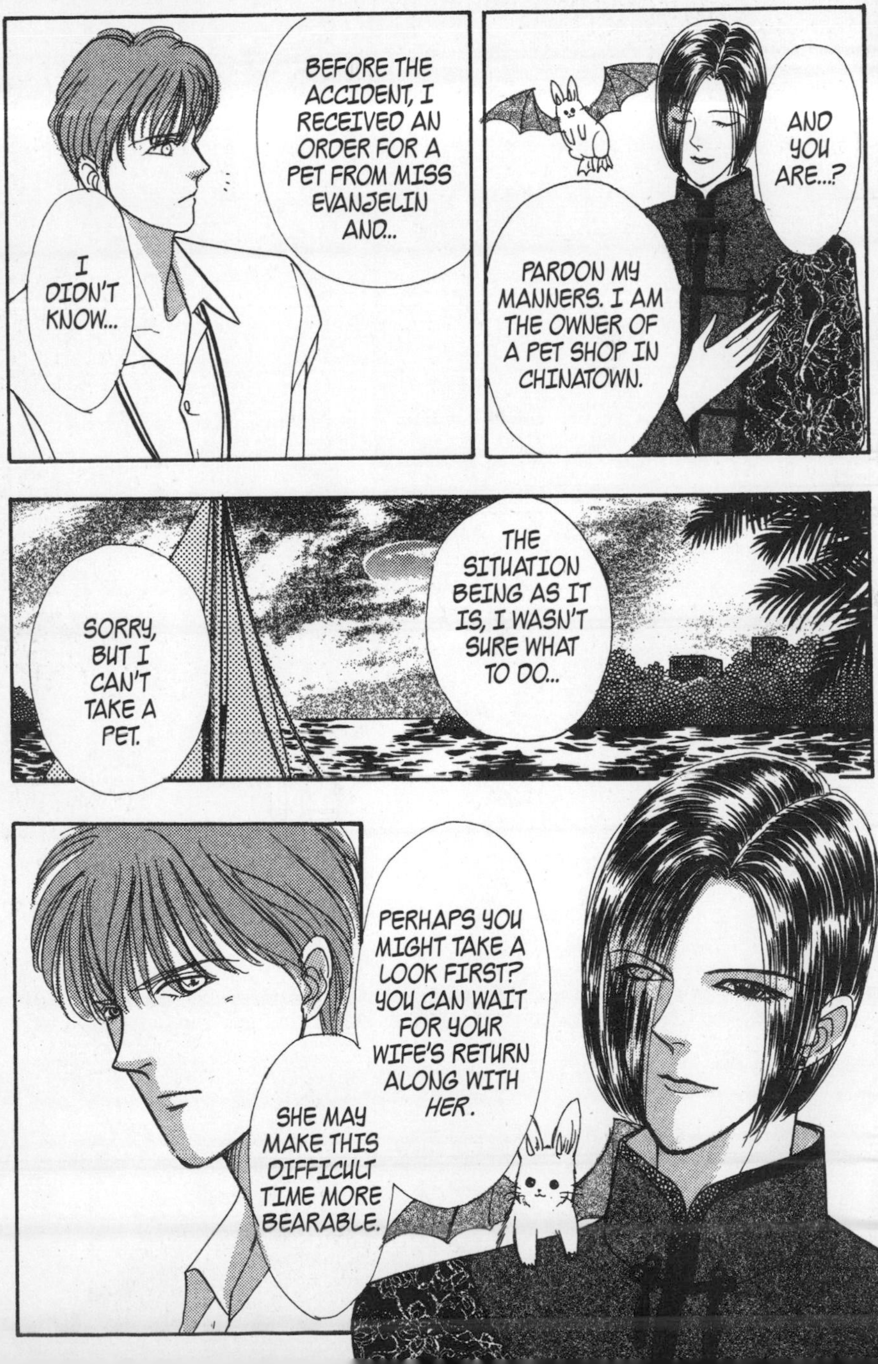
AND YOU ARE...?
PARDON MY MANNERS. I AM THE OWNER OF A PET SHOP IN CHINATOWN.
BEFORE THE ACCIDENT, I RECEIVED AN ORDER FOR A PET FROM MISS EVANJELIN AND...
I DIDN'T KNOW...
THE SITUATION BEING AS IT IS, I WASN'T SURE WHAT TO DO...
SORRY, BUT I CAN'T TAKE A PET.
PERHAPS YOU MIGHT TAKE A LOOK FIRST? YOU CAN WAIT FOR YOUR WIFE'S RETURN ALONG WITH *HER*.
SHE MAY MAKE THIS DIFFICULT TIME MORE BEARABLE.

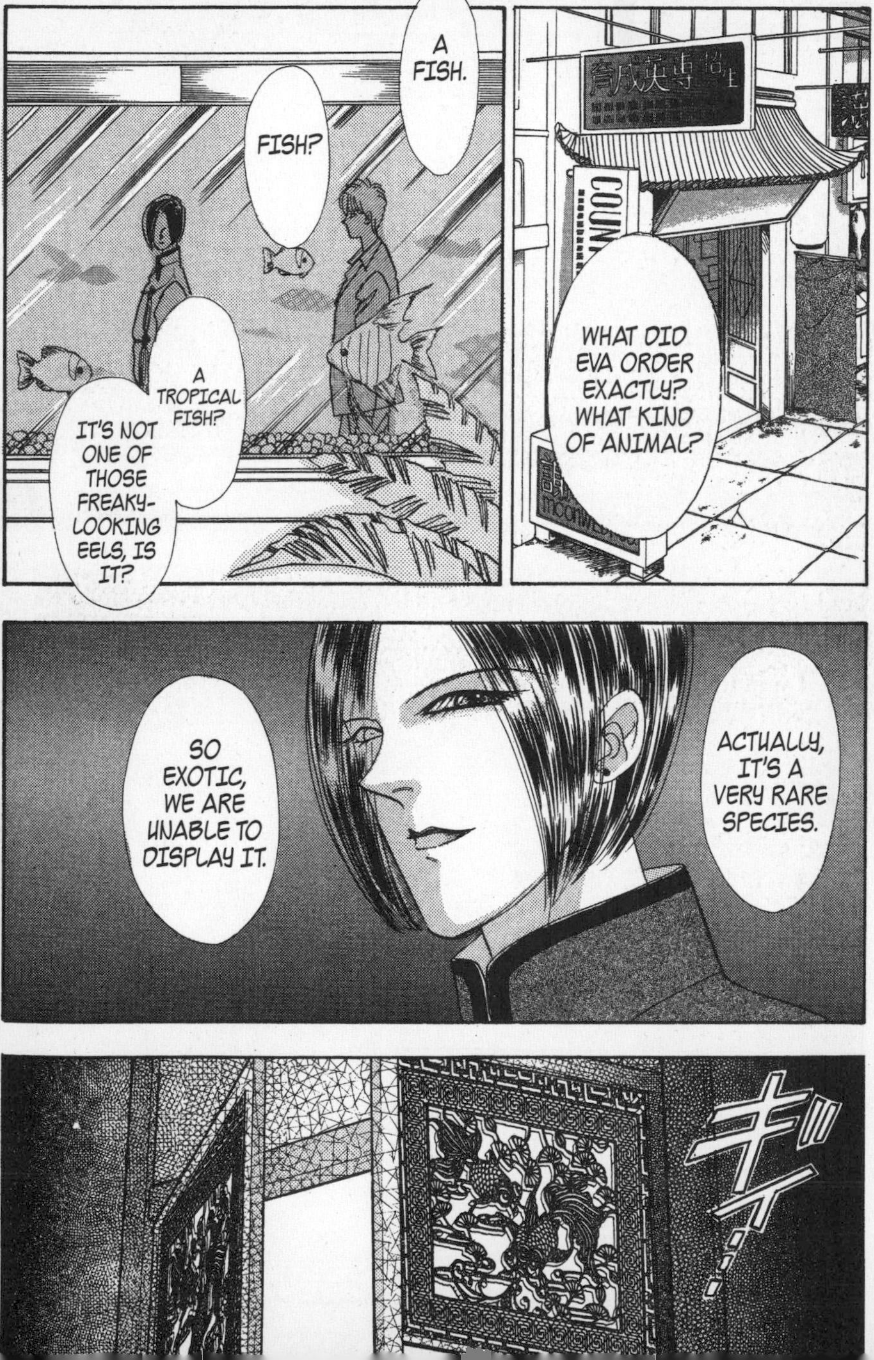
WHAT DID EVA ORDER EXACTLY? WHAT KIND OF ANIMAL?
A FISH.
FISH?
A TROPICAL FISH?
IT'S NOT ONE OF THOSE FREAKY-LOOKING EELS, IS IT?
ACTUALLY, IT'S A VERY RARE SPECIES.
SO EXOTIC, WE ARE UNABLE TO DISPLAY IT.

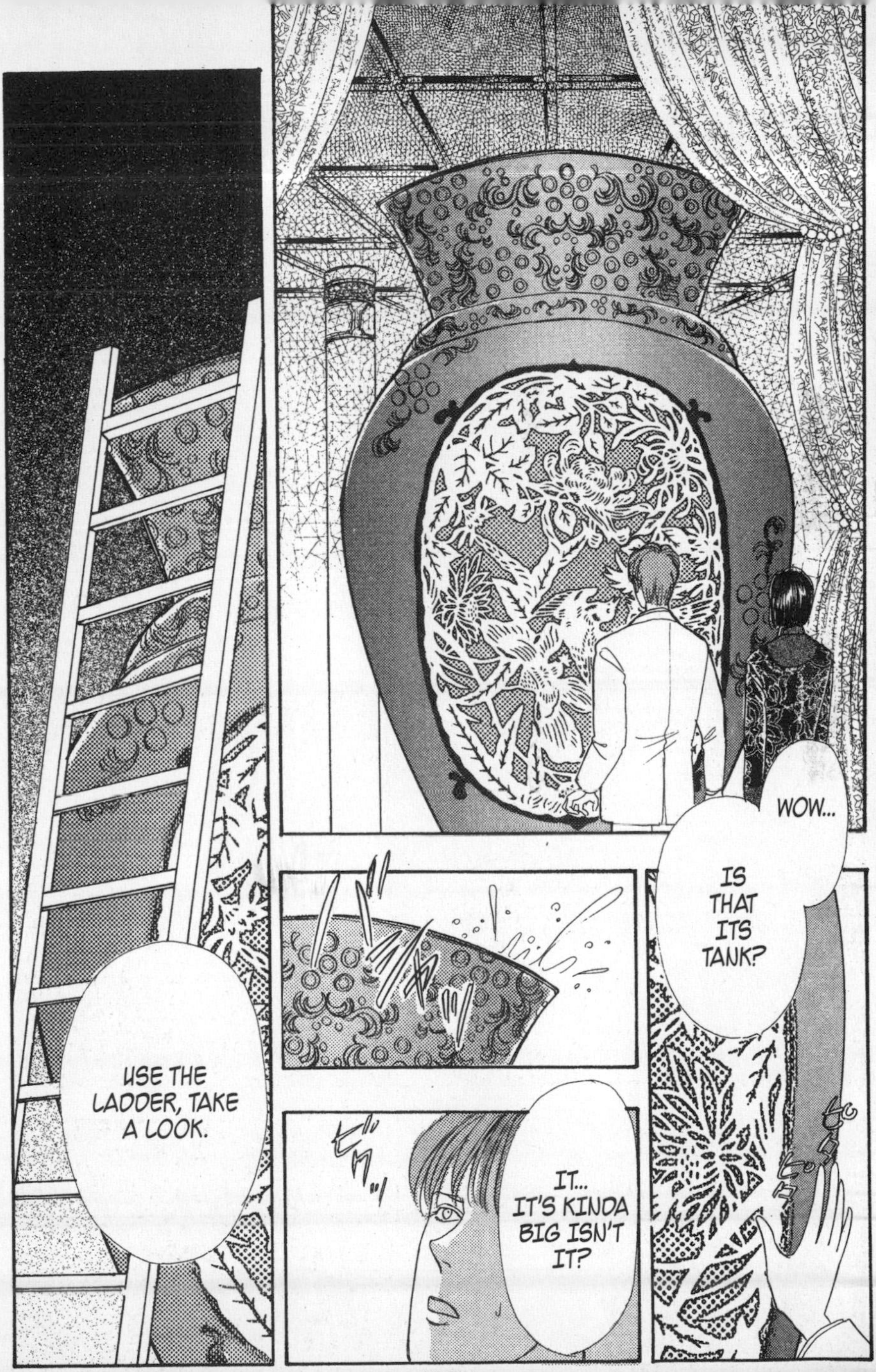
WOW...
IS THAT ITS TANK?
IT... IT'S KINDA BIG ISN'T IT?
USE THE LADDER, TAKE A LOOK.

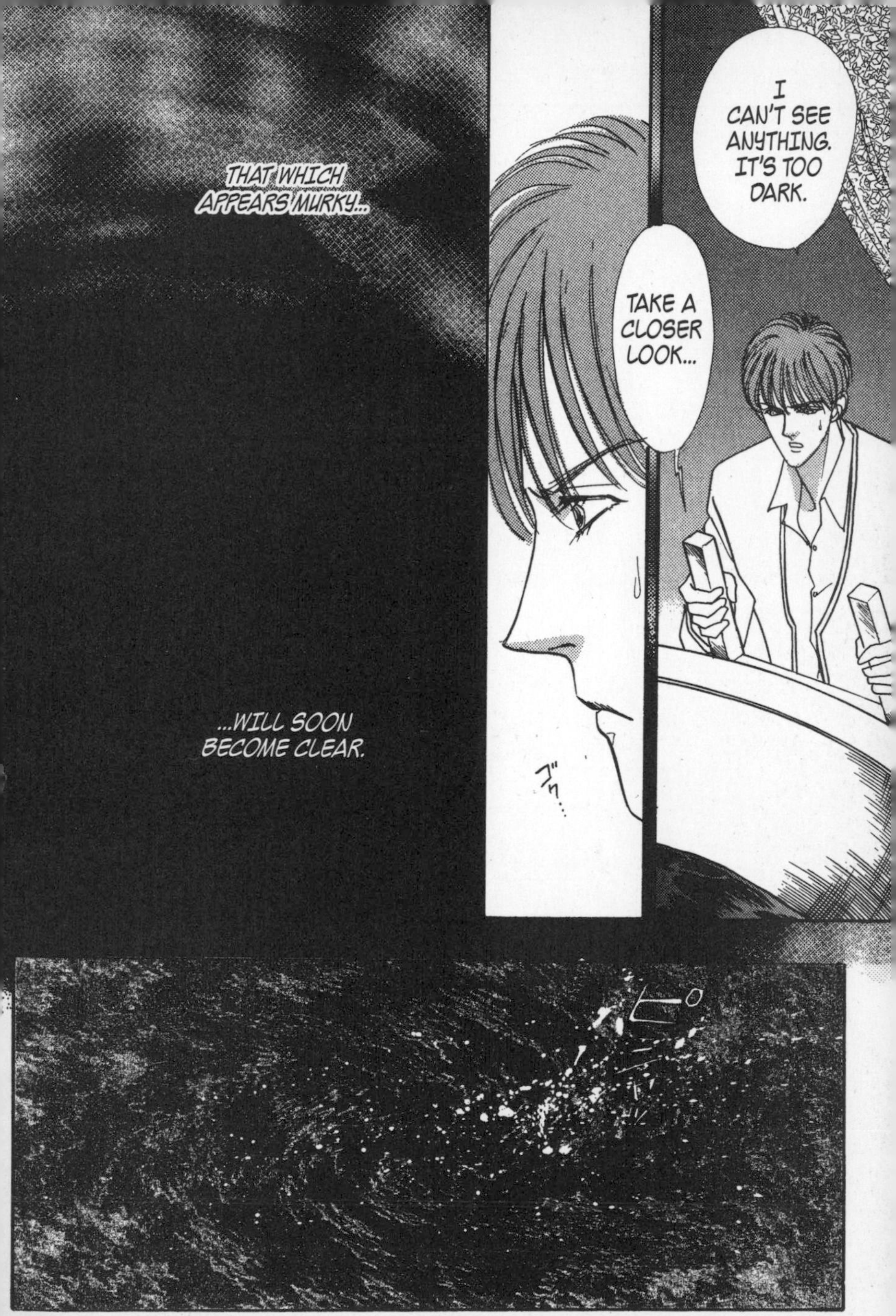
I CAN'T SEE ANYTHING. IT'S TOO DARK.
TAKE A CLOSER LOOK...
ゴク…
THAT WHICH APPEARS MURKY...
...WILL SOON BECOME CLEAR.
ピ

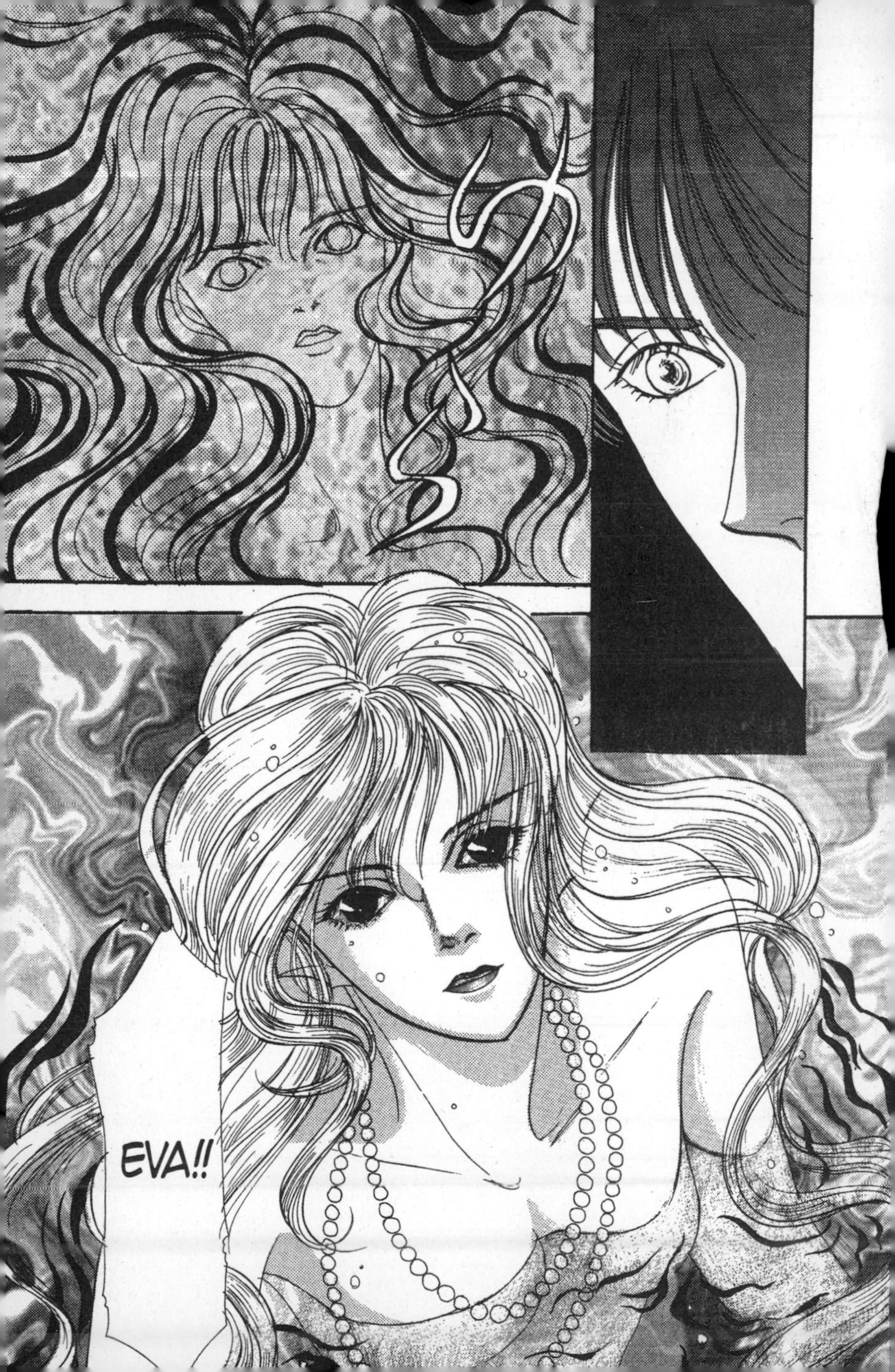
EVA!!

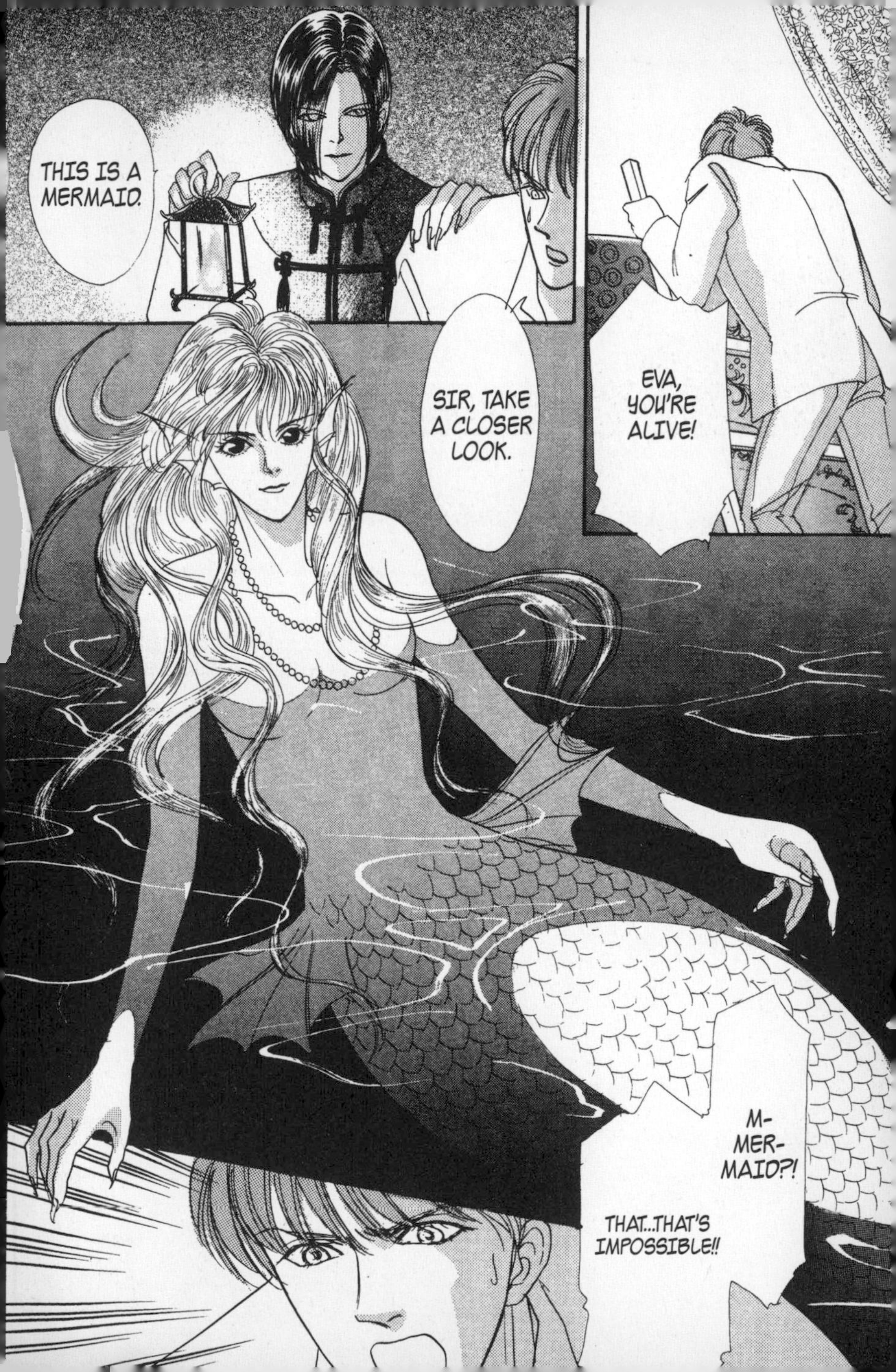
EVA, YOU'RE ALIVE!
THIS IS A MERMAID.
SIR, TAKE A CLOSER LOOK.
M-MER-MAID?!
THAT...THAT'S IMPOSSIBLE!!

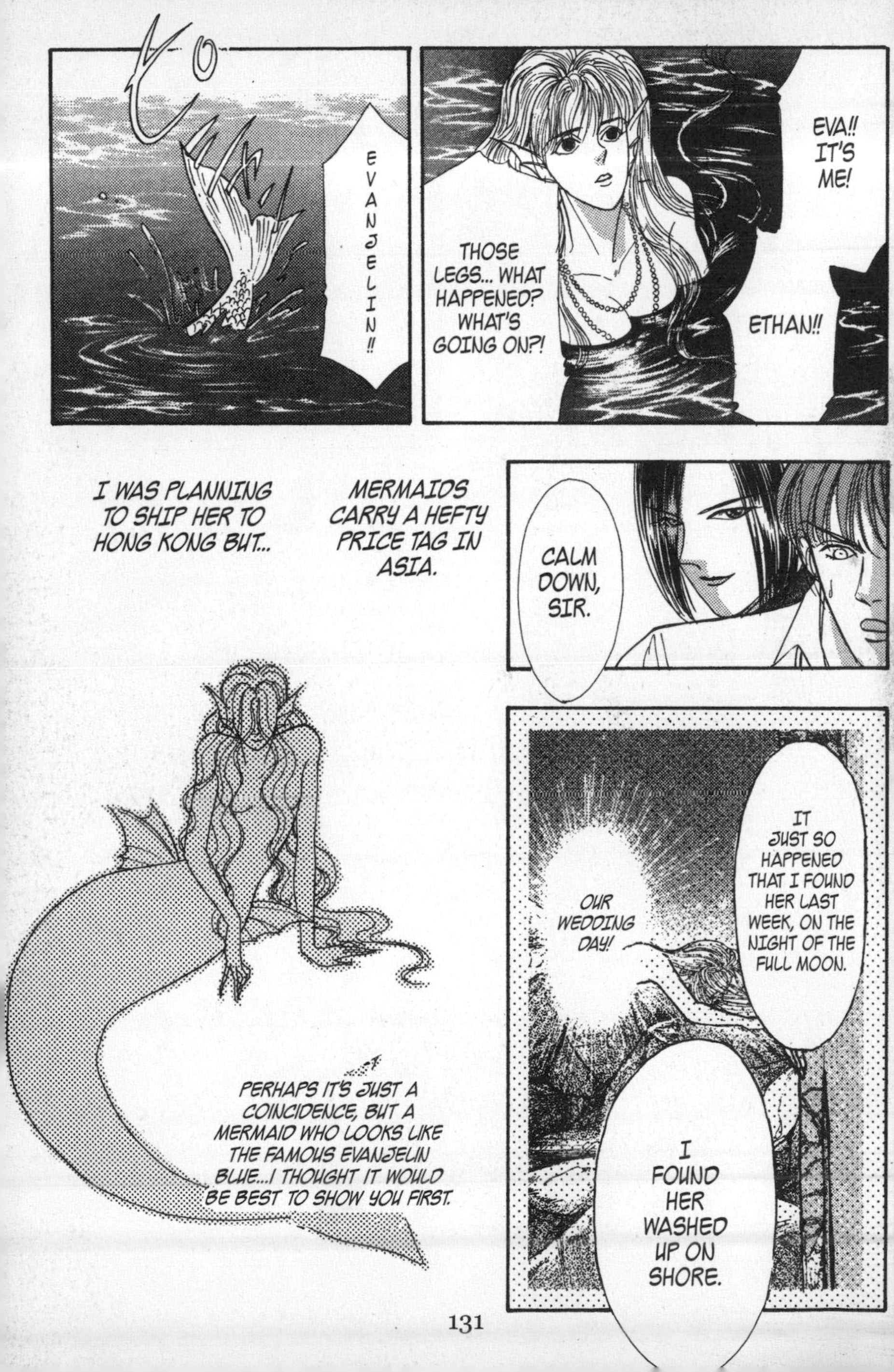
EVA!! IT'S ME!
ETHAN!!
THOSE LEGS... WHAT HAPPENED? WHAT'S GOING ON?!
EVANJELIN!!
CALM DOWN, SIR.
MERMAIDS CARRY A HEFTY PRICE TAG IN ASIA.
I WAS PLANNING TO SHIP HER TO HONG KONG BUT...
IT JUST SO HAPPENED THAT I FOUND HER LAST WEEK, ON THE NIGHT OF THE FULL MOON.
OUR WEDDING DAY!
I FOUND HER WASHED UP ON SHORE.
PERHAPS IT'S JUST A COINCIDENCE, BUT A MERMAID WHO LOOKS LIKE THE FAMOUS EVANJELIN BLUE...I THOUGHT IT WOULD BE BEST TO SHOW YOU FIRST.

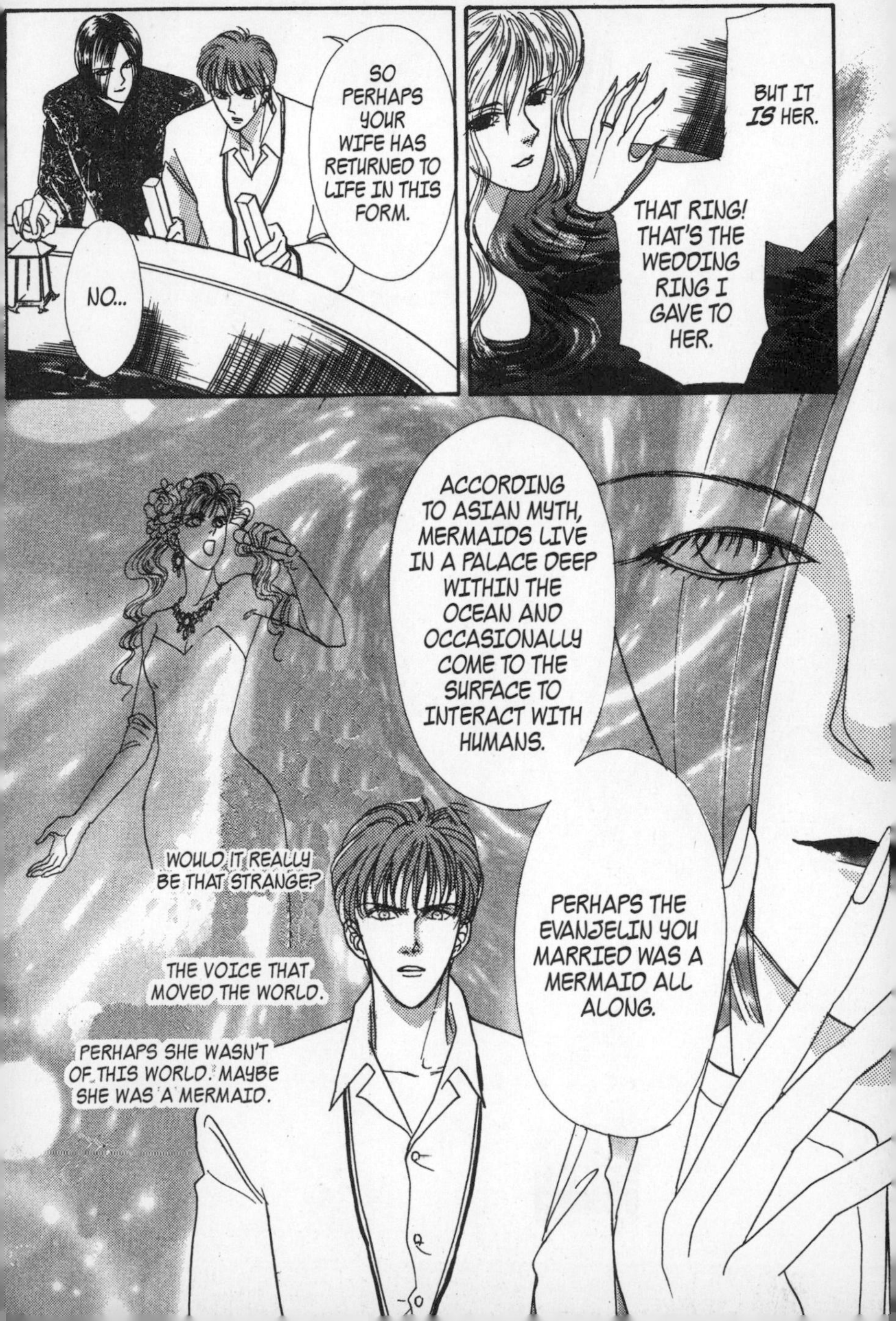
BUT IT *IS* HER.
THAT RING! THAT'S THE WEDDING RING I GAVE TO HER.
SO PERHAPS YOUR WIFE HAS RETURNED TO LIFE IN THIS FORM.
NO...
ACCORDING TO ASIAN MYTH, MERMAIDS LIVE IN A PALACE DEEP WITHIN THE OCEAN AND OCCASIONALLY COME TO THE SURFACE TO INTERACT WITH HUMANS.
PERHAPS THE EVANJELIN YOU MARRIED WAS A MERMAID ALL ALONG.
WOULD IT REALLY BE THAT STRANGE?
THE VOICE THAT MOVED THE WORLD.
PERHAPS SHE WASN'T OF THIS WORLD. MAYBE SHE WAS A MERMAID.

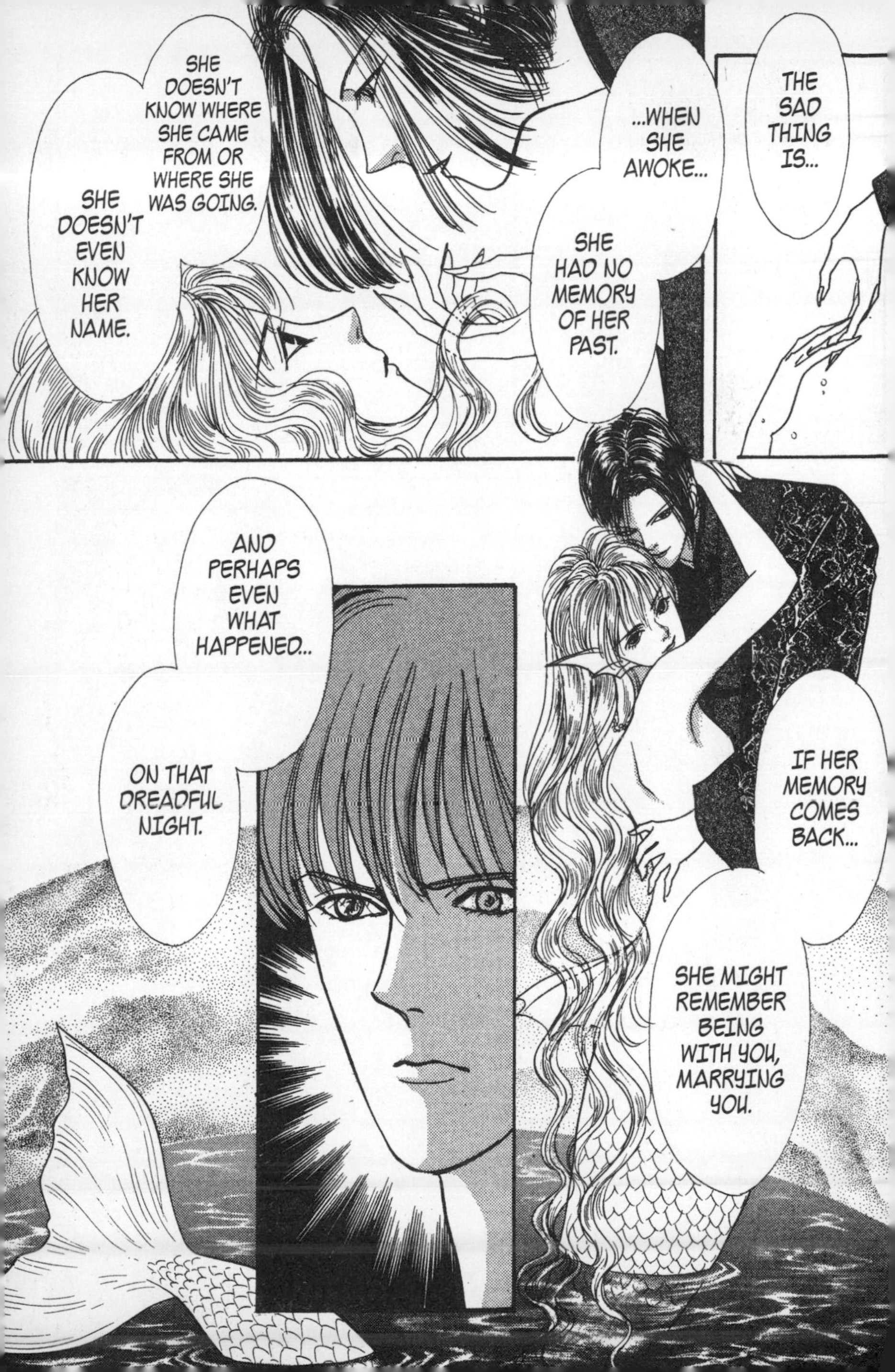
THE SAD THING IS...
...WHEN SHE AWOKE...
SHE HAD NO MEMORY OF HER PAST.
SHE DOESN'T KNOW WHERE SHE CAME FROM OR WHERE SHE WAS GOING.
SHE DOESN'T EVEN KNOW HER NAME.
IF HER MEMORY COMES BACK...
SHE MIGHT REMEMBER BEING WITH YOU, MARRYING YOU.
AND PERHAPS EVEN WHAT HAPPENED...
ON THAT DREADFUL NIGHT.

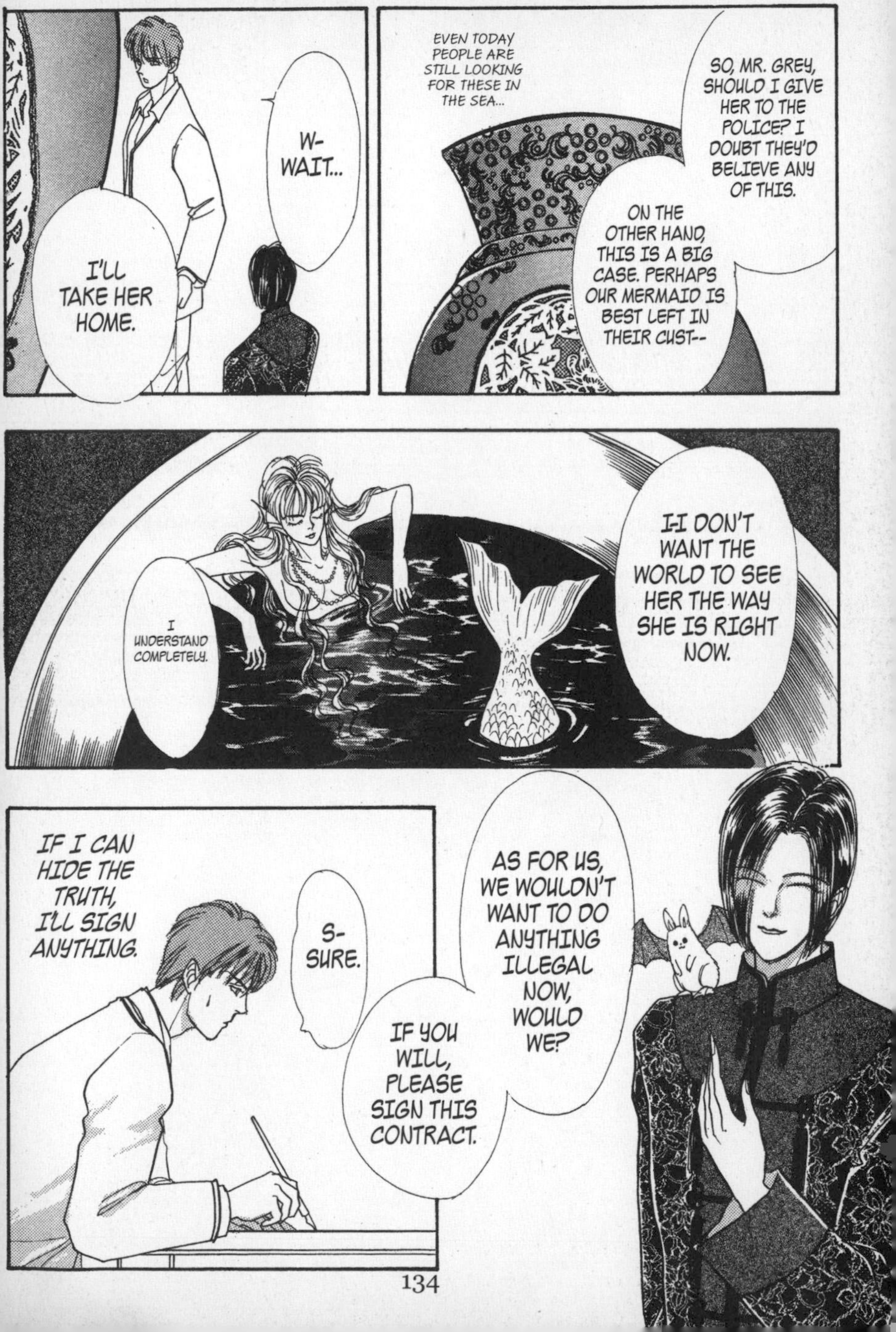
SO, MR. GREY, SHOULD I GIVE HER TO THE POLICE? I DOUBT THEY'D BELIEVE ANY OF THIS.
EVEN TODAY PEOPLE ARE STILL LOOKING FOR THESE IN THE SEA...
ON THE OTHER HAND, THIS IS A BIG CASE. PERHAPS OUR MERMAID IS BEST LEFT IN THEIR CUST--
W-WAIT...
I'LL TAKE HER HOME.
I-I DON'T WANT THE WORLD TO SEE HER THE WAY SHE IS RIGHT NOW.
I UNDERSTAND COMPLETELY.
AS FOR US, WE WOULDN'T WANT TO DO ANYTHING ILLEGAL NOW, WOULD WE?
IF YOU WILL, PLEASE SIGN THIS CONTRACT.
S-SURE.
IF I CAN HIDE THE TRUTH, I'LL SIGN ANYTHING.

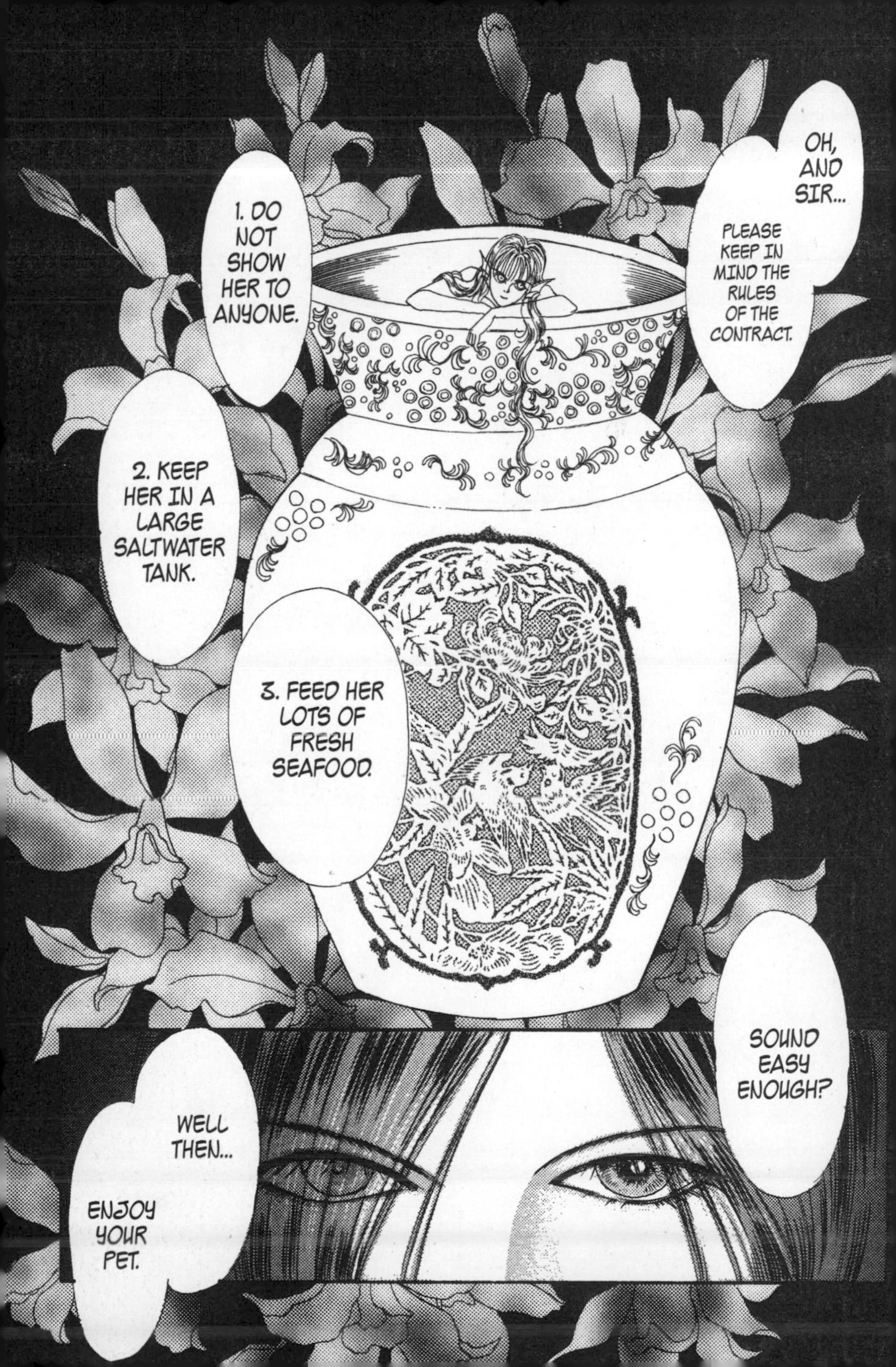
OH, AND SIR...
PLEASE KEEP IN MIND THE RULES OF THE CONTRACT.
1. DO NOT SHOW HER TO ANYONE.
2. KEEP HER IN A LARGE SALTWATER TANK.
3. FEED HER LOTS OF FRESH SEAFOOD.
SOUND EASY ENOUGH?
WELL THEN...
ENJOY YOUR PET.

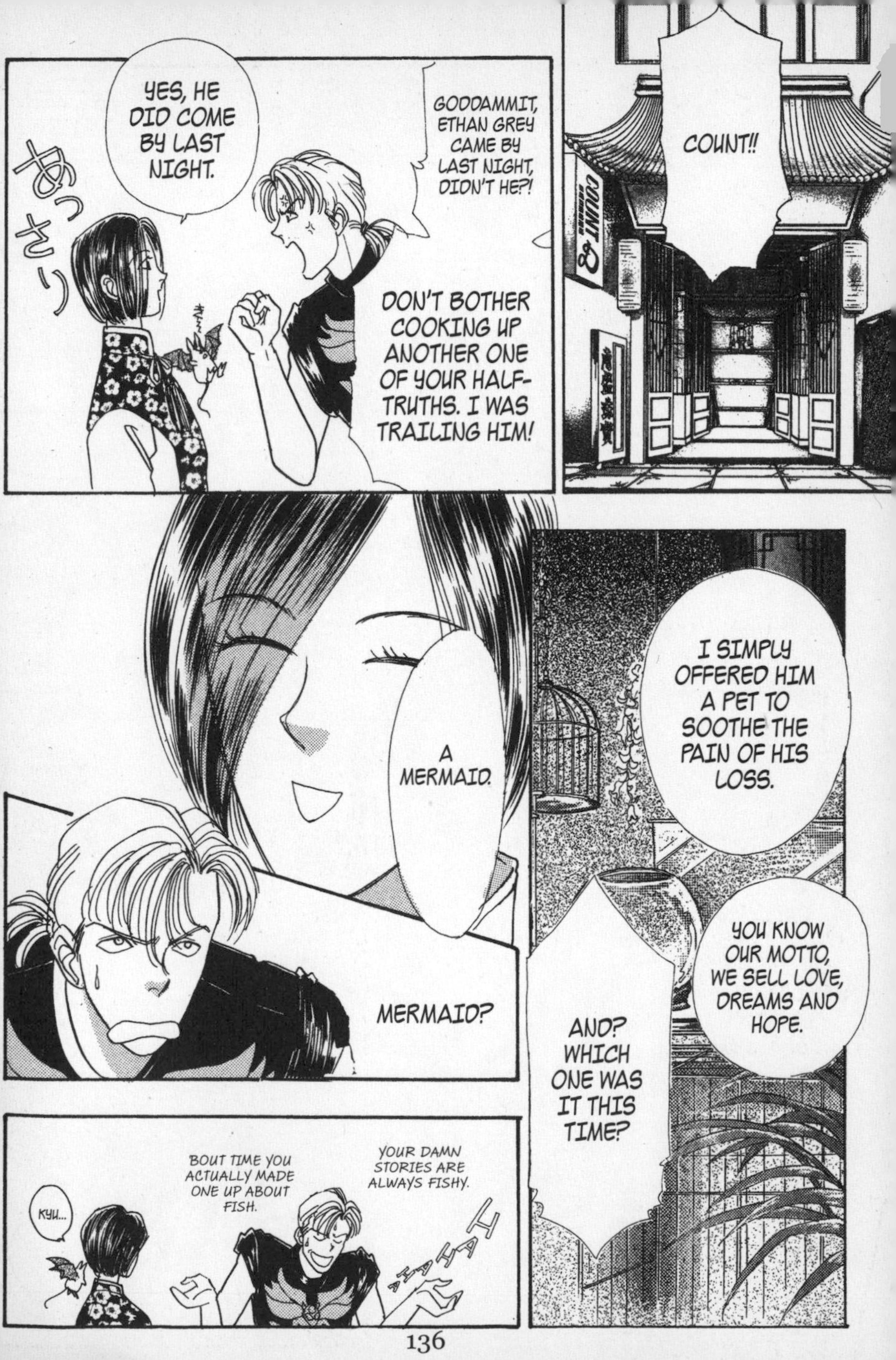
COUNT!!
GODDAMMIT, ETHAN GREY CAME BY LAST NIGHT, DIDN'T HE?!
YES, HE DID COME BY LAST NIGHT.
あっさり
DON'T BOTHER COOKING UP ANOTHER ONE OF YOUR HALF-TRUTHS. I WAS TRAILING HIM!
I SIMPLY OFFERED HIM A PET TO SOOTHE THE PAIN OF HIS LOSS.
YOU KNOW OUR MOTTO, WE SELL LOVE, DREAMS AND HOPE.
AND? WHICH ONE WAS IT THIS TIME?
A MERMAID.
MERMAID?
YOUR DAMN STORIES ARE ALWAYS FISHY.
BOUT TIME YOU ACTUALLY MADE ONE UP ABOUT FISH.
KYU...

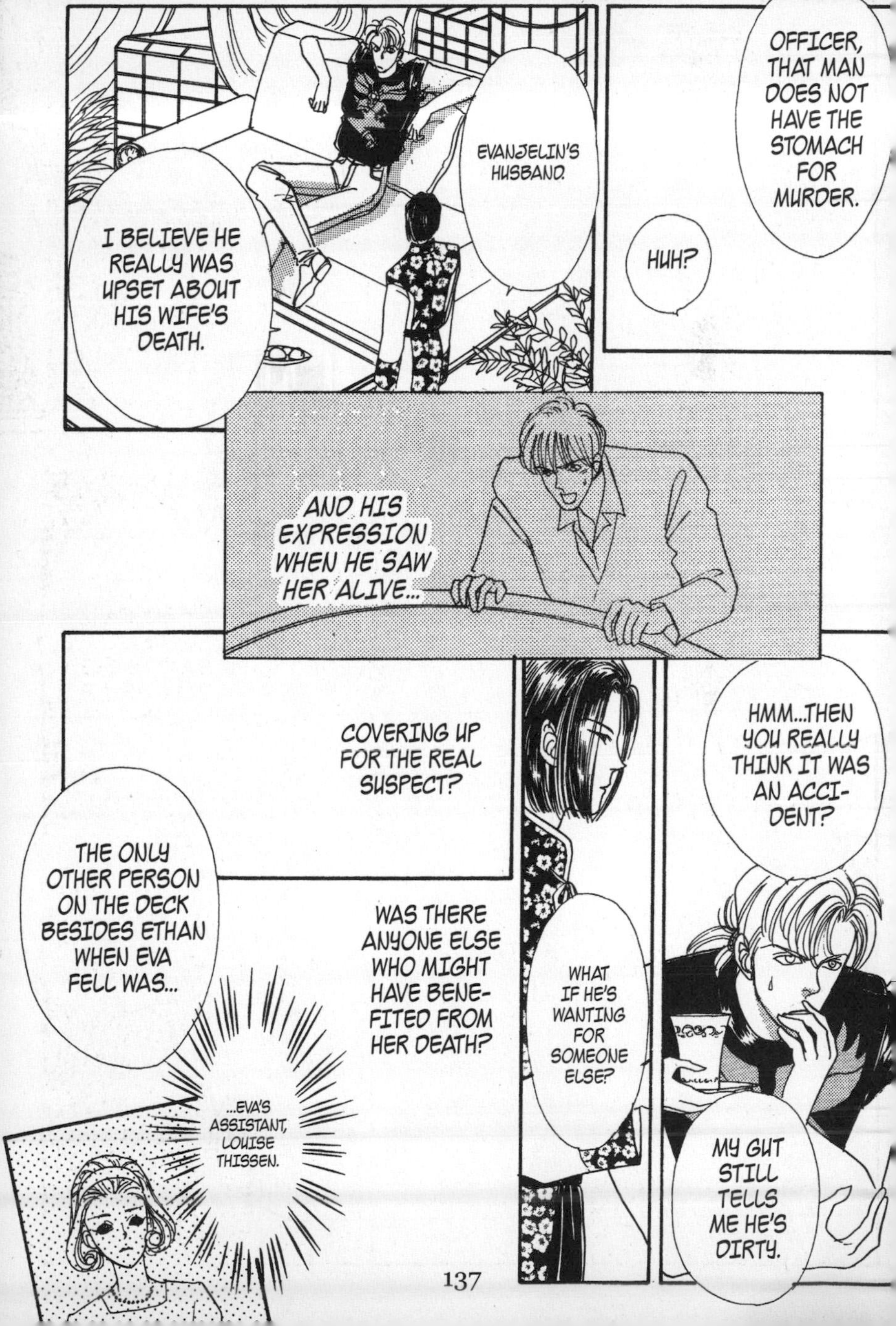
OFFICER, THAT MAN DOES NOT HAVE THE STOMACH FOR MURDER.
HUH?
EVANJELIN'S HUSBAND.
I BELIEVE HE REALLY WAS UPSET ABOUT HIS WIFE'S DEATH.
AND HIS EXPRESSION WHEN HE SAW HER ALIVE...
HMM...THEN YOU REALLY THINK IT WAS AN ACCI-DENT?
MY GUT STILL TELLS ME HE'S DIRTY.
WHAT IF HE'S WANTING FOR SOMEONE ELSE?
COVERING UP FOR THE REAL SUSPECT?
WAS THERE ANYONE ELSE WHO MIGHT HAVE BENE-FITED FROM HER DEATH?
THE ONLY OTHER PERSON ON THE DECK BESIDES ETHAN WHEN EVA FELL WAS...
...EVA'S ASSISTANT, LOUISE THISSEN.

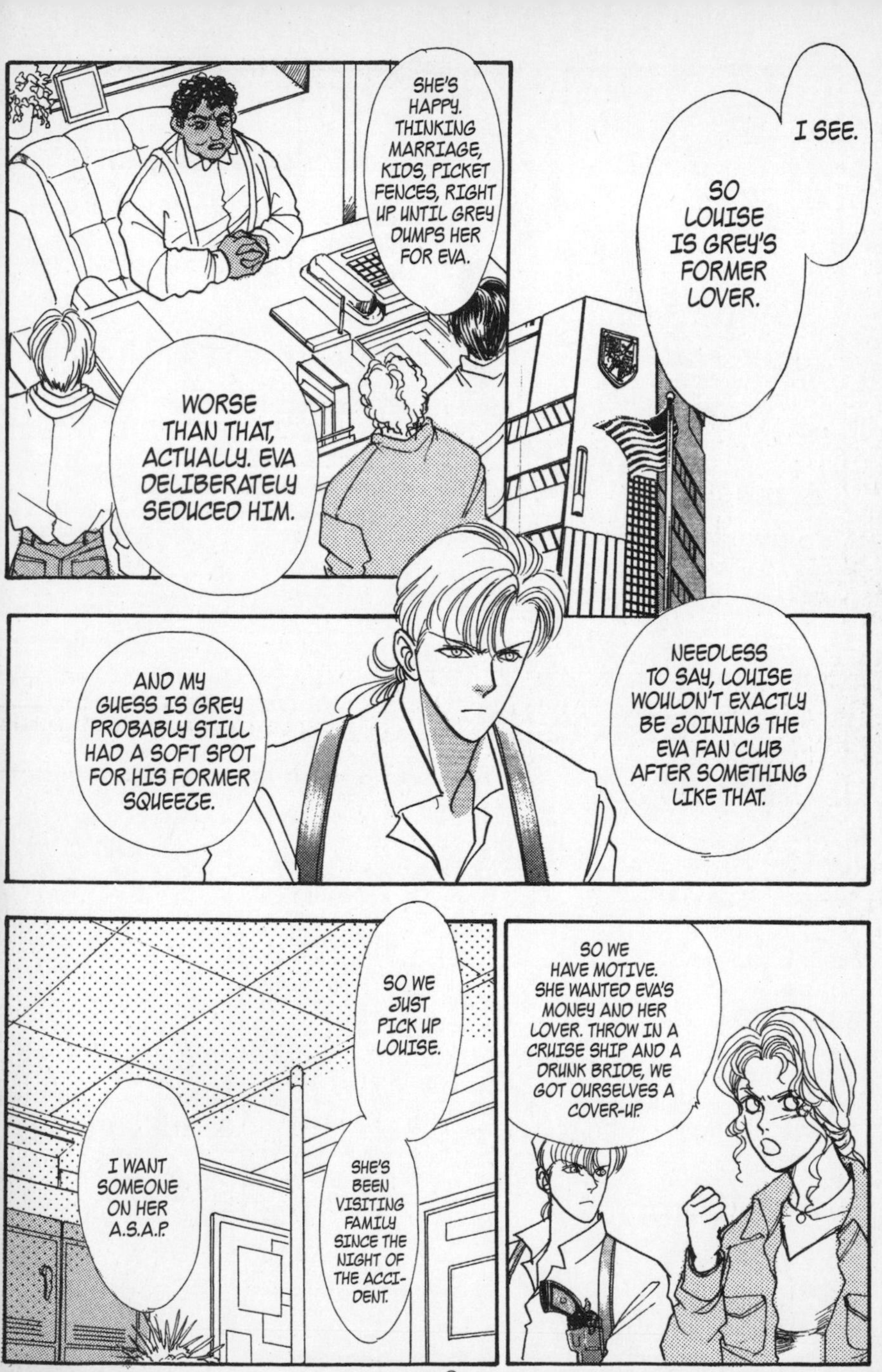
I SEE.
SO LOUISE IS GREY'S FORMER LOVER.
SHE'S HAPPY. THINKING MARRIAGE, KIDS, PICKET FENCES, RIGHT UP UNTIL GREY DUMPS HER FOR EVA.
WORSE THAN THAT, ACTUALLY. EVA DELIBERATELY SEDUCED HIM.
NEEDLESS TO SAY, LOUISE WOULDN'T EXACTLY BE JOINING THE EVA FAN CLUB AFTER SOMETHING LIKE THAT.
AND MY GUESS IS GREY PROBABLY STILL HAD A SOFT SPOT FOR HIS FORMER SQUEEZE.
SO WE HAVE MOTIVE. SHE WANTED EVA'S MONEY AND HER LOVER. THROW IN A CRUISE SHIP AND A DRUNK BRIDE, WE GOT OURSELVES A COVER-UP.
SO WE JUST PICK UP LOUISE.
SHE'S BEEN VISITING FAMILY SINCE THE NIGHT OF THE ACCI-DENT.
I WANT SOMEONE ON HER A.S.A.P.

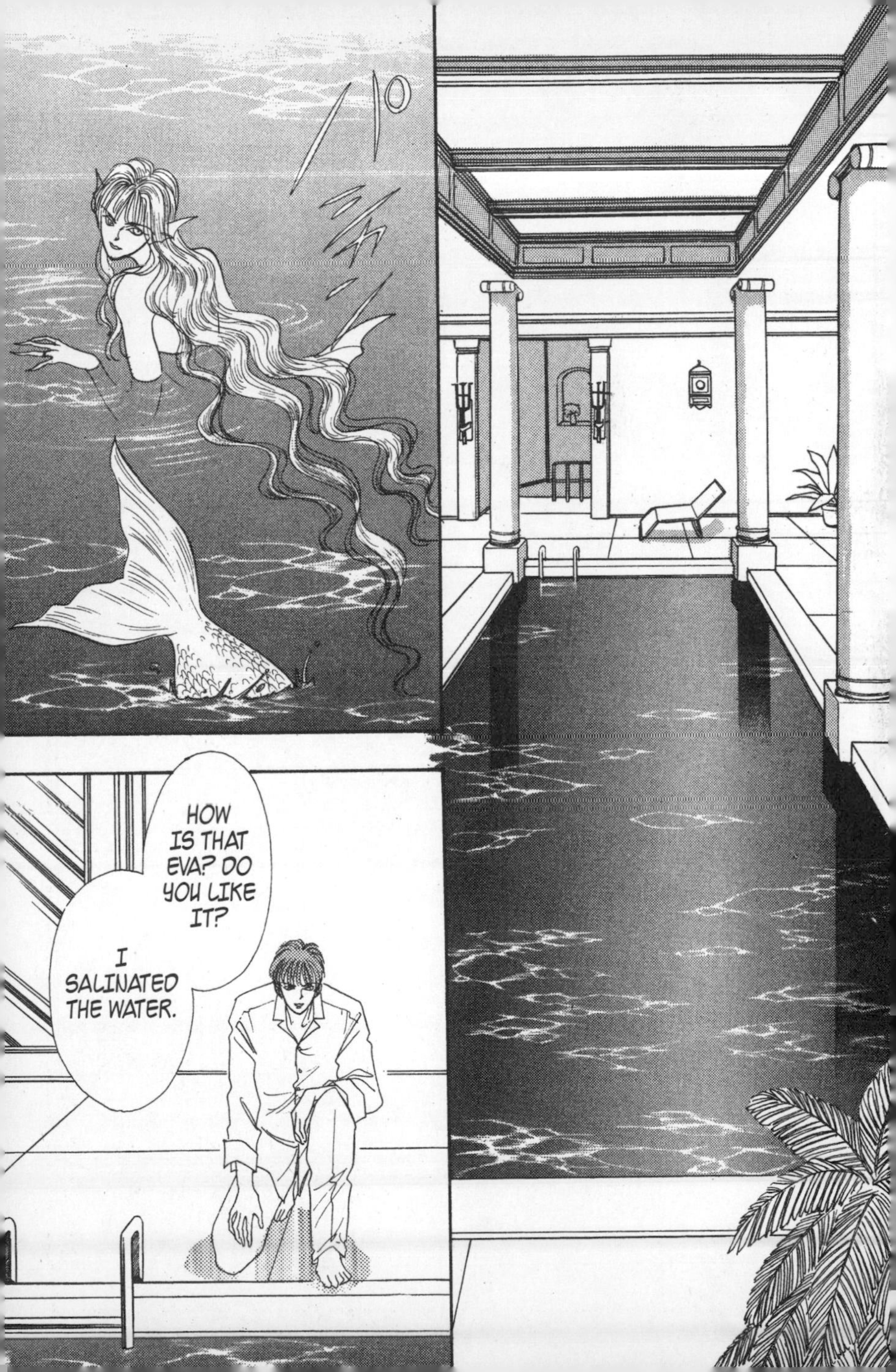
HOW IS THAT EVA? DO YOU LIKE IT?
I SALINATED THE WATER.

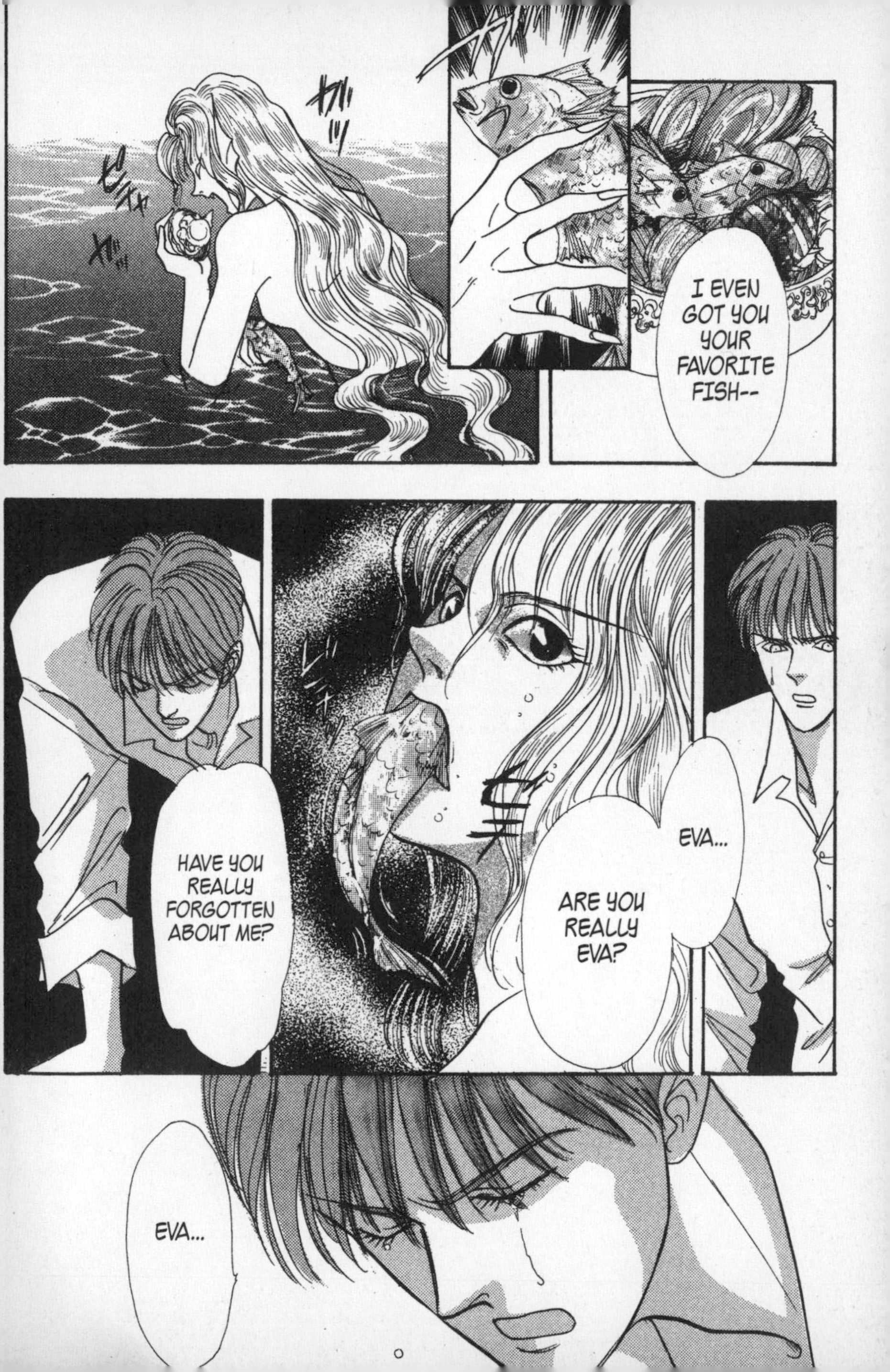
I EVEN GOT YOU YOUR FAVORITE FISH--
EVA...
ARE YOU REALLY EVA?
HAVE YOU REALLY FORGOTTEN ABOUT ME?
EVA...

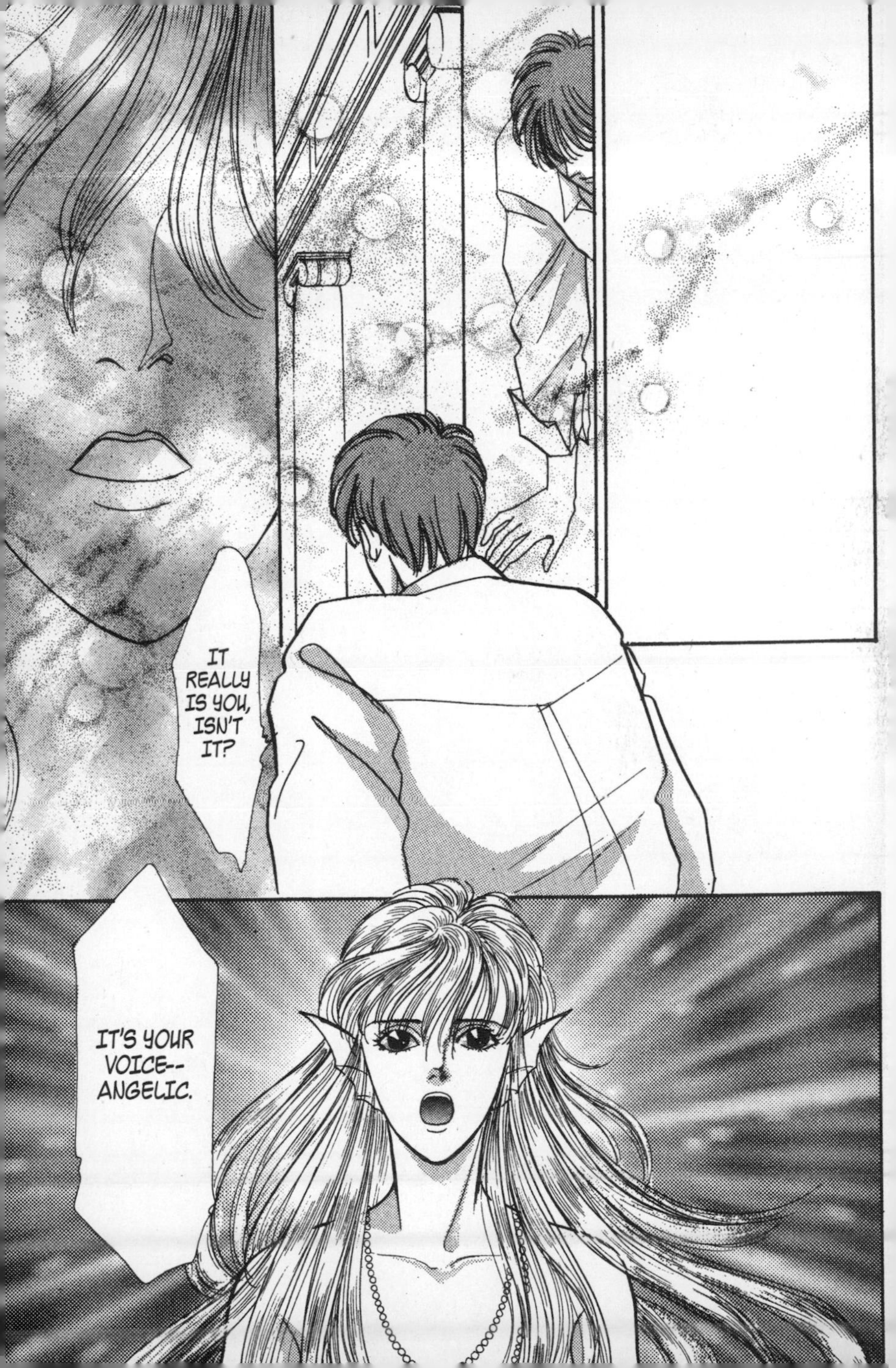
IT REALLY IS YOU, ISN'T IT?
IT'S YOUR VOICE--ANGELIC.

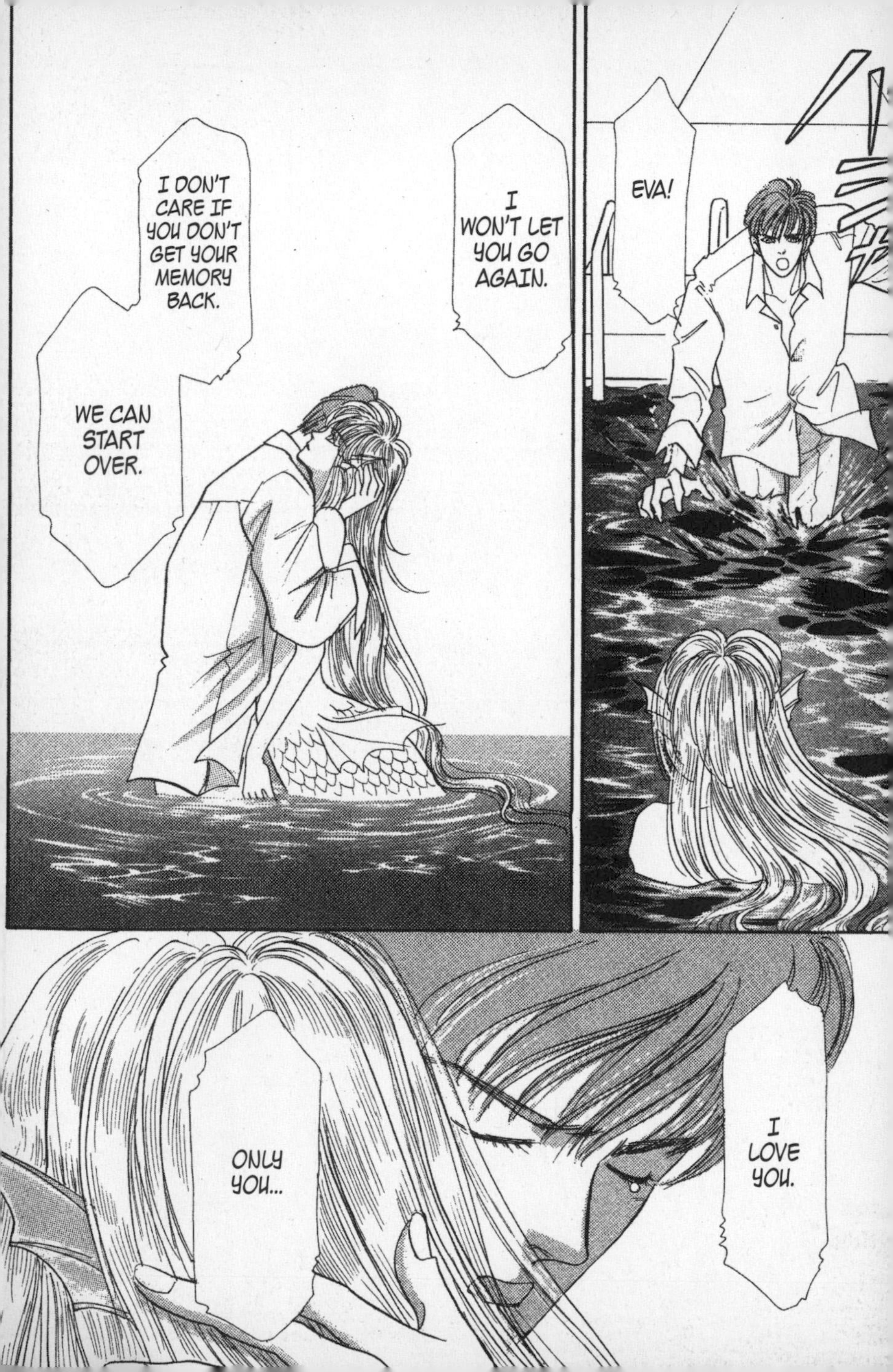
EVA!
I WON'T LET YOU GO AGAIN.
I DON'T CARE IF YOU DON'T GET YOUR MEMORY BACK.
WE CAN START OVER.
I LOVE YOU.
ONLY YOU...

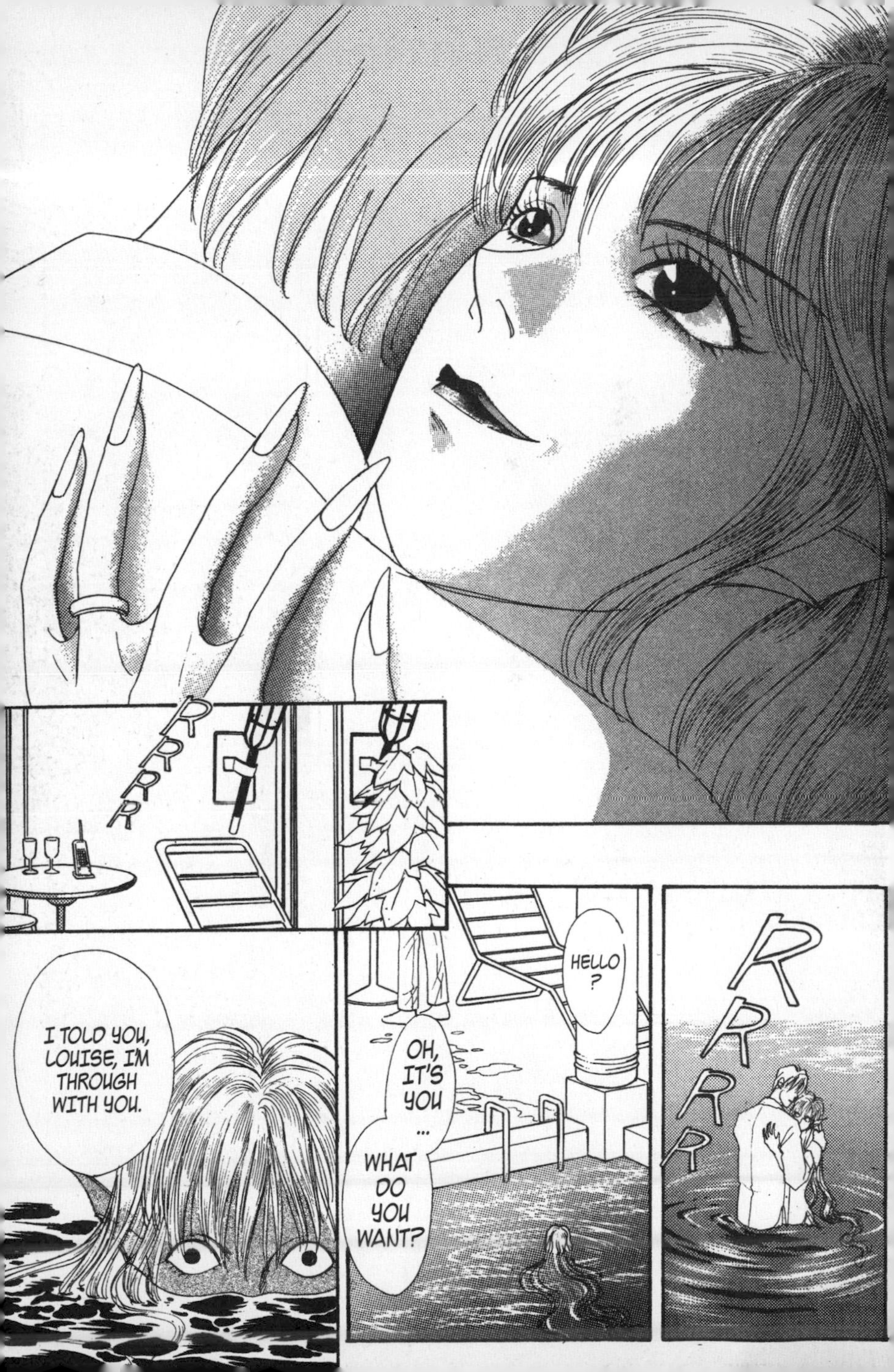
RRRRR
RRRRR
HELLO?
OH, IT'S YOU ...
WHAT DO YOU WANT?
I TOLD YOU, LOUISE, I'M THROUGH WITH YOU.

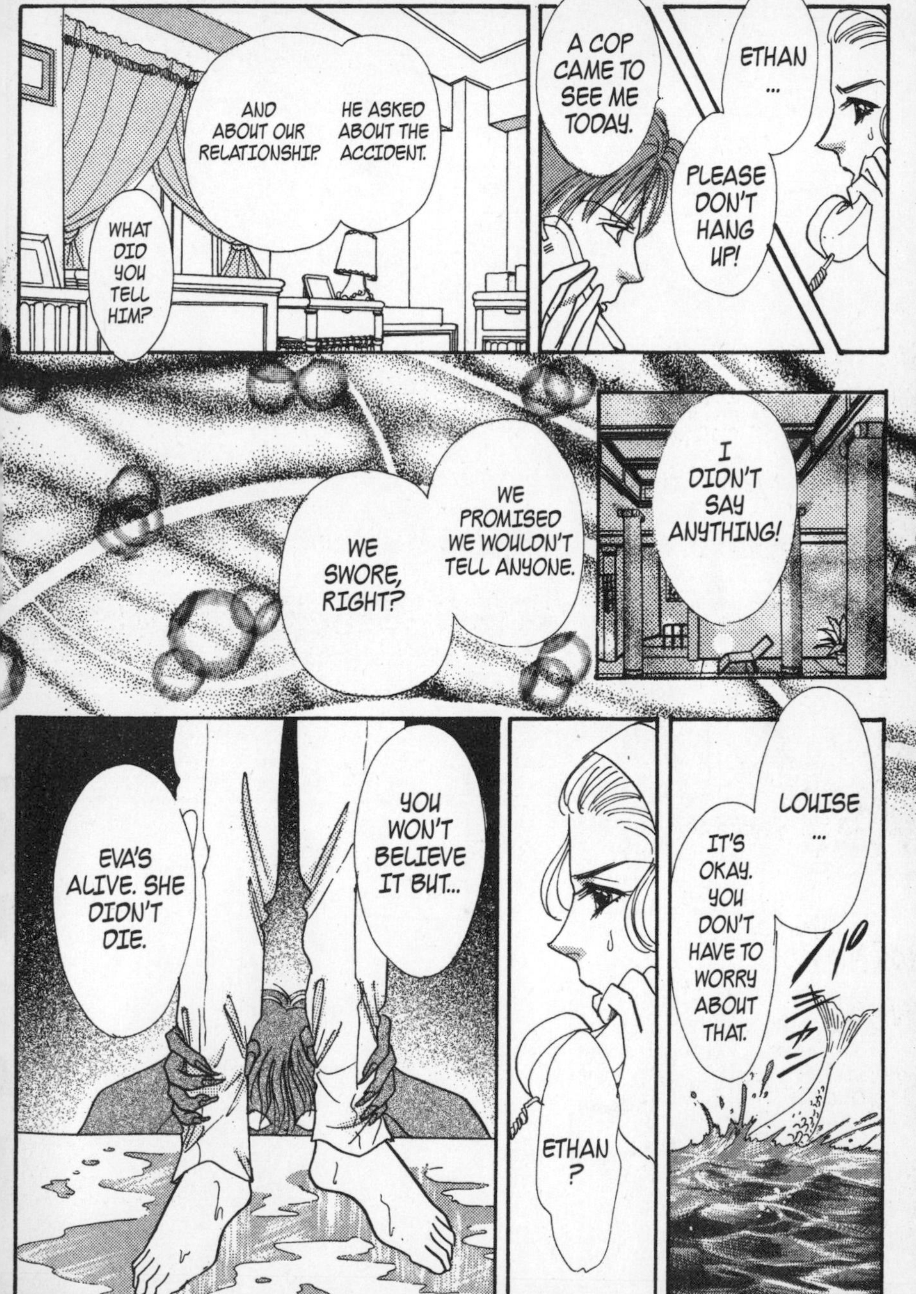
ETHAN ...
PLEASE DON'T HANG UP!
A COP CAME TO SEE ME TODAY.
HE ASKED ABOUT THE ACCIDENT.
AND ABOUT OUR RELATIONSHIP.
WHAT DID YOU TELL HIM?
I DIDN'T SAY ANYTHING!
WE PROMISED WE WOULDN'T TELL ANYONE.
WE SWORE, RIGHT?
LOUISE ...
IT'S OKAY. YOU DON'T HAVE TO WORRY ABOUT THAT.
ETHAN ?
YOU WON'T BELIEVE IT BUT...
EVA'S ALIVE. SHE DIDN'T DIE.

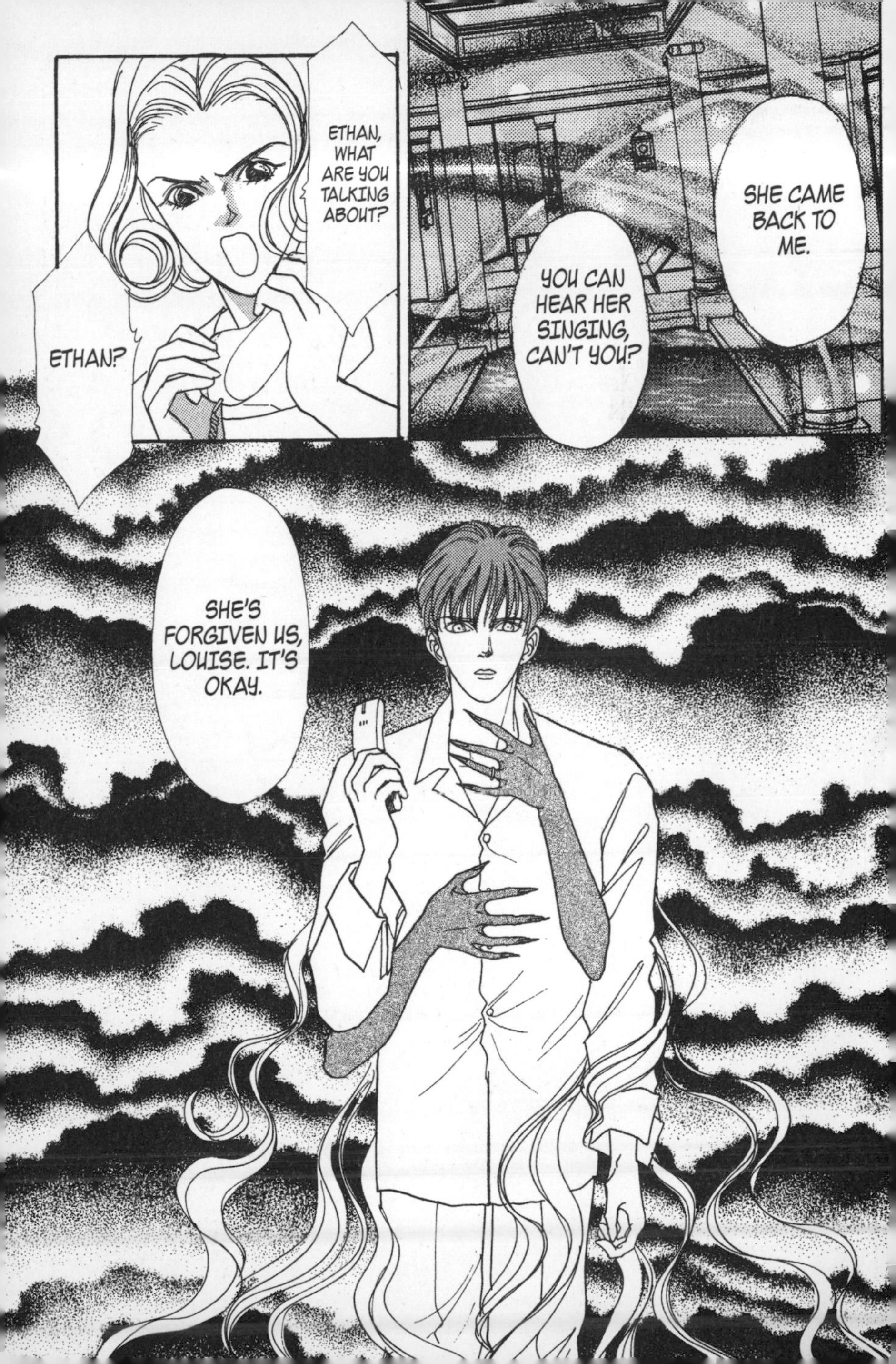
SHE CAME BACK TO ME.
YOU CAN HEAR HER SINGING, CAN'T YOU?
ETHAN, WHAT ARE YOU TALKING ABOUT?
ETHAN?
SHE'S FORGIVEN US, LOUISE. IT'S OKAY.

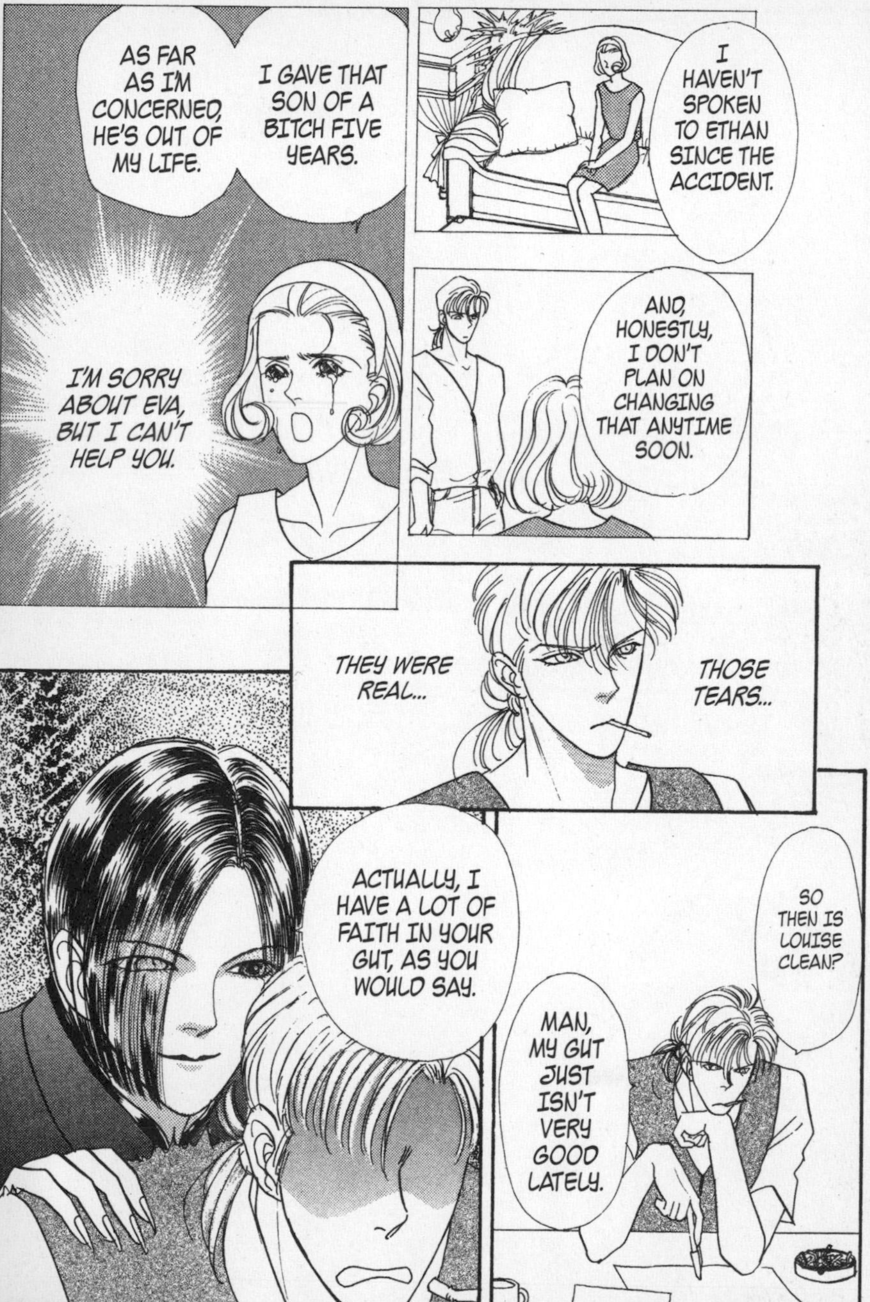
I HAVEN'T SPOKEN TO ETHAN SINCE THE ACCIDENT.
AND, HONESTLY, I DON'T PLAN ON CHANGING THAT ANYTIME SOON.
I GAVE THAT SON OF A BITCH FIVE YEARS.
AS FAR AS I'M CONCERNED, HE'S OUT OF MY LIFE.
I'M SORRY ABOUT EVA, BUT I CAN'T HELP YOU.
THOSE TEARS...
THEY WERE REAL...
SO THEN IS LOUISE CLEAN?
MAN, MY GUT JUST ISN'T VERY GOOD LATELY.
ACTUALLY, I HAVE A LOT OF FAITH IN YOUR GUT, AS YOU WOULD SAY.

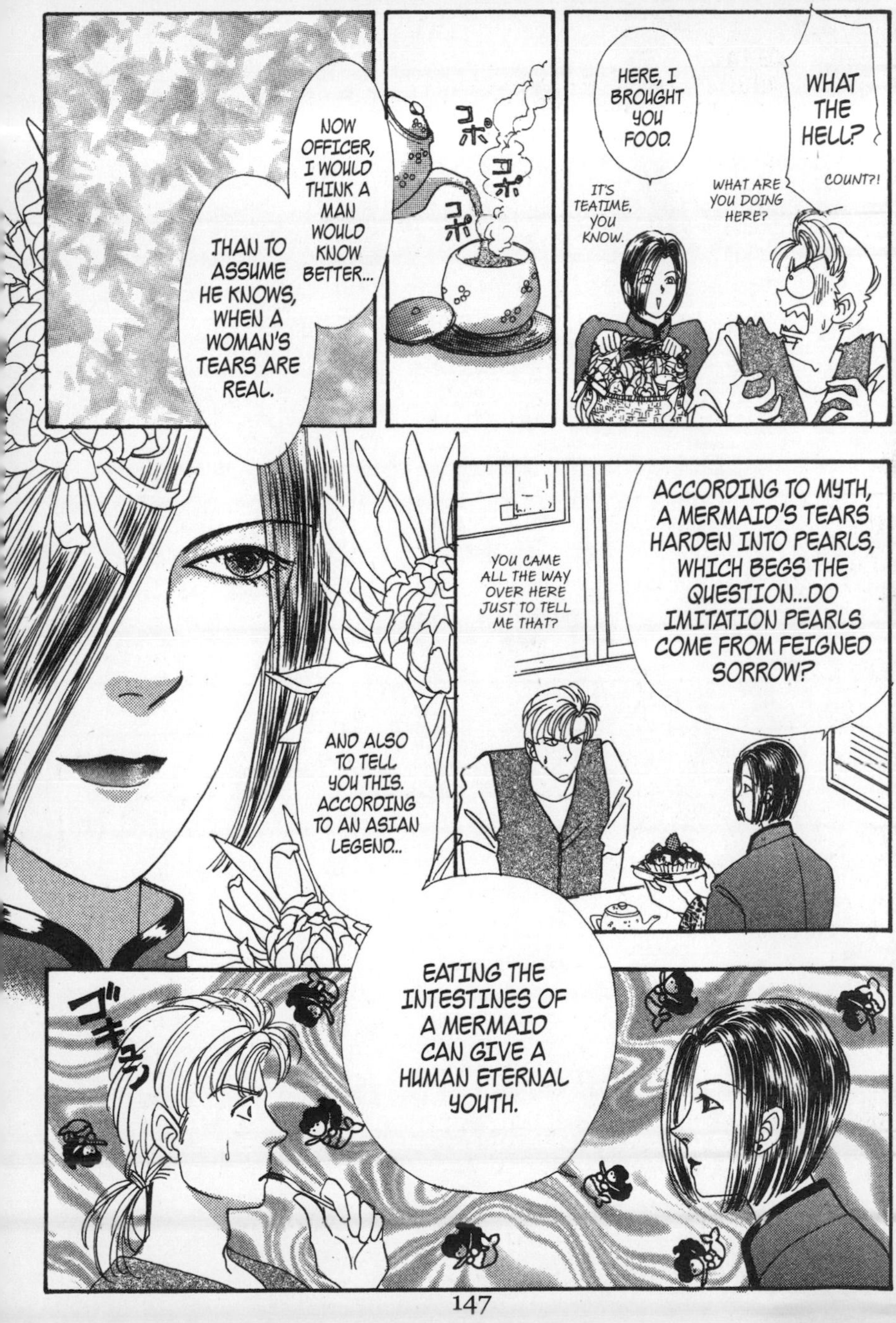
WHAT THE HELL?
COUNT?!
WHAT ARE YOU DOING HERE?
HERE, I BROUGHT YOU FOOD.
IT'S TEATIME, YOU KNOW.
コポ
コポ
コポ
NOW OFFICER, I WOULD THINK A MAN WOULD KNOW BETTER...
THAN TO ASSUME HE KNOWS, WHEN A WOMAN'S TEARS ARE REAL.
ACCORDING TO MYTH, A MERMAID'S TEARS HARDEN INTO PEARLS, WHICH BEGS THE QUESTION...DO IMITATION PEARLS COME FROM FEIGNED SORROW?
YOU CAME ALL THE WAY OVER HERE JUST TO TELL ME THAT?
AND ALSO TO TELL YOU THIS. ACCORDING TO AN ASIAN LEGEND...
EATING THE INTESTINES OF A MERMAID CAN GIVE A HUMAN ETERNAL YOUTH.

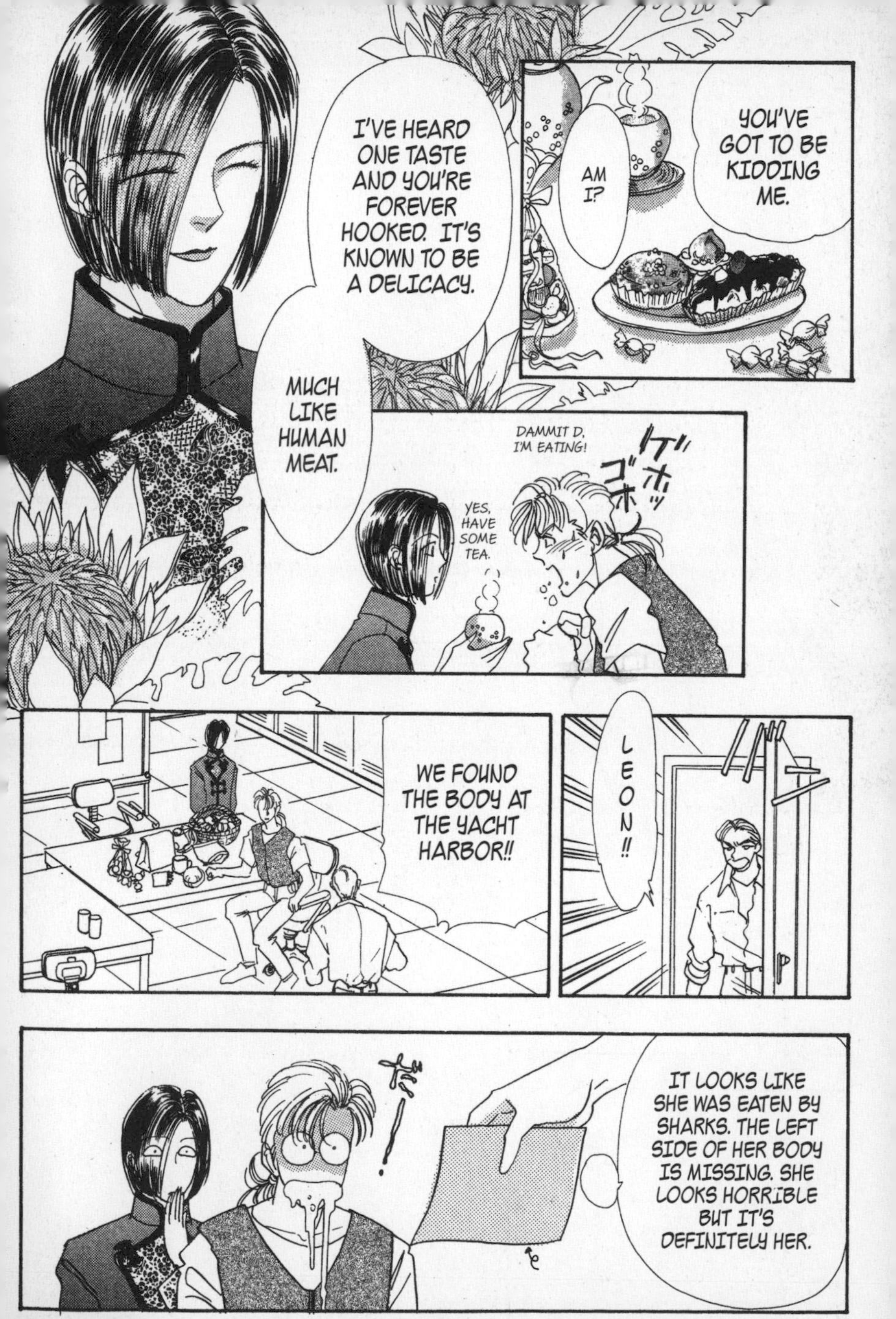

YOU'VE GOT TO BE KIDDING ME.
AM I?
I'VE HEARD ONE TASTE AND YOU'RE FOREVER HOOKED. IT'S KNOWN TO BE A DELICACY.
MUCH LIKE HUMAN MEAT.
DAMMIT D, I'M EATING!
ゲホッ ゴホッ
YES, HAVE SOME TEA.
LEON!!
WE FOUND THE BODY AT THE YACHT HARBOR!!
IT LOOKS LIKE SHE WAS EATEN BY SHARKS. THE LEFT SIDE OF HER BODY IS MISSING. SHE LOOKS HORRIBLE BUT IT'S DEFINITELY HER.

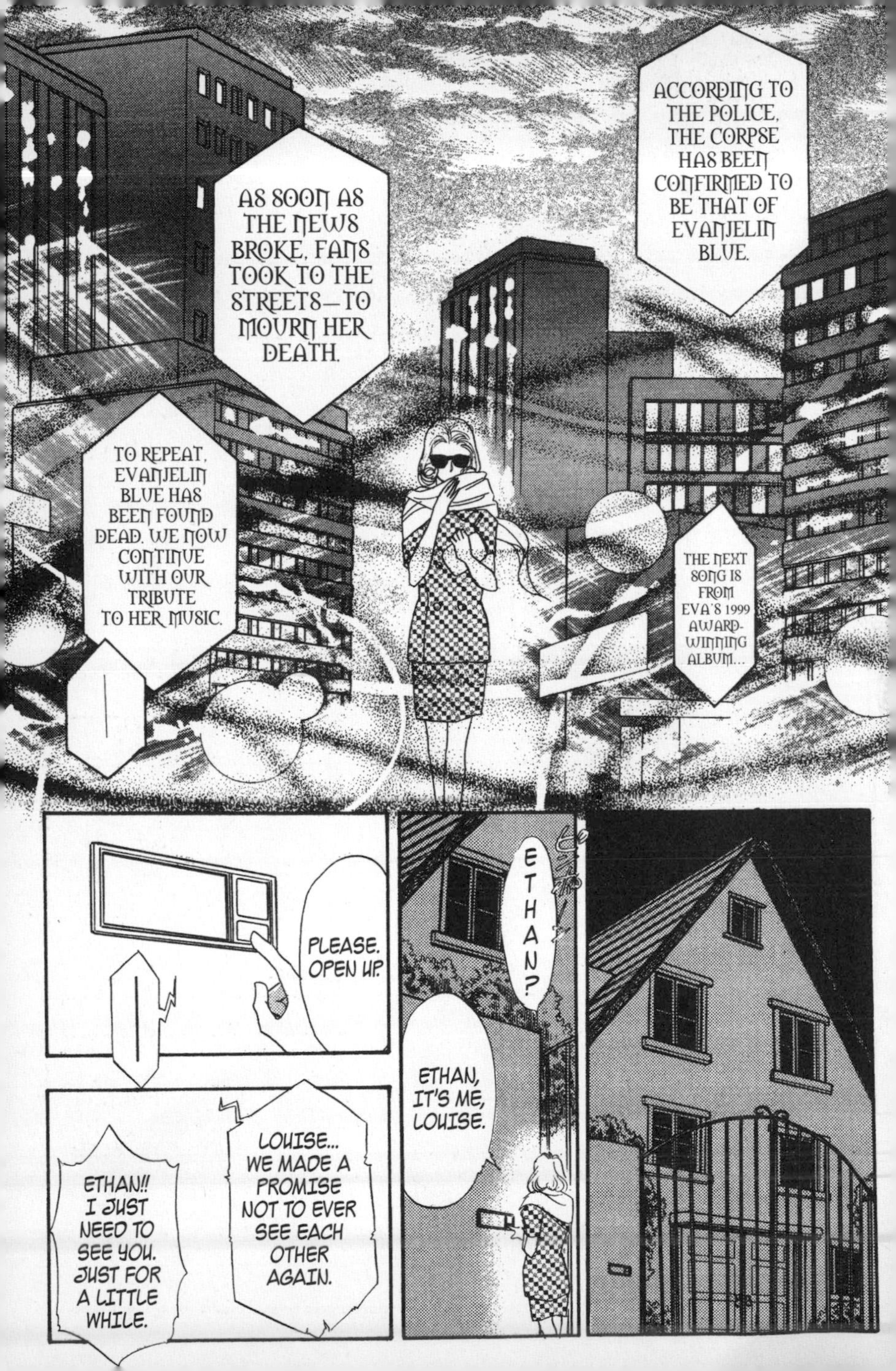
ACCORDING TO THE POLICE, THE CORPSE HAS BEEN CONFIRMED TO BE THAT OF EVANJELIN BLUE.
AS SOON AS THE NEWS BROKE, FANS TOOK TO THE STREETS—TO MOURN HER DEATH.
THE NEXT SONG IS FROM EVA'S 1999 AWARD-WINNING ALBUM...
TO REPEAT, EVANJELIN BLUE HAS BEEN FOUND DEAD. WE NOW CONTINUE WITH OUR TRIBUTE TO HER MUSIC.
ETHAN?
ETHAN, IT'S ME, LOUISE.
PLEASE. OPEN UP.
LOUISE... WE MADE A PROMISE NOT TO EVER SEE EACH OTHER AGAIN.
ETHAN!! I JUST NEED TO SEE YOU. JUST FOR A LITTLE WHILE.

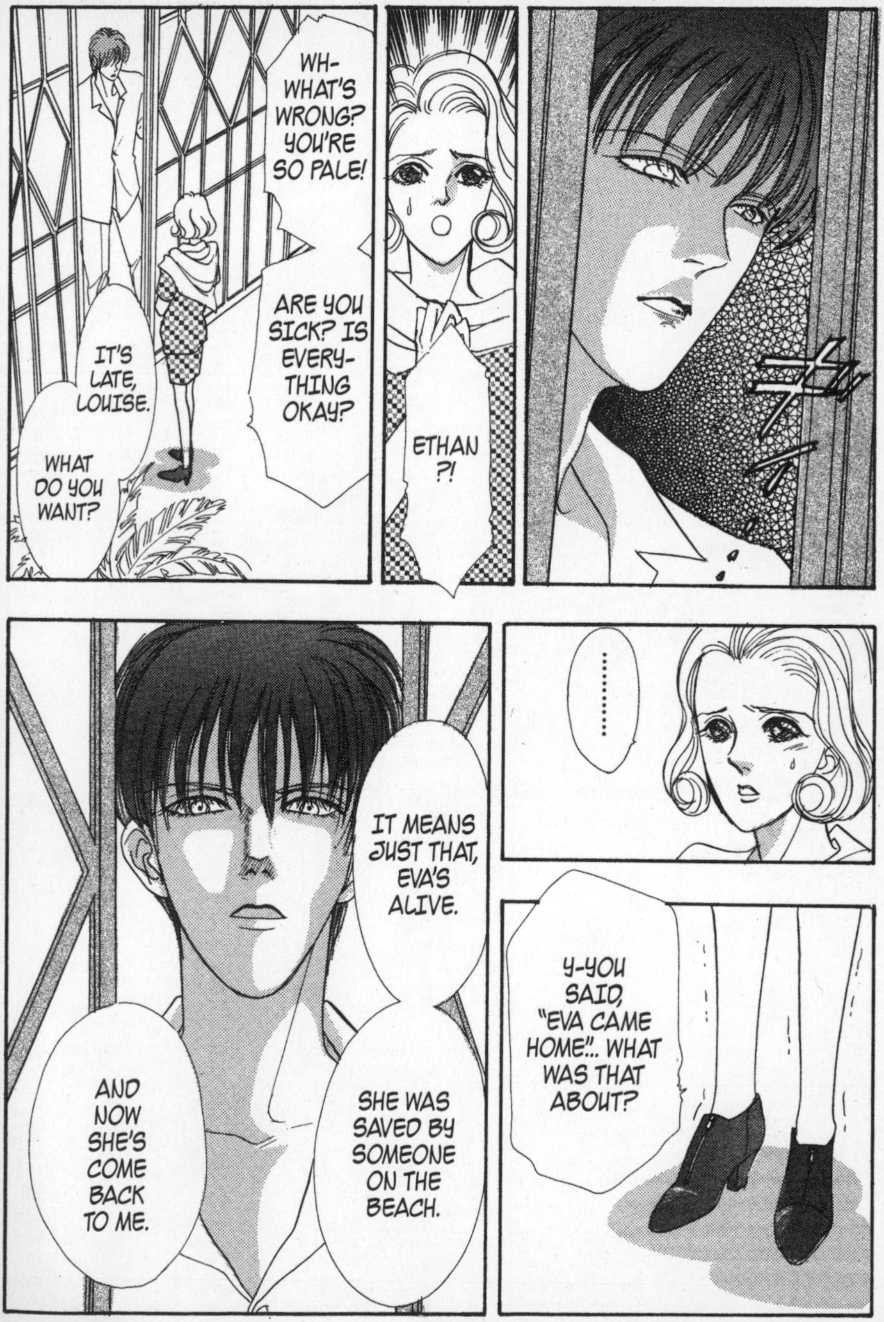
WH-WHAT'S WRONG? YOU'RE SO PALE!
ARE YOU SICK? IS EVERYTHING OKAY?
ETHAN ?!
IT'S LATE, LOUISE.
WHAT DO YOU WANT?
......
Y-YOU SAID, "EVA CAME HOME"... WHAT WAS THAT ABOUT?
IT MEANS JUST THAT, EVA'S ALIVE.
SHE WAS SAVED BY SOMEONE ON THE BEACH.
AND NOW SHE'S COME BACK TO ME.

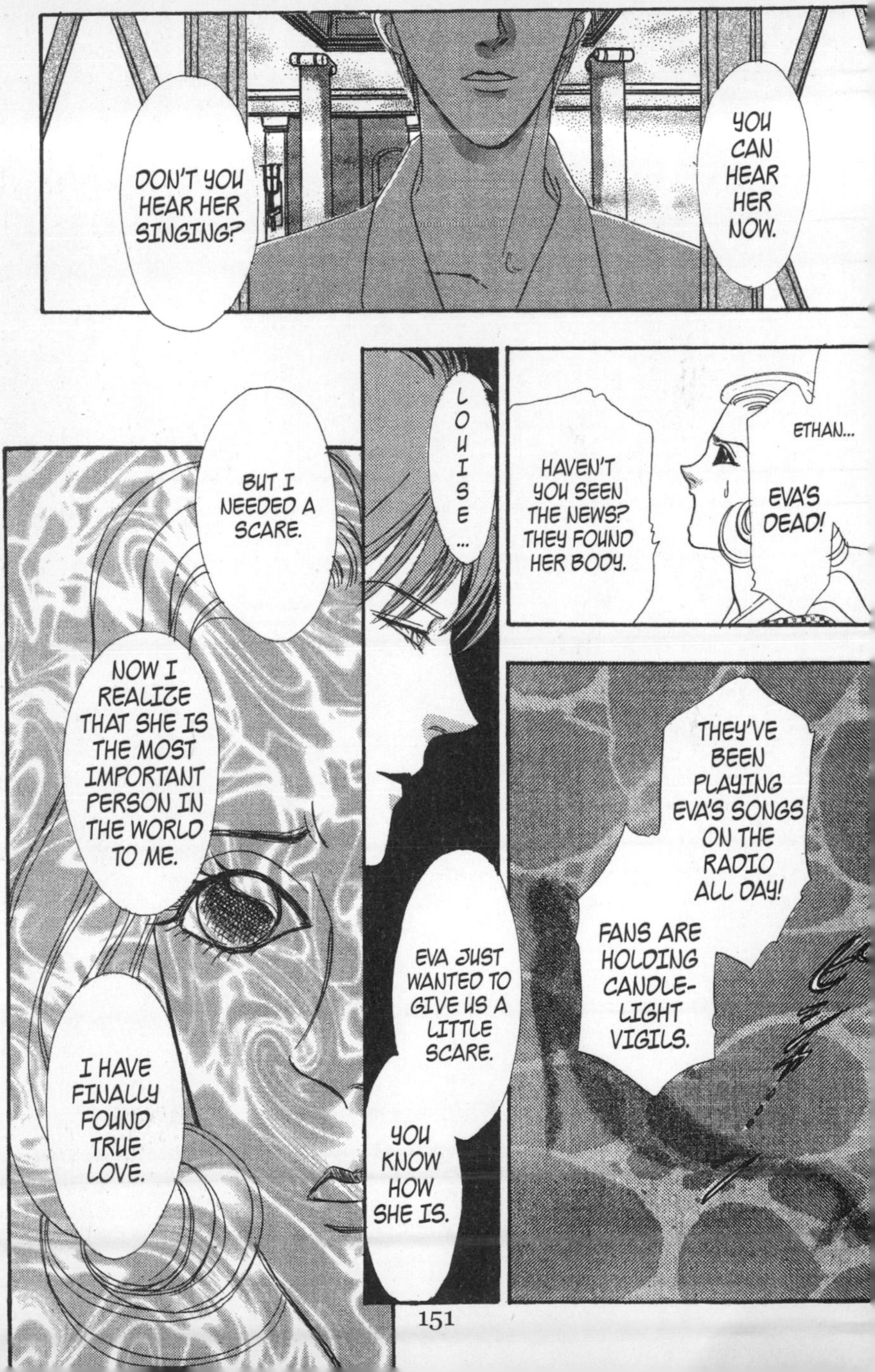
YOU CAN HEAR HER NOW.
DON'T YOU HEAR HER SINGING?
ETHAN...
EVA'S DEAD!
HAVEN'T YOU SEEN THE NEWS? THEY FOUND HER BODY.
THEY'VE BEEN PLAYING EVA'S SONGS ON THE RADIO ALL DAY!
FANS ARE HOLDING CANDLE-LIGHT VIGILS.
LOUISE...
EVA JUST WANTED TO GIVE US A LITTLE SCARE.
YOU KNOW HOW SHE IS.
BUT I NEEDED A SCARE.
NOW I REALIZE THAT SHE IS THE MOST IMPORTANT PERSON IN THE WORLD TO ME.
I HAVE FINALLY FOUND TRUE LOVE.

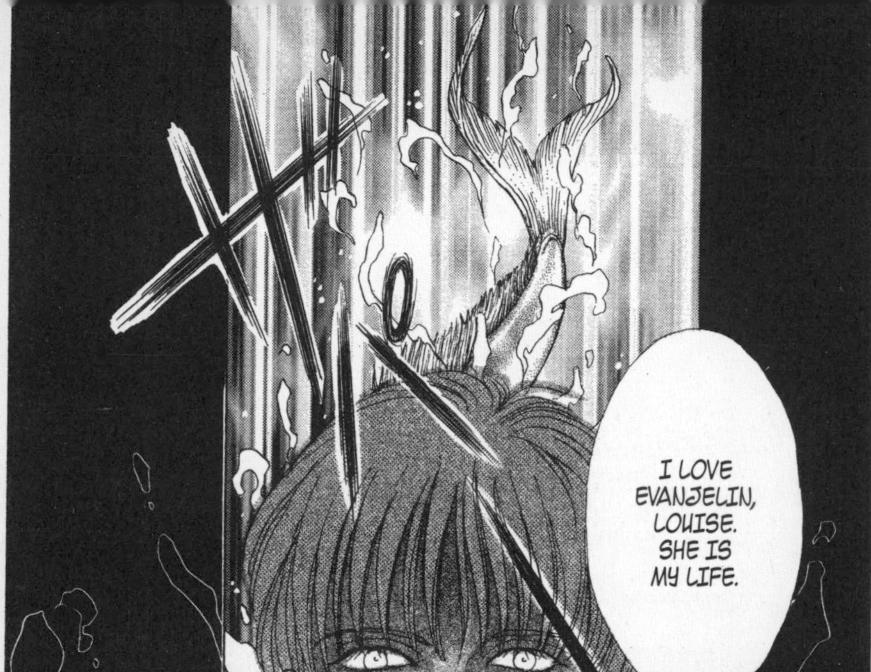
I LOVE EVANJELIN, LOUISE. SHE IS MY LIFE.
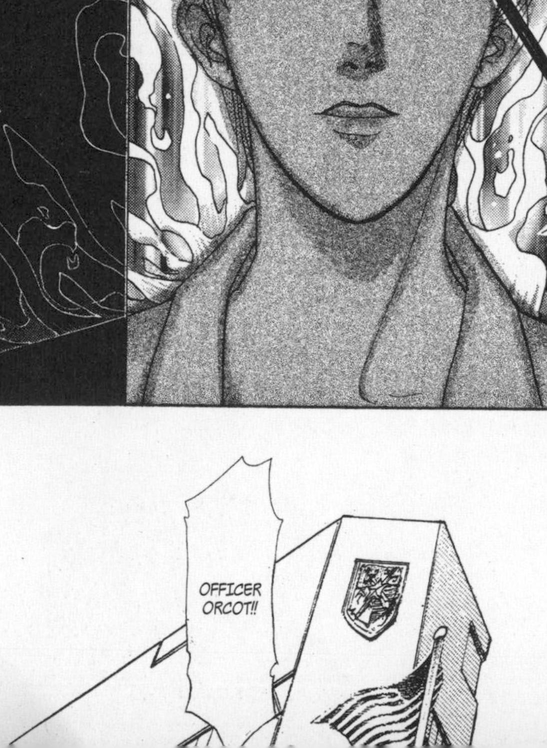
OFFICER ORCOT!!

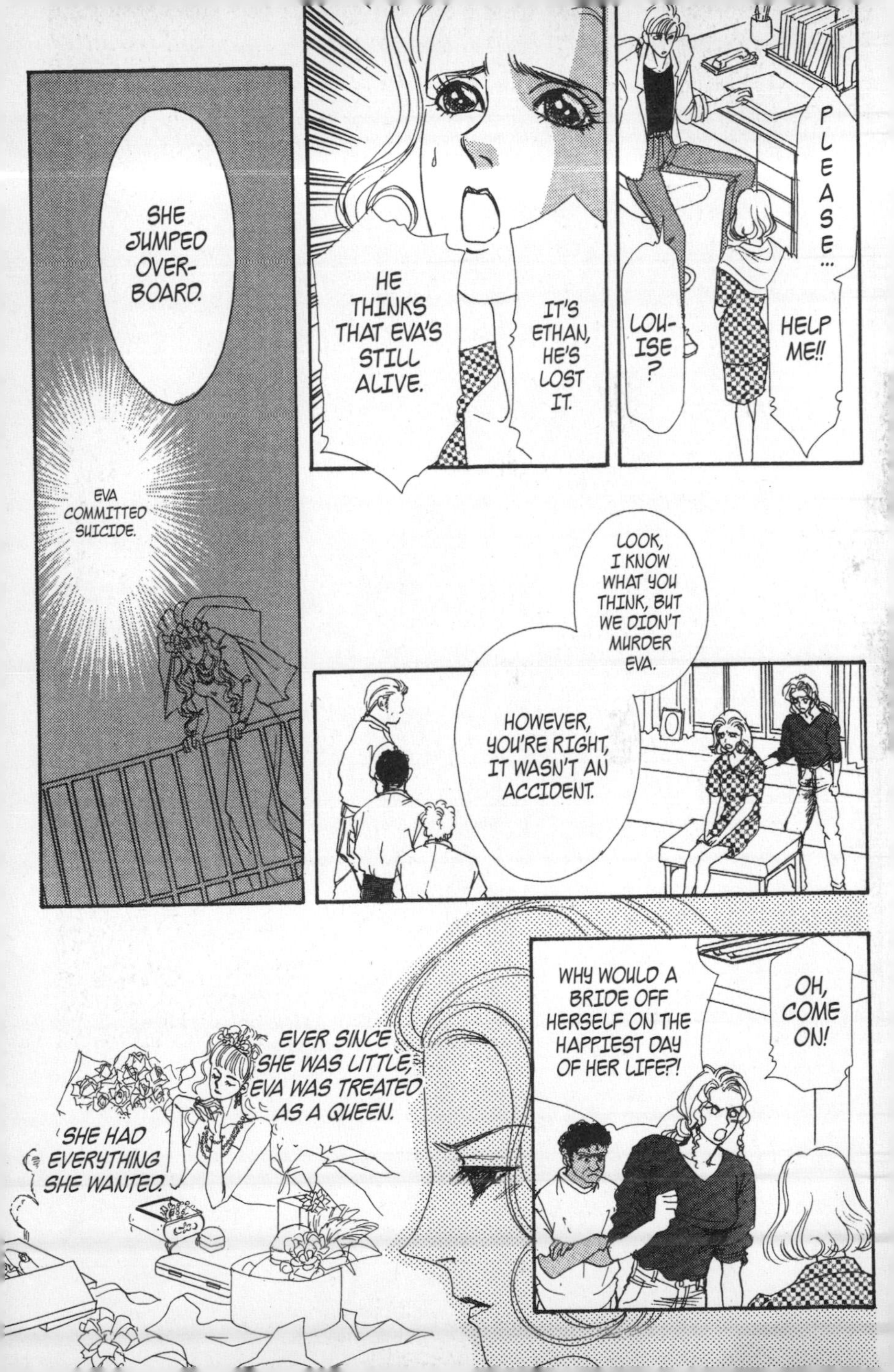
PLEASE...
HELP ME!!
LOU-ISE?
IT'S ETHAN, HE'S LOST IT.
HE THINKS THAT EVA'S STILL ALIVE.
LOOK, I KNOW WHAT YOU THINK, BUT WE DIDN'T MURDER EVA.
HOWEVER, YOU'RE RIGHT, IT WASN'T AN ACCIDENT.
SHE JUMPED OVER-BOARD.
EVA COMMITTED SUICIDE.
OH, COME ON!
WHY WOULD A BRIDE OFF HERSELF ON THE HAPPIEST DAY OF HER LIFE?!
EVER SINCE SHE WAS LITTLE, EVA WAS TREATED AS A QUEEN.
SHE HAD EVERYTHING SHE WANTED.

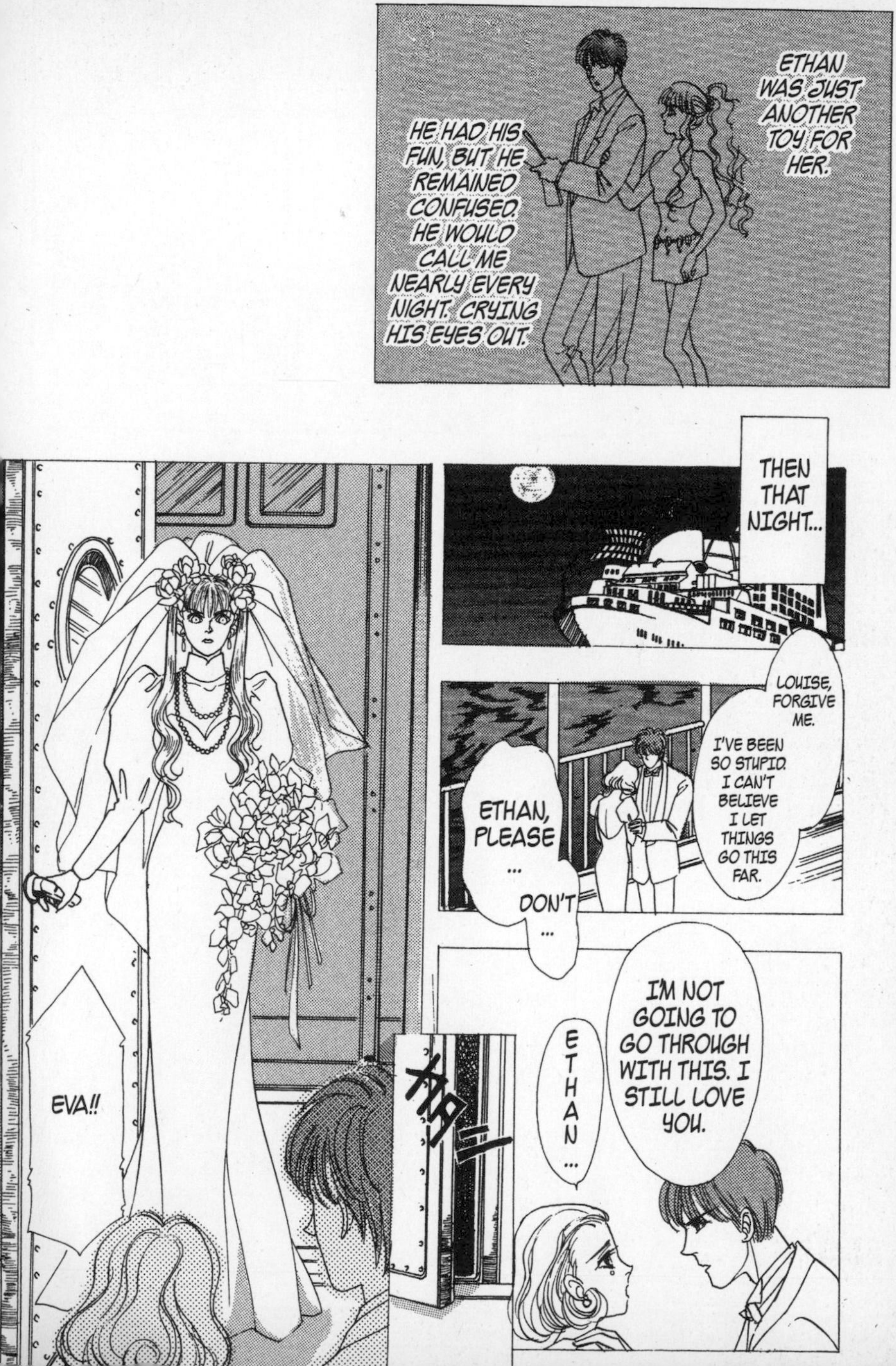
ETHAN WAS JUST ANOTHER TOY FOR HER.
HE HAD HIS FUN, BUT HE REMAINED CONFUSED. HE WOULD CALL ME NEARLY EVERY NIGHT. CRYING HIS EYES OUT.
THEN THAT NIGHT...
LOUISE, FORGIVE ME.
I'VE BEEN SO STUPID. I CAN'T BELIEVE I LET THINGS GO THIS FAR.
ETHAN, PLEASE ... DON'T ...
I'M NOT GOING TO GO THROUGH WITH THIS. I STILL LOVE YOU.
ETHAN ...
EVA!!

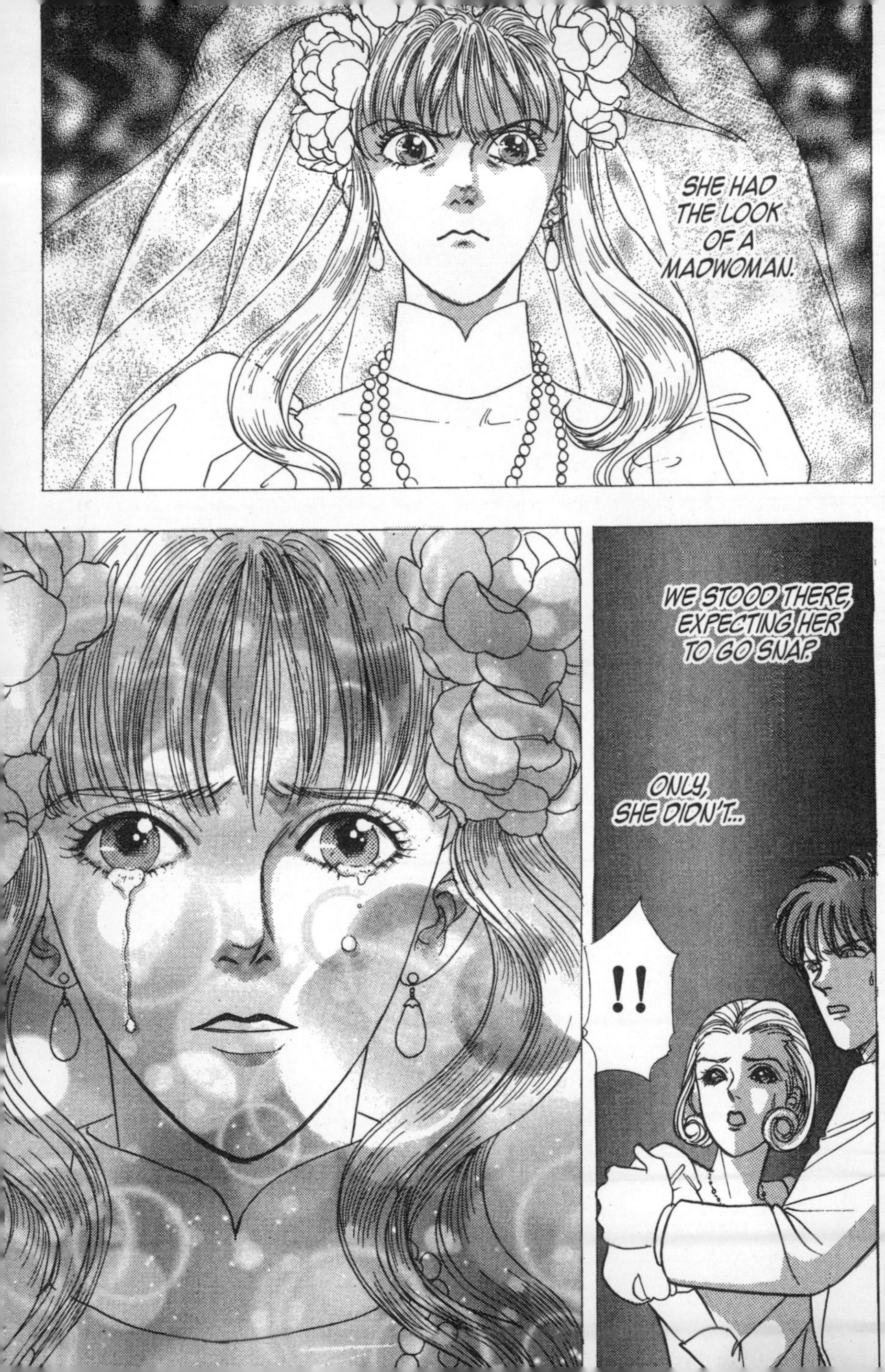
SHE HAD THE LOOK OF A MADWOMAN.
WE STOOD THERE, EXPECTING HER TO GO SNAP.
ONLY, SHE DIDN'T...
!!

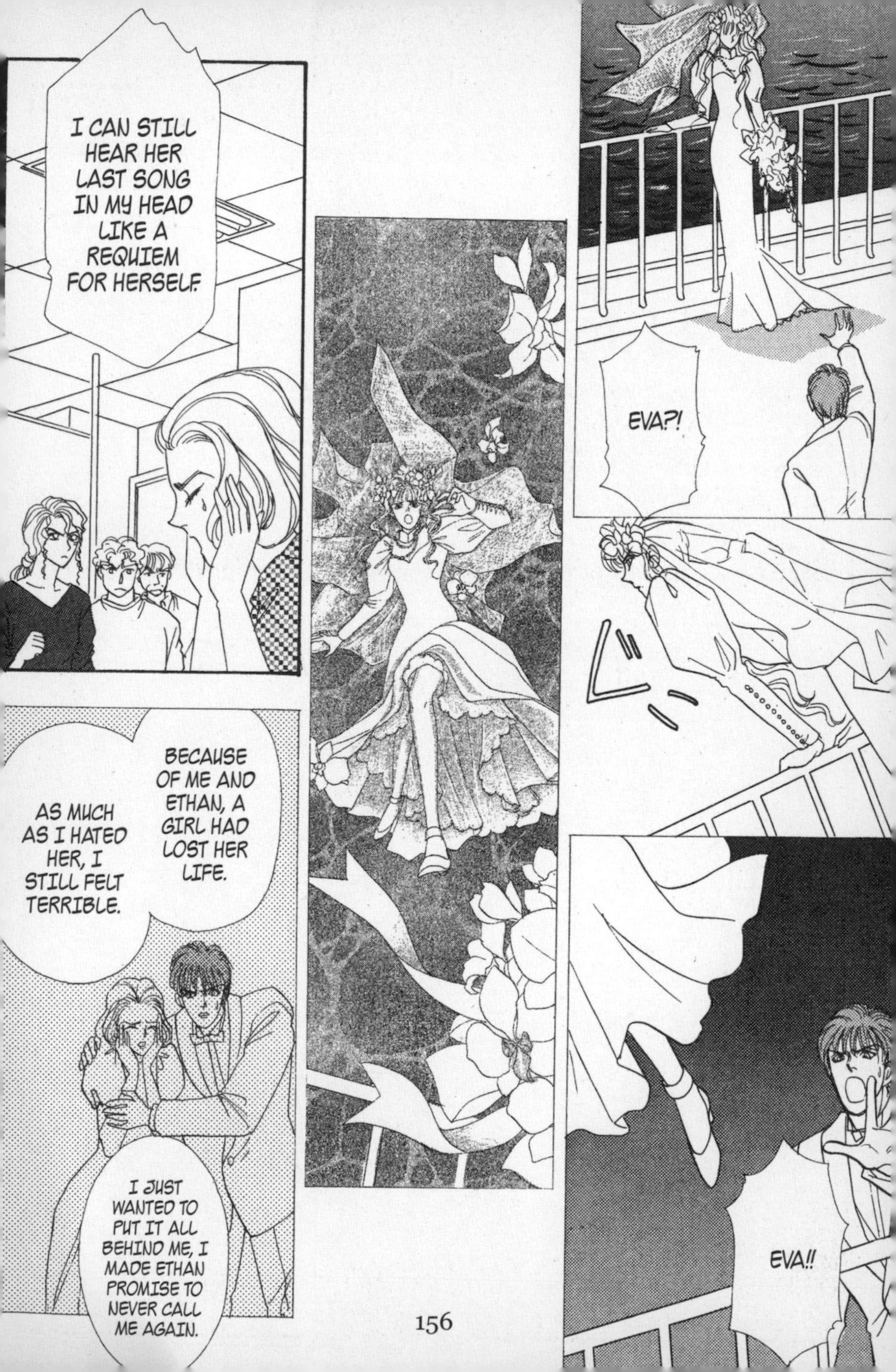

EVA?!
EVA!!
I CAN STILL HEAR HER LAST SONG IN MY HEAD LIKE A REQUIEM FOR HERSELF.
BECAUSE OF ME AND ETHAN, A GIRL HAD LOST HER LIFE.
AS MUCH AS I HATED HER, I STILL FELT TERRIBLE.
I JUST WANTED TO PUT IT ALL BEHIND ME, I MADE ETHAN PROMISE TO NEVER CALL ME AGAIN.

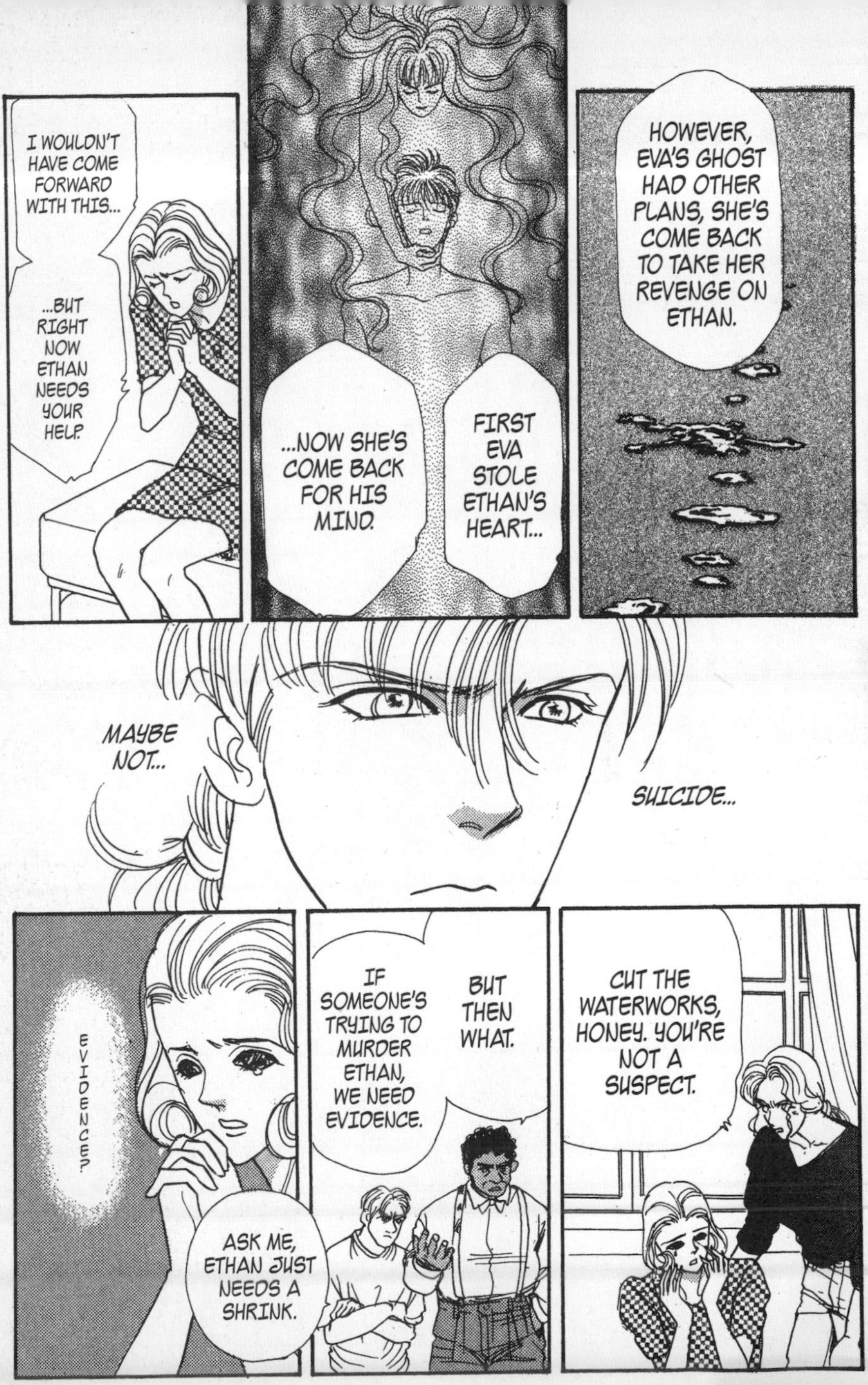
HOWEVER, EVA'S GHOST HAD OTHER PLANS, SHE'S COME BACK TO TAKE HER REVENGE ON ETHAN.
FIRST EVA STOLE ETHAN'S HEART...
...NOW SHE'S COME BACK FOR HIS MIND.
I WOULDN'T HAVE COME FORWARD WITH THIS...
...BUT RIGHT NOW ETHAN NEEDS YOUR HELP.
SUICIDE...
MAYBE NOT...
CUT THE WATERWORKS, HONEY. YOU'RE NOT A SUSPECT.
BUT THEN WHAT.
IF SOMEONE'S TRYING TO MURDER ETHAN, WE NEED EVIDENCE.
ASK ME, ETHAN JUST NEEDS A SHRINK.
EVIDENCE?

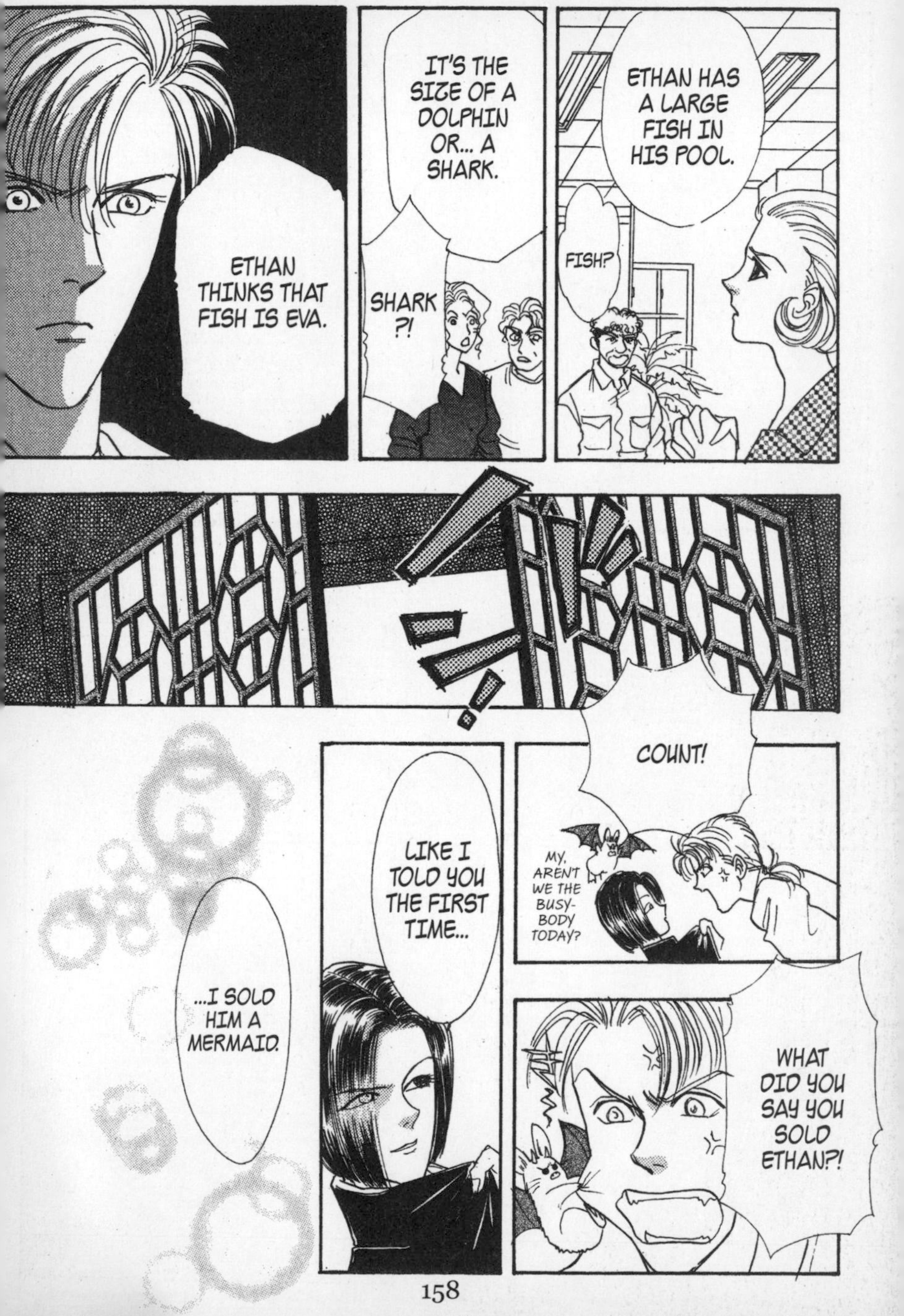
ETHAN HAS A LARGE FISH IN HIS POOL.
FISH?
IT'S THE SIZE OF A DOLPHIN OR... A SHARK.
SHARK?!
ETHAN THINKS THAT FISH IS EVA.
COUNT!
MY, AREN'T WE THE BUSY-BODY TODAY?
WHAT DID YOU SAY YOU SOLD ETHAN?!
LIKE I TOLD YOU THE FIRST TIME...
...I SOLD HIM A MERMAID.

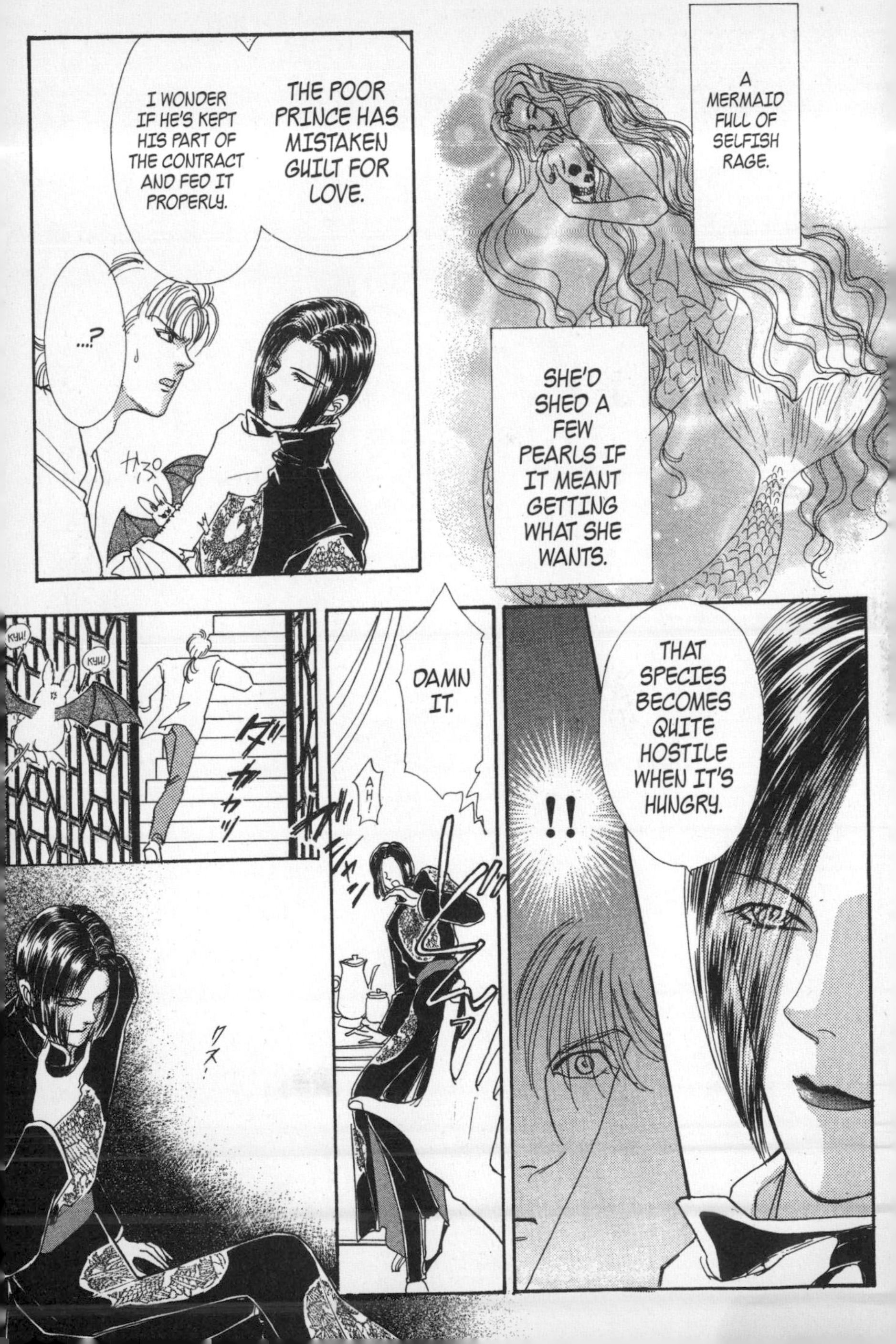
A MERMAID FULL OF SELFISH RAGE.
SHE'D SHED A FEW PEARLS IF IT MEANT GETTING WHAT SHE WANTS.
THE POOR PRINCE HAS MISTAKEN GUILT FOR LOVE.
I WONDER IF HE'S KEPT HIS PART OF THE CONTRACT AND FED IT PROPERLY.
...?
THAT SPECIES BECOMES QUITE HOSTILE WHEN IT'S HUNGRY.
!!
DAMN IT.
AH!
KYU!
KYU!
クス

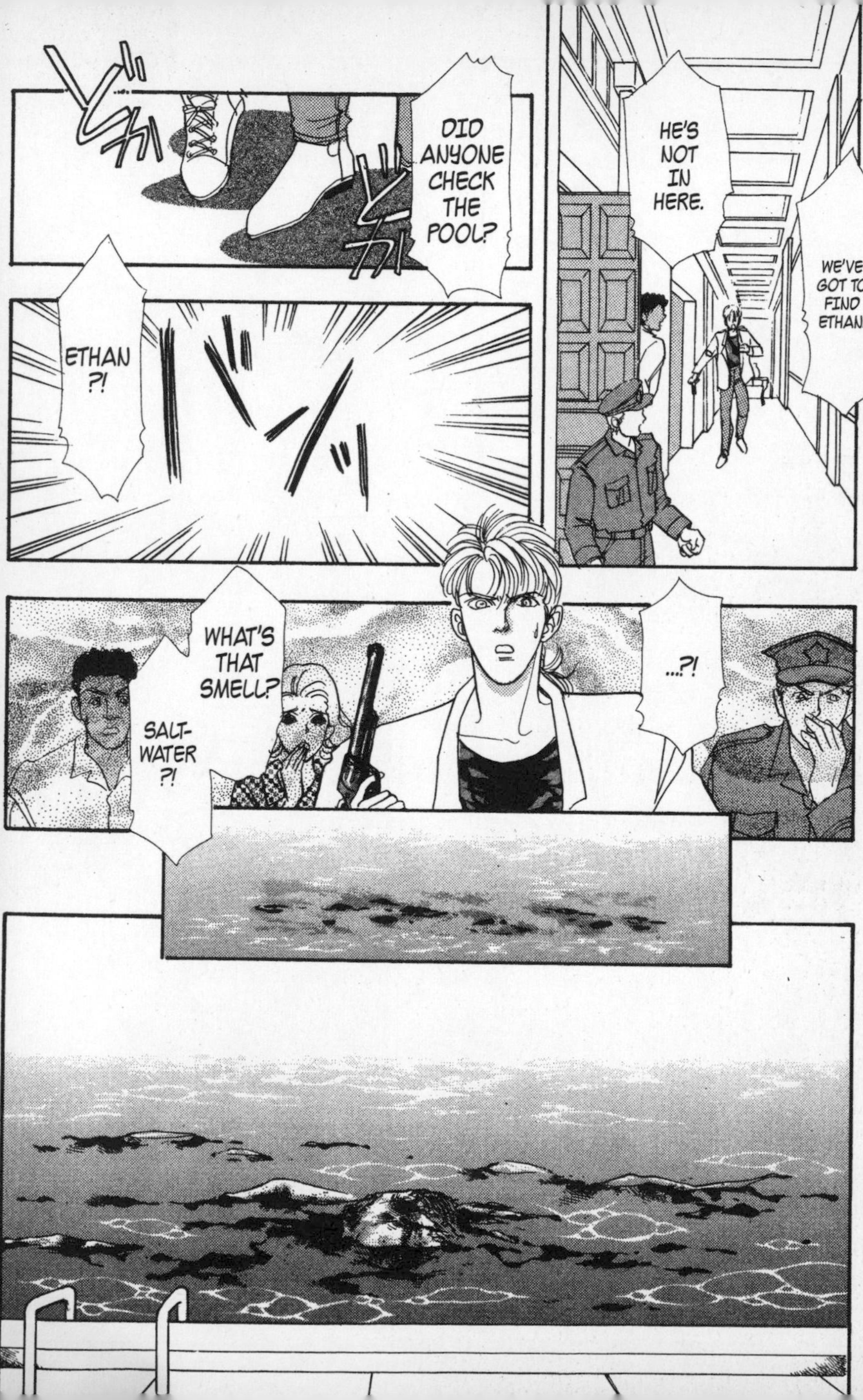

HE'S NOT IN HERE.
WE'VE GOT TO FIND ETHAN.
DID ANYONE CHECK THE POOL?
ETHAN ?!
...?!
WHAT'S THAT SMELL?
SALT-WATER ?!

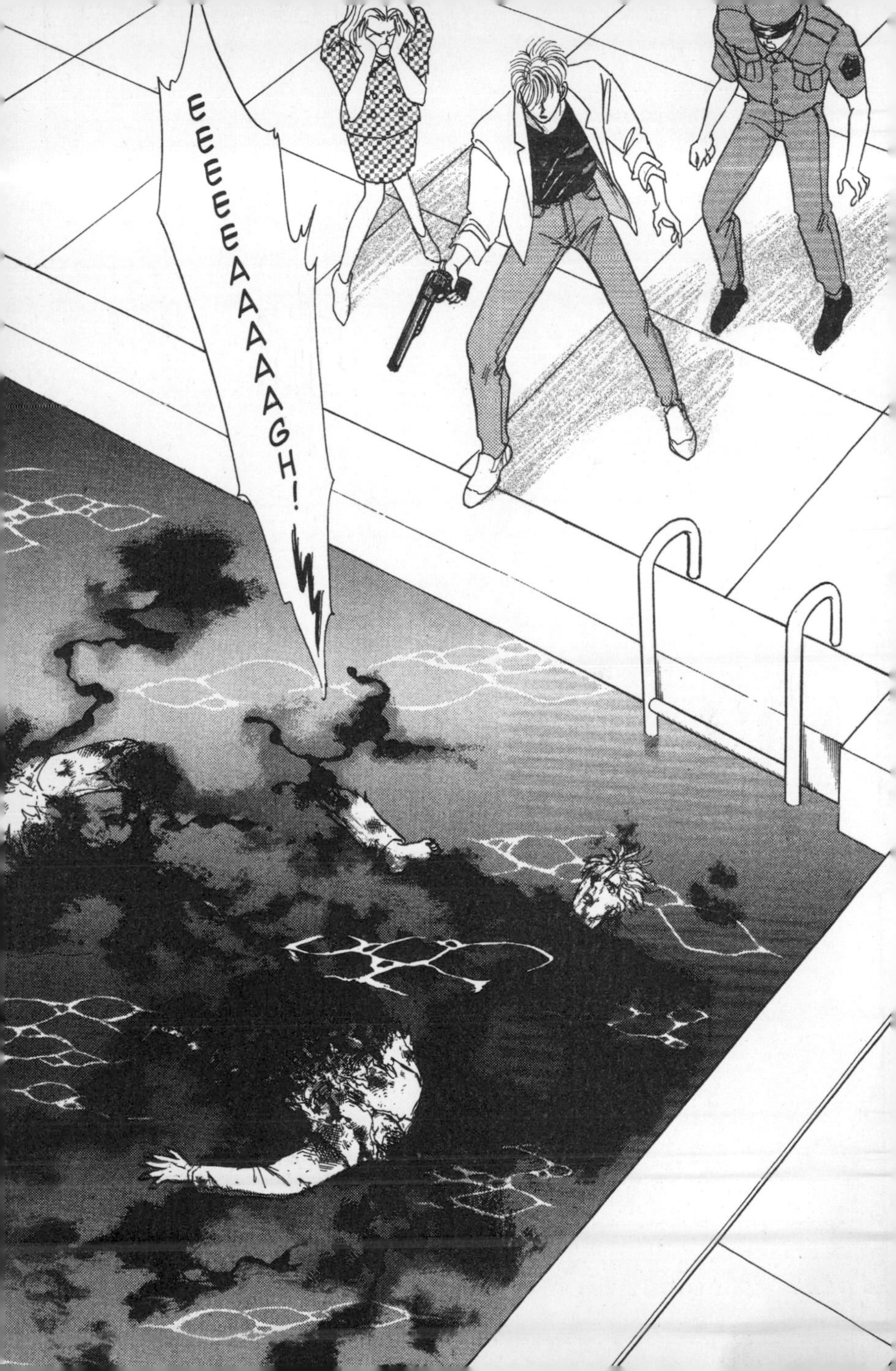
EEEEEEAAAAAAGH!

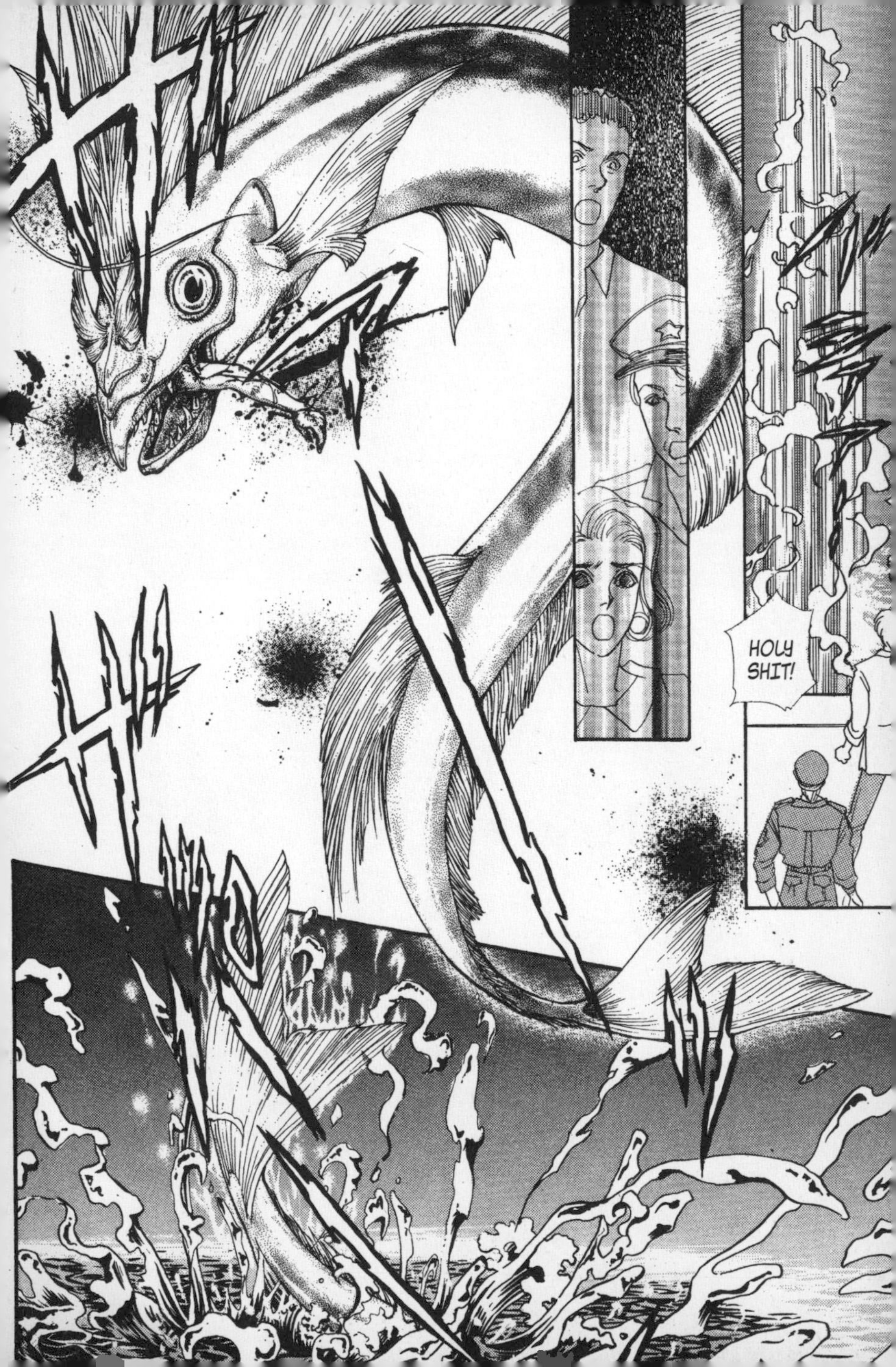
HOLY SHIT!

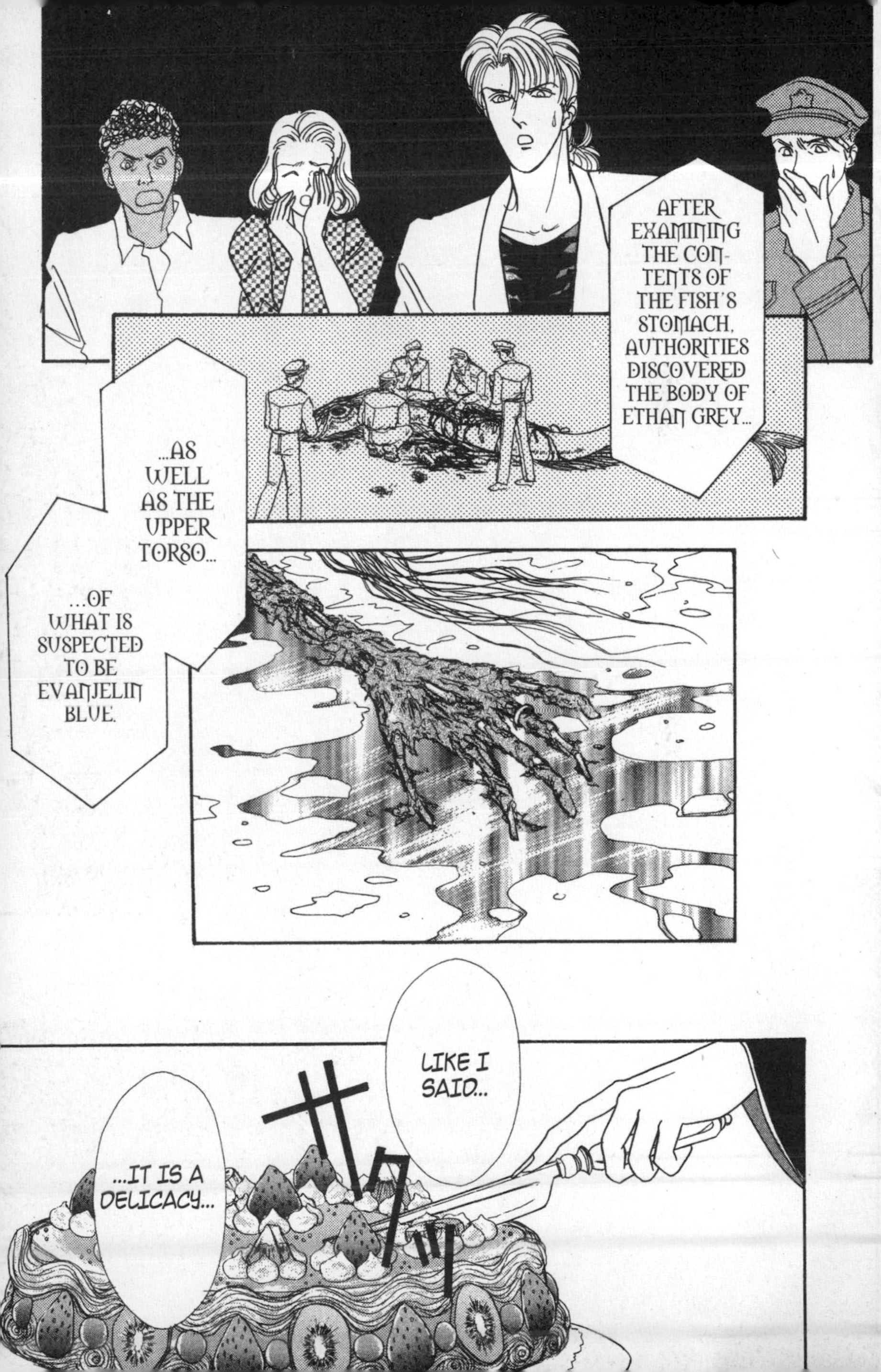
AFTER EXAMINING THE CON- TENTS OF THE FISH'S STOMACH, AUTHORITIES DISCOVERED THE BODY OF ETHAN GREY...
...AS WELL AS THE UPPER TORSO...
...OF WHAT IS SUSPECTED TO BE EVANJELIN BLUE.
LIKE I SAID...
...IT IS A DELICACY...

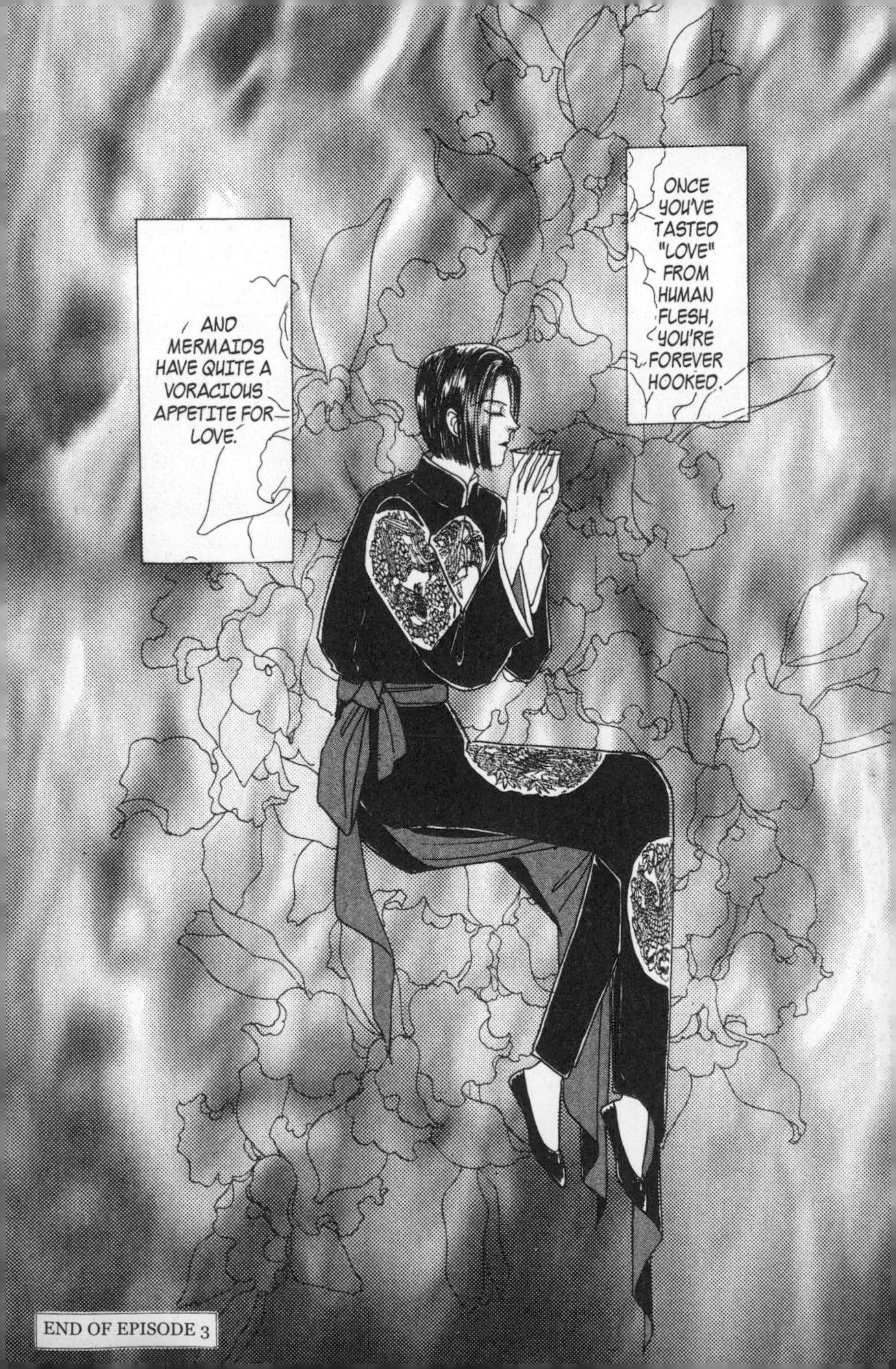
ONCE YOU'VE TASTED "LOVE" FROM HUMAN FLESH, YOU'RE FOREVER HOOKED.
AND MERMAIDS HAVE QUITE A VORACIOUS APPETITE FOR LOVE.
END OF EPISODE 3

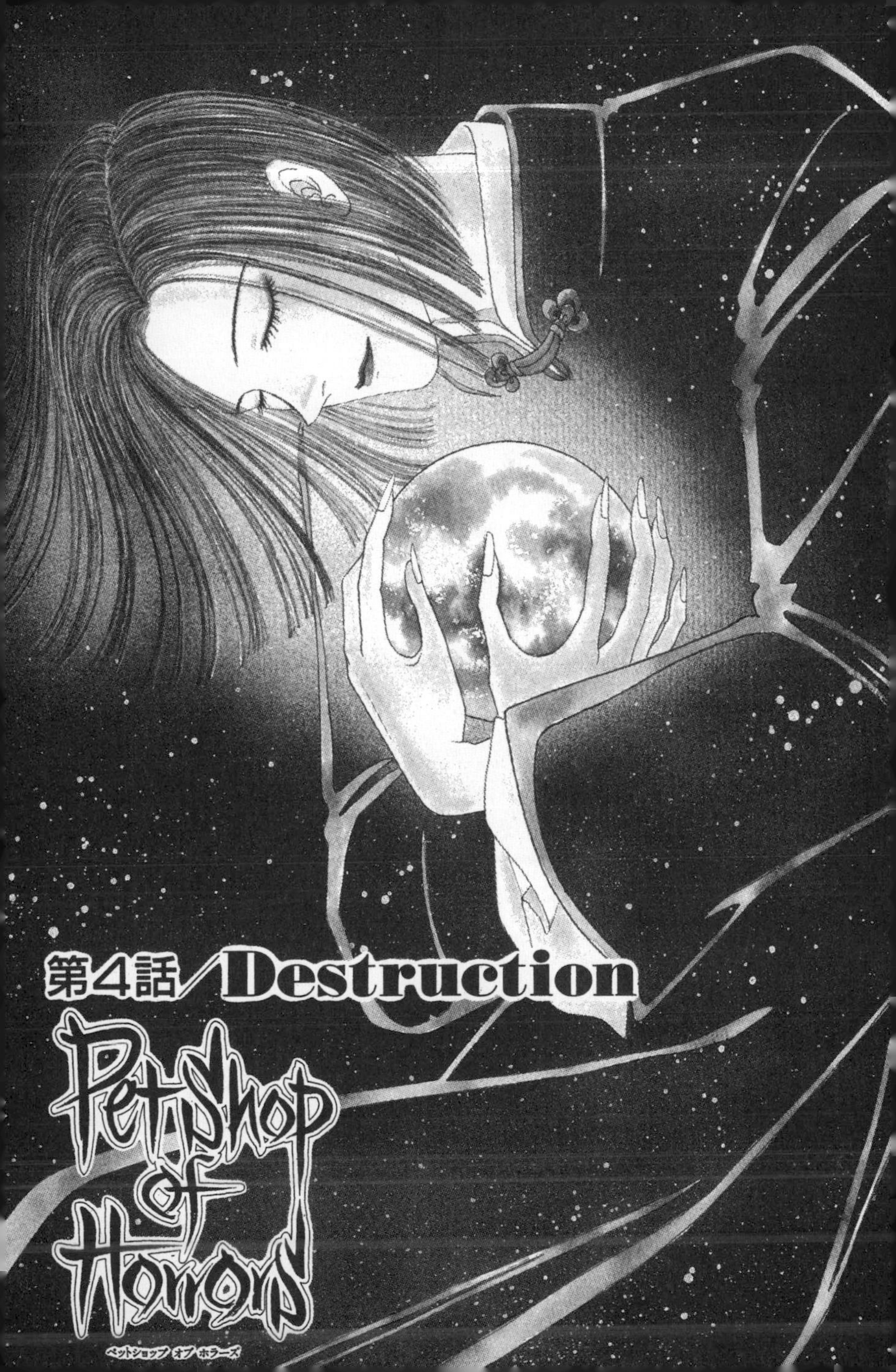
第4話／Destruction
Pet Shop of Horrors
ペットショップ オブ ホラーズ

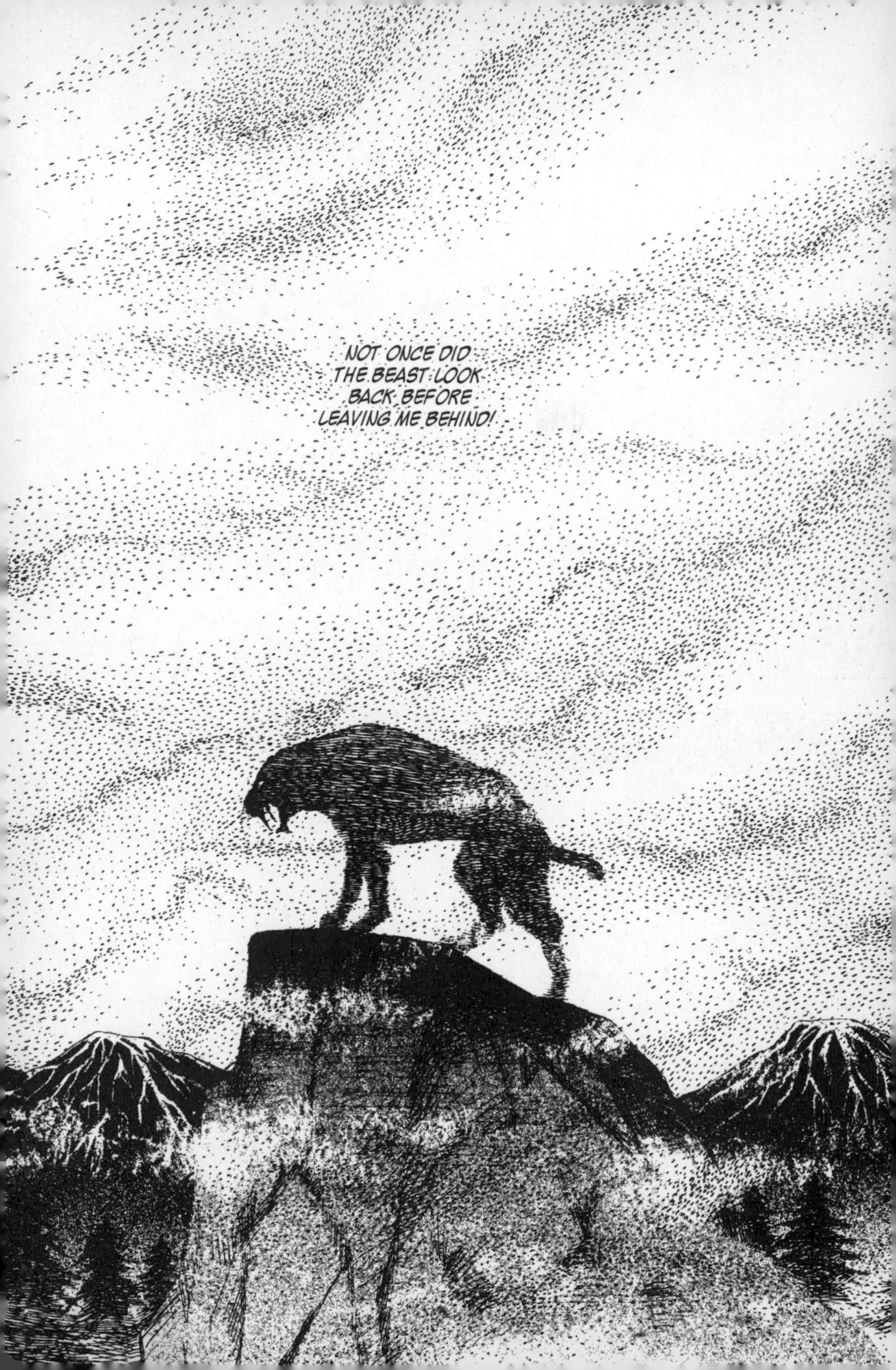
NOT ONCE DID THE BEAST LOOK BACK BEFORE LEAVING ME BEHIND!

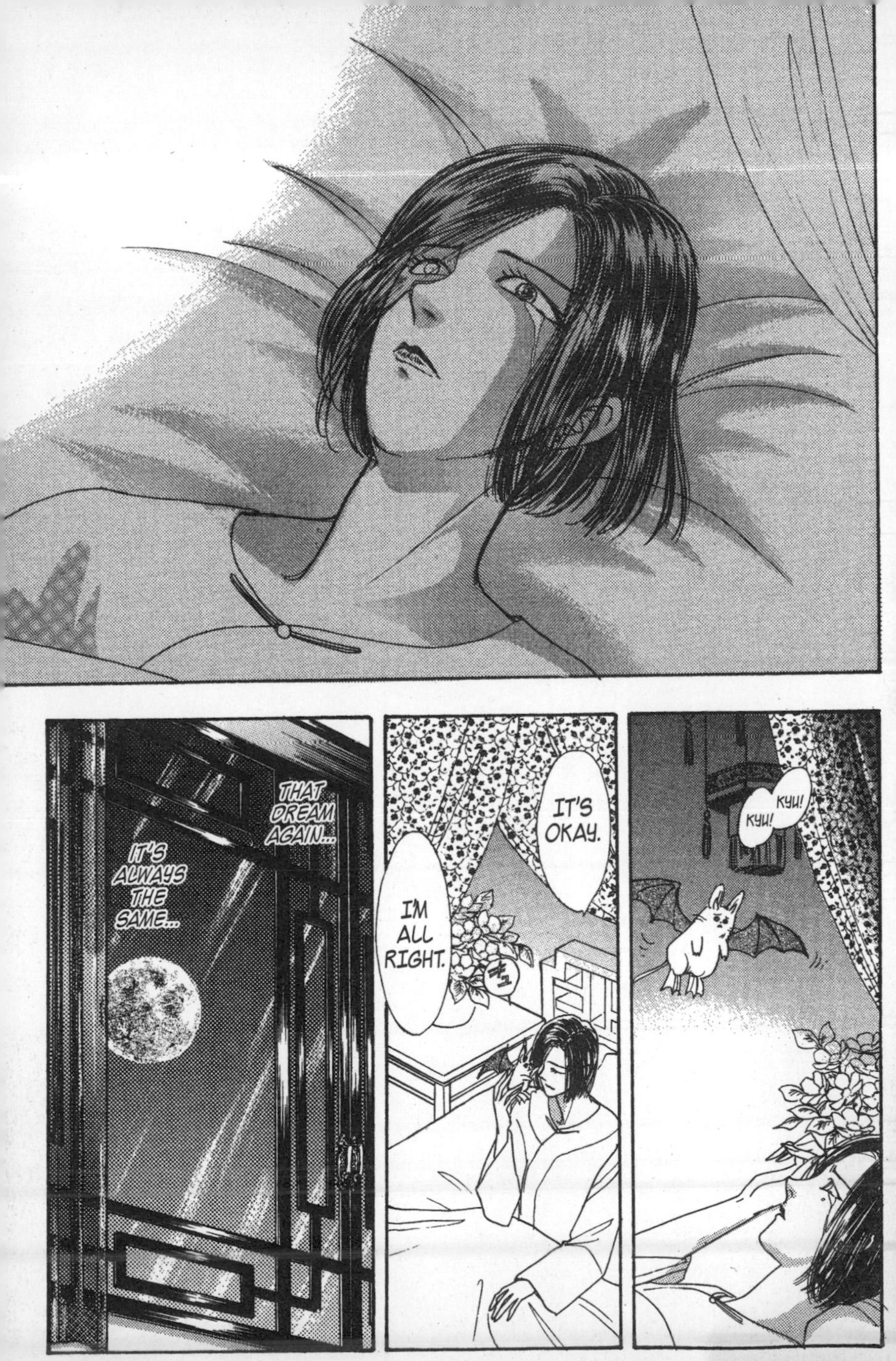
KYU!
KYU!
IT'S OKAY.
I'M ALL RIGHT.
THAT DREAM AGAIN...
IT'S ALWAYS THE SAME...

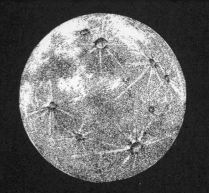

ONCE
AGAIN...

...ANOTHER
SPECIES
DISAPPEARS.

HUH
?

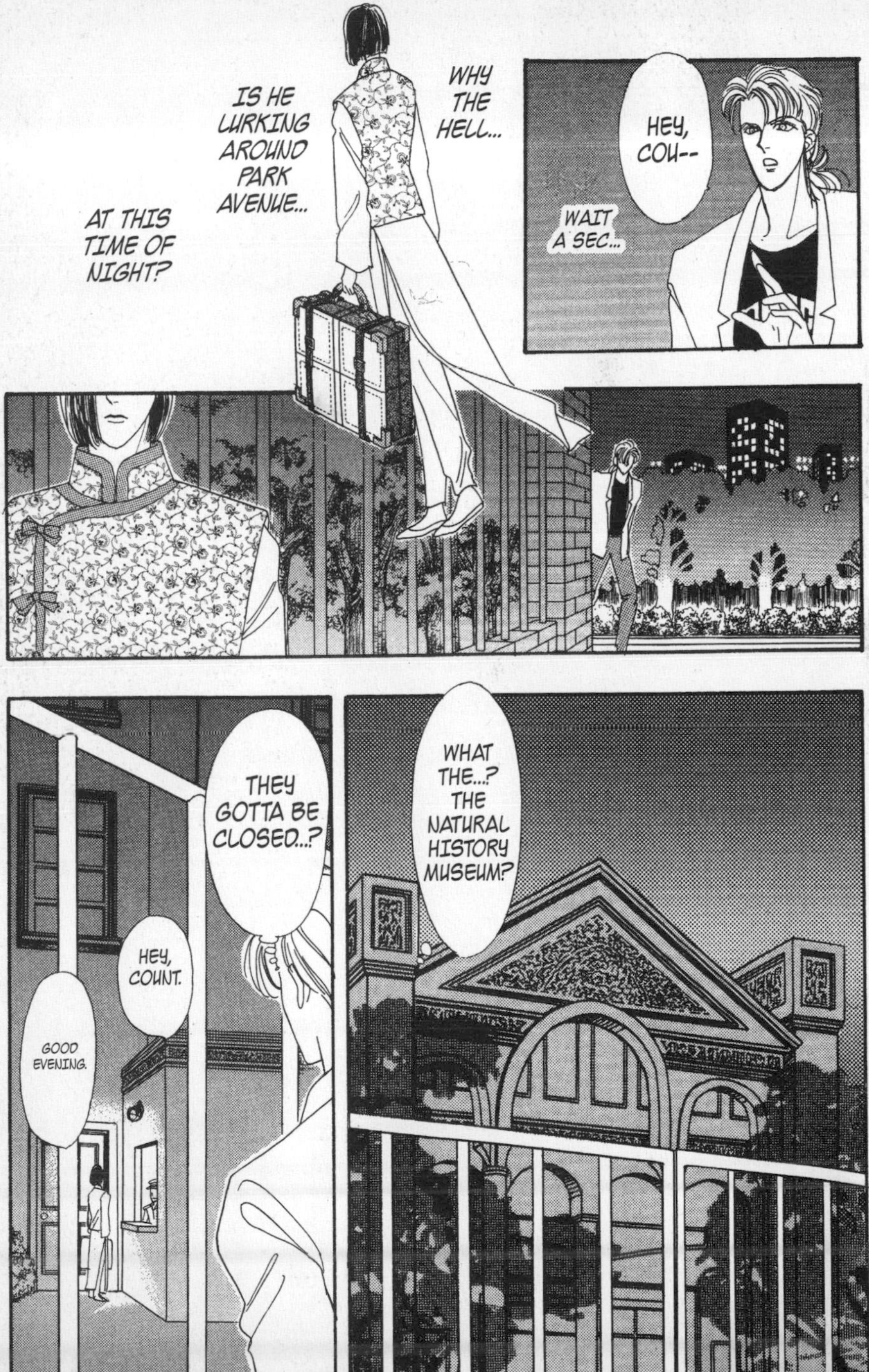
HEY, COU--
WAIT A SEC...
WHY THE HELL...
IS HE LURKING AROUND PARK AVENUE...
AT THIS TIME OF NIGHT?
WHAT THE...? THE NATURAL HISTORY MUSEUM?
THEY GOTTA BE CLOSED...?
HEY, COUNT.
GOOD EVENING.

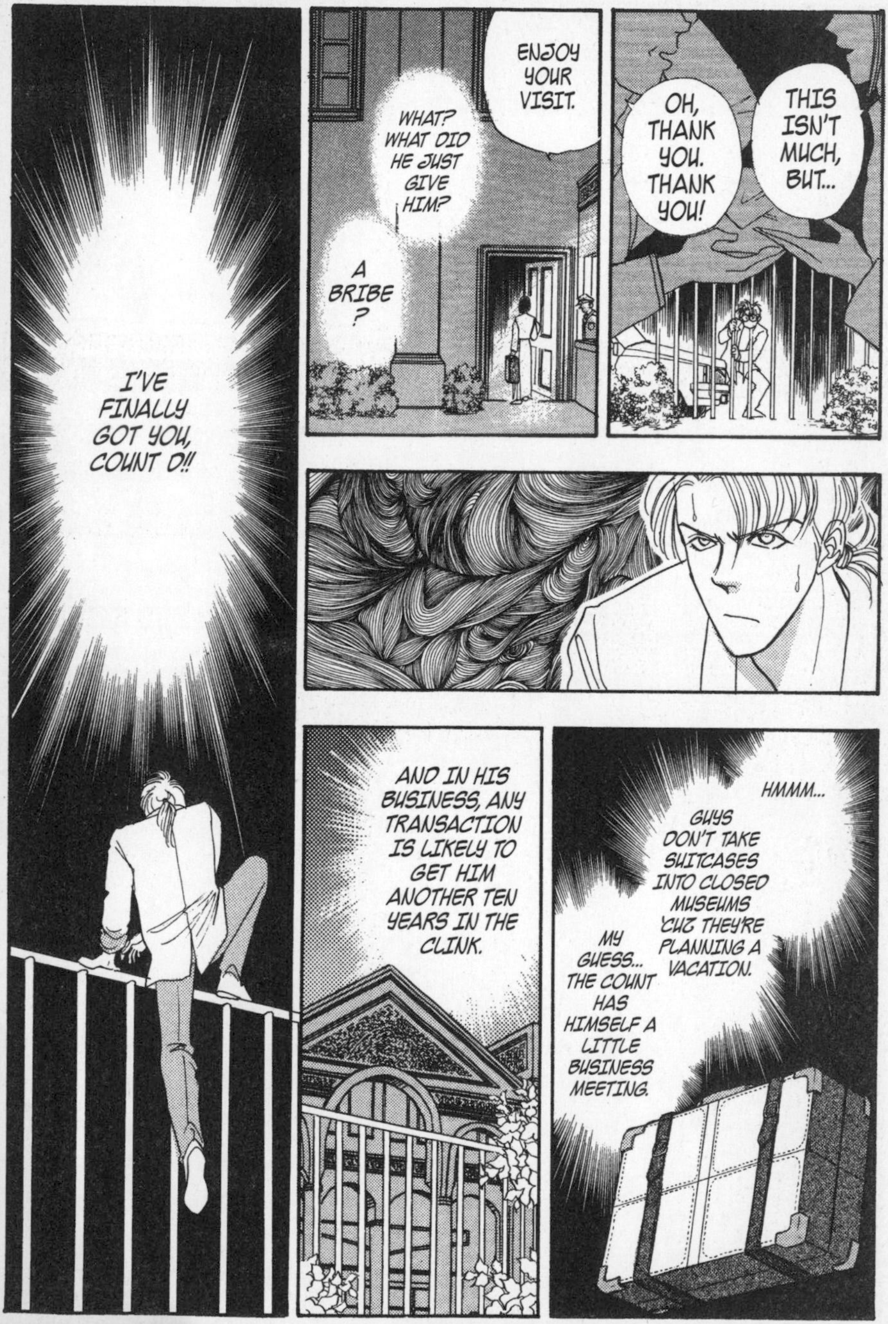
THIS ISN'T MUCH, BUT...
OH, THANK YOU. THANK YOU!
ENJOY YOUR VISIT.
WHAT? WHAT DID HE JUST GIVE HIM?
A BRIBE?
HMMM...
GUYS DON'T TAKE SUITCASES INTO CLOSED MUSEUMS 'CUZ THEY'RE PLANNING A VACATION.
MY GUESS... THE COUNT HAS HIMSELF A LITTLE BUSINESS MEETING.
AND IN HIS BUSINESS, ANY TRANSACTION IS LIKELY TO GET HIM ANOTHER TEN YEARS IN THE CLINK.
I'VE FINALLY GOT YOU, COUNT D!!

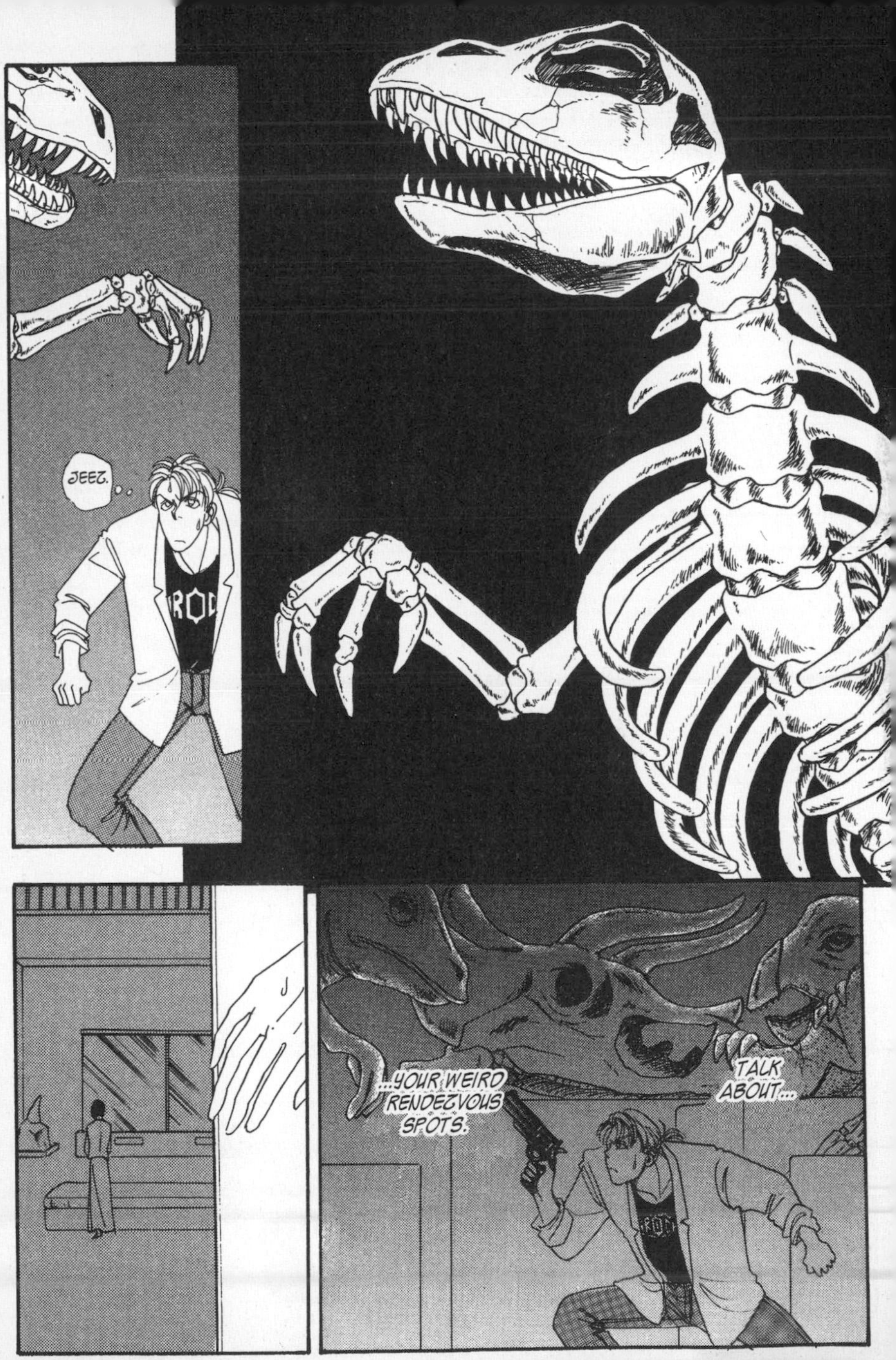
JEEZ.
TALK ABOUT...
...YOUR WEIRD RENDEZVOUS SPOTS.

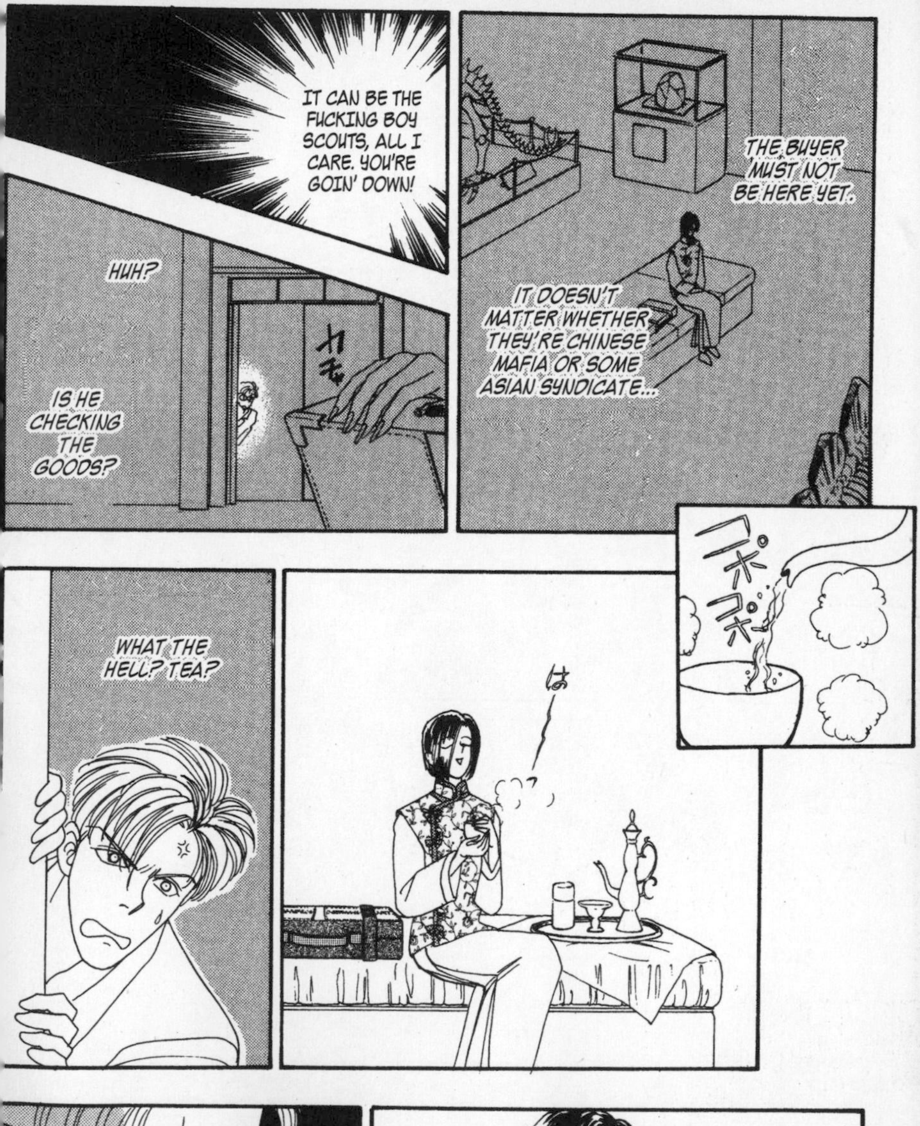
THE BUYER MUST NOT BE HERE YET.
IT DOESN'T MATTER WHETHER THEY'RE CHINESE MAFIA OR SOME ASIAN SYNDICATE...
IT CAN BE THE FUCKING BOY SCOUTS, ALL I CARE. YOU'RE GOIN' DOWN!
HUH?
IS HE CHECKING THE GOODS?
は—
WHAT THE HELL? TEA?
EH...IT'S A RUSE.
ふわ…
PROBABLY TRYING NOT TO SPOOK THE BUYER.
HUH?

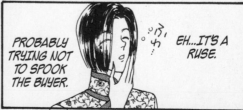

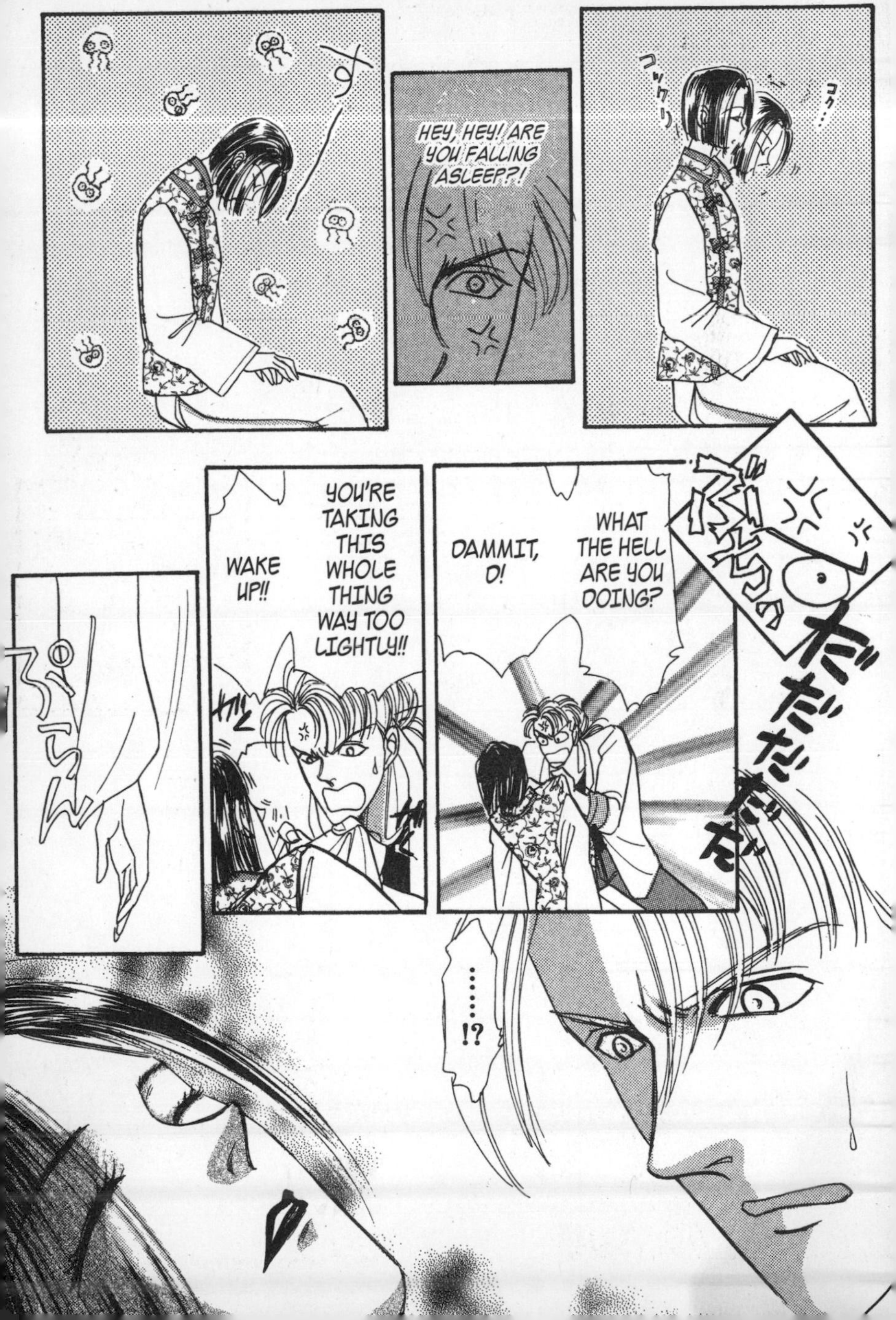
コックリ
コク…
HEY, HEY! ARE YOU FALLING ASLEEP?!
WHAT THE HELL ARE YOU DOING?
DAMMIT, D!
YOU'RE TAKING THIS WHOLE THING WAY TOO LIGHTLY!!
WAKE UP!!
......!?

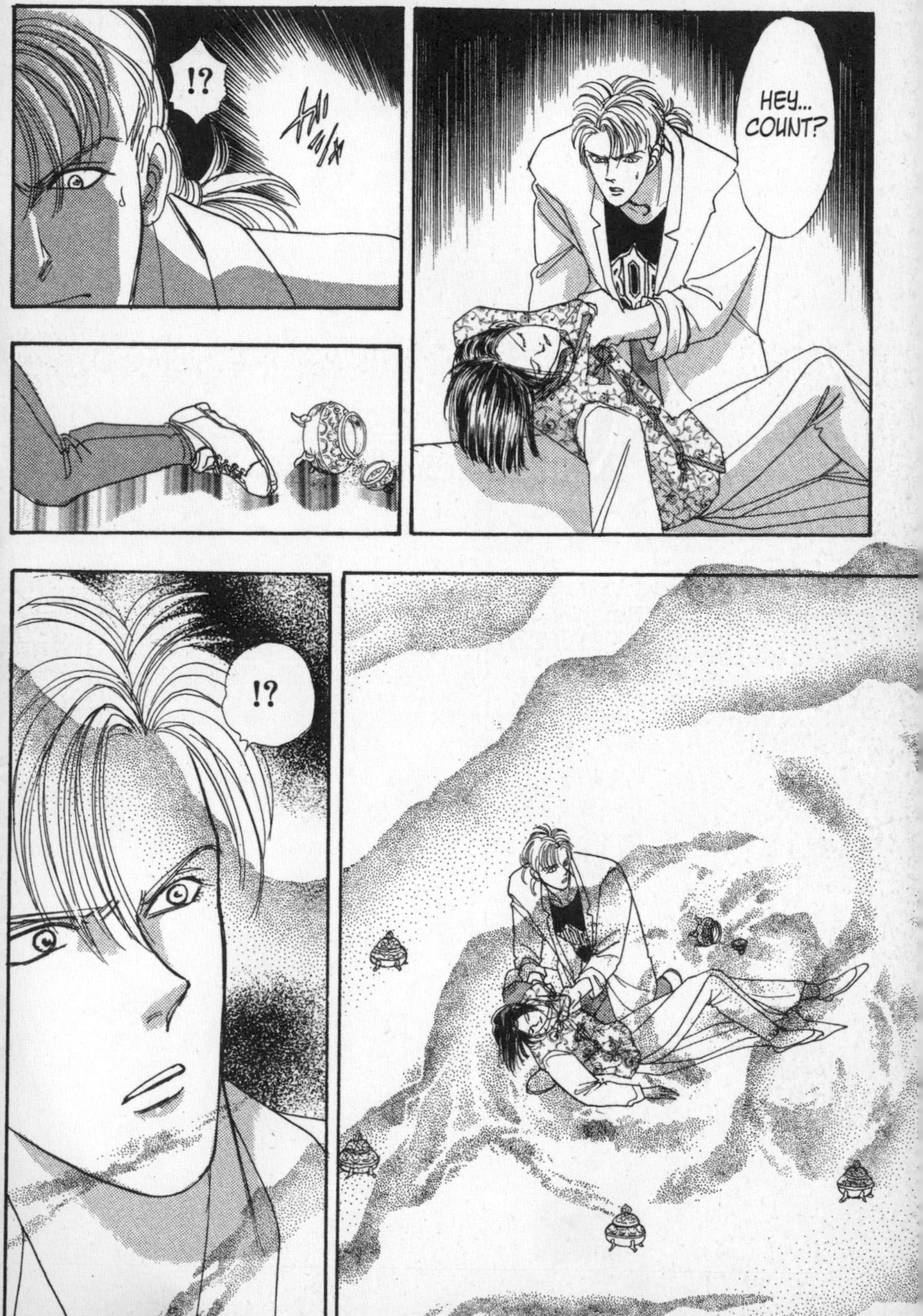
HEY... COUNT?
!?
!?

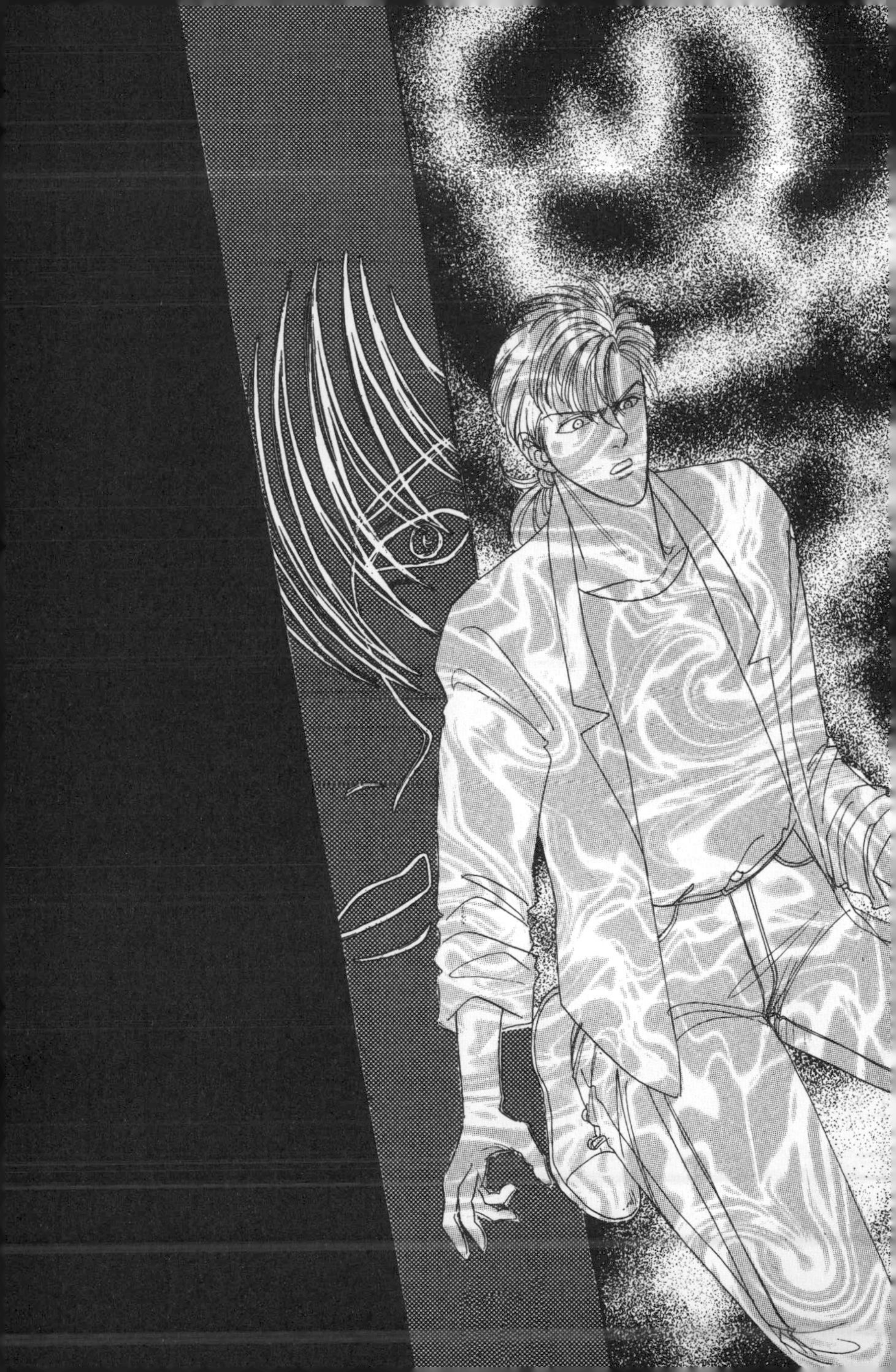

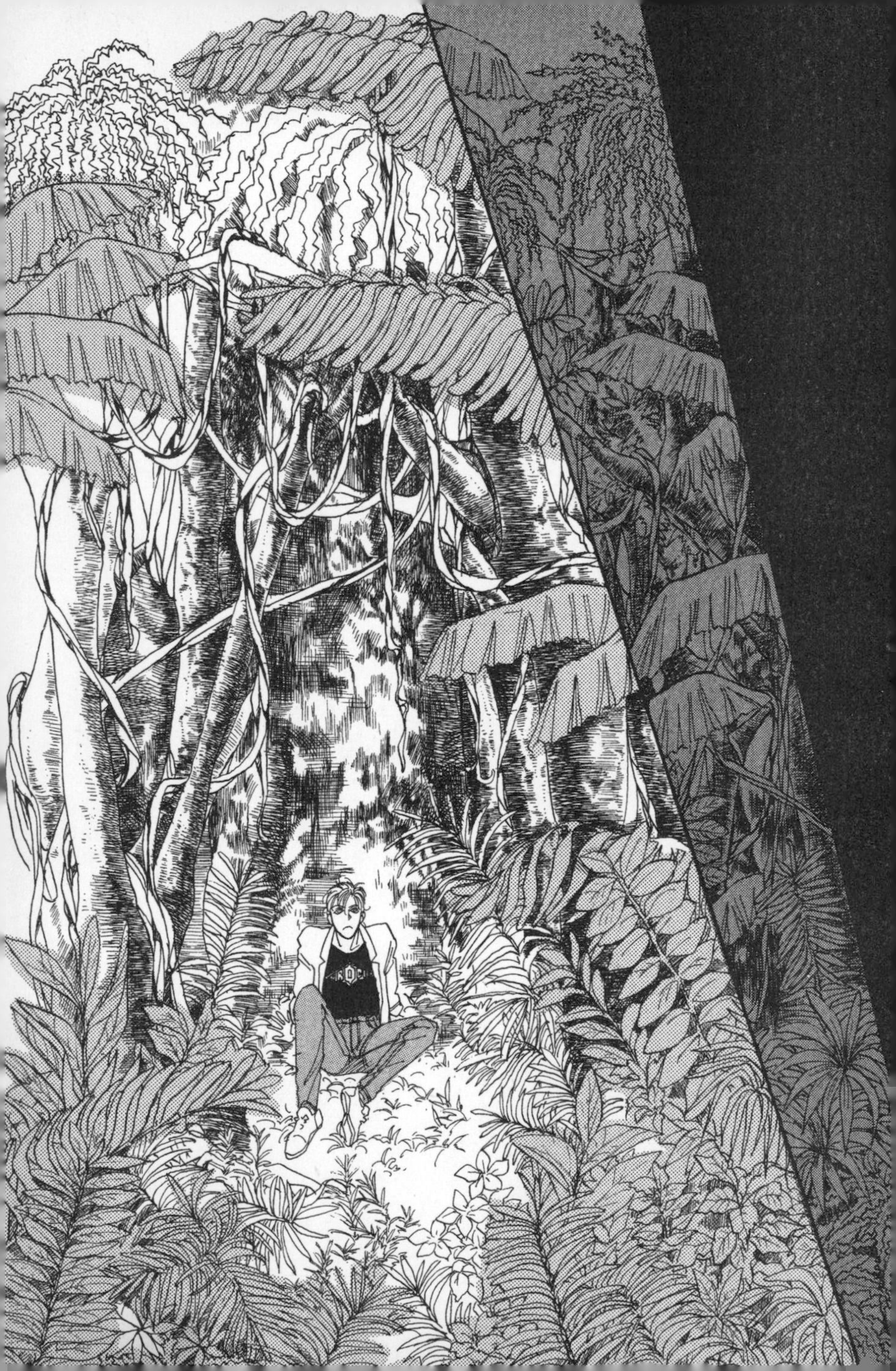

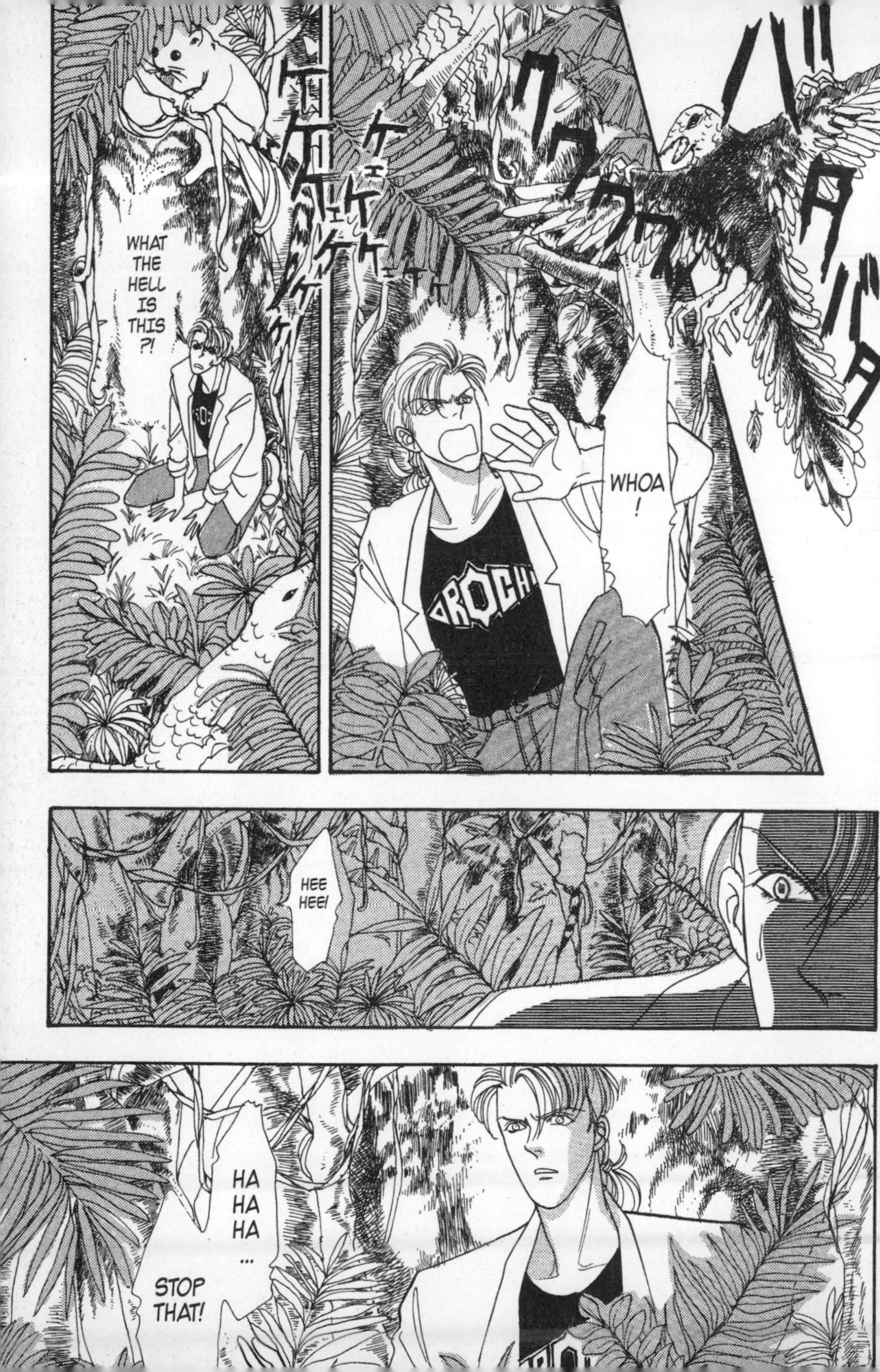
バタバタ
WHOA!
WHAT THE HELL IS THIS?!
HEE HEE!
HA HA HA...
STOP THAT!

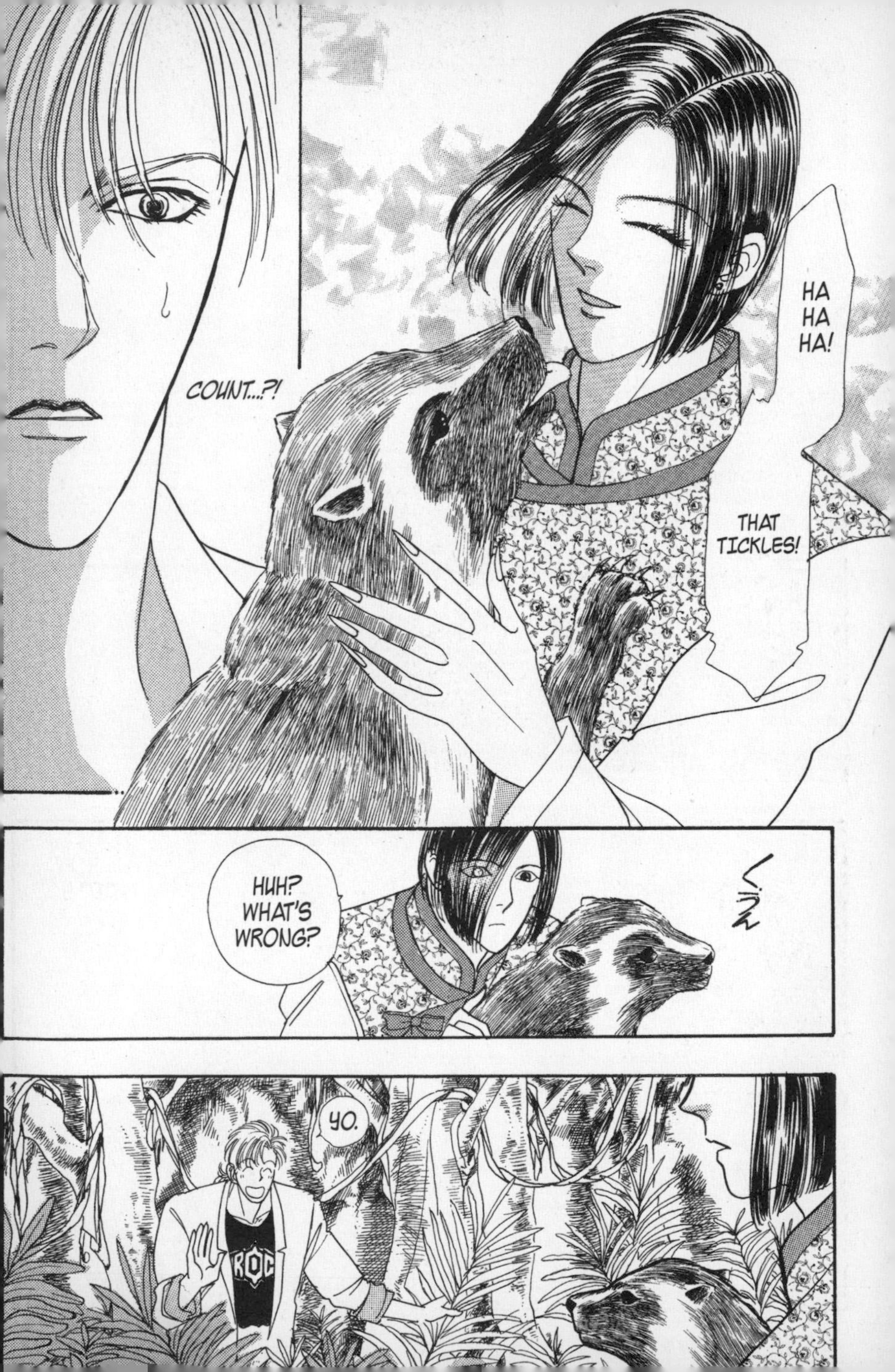
HA HA HA!
THAT TICKLES!
COUNT...?!
HUH? WHAT'S WRONG?
YO.

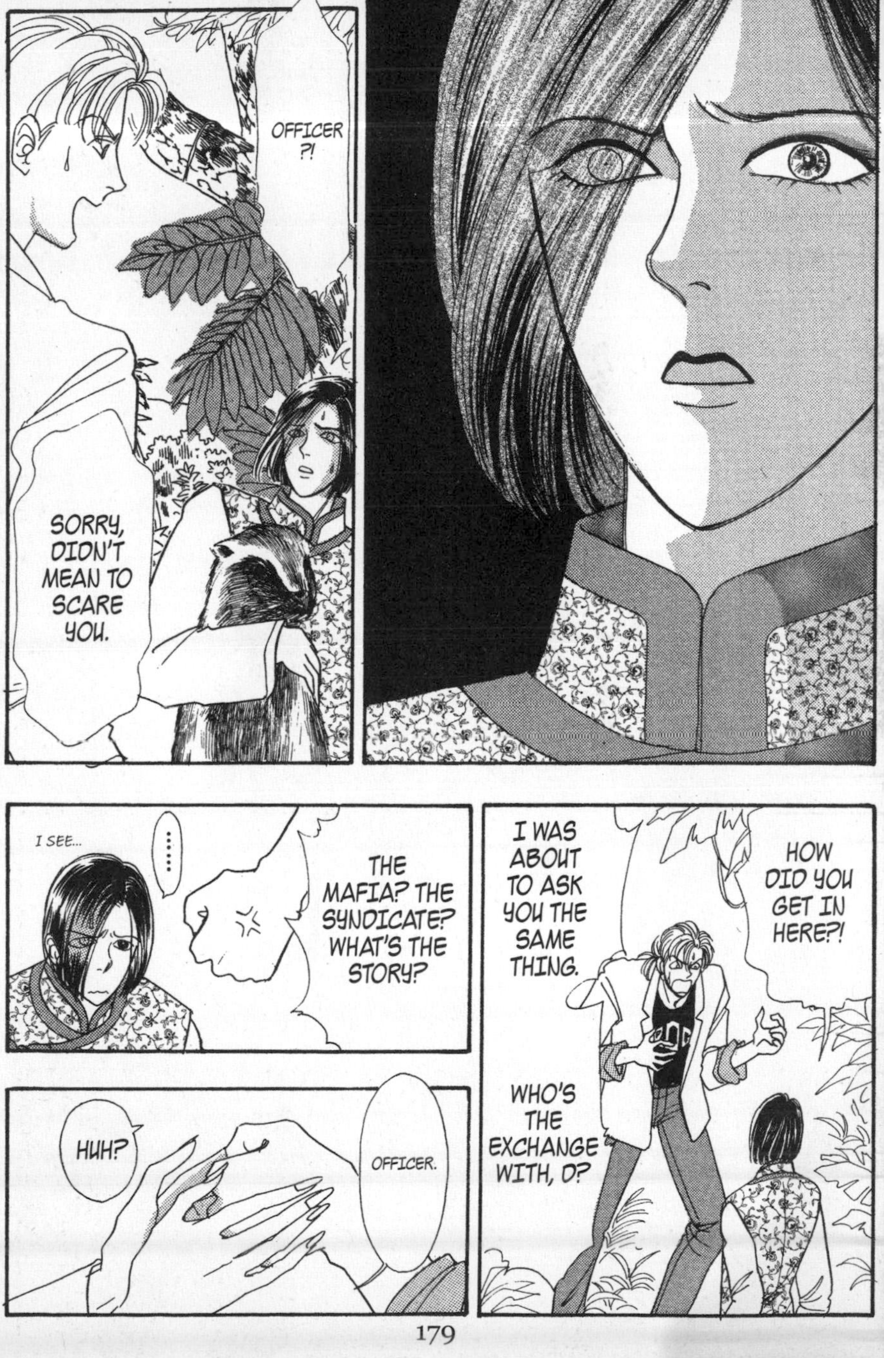
OFFICER ?!
SORRY, DIDN'T MEAN TO SCARE YOU.
HOW DID YOU GET IN HERE?!
I WAS ABOUT TO ASK YOU THE SAME THING.
WHO'S THE EXCHANGE WITH, D?
THE MAFIA? THE SYNDICATE? WHAT'S THE STORY?
......
I SEE...
OFFICER.
HUH?

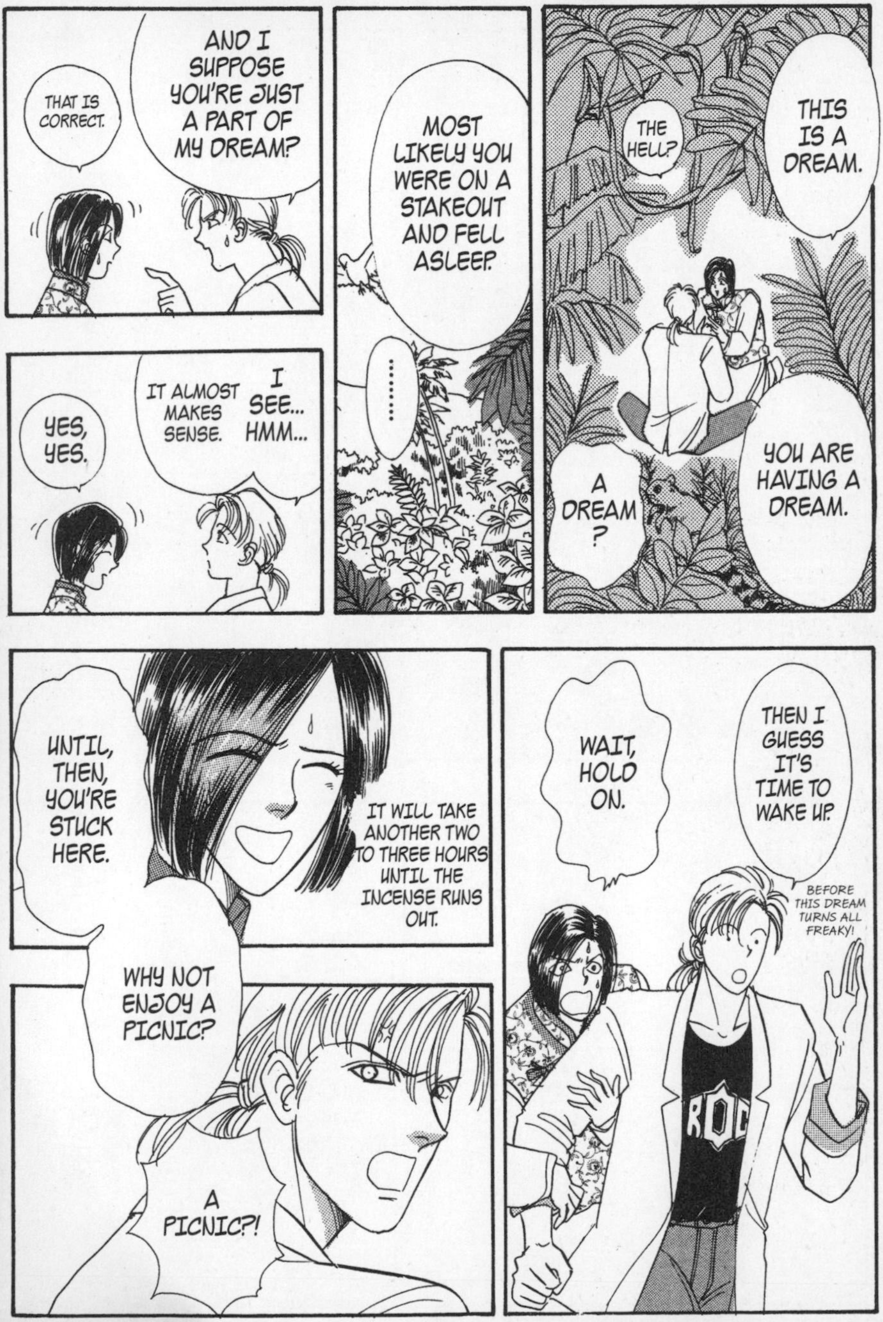
THIS IS A DREAM.
THE HELL?
YOU ARE HAVING A DREAM.
A DREAM?
MOST LIKELY YOU WERE ON A STAKEOUT AND FELL ASLEEP.
......
AND I SUPPOSE YOU'RE JUST A PART OF MY DREAM?
THAT IS CORRECT.
I SEE... HMM...
IT ALMOST MAKES SENSE.
YES, YES.
THEN I GUESS IT'S TIME TO WAKE UP.
WAIT, HOLD ON.
BEFORE THIS DREAM TURNS ALL FREAKY!
IT WILL TAKE ANOTHER TWO TO THREE HOURS UNTIL THE INCENSE RUNS OUT.
UNTIL, THEN, YOU'RE STUCK HERE.
WHY NOT ENJOY A PICNIC?
A PICNIC?!

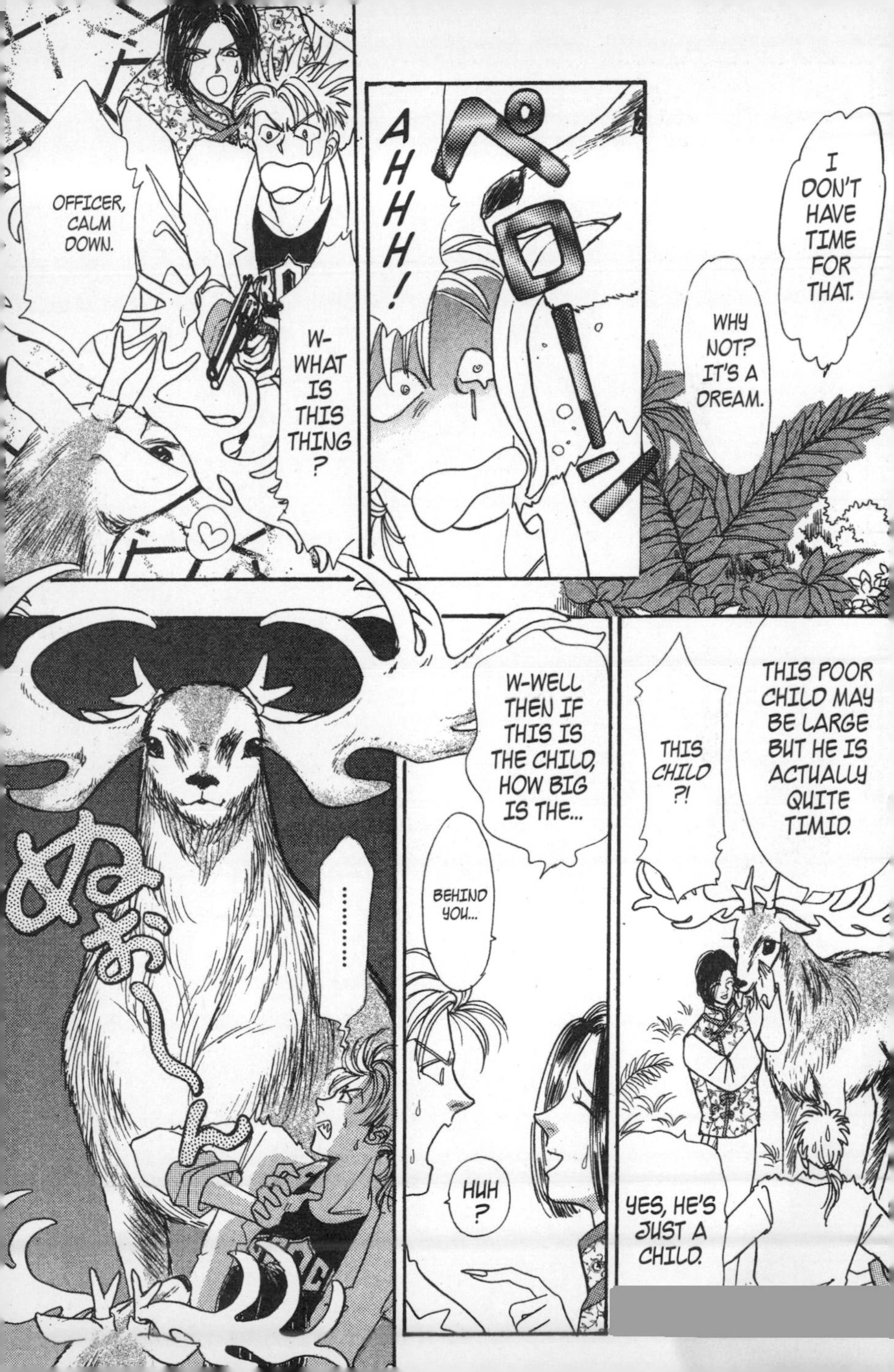

I DON'T HAVE TIME FOR THAT.
WHY NOT? IT'S A DREAM.
AHHHH!
W-WHAT IS THIS THING?
OFFICER, CALM DOWN.
THIS POOR CHILD MAY BE LARGE BUT HE IS ACTUALLY QUITE TIMID.
THIS CHILD?!
YES, HE'S JUST A CHILD.
W-WELL THEN IF THIS IS THE CHILD, HOW BIG IS THE...
BEHIND YOU...
HUH?
....

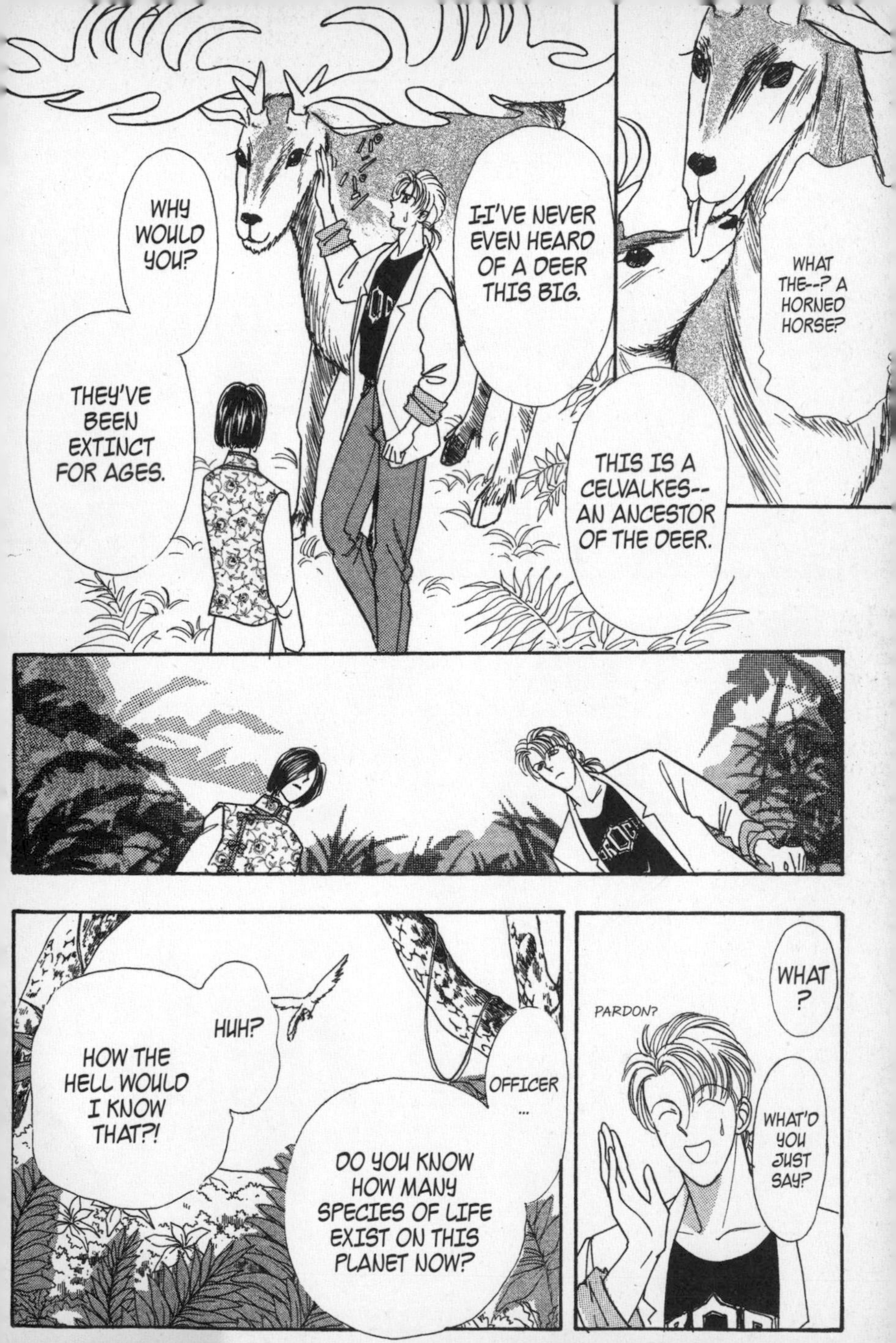
WHAT THE--? A HORNED HORSE?
THIS IS A CELVALKES-- AN ANCESTOR OF THE DEER.
I-I'VE NEVER EVEN HEARD OF A DEER THIS BIG.
WHY WOULD YOU?
THEY'VE BEEN EXTINCT FOR AGES.
WHAT ?
PARDON?
WHAT'D YOU JUST SAY?
OFFICER ...
DO YOU KNOW HOW MANY SPECIES OF LIFE EXIST ON THIS PLANET NOW?
HUH?
HOW THE HELL WOULD I KNOW THAT?!

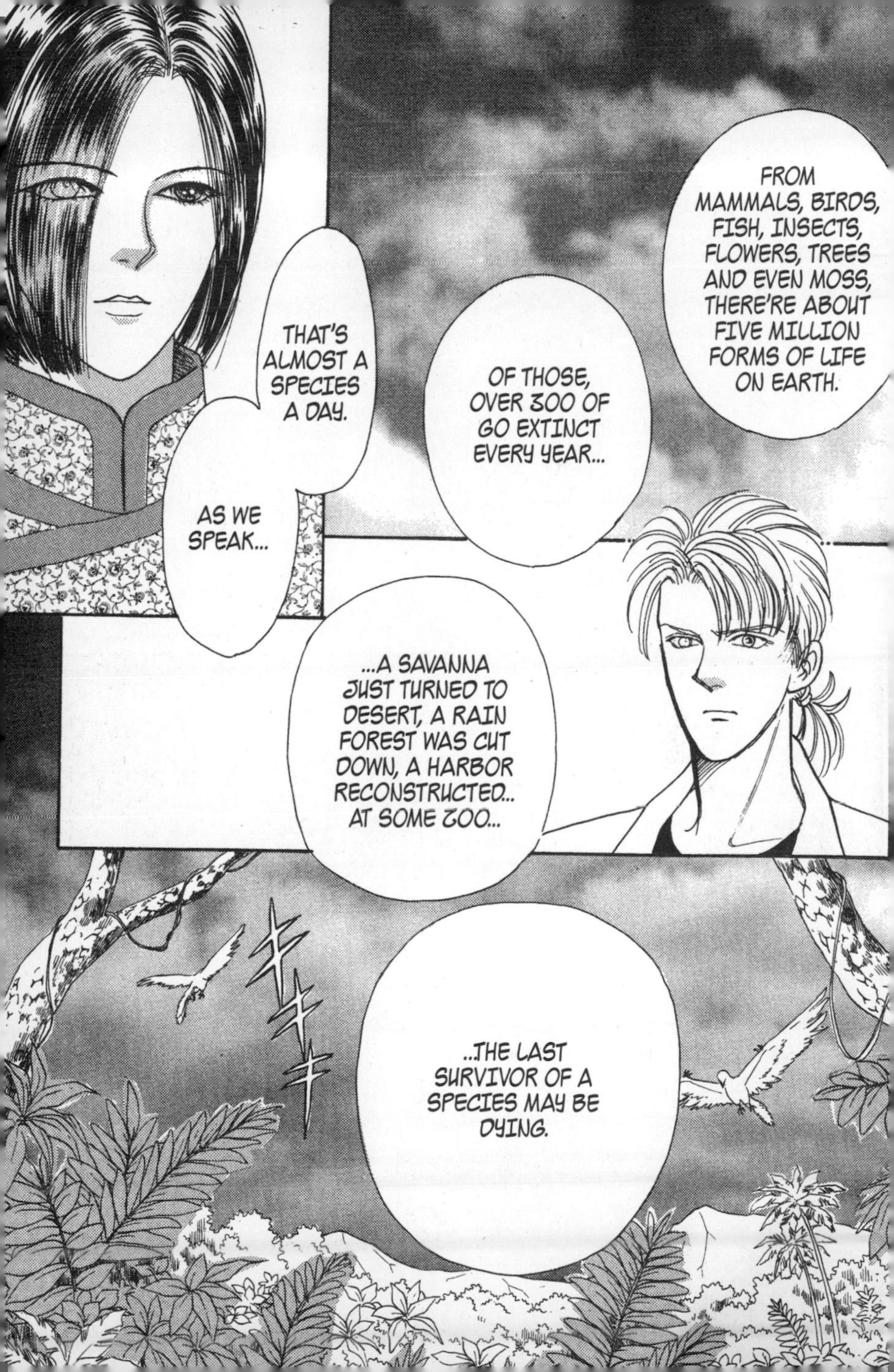
FROM MAMMALS, BIRDS, FISH, INSECTS, FLOWERS, TREES AND EVEN MOSS, THERE'RE ABOUT FIVE MILLION FORMS OF LIFE ON EARTH.
OF THOSE, OVER 300 OF GO EXTINCT EVERY YEAR...
THAT'S ALMOST A SPECIES A DAY.
AS WE SPEAK...
...A SAVANNA JUST TURNED TO DESERT, A RAIN FOREST WAS CUT DOWN, A HARBOR RECONSTRUCTED... AT SOME ZOO...
...THE LAST SURVIVOR OF A SPECIES MAY BE DYING.

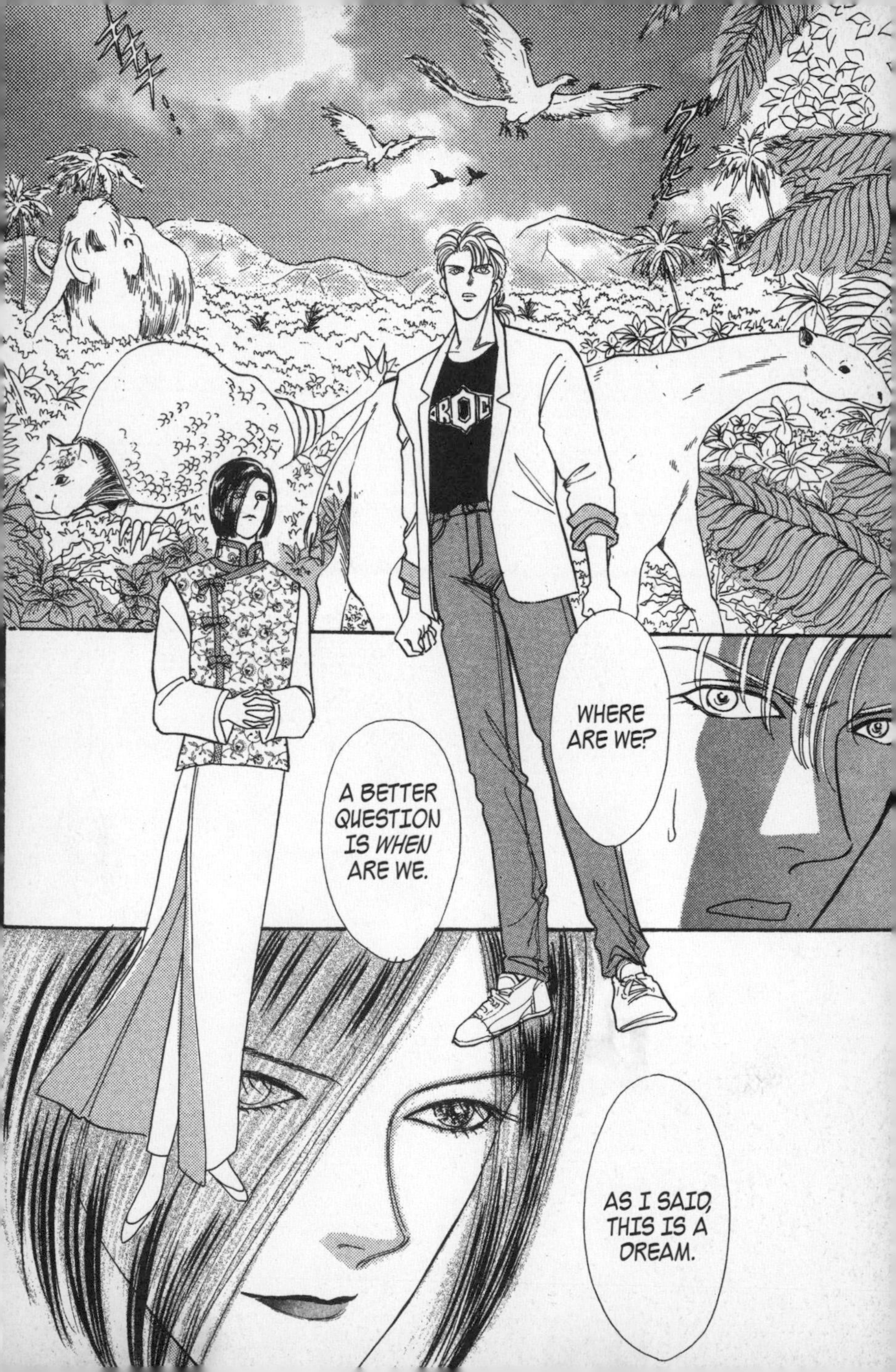
WHERE ARE WE?
A BETTER QUESTION IS *WHEN* ARE WE.
AS I SAID, THIS IS A DREAM.

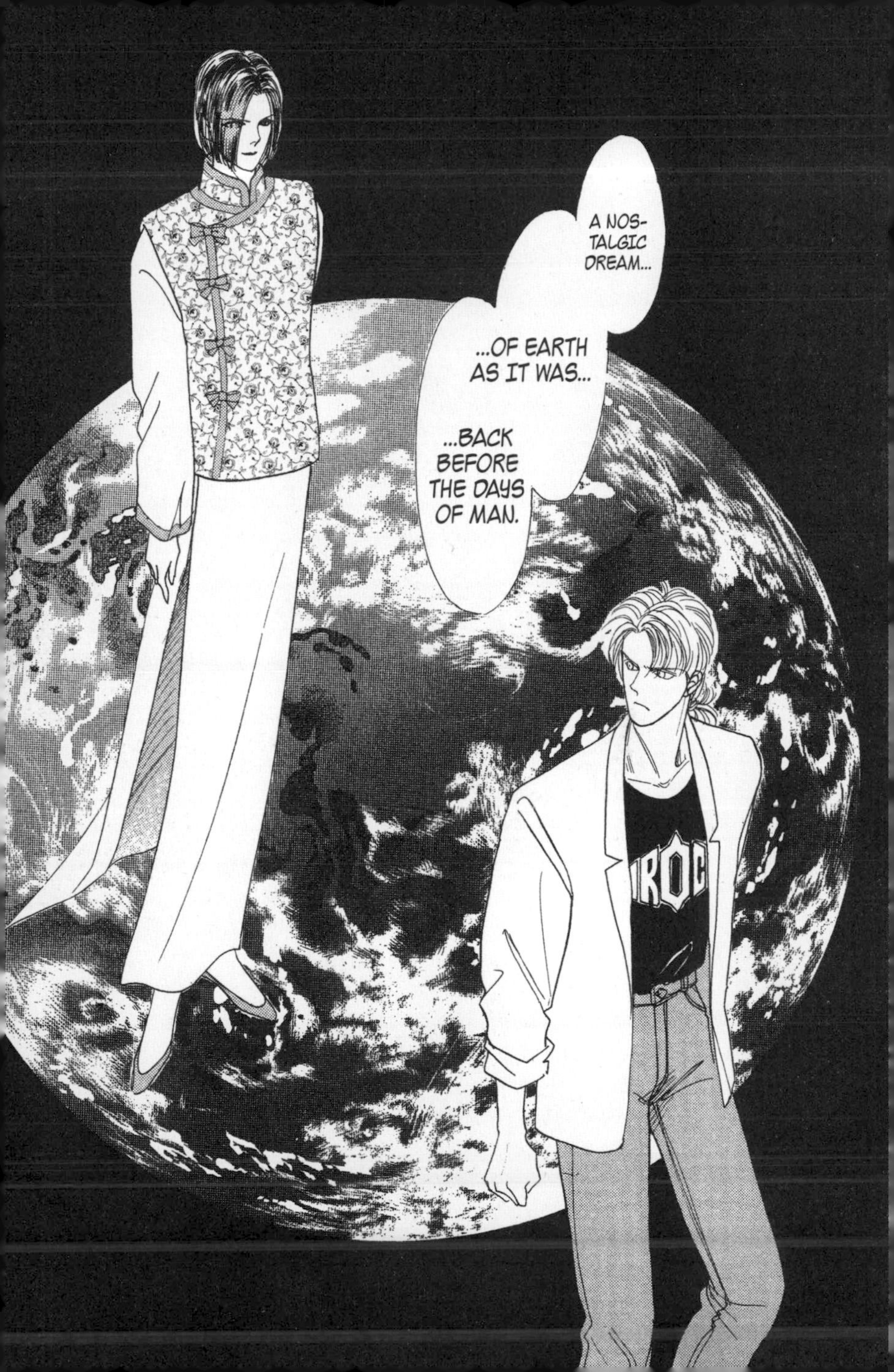
A NOS-
TALGIC
DREAM...
...OF EARTH
AS IT WAS...
...BACK
BEFORE
THE DAYS
OF MAN.

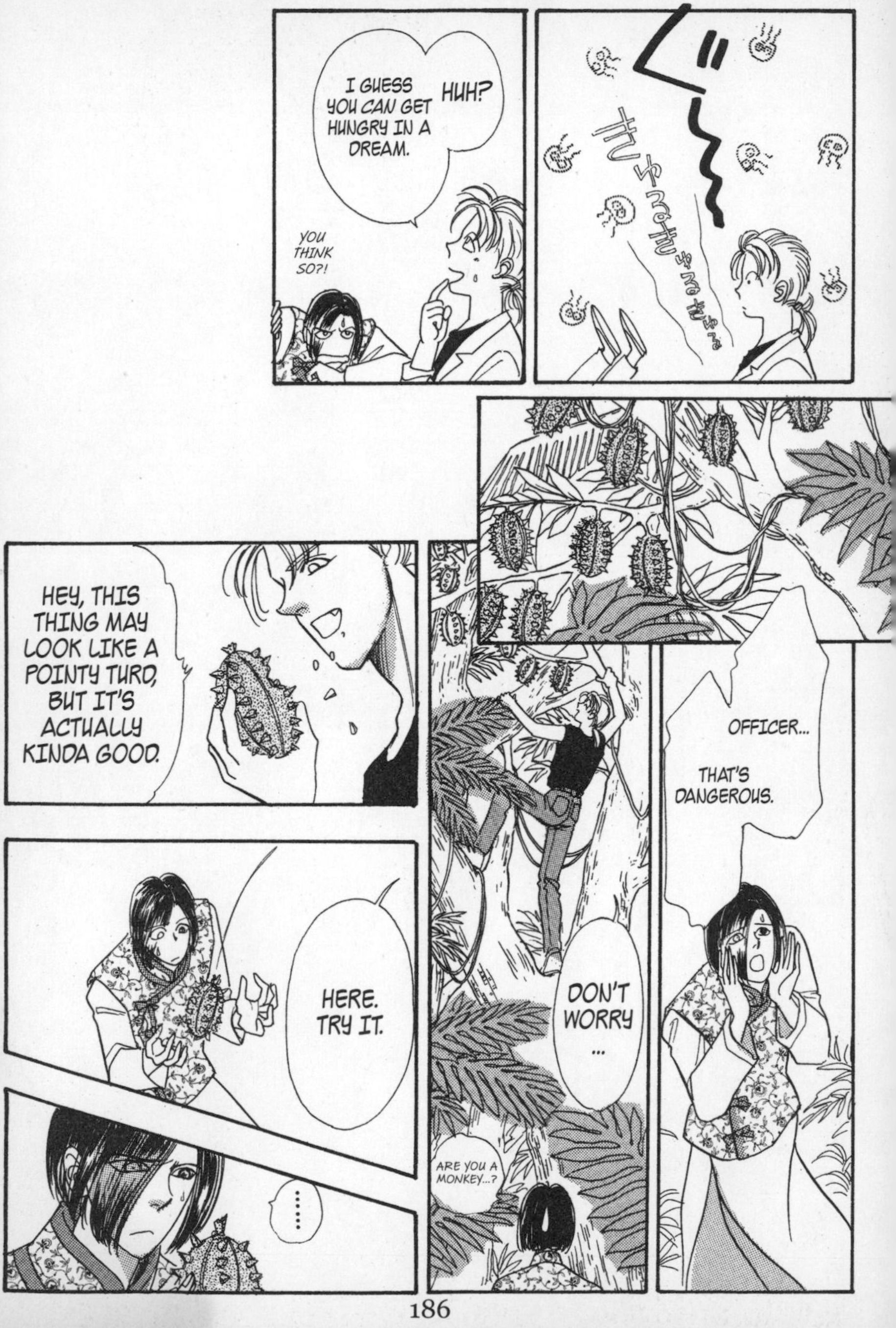
ぐ〜
きゅるきゅるきゅる
HUH?
I GUESS YOU CAN GET HUNGRY IN A DREAM.
YOU THINK SO?!
OFFICER...
THAT'S DANGEROUS.
DON'T WORRY ...
ARE YOU A MONKEY...?
HEY, THIS THING MAY LOOK LIKE A POINTY TURD, BUT IT'S ACTUALLY KINDA GOOD.
HERE. TRY IT.
......

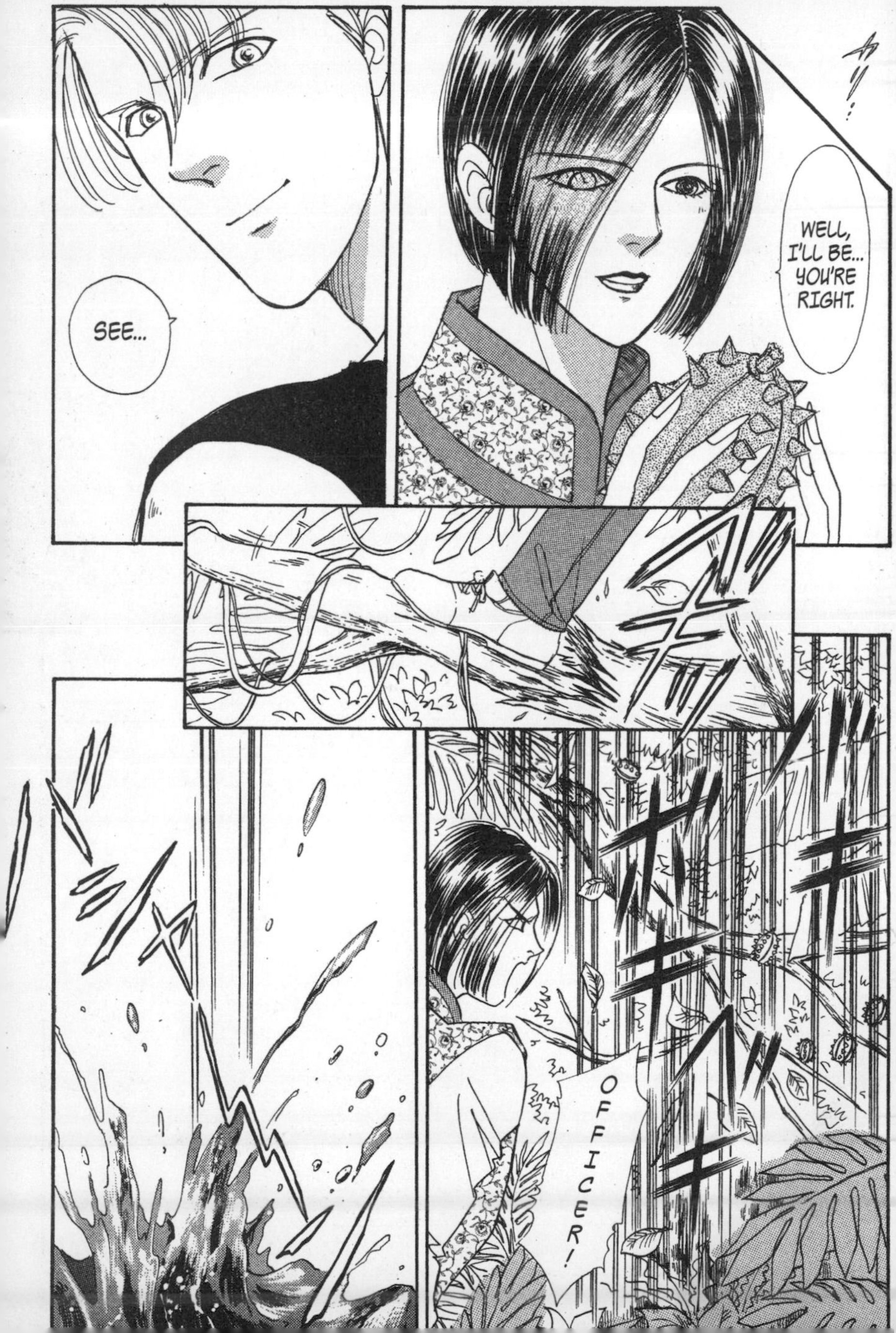
WELL, I'LL BE... YOU'RE RIGHT.
SEE...
OFFICER!

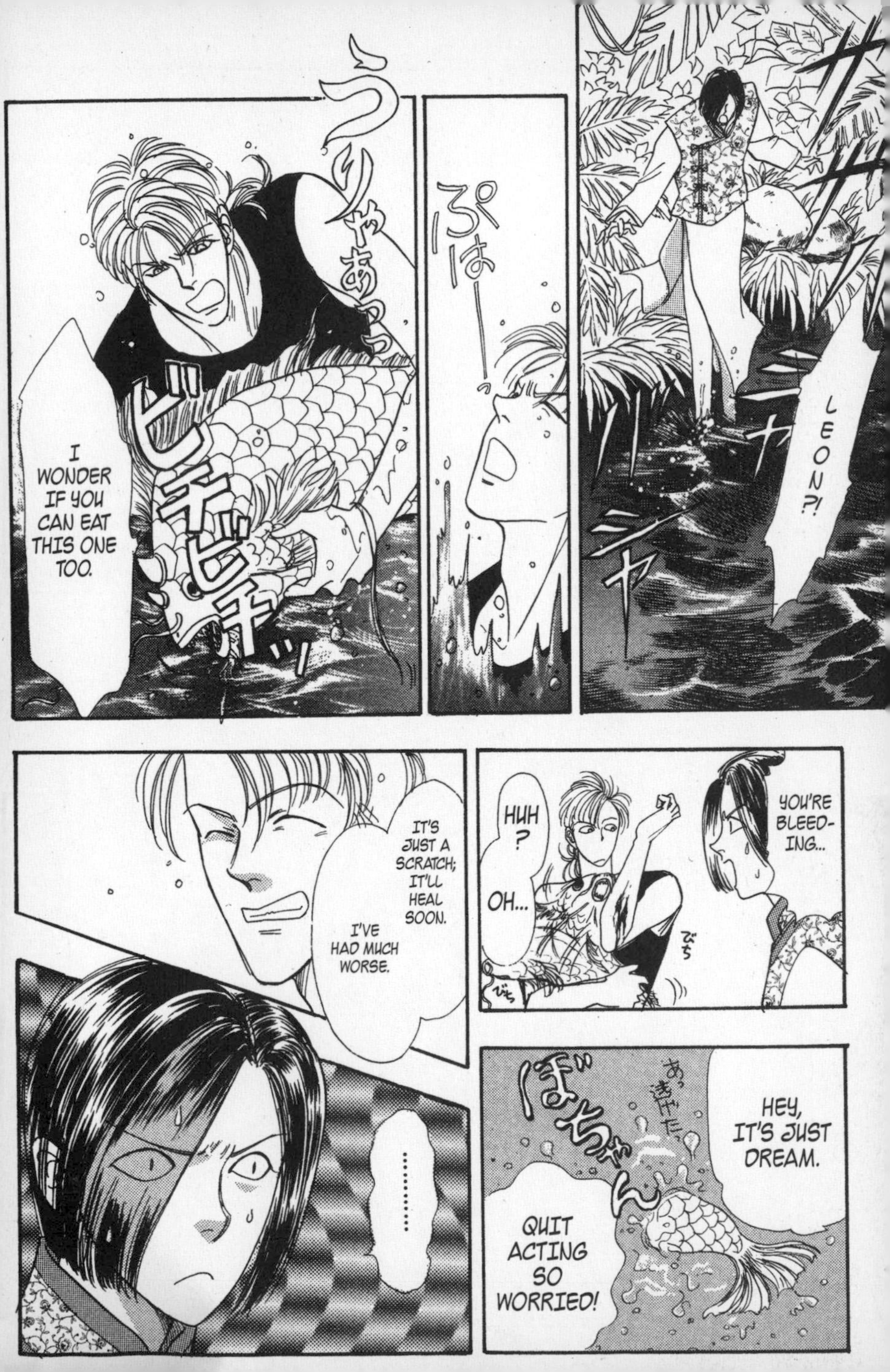
LEON?!
ぷはーっ
うりゃあっ
ビチビチッ
I WONDER IF YOU CAN EAT THIS ONE TOO.
YOU'RE BLEED-ING...
HUH?
OH...
IT'S JUST A SCRATCH; IT'LL HEAL SOON.
I'VE HAD MUCH WORSE.
......
HEY, IT'S JUST DREAM.
あっ逃げた
ぼちゃん
QUIT ACTING SO WORRIED!

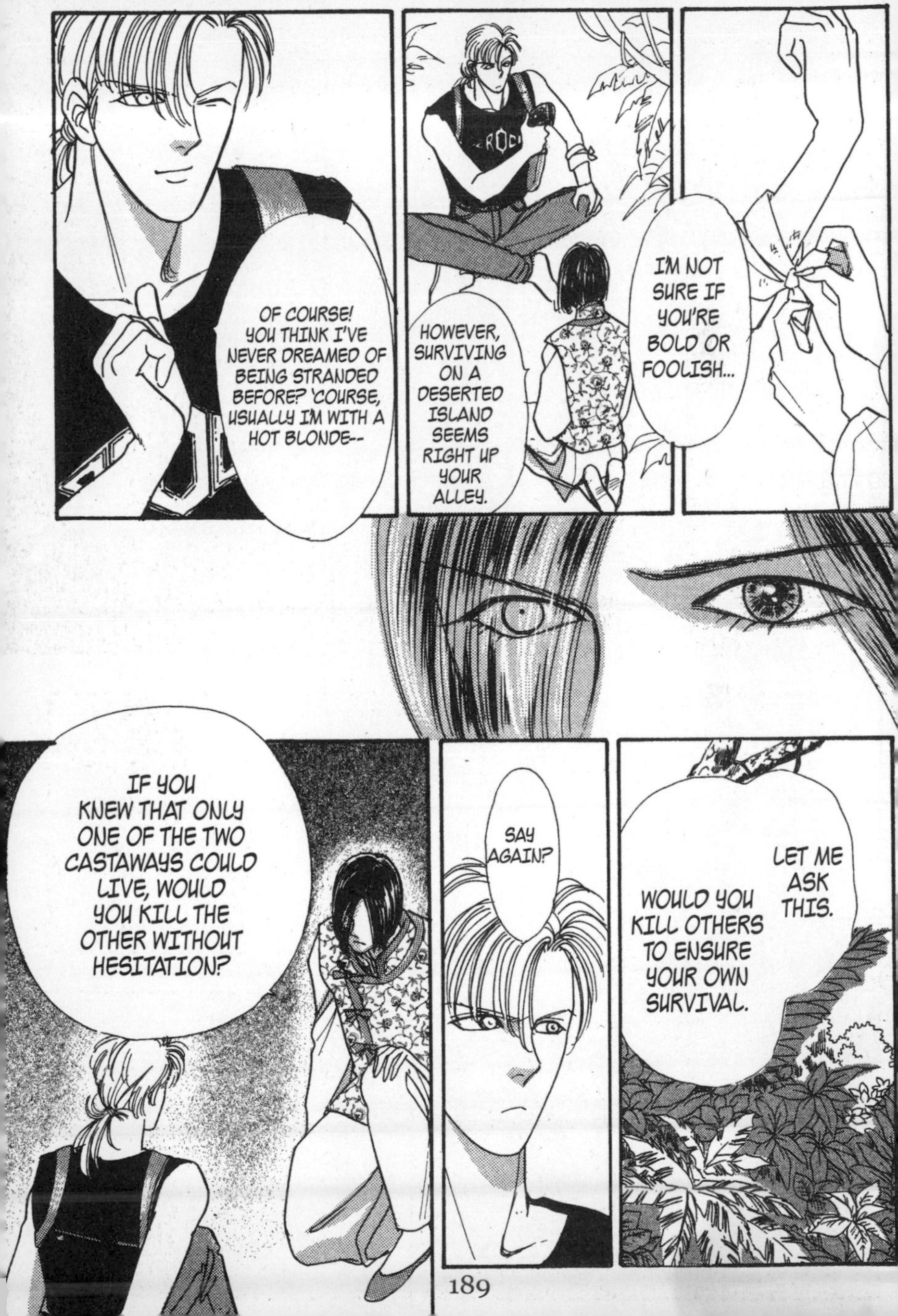
I'M NOT SURE IF YOU'RE BOLD OR FOOLISH...
HOWEVER, SURVIVING ON A DESERTED ISLAND SEEMS RIGHT UP YOUR ALLEY.
OF COURSE! YOU THINK I'VE NEVER DREAMED OF BEING STRANDED BEFORE? 'COURSE, USUALLY I'M WITH A HOT BLONDE--
LET ME ASK THIS.
WOULD YOU KILL OTHERS TO ENSURE YOUR OWN SURVIVAL.
SAY AGAIN?
IF YOU KNEW THAT ONLY ONE OF THE TWO CASTAWAYS COULD LIVE, WOULD YOU KILL THE OTHER WITHOUT HESITATION?

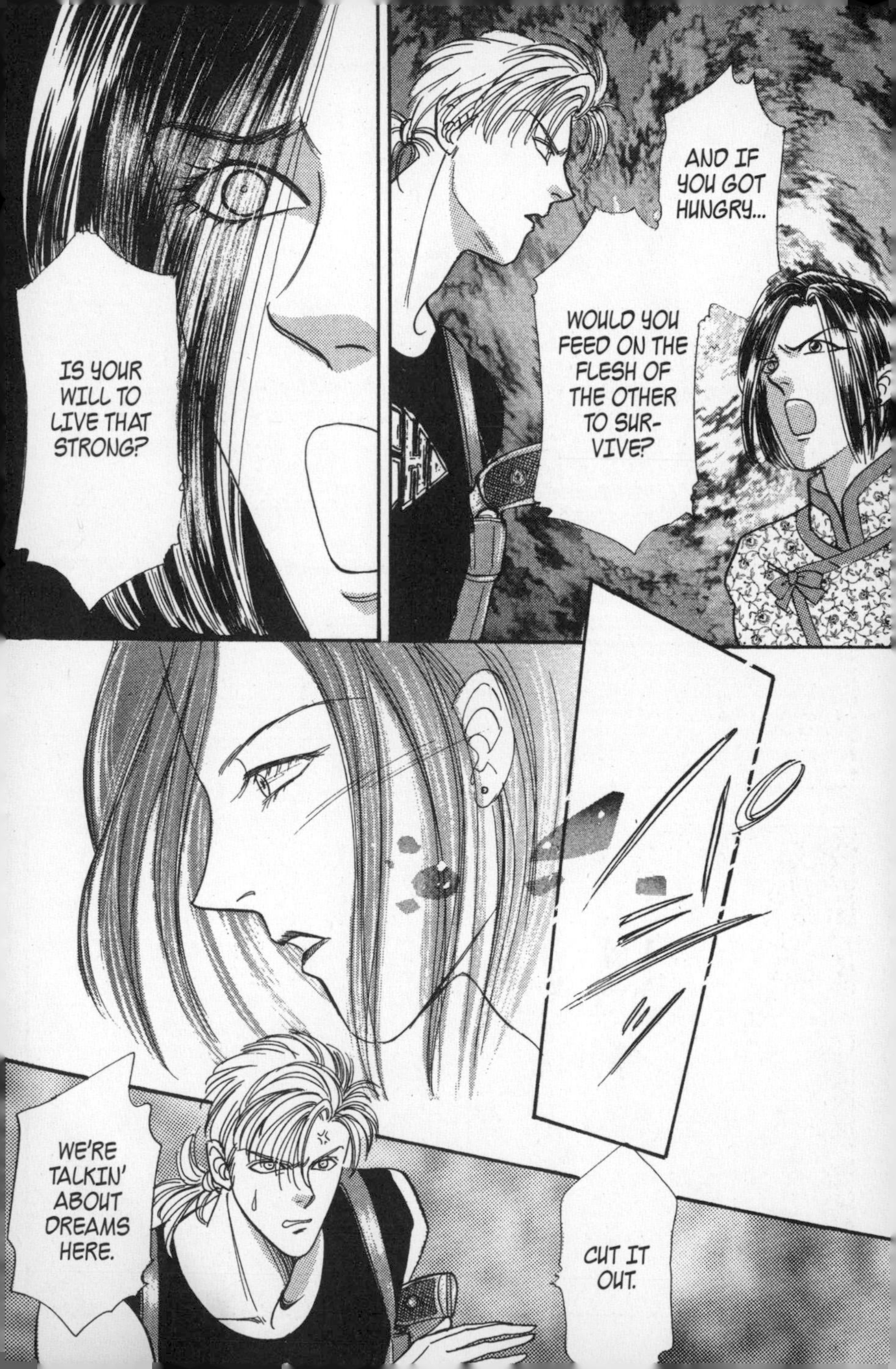
AND IF YOU GOT HUNGRY...
WOULD YOU FEED ON THE FLESH OF THE OTHER TO SUR-VIVE?
IS YOUR WILL TO LIVE THAT STRONG?
CUT IT OUT.
WE'RE TALKIN' ABOUT DREAMS HERE.

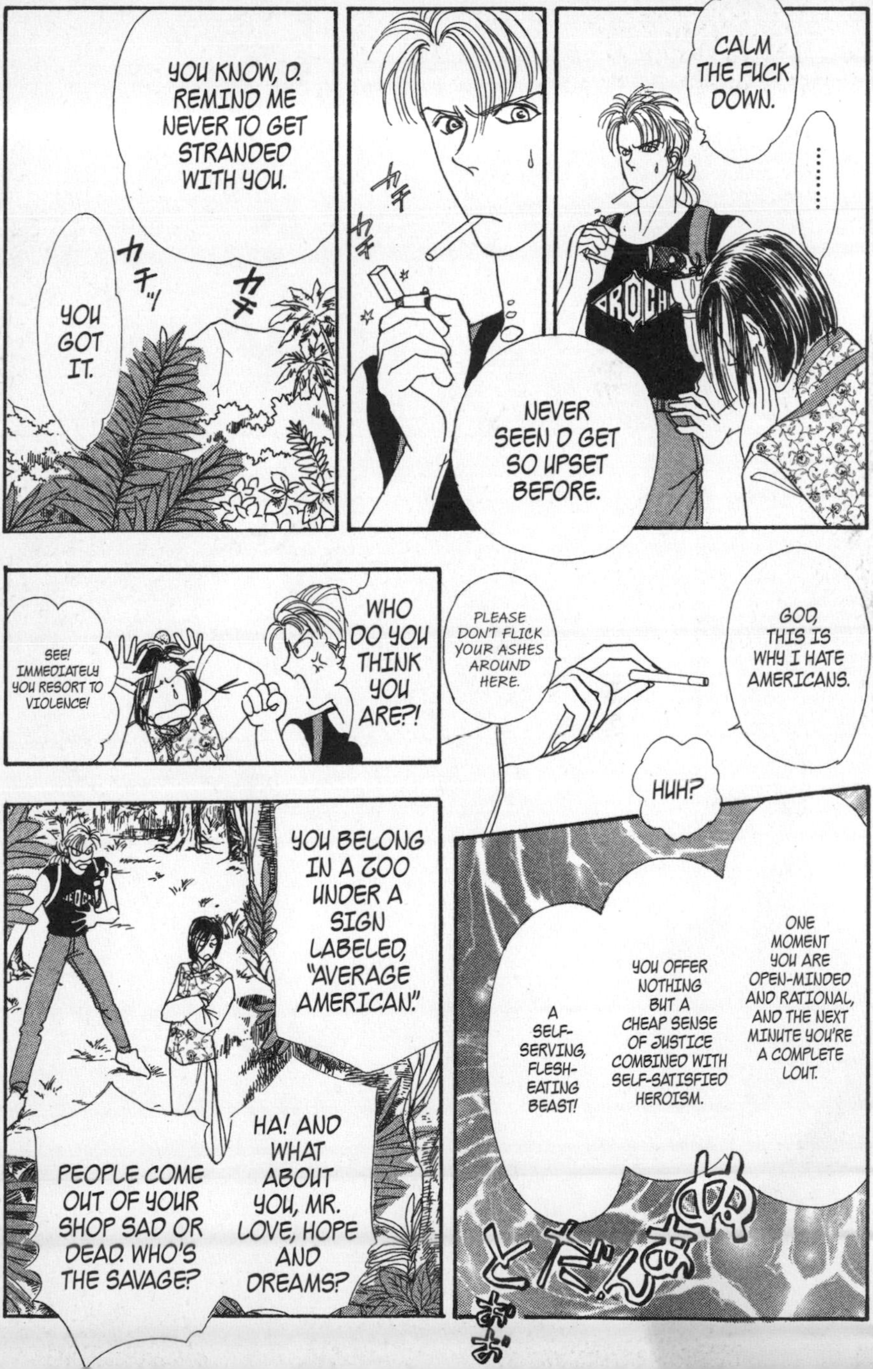
CALM THE FUCK DOWN.
......
カチ
カチ
NEVER SEEN D GET SO UPSET BEFORE.
YOU KNOW, D. REMIND ME NEVER TO GET STRANDED WITH YOU.
カチ
カチッ
YOU GOT IT.
GOD, THIS IS WHY I HATE AMERICANS.
PLEASE DON'T FLICK YOUR ASHES AROUND HERE.
WHO DO YOU THINK YOU ARE?!
SEE! IMMEDIATELY YOU RESORT TO VIOLENCE!
HUH?
ONE MOMENT YOU ARE OPEN-MINDED AND RATIONAL, AND THE NEXT MINUTE YOU'RE A COMPLETE LOUT.
YOU OFFER NOTHING BUT A CHEAP SENSE OF JUSTICE COMBINED WITH SELF-SATISFIED HEROISM.
A SELF-SERVING, FLESH-EATING BEAST!
YOU BELONG IN A ZOO UNDER A SIGN LABELED, "AVERAGE AMERICAN."
HA! AND WHAT ABOUT YOU, MR. LOVE, HOPE AND DREAMS?
PEOPLE COME OUT OF YOUR SHOP SAD OR DEAD. WHO'S THE SAVAGE?

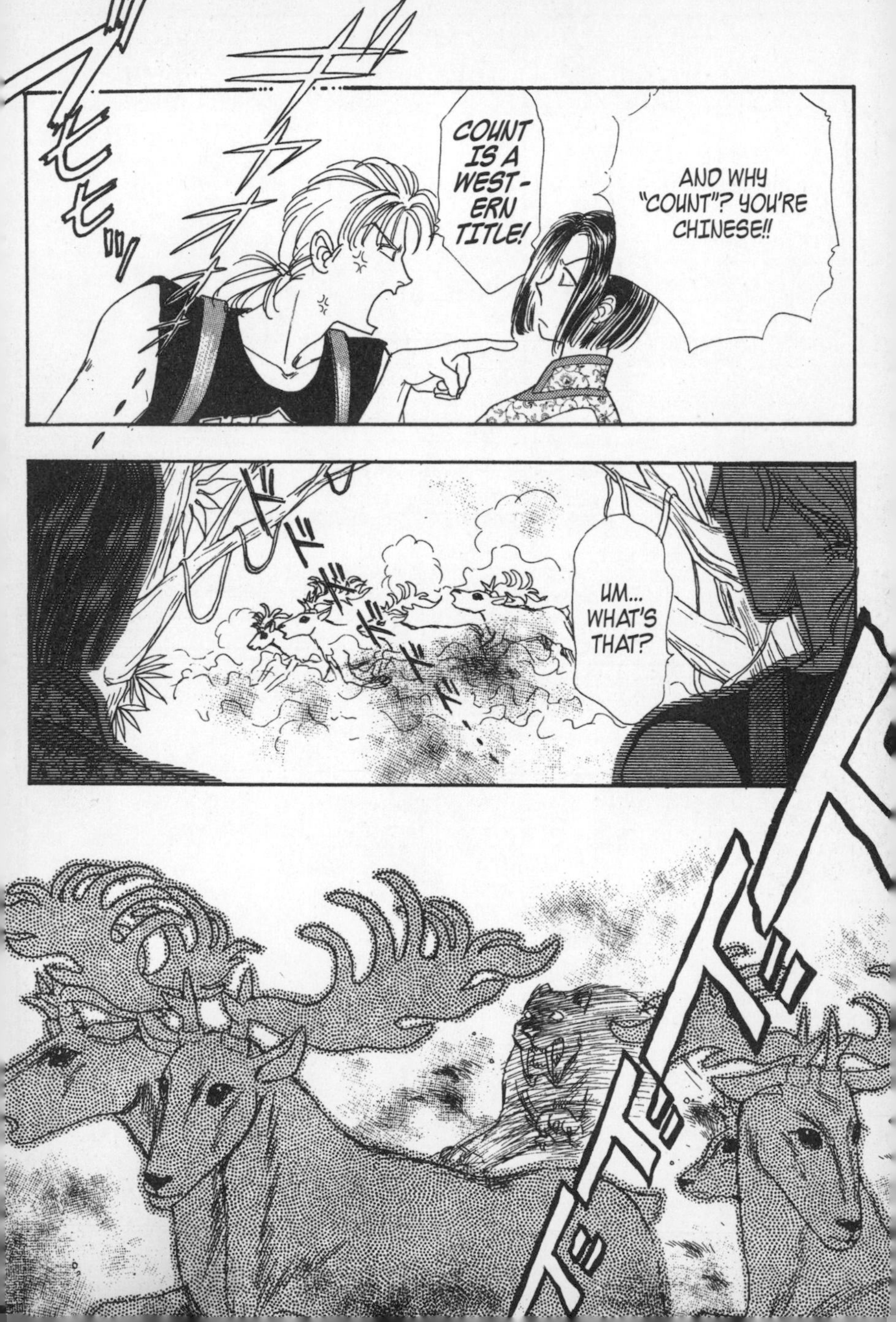
AND WHY "COUNT"? YOU'RE CHINESE!!
COUNT IS A WEST-ERN TITLE!
UM... WHAT'S THAT?

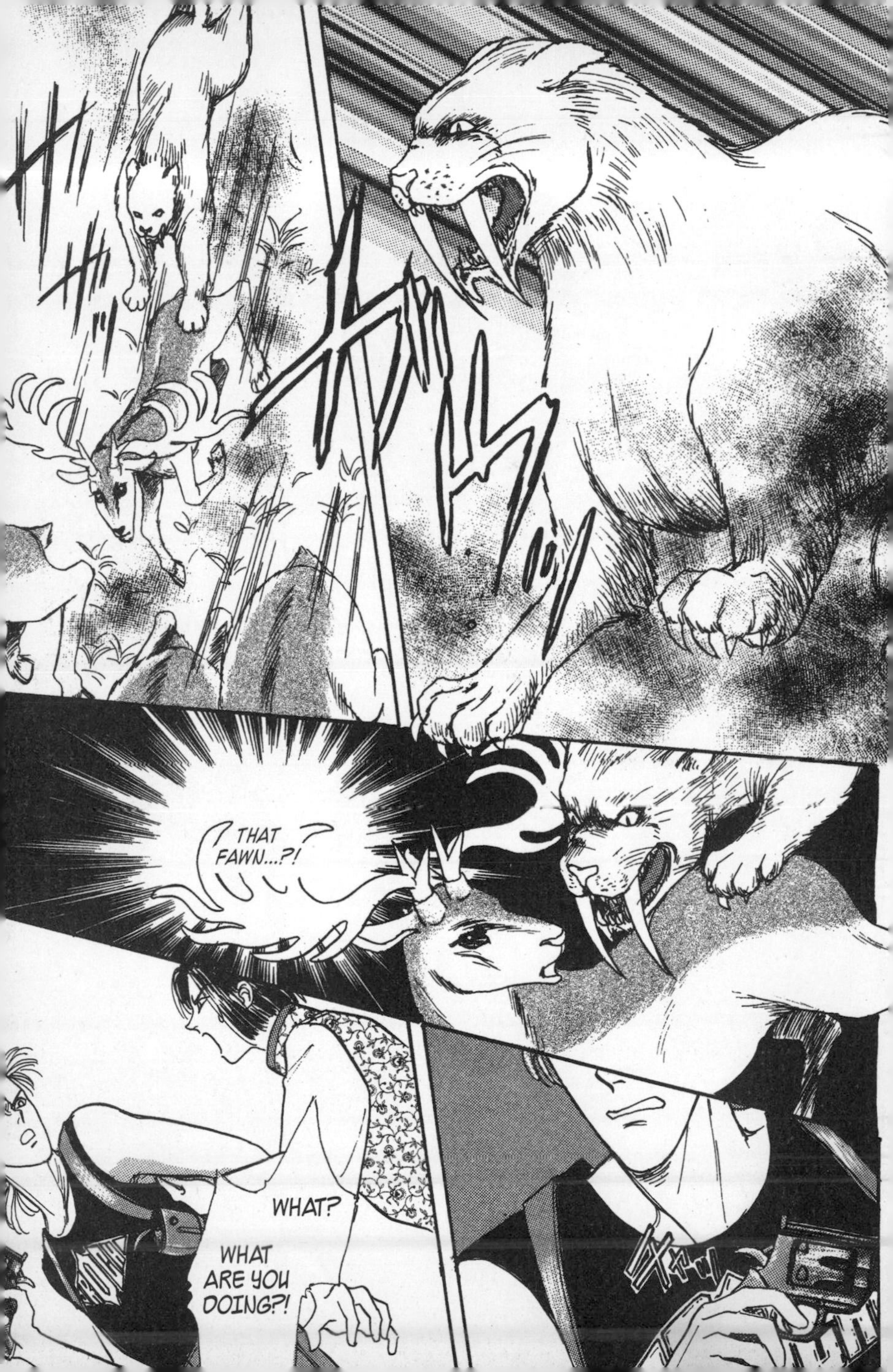
THAT FAWN...?!
WHAT?
WHAT ARE YOU DOING?!

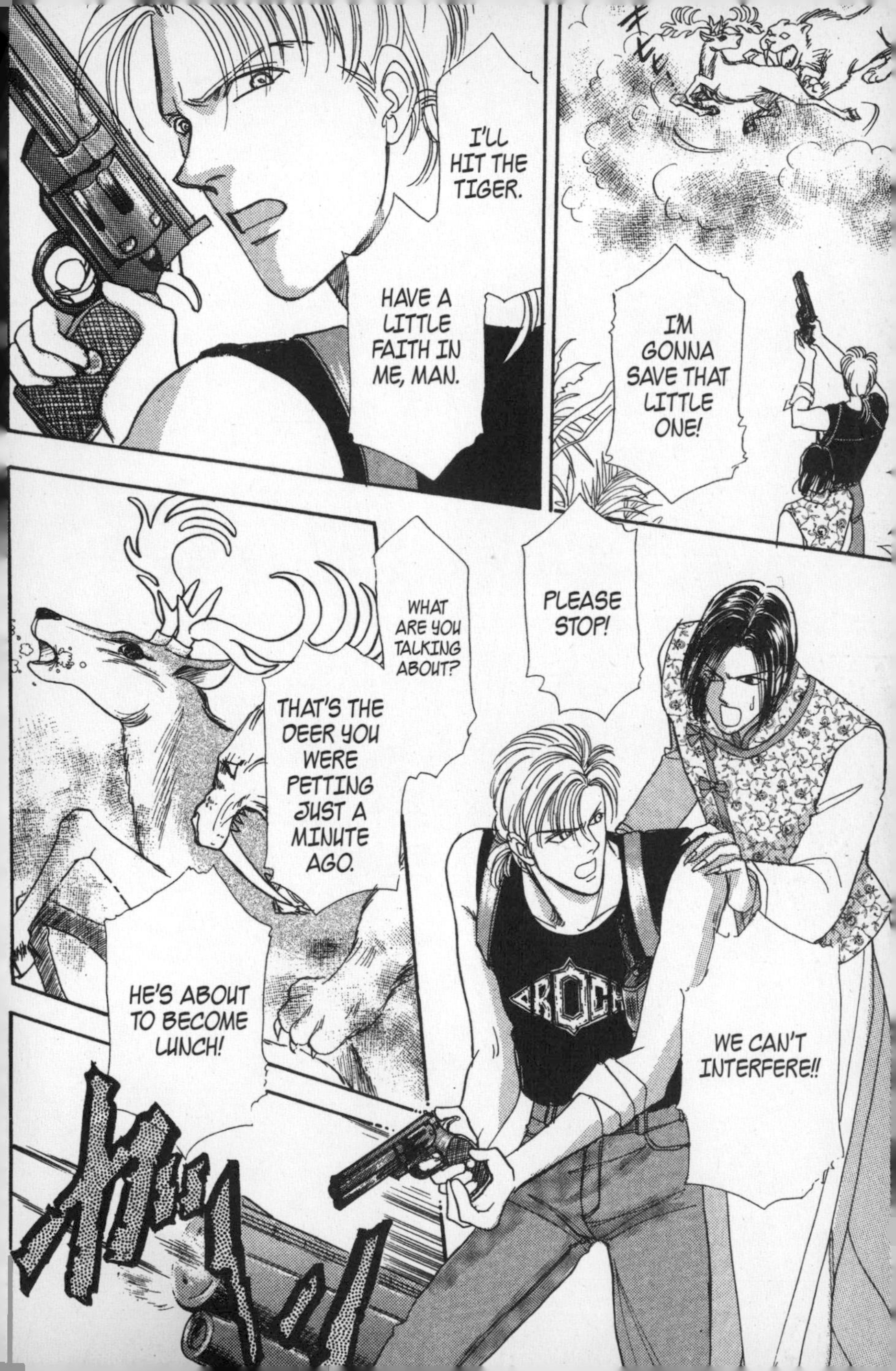
I'M GONNA SAVE THAT LITTLE ONE!
I'LL HIT THE TIGER.
HAVE A LITTLE FAITH IN ME, MAN.
PLEASE STOP!
WHAT ARE YOU TALKING ABOUT?
THAT'S THE DEER YOU WERE PETTING JUST A MINUTE AGO.
WE CAN'T INTERFERE!!
HE'S ABOUT TO BECOME LUNCH!

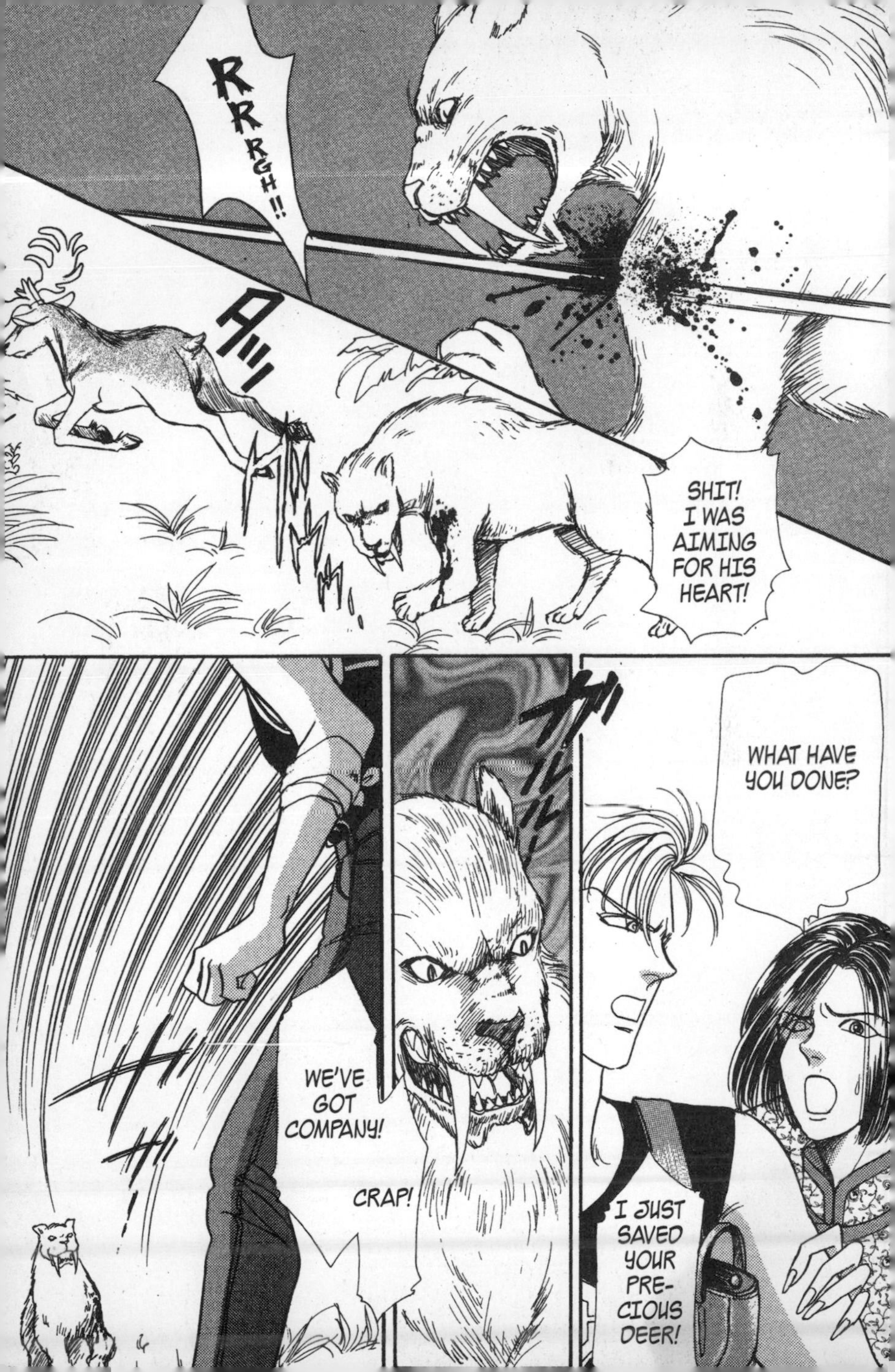
RRRGH!!
SHIT! I WAS AIMING FOR HIS HEART!
WHAT HAVE YOU DONE?
I JUST SAVED YOUR PRECIOUS DEER!
WE'VE GOT COMPANY!
CRAP!

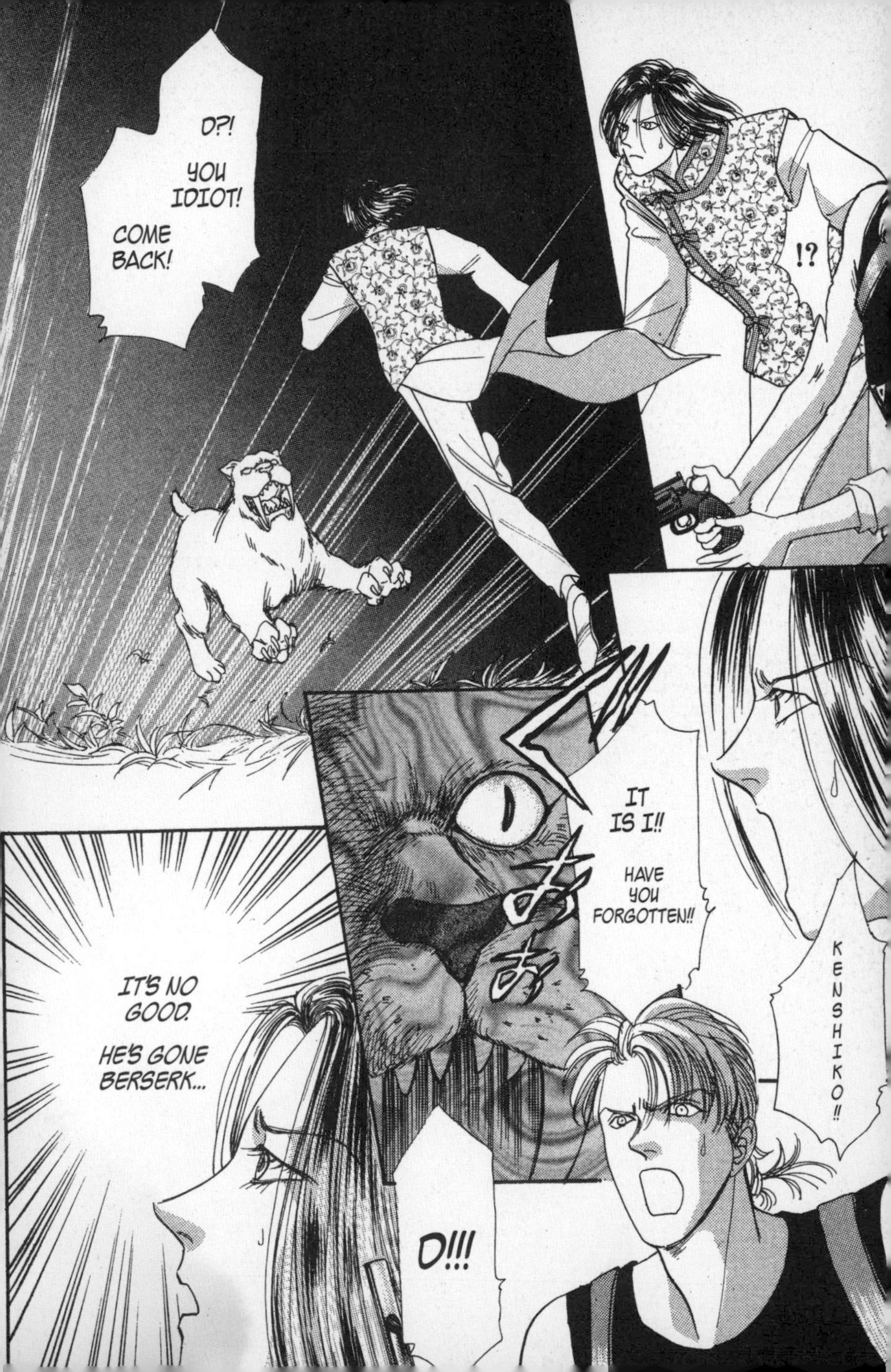
!?
D?!
YOU IDIOT!
COME BACK!
KENSHIKO!!
IT IS I!!
HAVE YOU FORGOTTEN!!
D!!!
IT'S NO GOOD.
HE'S GONE BERSERK...

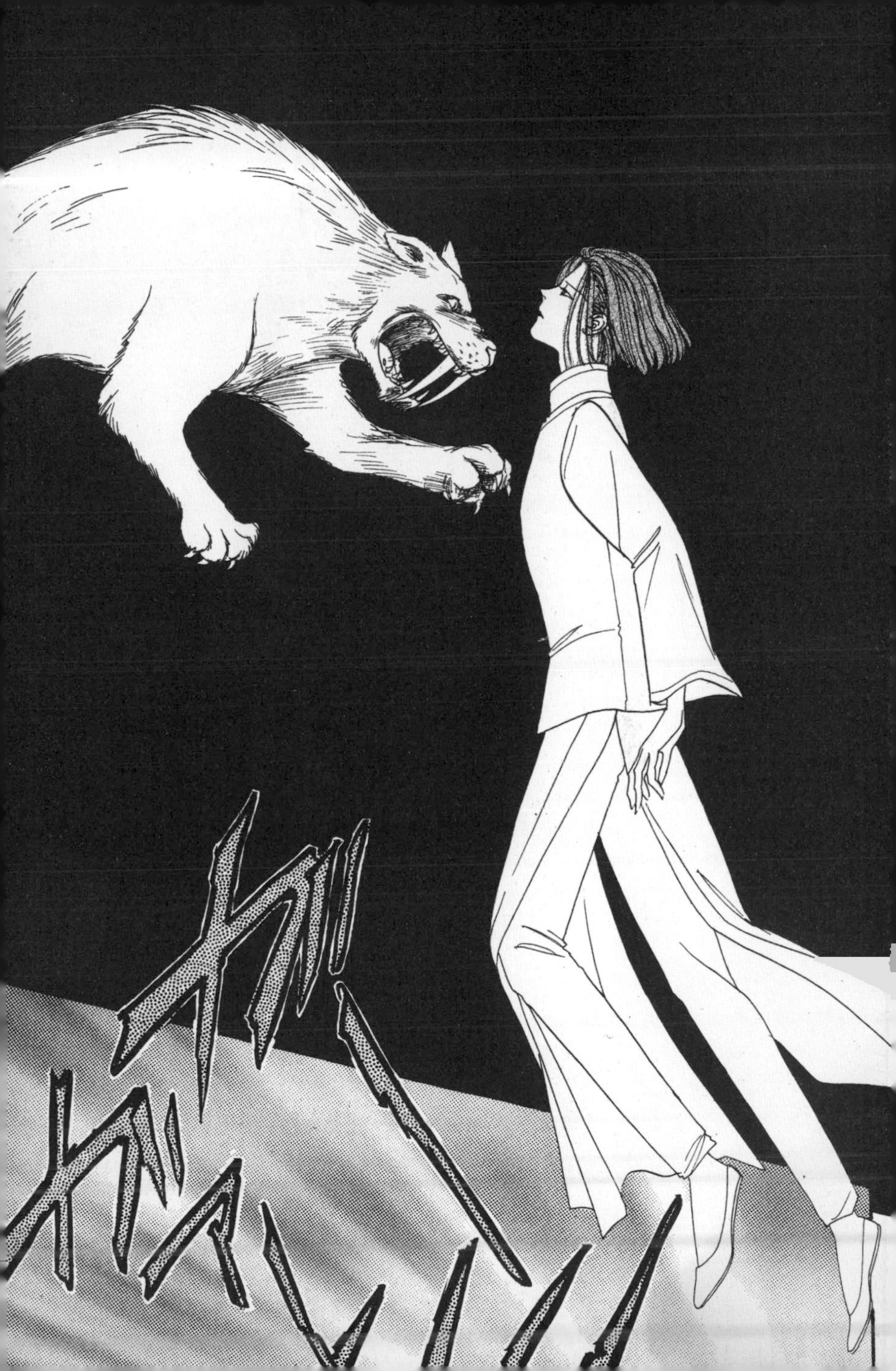

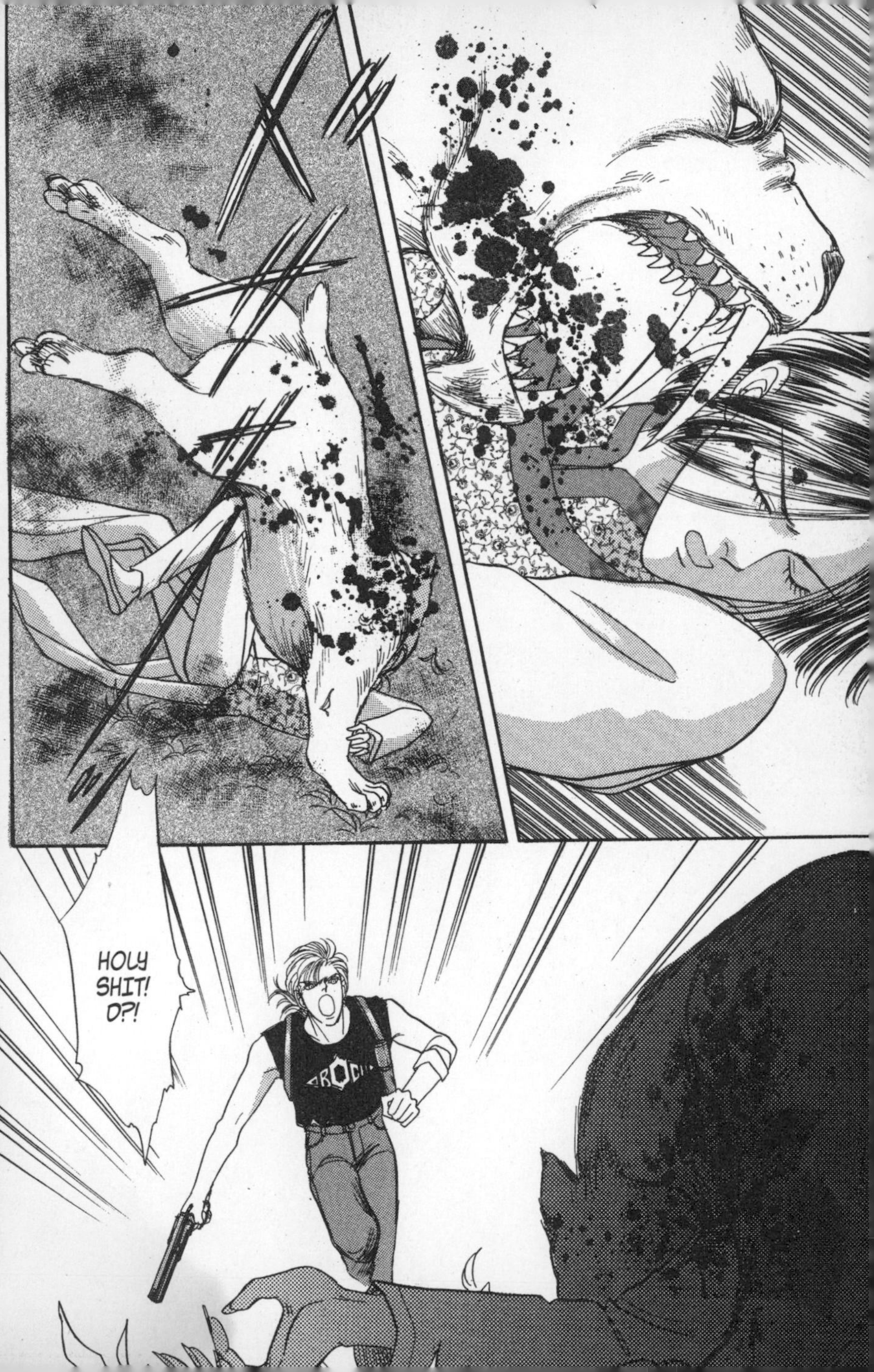
HOLY SHIT! D?!

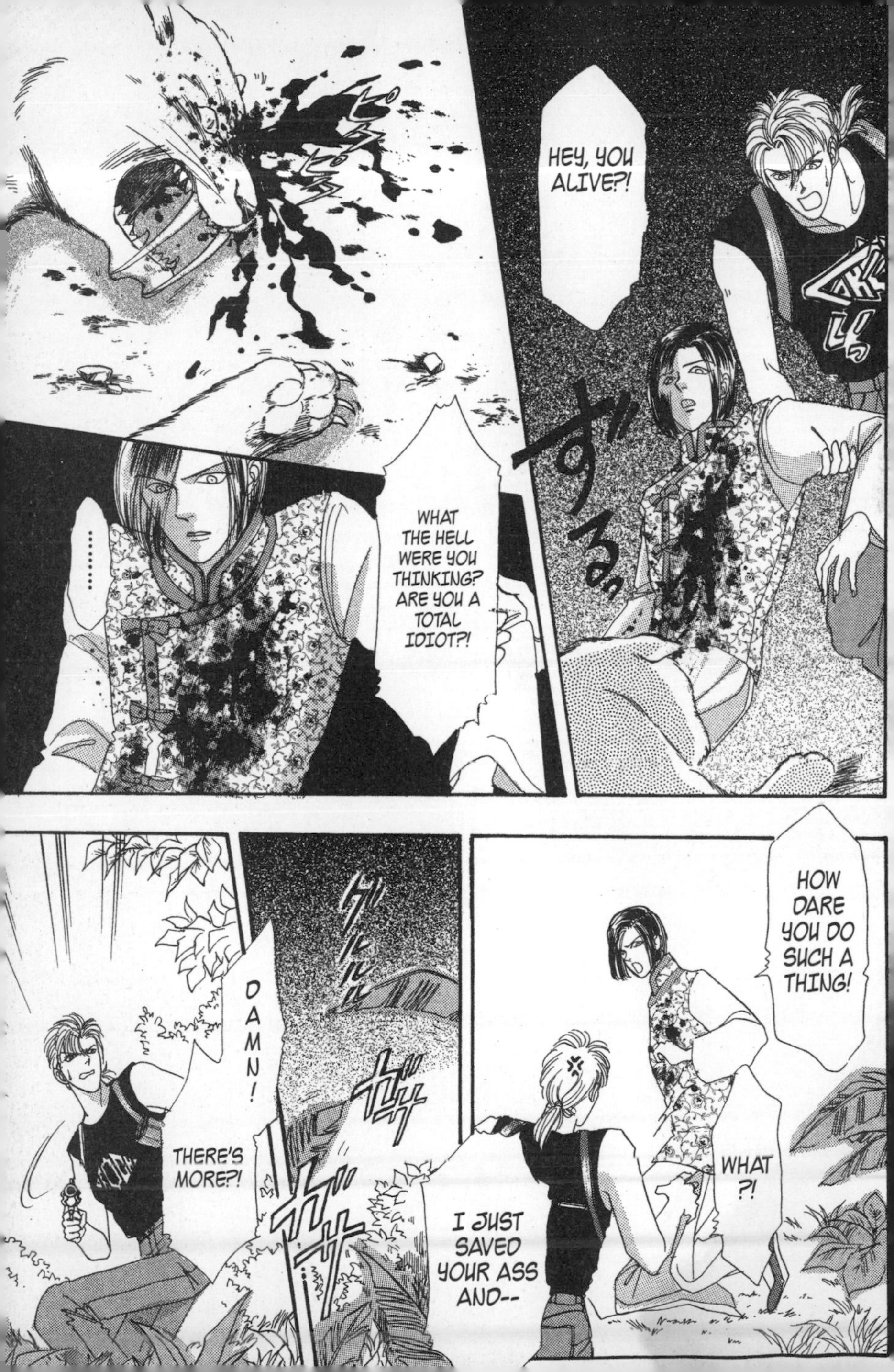

HEY, YOU ALIVE?!
WHAT THE HELL WERE YOU THINKING? ARE YOU A TOTAL IDIOT?!
......
HOW DARE YOU DO SUCH A THING!
WHAT?!
I JUST SAVED YOUR ASS AND--
DAMN!
THERE'S MORE?!

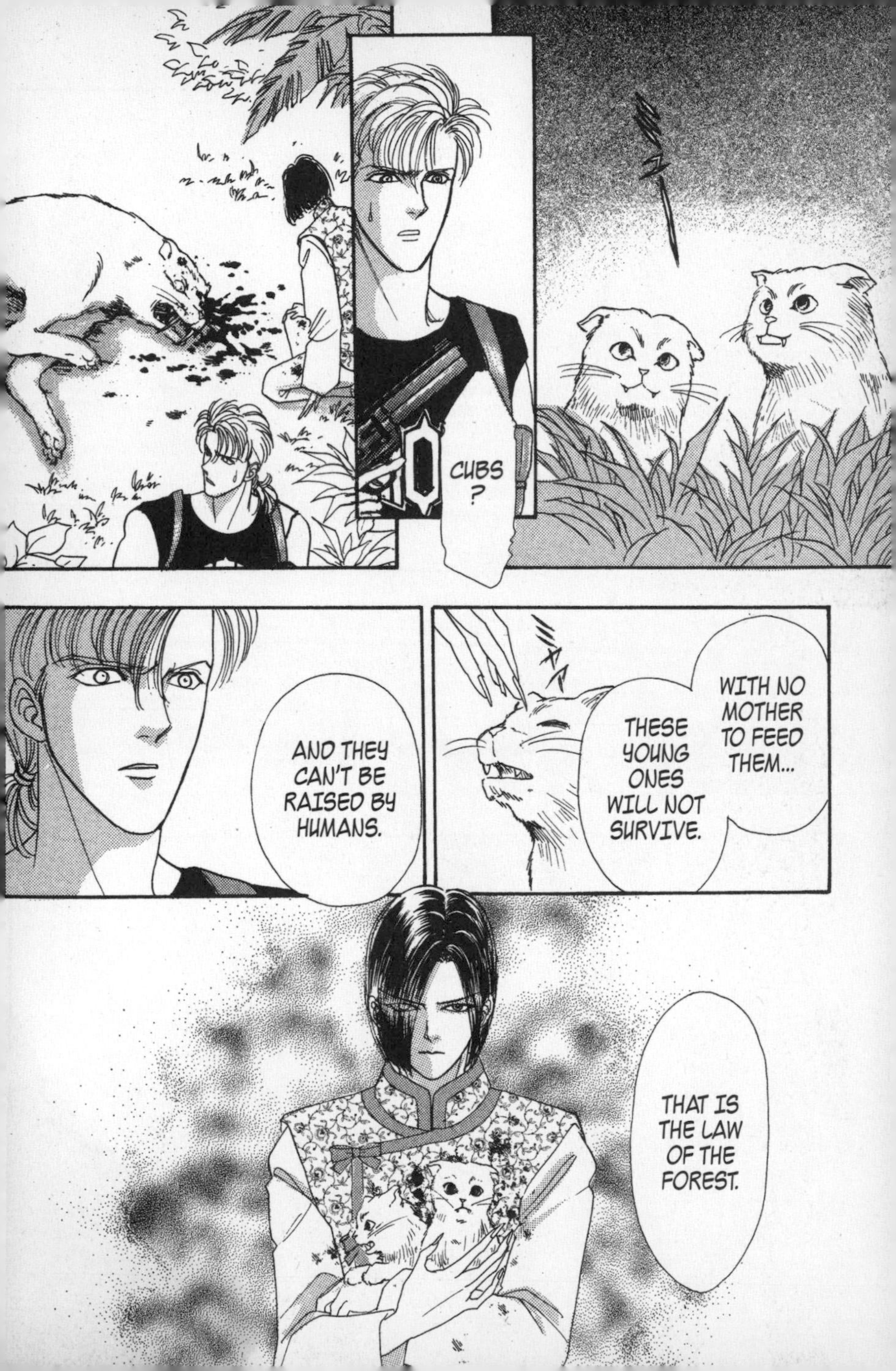
CUBS?
WITH NO MOTHER TO FEED THEM...
THESE YOUNG ONES WILL NOT SURVIVE.
AND THEY CAN'T BE RAISED BY HUMANS.
THAT IS THE LAW OF THE FOREST.

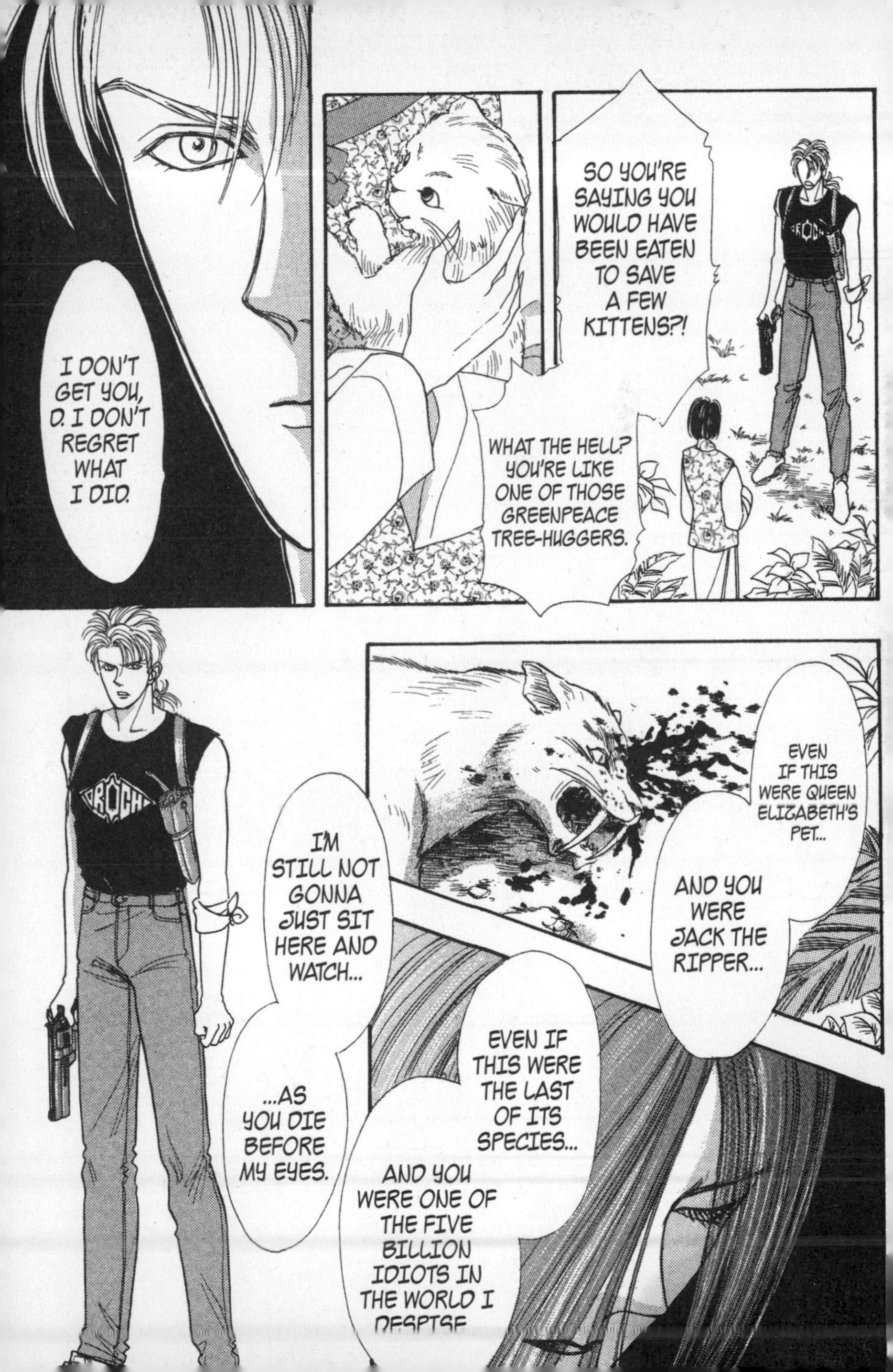
SO YOU'RE SAYING YOU WOULD HAVE BEEN EATEN TO SAVE A FEW KITTENS?!
WHAT THE HELL? YOU'RE LIKE ONE OF THOSE GREENPEACE TREE-HUGGERS.
I DON'T GET YOU, D. I DON'T REGRET WHAT I DID.
EVEN IF THIS WERE QUEEN ELIZABETH'S PET...
AND YOU WERE JACK THE RIPPER...
EVEN IF THIS WERE THE LAST OF ITS SPECIES...
AND YOU WERE ONE OF THE FIVE BILLION IDIOTS IN THE WORLD I DESPISE
I'M STILL NOT GONNA JUST SIT HERE AND WATCH...
...AS YOU DIE BEFORE MY EYES.

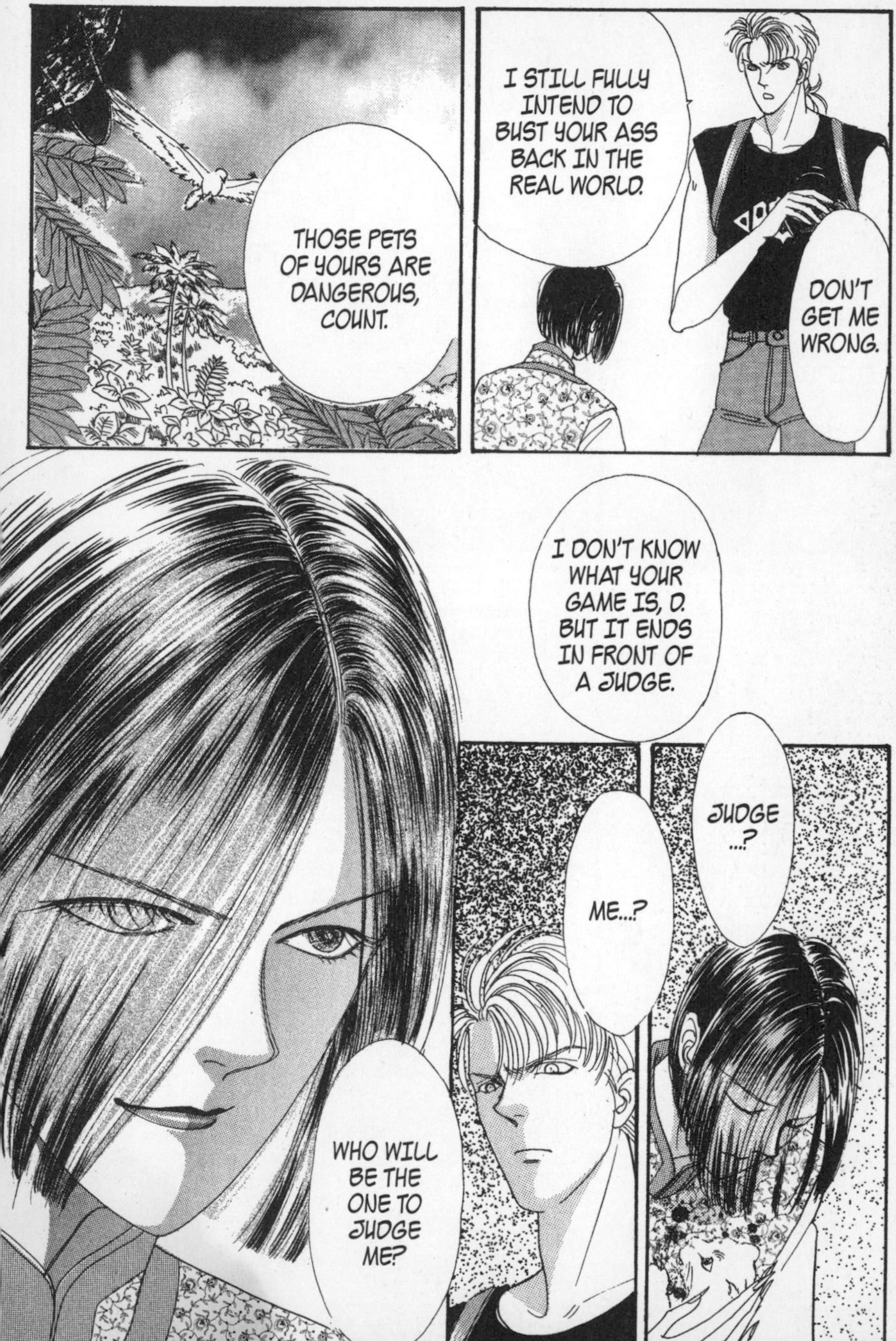
DON'T GET ME WRONG.
I STILL FULLY INTEND TO BUST YOUR ASS BACK IN THE REAL WORLD.
THOSE PETS OF YOURS ARE DANGEROUS, COUNT.
I DON'T KNOW WHAT YOUR GAME IS, D. BUT IT ENDS IN FRONT OF A JUDGE.
JUDGE ...?
ME...?
WHO WILL BE THE ONE TO JUDGE ME?

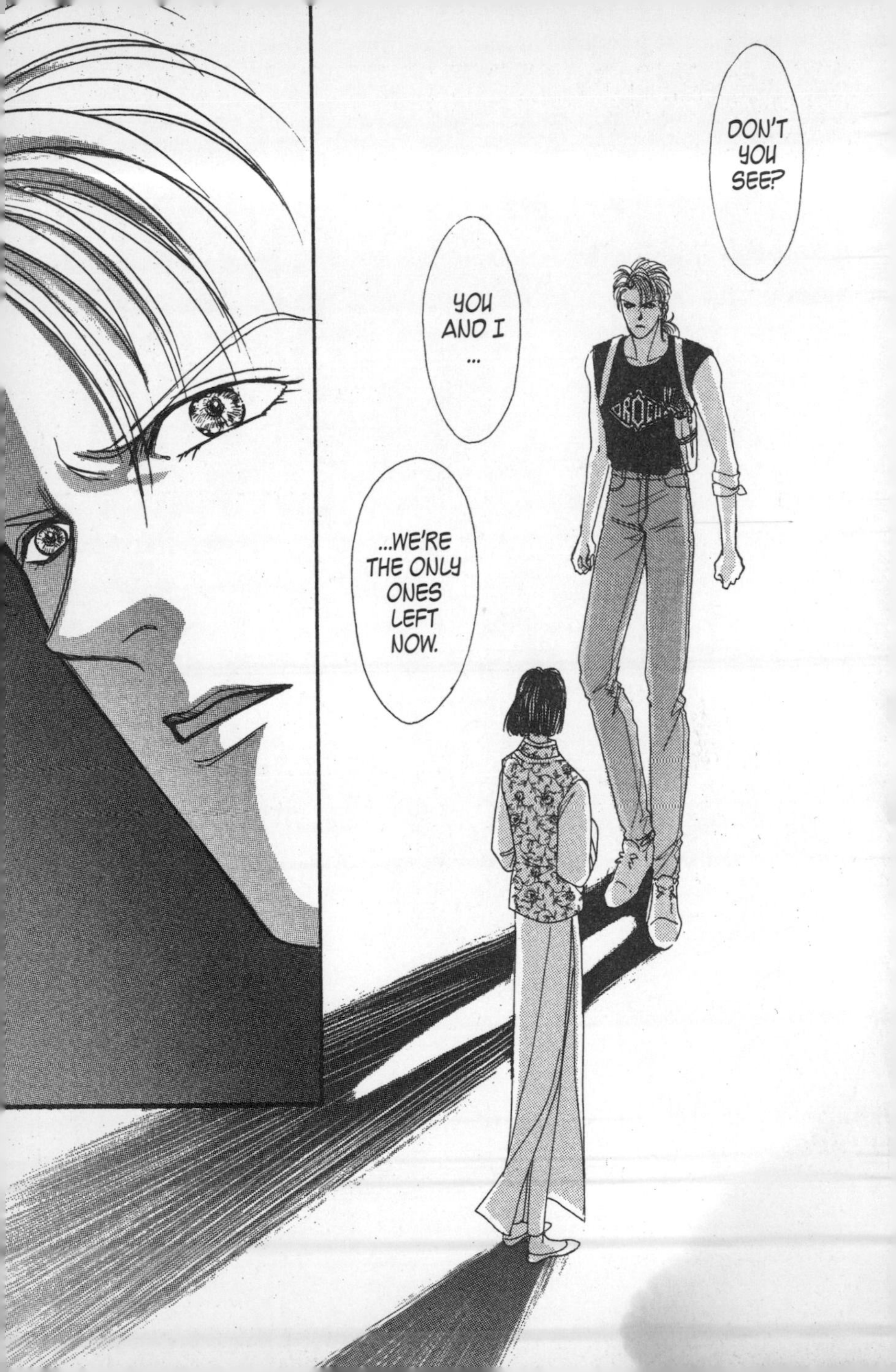
DON'T YOU SEE?
YOU AND I ...
...WE'RE THE ONLY ONES LEFT NOW.

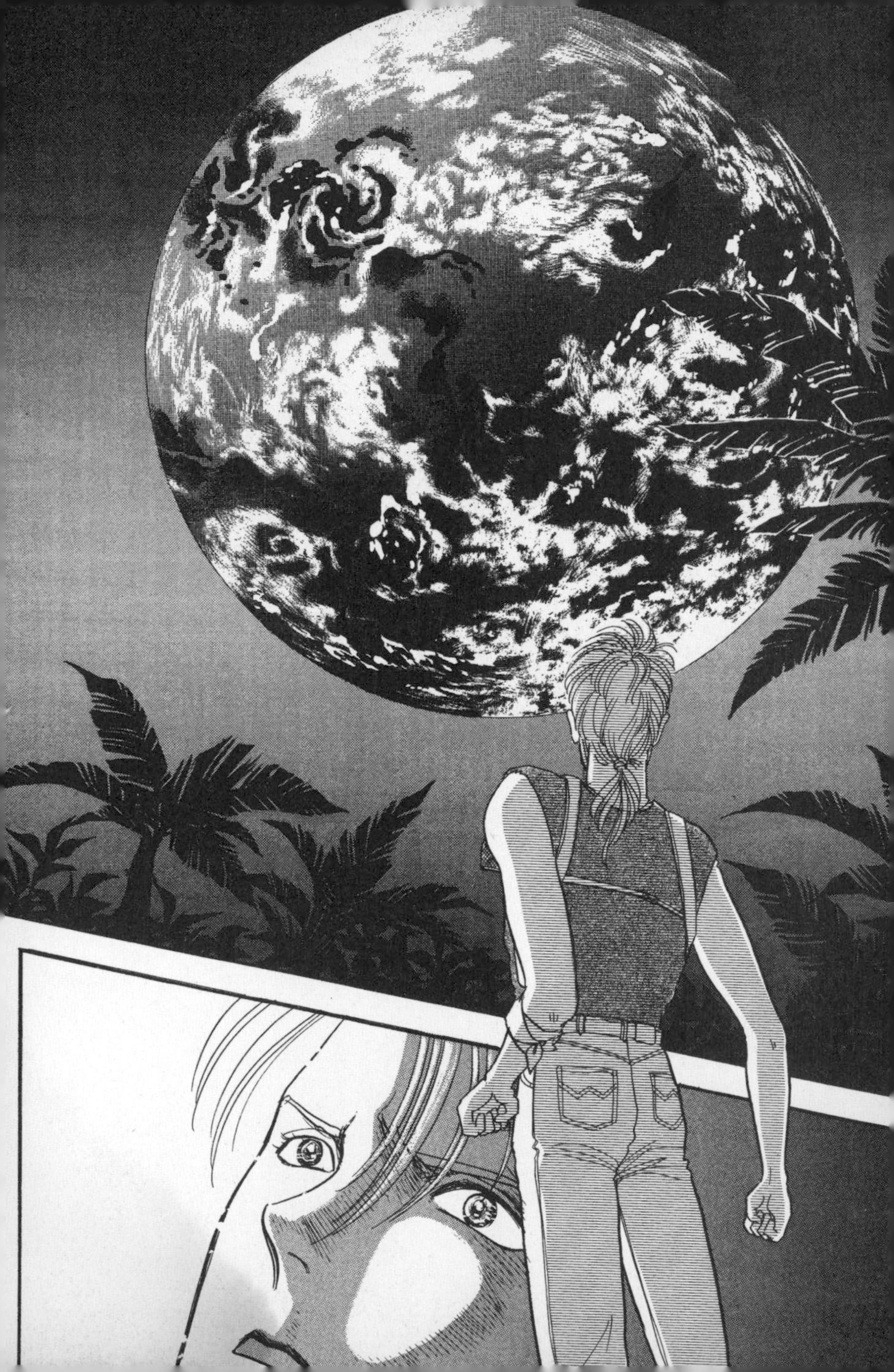

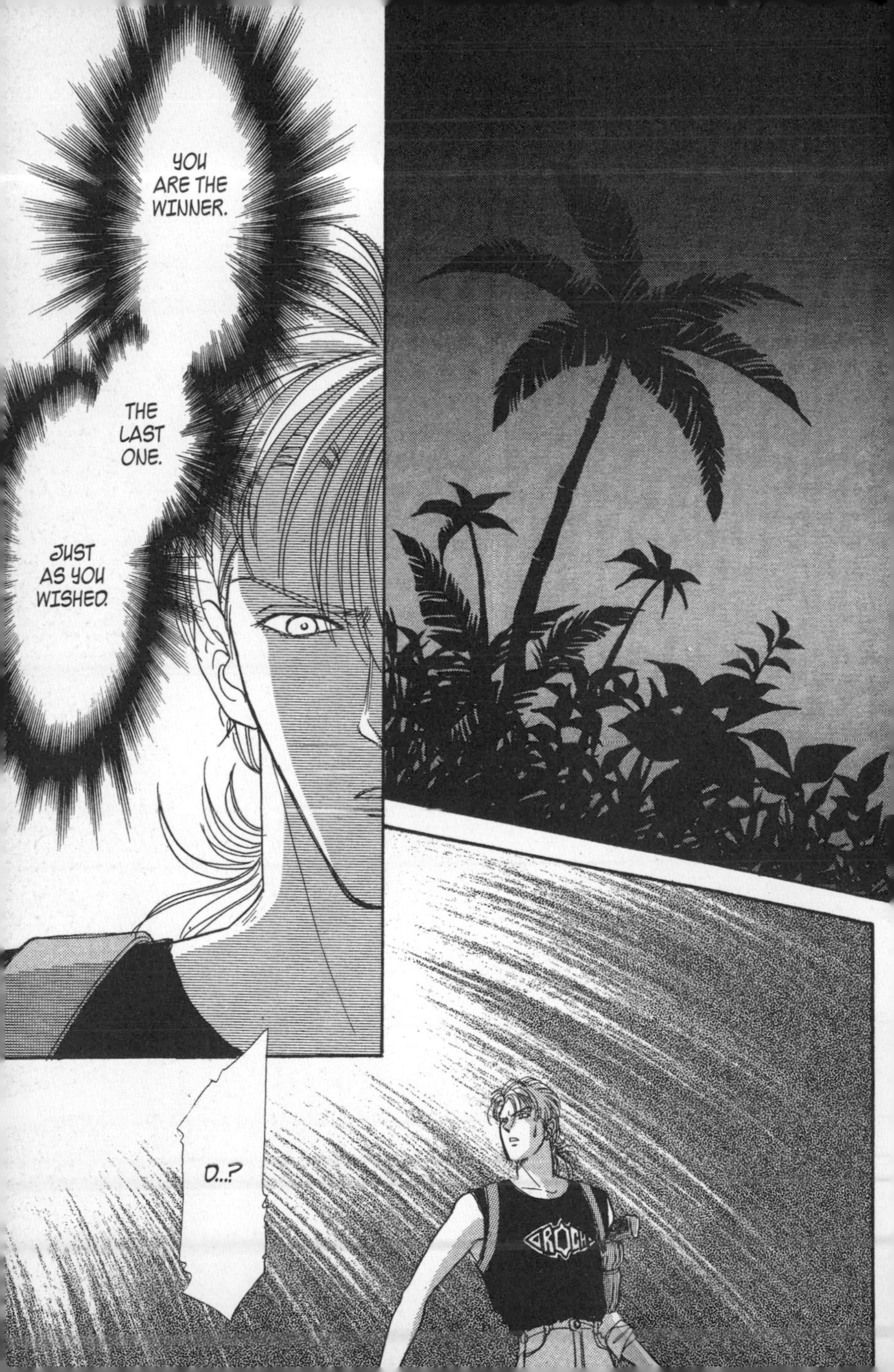
YOU ARE THE WINNER.
THE LAST ONE.
JUST AS YOU WISHED.
O..?

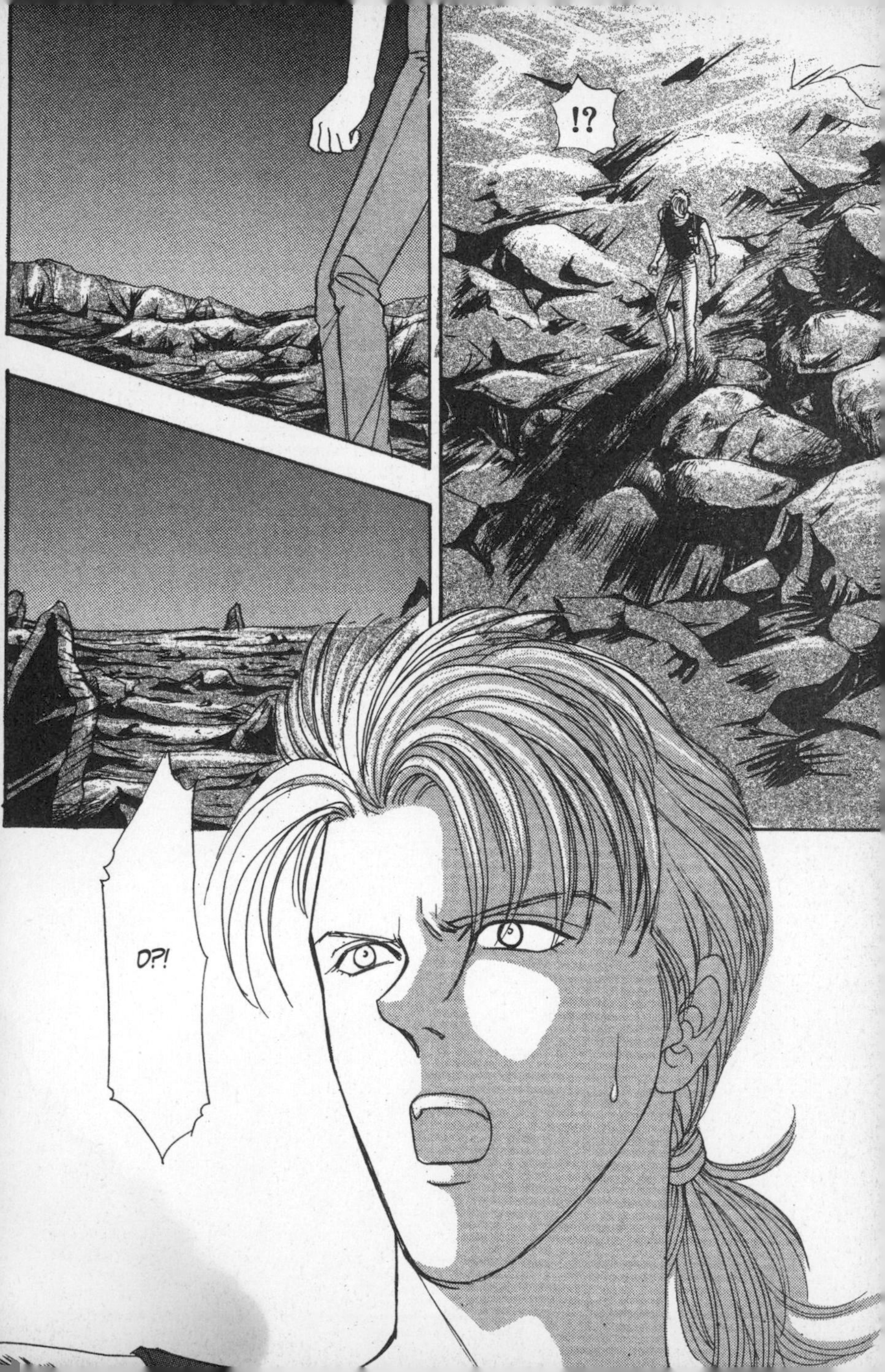
!?
O?!

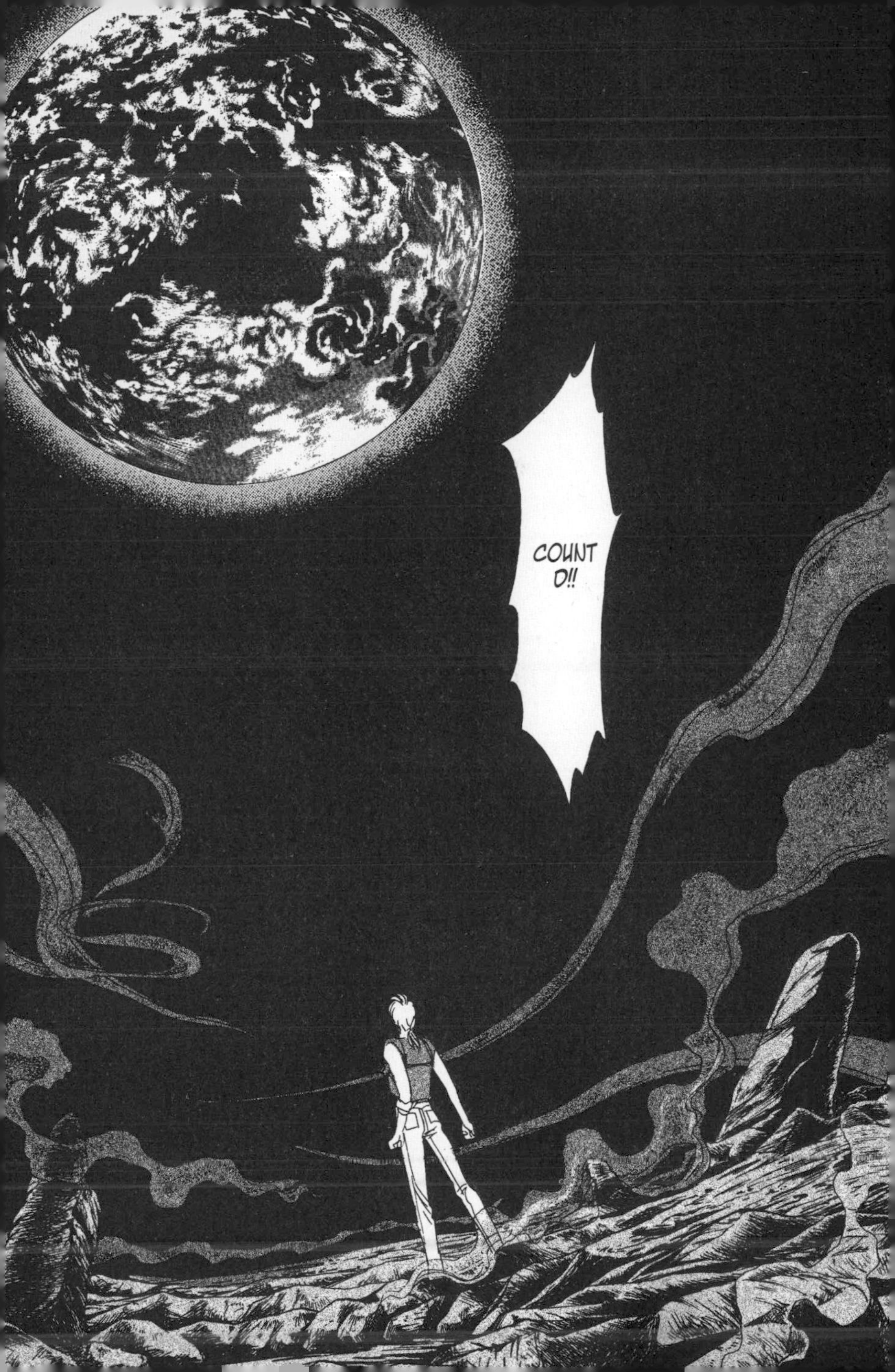
COUNT D!!

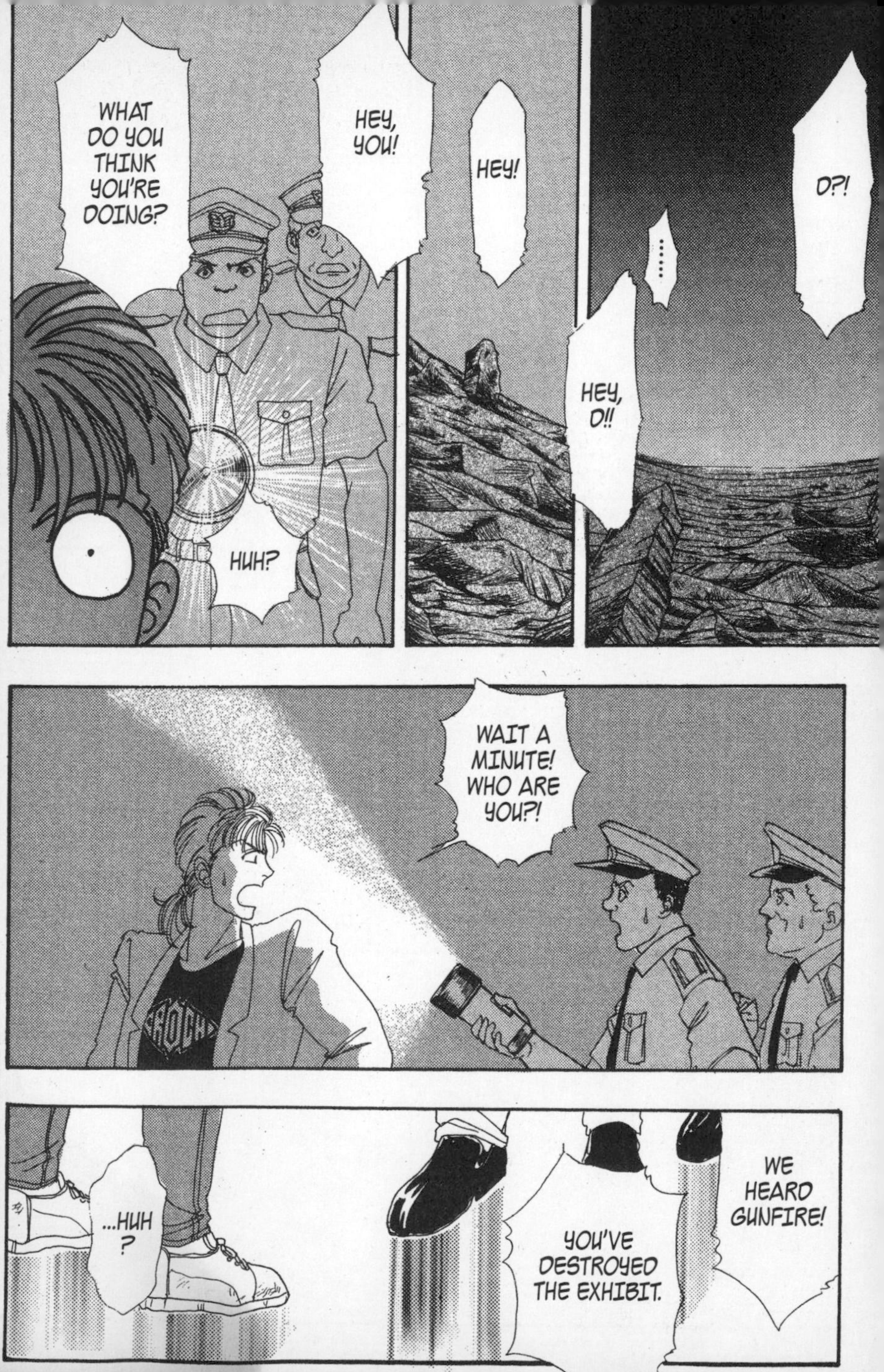
D?!
......
HEY, D!!
HEY!
HEY, YOU!
WHAT DO YOU THINK YOU'RE DOING?
HUH?
WAIT A MINUTE! WHO ARE YOU?!
WE HEARD GUNFIRE!
YOU'VE DESTROYED THE EXHIBIT.
...HUH?

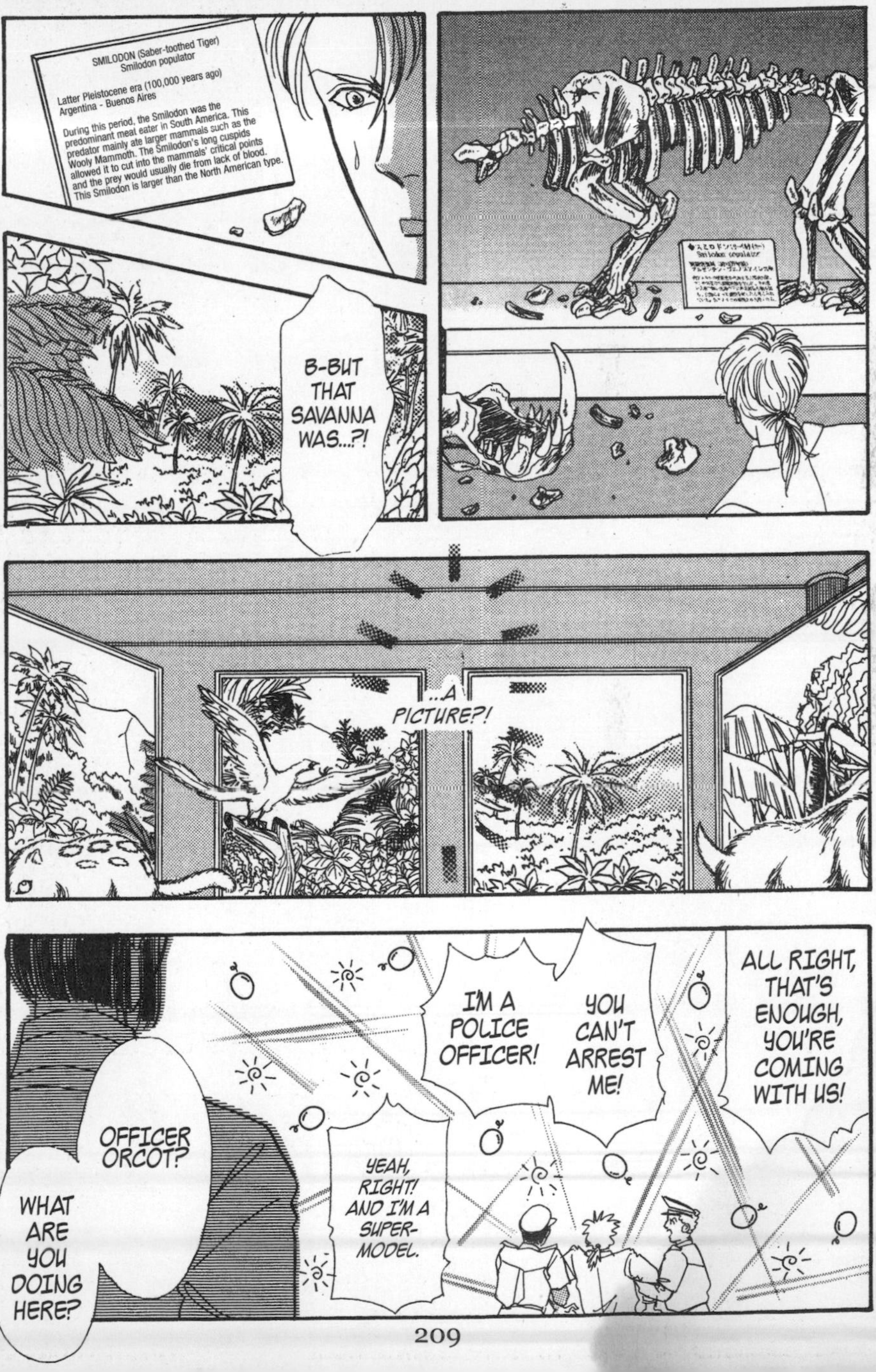
SMILODON (Saber-toothed Tiger)
Smilodon populator
Latter Pleistocene era (100,000 years ago)
Argentina - Buenos Aires
During this period, the Smilodon was the predominant meat eater in South America. This predator mainly ate larger mammals such as the Wooly Mammoth. The Smilodon's long cuspids allowed it to cut into the mammals' critical points and the prey would usually die from lack of blood. This Smilodon is larger than the North American type.
B-BUT THAT SAVANNA WAS...?!
...A PICTURE?!
ALL RIGHT, THAT'S ENOUGH, YOU'RE COMING WITH US!
YOU CAN'T ARREST ME!
I'M A POLICE OFFICER!
YEAH, RIGHT! AND I'M A SUPER-MODEL.
OFFICER ORCOT?
WHAT ARE YOU DOING HERE?

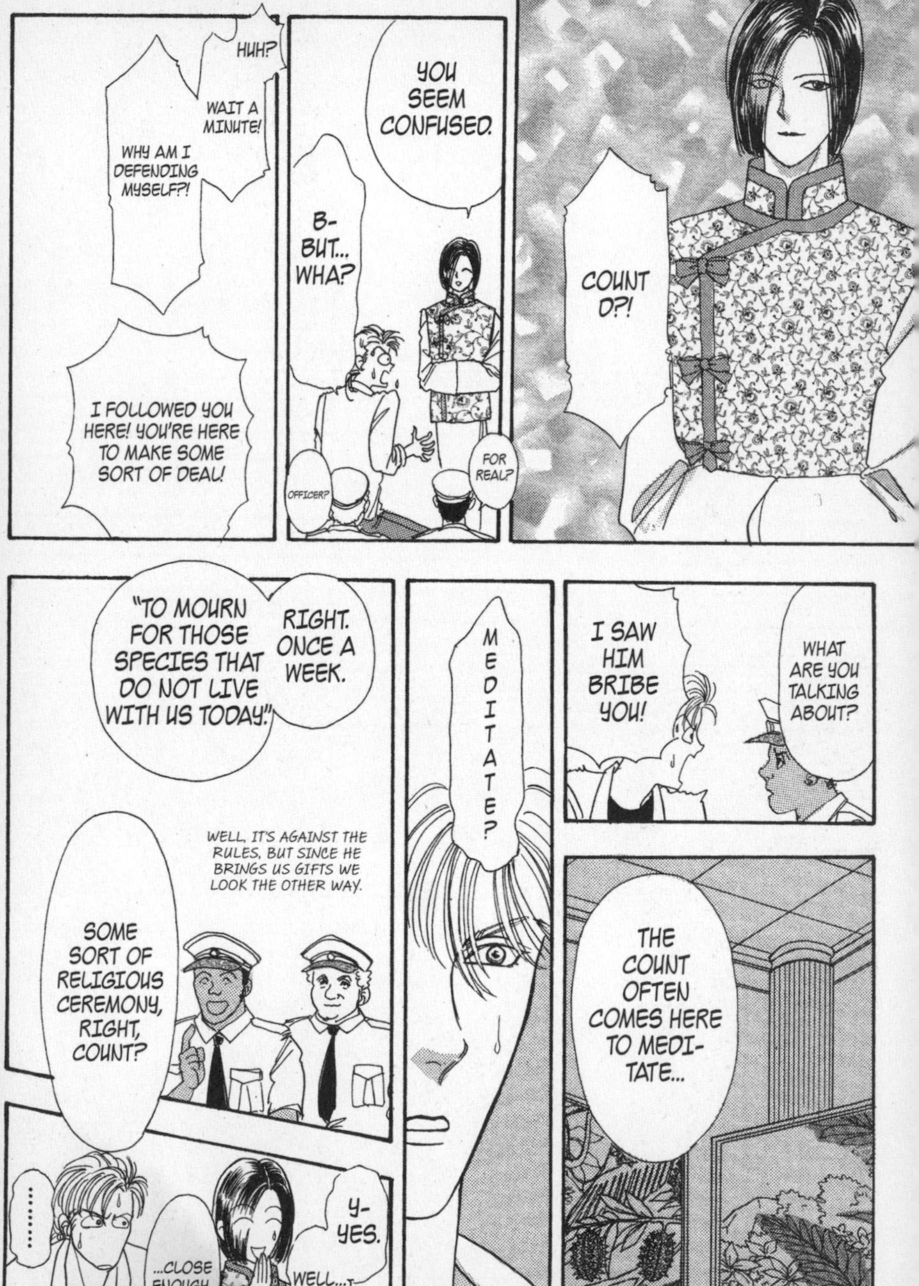
COUNT D?!
YOU SEEM CONFUSED.
B-BUT... WHA?
FOR REAL?
OFFICER?
HUH?
WAIT A MINUTE!
WHY AM I DEFENDING MYSELF?!
I FOLLOWED YOU HERE! YOU'RE HERE TO MAKE SOME SORT OF DEAL!
WHAT ARE YOU TALKING ABOUT?
I SAW HIM BRIBE YOU!
THE COUNT OFTEN COMES HERE TO MEDI-TATE...
MEDITATE?
RIGHT. ONCE A WEEK.
"TO MOURN FOR THOSE SPECIES THAT DO NOT LIVE WITH US TODAY."
SOME SORT OF RELIGIOUS CEREMONY, RIGHT, COUNT?
WELL, IT'S AGAINST THE RULES, BUT SINCE HE BRINGS US GIFTS WE LOOK THE OTHER WAY.
Y-YES.
WELL...
...CLOSE ENOUGH.
......

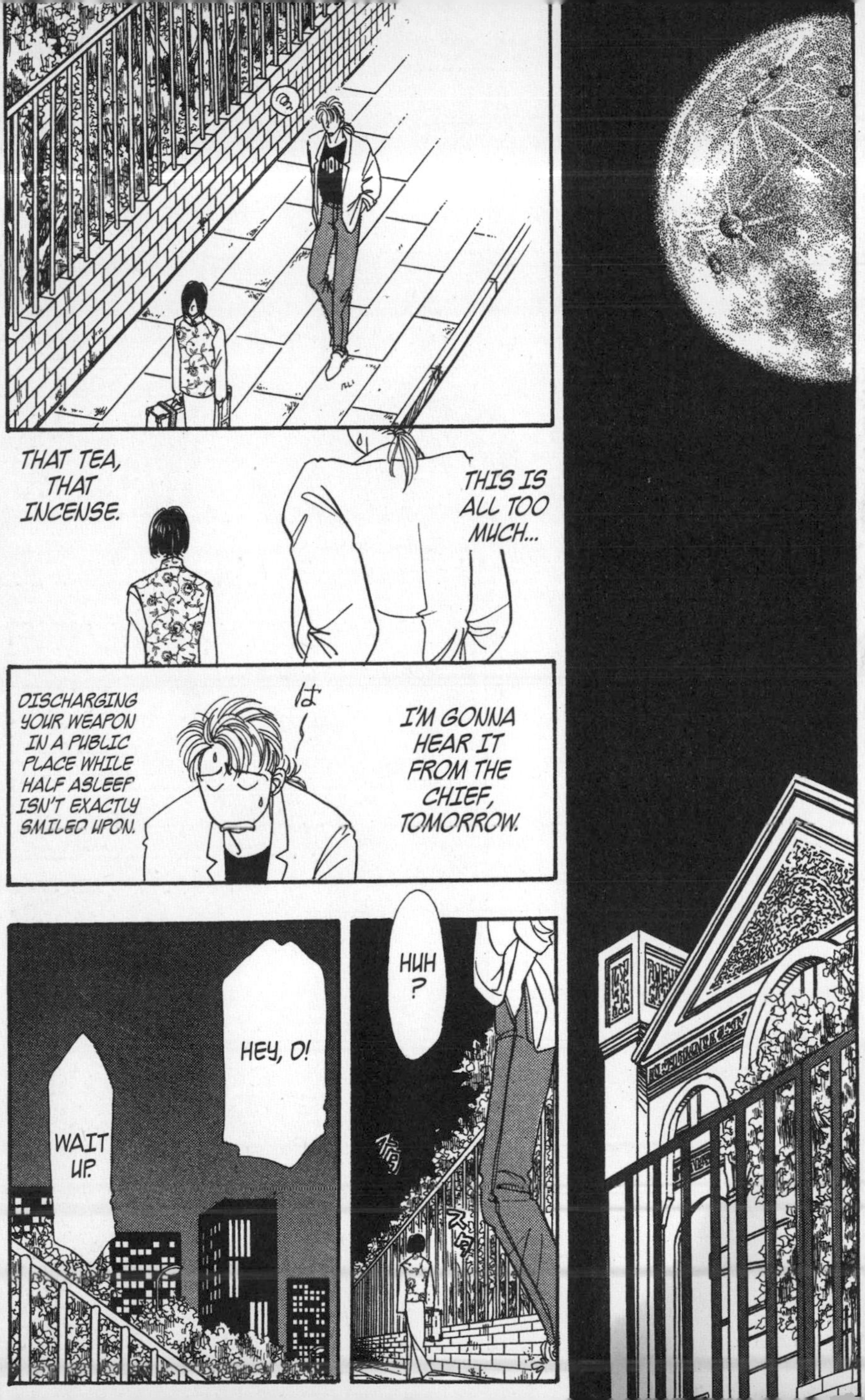
THIS IS ALL TOO MUCH...
THAT TEA, THAT INCENSE.
I'M GONNA HEAR IT FROM THE CHIEF, TOMORROW.
は
DISCHARGING YOUR WEAPON IN A PUBLIC PLACE WHILE HALF ASLEEP ISN'T EXACTLY SMILED UPON.
HUH?
HEY, D!
WAIT UP.

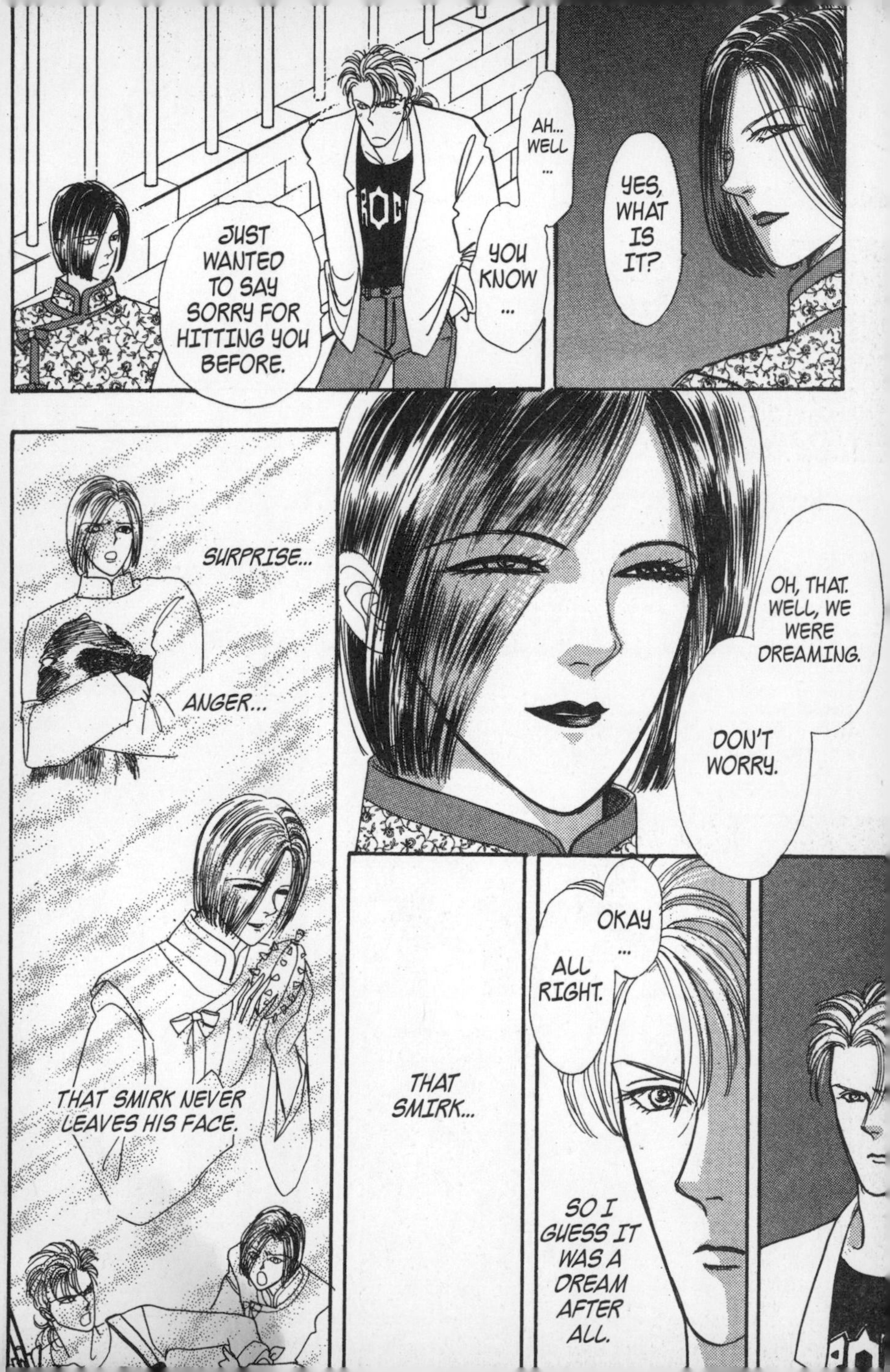
YES, WHAT IS IT?
AH... WELL ...
YOU KNOW ...
JUST WANTED TO SAY SORRY FOR HITTING YOU BEFORE.
OH, THAT. WELL, WE WERE DREAMING.
DON'T WORRY.
OKAY ...
ALL RIGHT.
SO I GUESS IT WAS A DREAM AFTER ALL.
THAT SMIRK...
SURPRISE...
ANGER...
THAT SMIRK NEVER LEAVES HIS FACE.

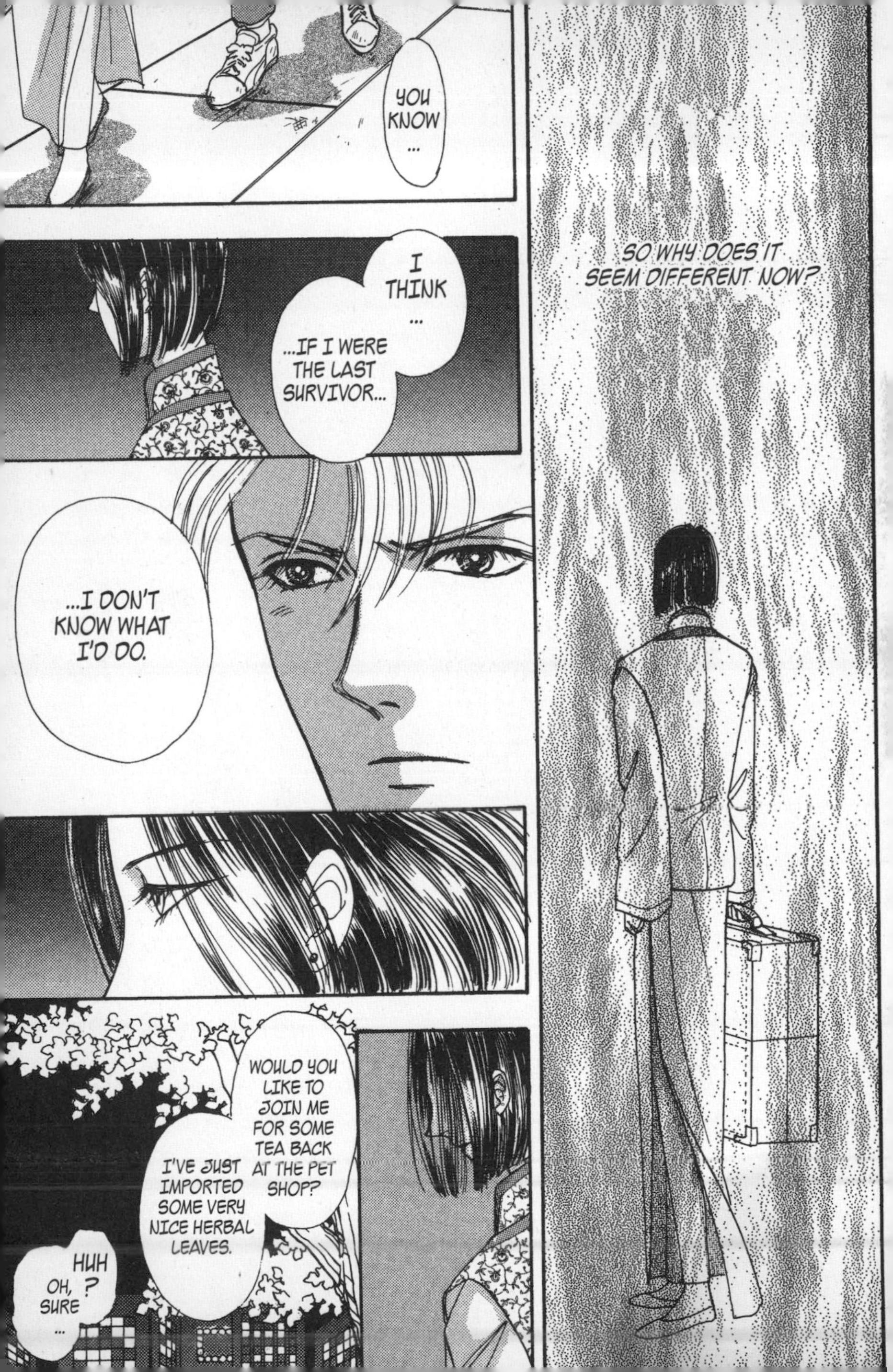
SO WHY DOES IT SEEM DIFFERENT NOW?
YOU KNOW ...
I THINK ...
...IF I WERE THE LAST SURVIVOR...
...I DON'T KNOW WHAT I'D DO.
WOULD YOU LIKE TO JOIN ME FOR SOME TEA BACK AT THE PET SHOP?
I'VE JUST IMPORTED SOME VERY NICE HERBAL LEAVES.
HUH ?
OH, SURE ...

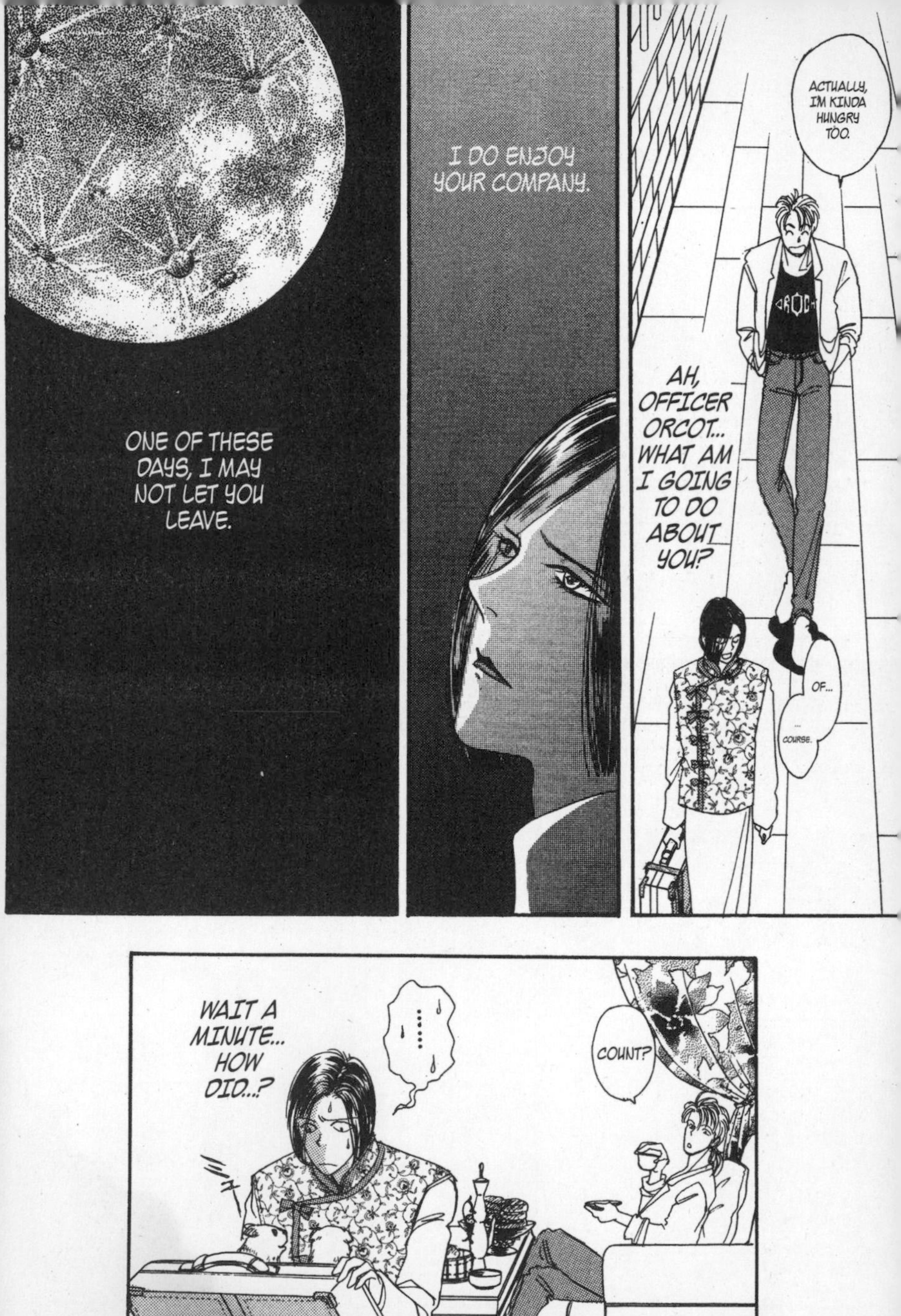
ACTUALLY, I'M KINDA HUNGRY TOO.
AH, OFFICER ORCOT... WHAT AM I GOING TO DO ABOUT YOU?
OF...
...COURSE.
I DO ENJOY YOUR COMPANY.
ONE OF THESE DAYS, I MAY NOT LET YOU LEAVE.
COUNT?
......
WAIT A MINUTE... HOW DID...?

END OF EPISODE 4

PET CATALOG

ペットカタログ

No.2

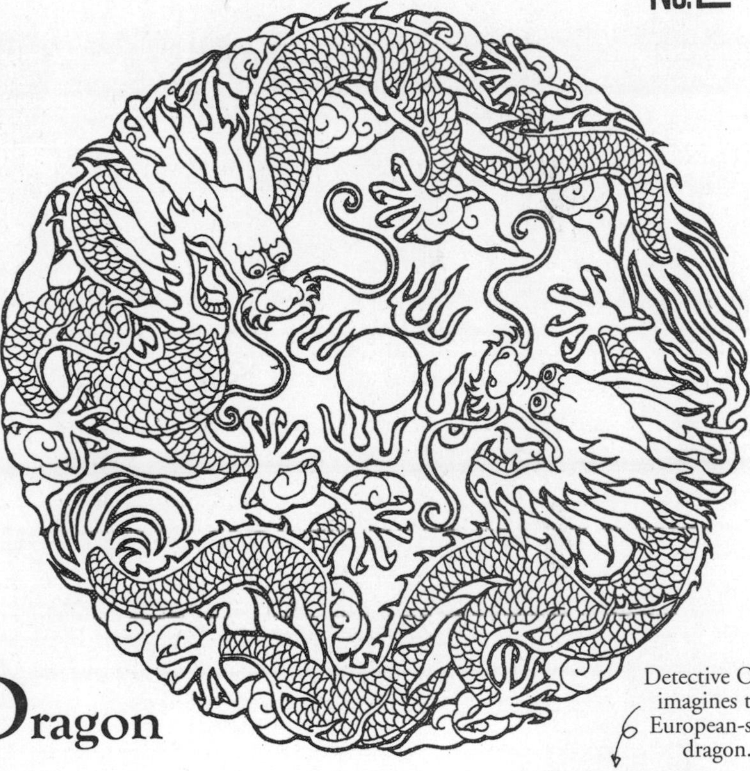

Dragon

Detective Orcot imagines this European-style dragon.

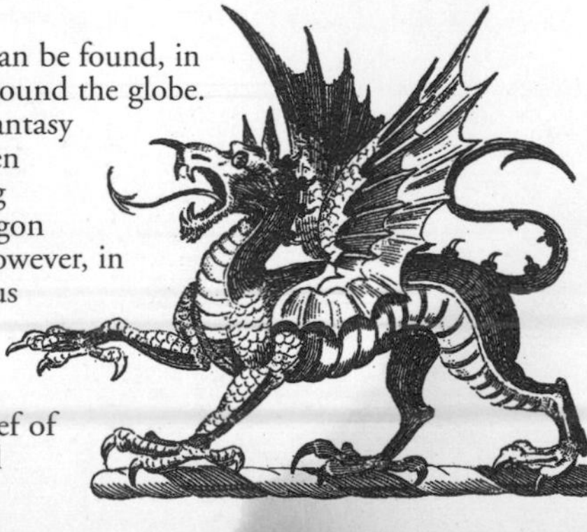

The dragon is a mythical creature that can be found, in one form or another, in folklore from around the globe. In popular culture (television, movies, fantasy role-playing games, etc.) the dragon often appears as a large, winged, fire-breathing reptile such as the Red Dragon from Lord of the Rings. However, in many Asian cultures, various types of dragons color the folkloric landscape. In Japan, the 17th Century sculptor Jingoro Hidari's relief of a dragon (shown above, actual size) captures the archetypical Asian dragon.

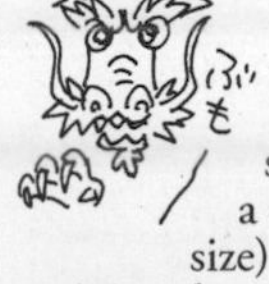

Lady & cats

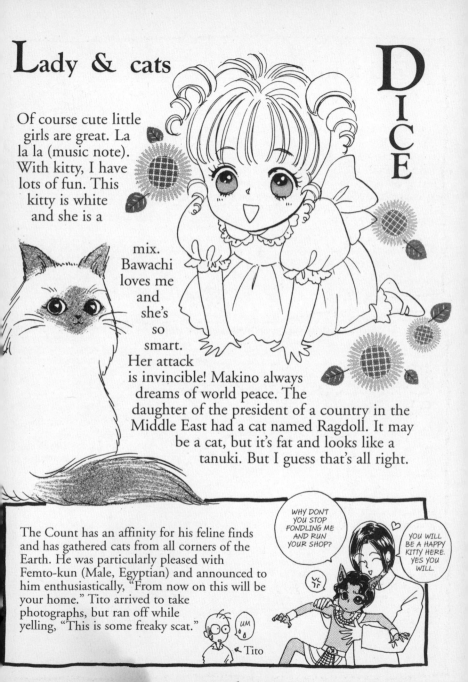

DICE

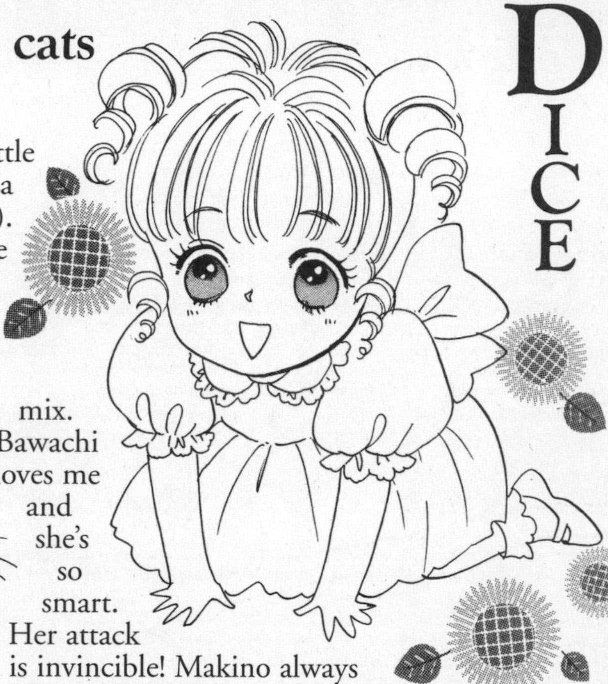

Of course cute little girls are great. La la la (music note). With kitty, I have lots of fun. This kitty is white and she is a mix. Bawachi loves me and she's so smart. Her attack is invincible! Makino always dreams of world peace. The daughter of the president of a country in the Middle East had a cat named Ragdoll. It may be a cat, but it's fat and looks like a tanuki. But I guess that's all right.

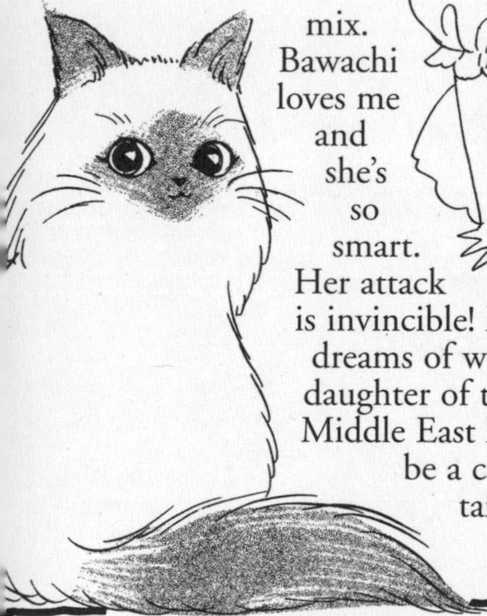

The Count has an affinity for his feline finds and has gathered cats from all corners of the Earth. He was particularly pleased with Femto-kun (Male, Egyptian) and announced to him enthusiastically, "From now on this will be your home." Tito arrived to take photographs, but ran off while yelling, "This is some freaky scat."

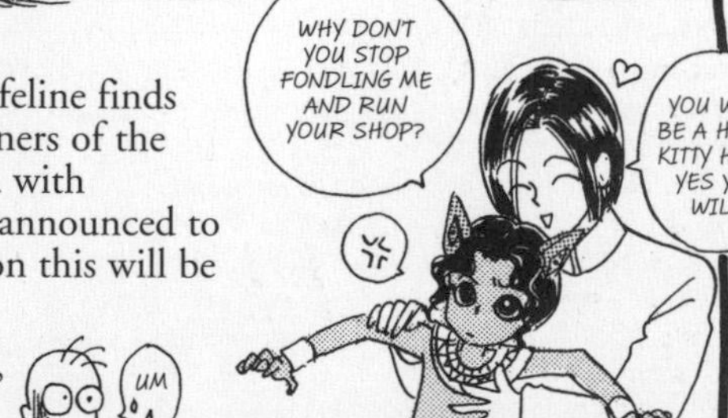
YOU WILL BE A HAPPY KITTY HERE. YES YOU WILL.
WHY DON'T YOU STOP FONDLING ME AND RUN YOUR SHOP?
UM
Tito

Delicious(人魚)

Merpeople

These are mysterious giant fish, definitely a weird phenomenon. Rumor has it hat they can only be found in the Dragon King's palace deep within the crevices of the ocean floor. But they don't look like your average, standard variety fish like the one pictured to the right. These creatures look more human. So the question is…how did Count D get a jar large enough to hold one into his shop? I gotta ask him about that.

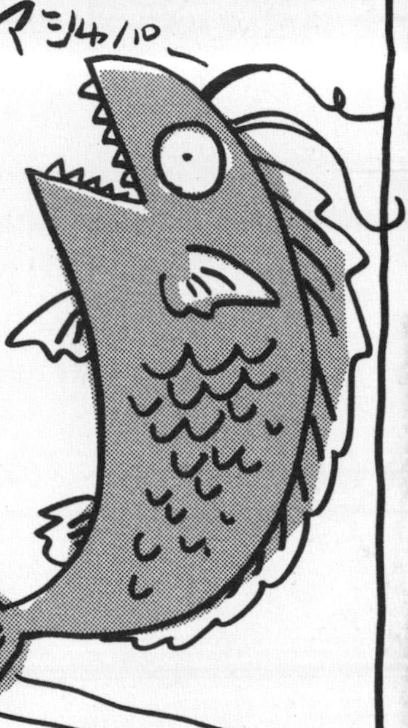

Destruction(サーベルタイガー)

Saber-toothed Tiger

Scientific Name: Smilodon
Japanese Name: Kenshiko
(the name is a bit simple)

This animal lived 3 million years ago and became extinct 10 thousand years ago. It had short fangs on its bottom jaw and larger fangs on its top jaw that were protected by a sack-like lip. Its front legs were longer than its hind legs, making him look slightly clumsy. (Akino thought this was a regular cat?)

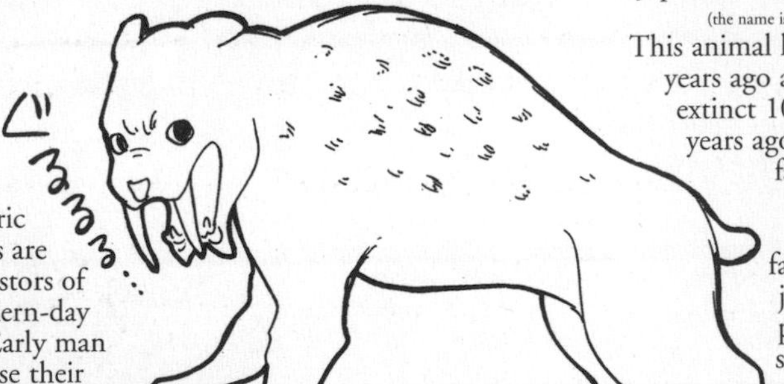
ぐるるる…

These prehistoric creatures are the ancestors of the modern-day puma. Early man would use their thick pelts as coats…dying them pink, emblazoning them with purple stripes, and unloading them at Gloomingdales for way more than they were worth.

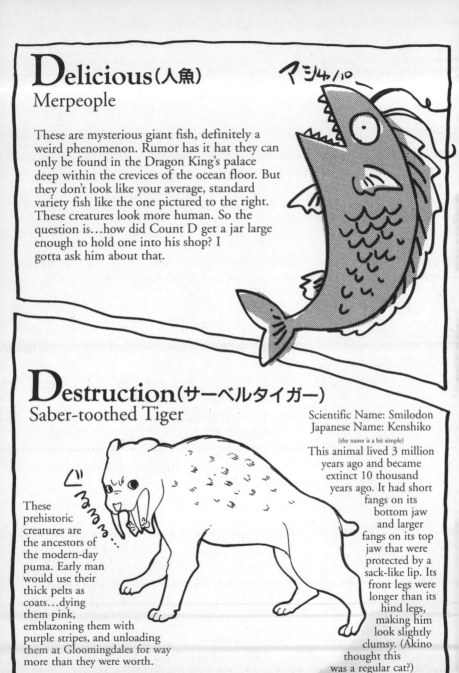

Leon Orcot

Gender: Male

Nationality: American

Age: 24… maybe?

Height: 184 cm

Weight: 72 kg

Occupation: Detective

Attributes: ?

Fighting Style: With a gun

Hobby: Wearing T-shirts with strange things on them.

Favorite food: Hamburger with a cola

Dislikes: Nothing

Favorite music: Hard Rock (Somehow it makes me smile)

Favorite type of girl: A glamorous blonde or red-haired beauty

Favorite sport: American football

Personality: Easily angered

Rival: Q-chan

He has undergone the most drastic change since the early incarnations of his character. He was supposed to be a flashy, hip detective like Tubbs on Miami Vice, but he eventually became an inquisitive Dick like Mike Hammer.

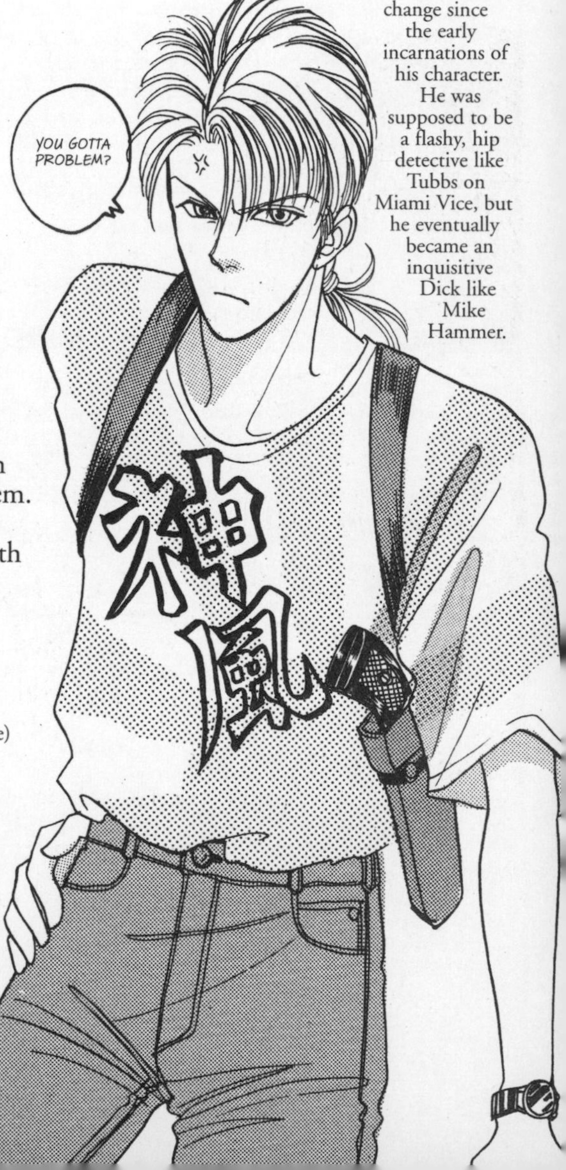
YOU GOTTA PROBLEM?

Next issue...

The Count is at it again. This time he attempts assassination with his own hands?! Who is this father, that aggravates him so? Count D shows mockery towards humans, even to a little girl who knows no better. But one happens to grab his heart?! A man?! He doesn't seem to be a 'normal' human, but then what? It seems that the Count also has to deal with his grandfather's customers as well, but what course of action will he take? Things become even more mysterious as we learn more about who the Count is (or what).

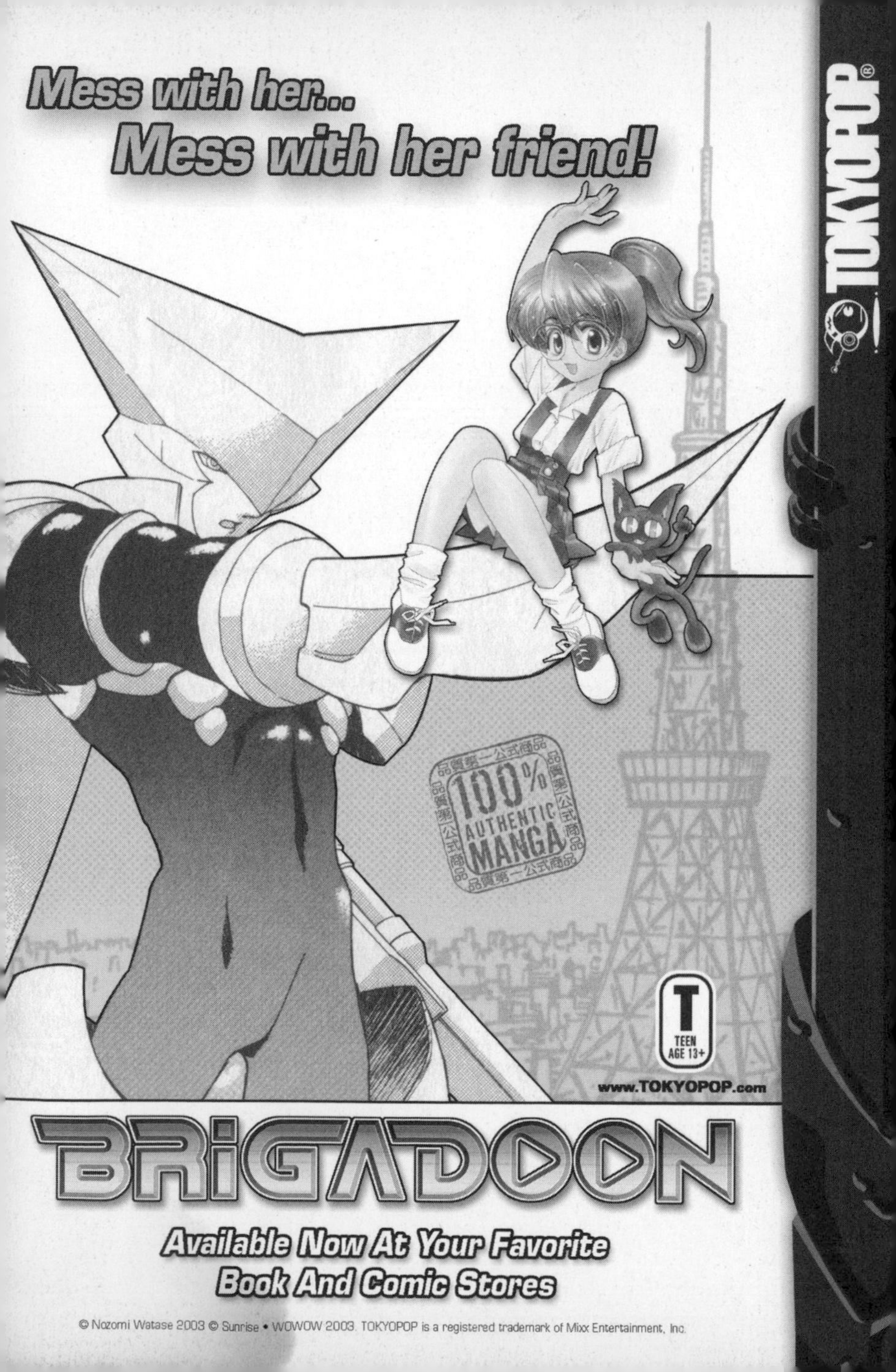
Mess with her...
Mess with her friend!
TOKYOPOP®
100% AUTHENTIC MANGA
T
TEEN AGE 13+
www.TOKYOPOP.com
BRIGADOON
Available Now At Your Favorite
Book And Comic Stores
© Nozomi Watase 2003 © Sunrise • WOWOW 2003. TOKYOPOP is a registered trademark of Mixx Entertainment, Inc.

Under the Glass Moon

By Ko Ya-Seong

Black Magic Meets Red-Hot Romance

Available Now At Your Favorite Book and Comic Stores!

OT
OLDER TEEN
AGE 16+

www.TOKYOPOP.com

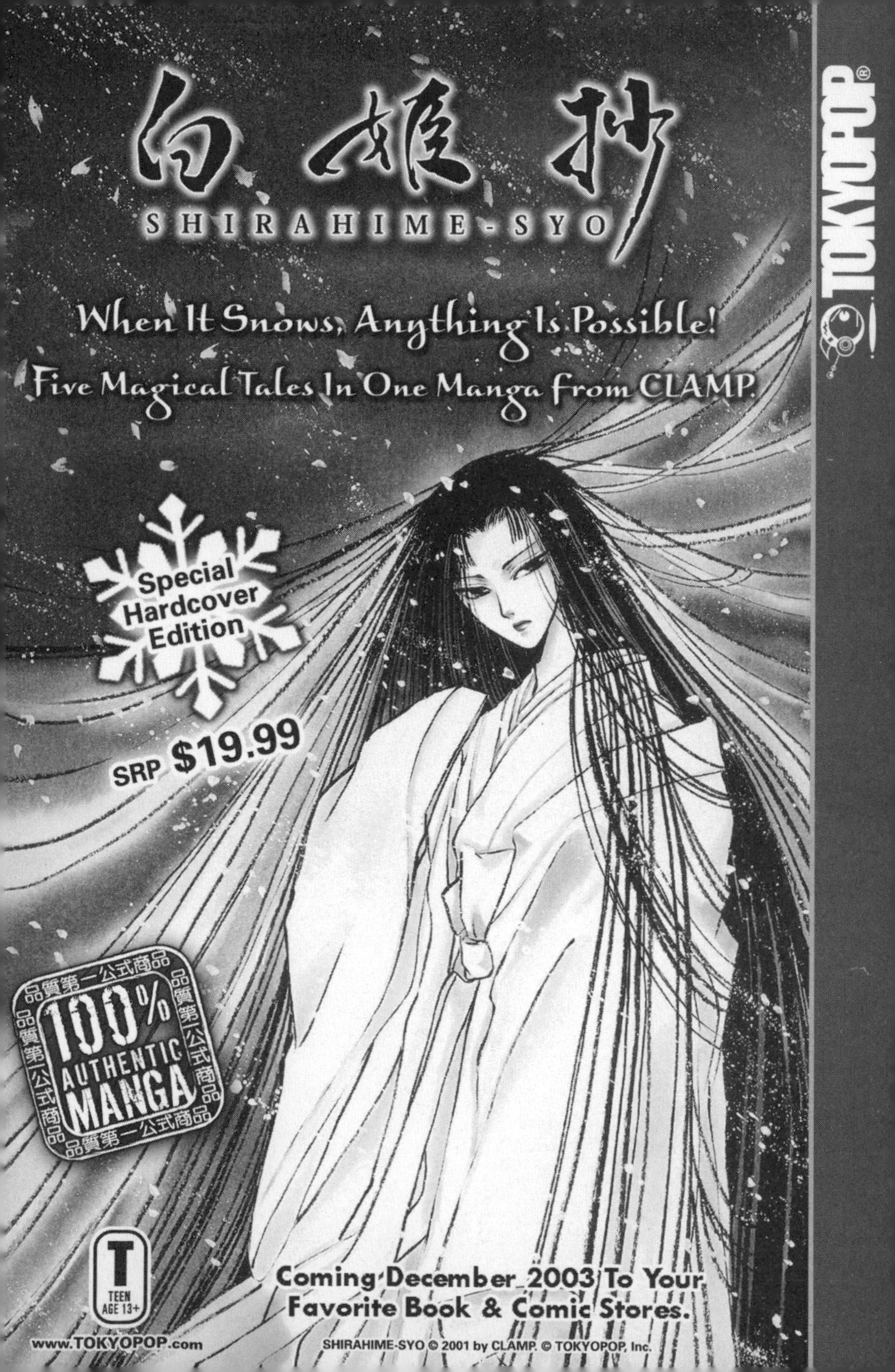
白姫抄
SHIRAHIME-SYO
When It Snows, Anything Is Possible!
Five Magical Tales In One Manga from CLAMP.
Special Hardcover Edition
SRP $19.99
品質第一公式商品
100% AUTHENTIC MANGA
T TEEN AGE 13+
Coming December 2003 To Your Favorite Book & Comic Stores.
www.TOKYOPOP.com
SHIRAHIME-SYO © 2001 by CLAMP. © TOKYOPOP, Inc.
TOKYOPOP

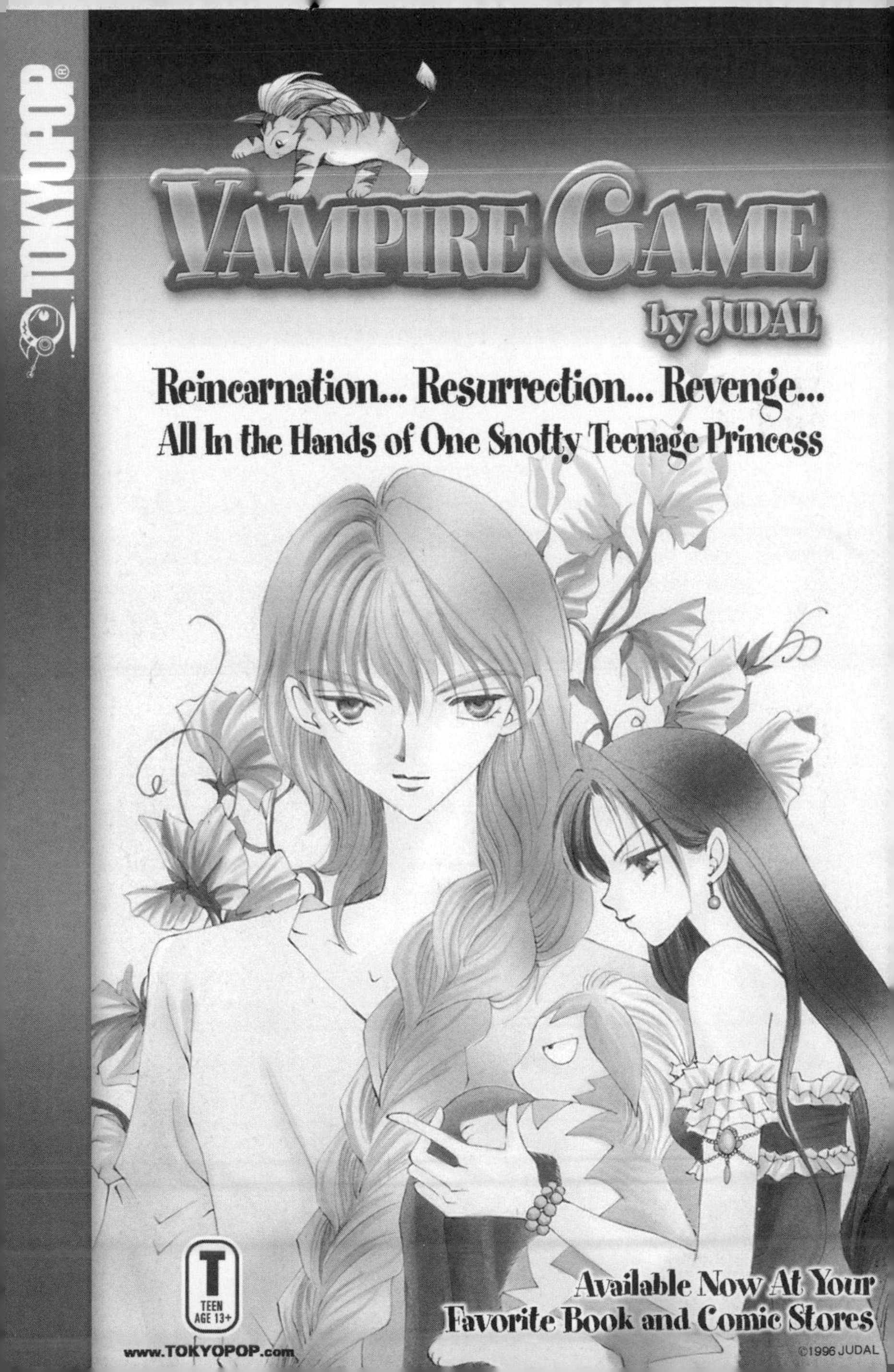
TOKYOPOP®
VAMPIRE GAME
by JUDAL
Reincarnation... Resurrection... Revenge...
All In the Hands of One Snotty Teenage Princess
T
TEEN
AGE 13+
Available Now At Your
Favorite Book and Comic Stores
www.TOKYOPOP.com
©1996 JUDAL

STOP!

This is the back of the book.
You wouldn't want to spoil a great ending!

This book is printed "manga-style," in the authentic Japanese right-to-left format. Since none of the artwork has been flipped or altered, readers get to experience the story just as the creator intended. You've been asking for it, so TOKYOPOP® delivered: authentic, hot-off-the-press, and far more fun!

DIRECTIONS

If this is your first time reading manga-style, here's a quick guide to help you understand how it works.

It's easy... just start in the top right panel and follow the numbers. Have fun, and look for more 100% authentic manga from TOKYOPOP®!